Food and Museums

Food and Museums

EDITED BY NINA LEVENT AND IRINA D. MIHALACHE

BLOOMSBURY ACADEMIC
LONDON • NEW YORK • OXFORD • NEW DELHI • SYDNEY

BLOOMSBURY ACADEMIC
Bloomsbury Publishing Plc
50 Bedford Square, London, WC1B 3DP, UK

BLOOMSBURY, BLOOMSBURY ACADEMIC
and the Diana logo are trademarks of Bloomsbury Publishing Plc

First published in Great Britain 2017
Paperback edition first published 2018

Cover design: Sharon Mah
Cover image © Joanna Parkin/Getty Images

A catalogue record for this book is available from the British Library.

ISBN: HB: 978-1-4742-6224-8
PB: 978-1-3500-7014-1
ePDF: 978-1-4742-6226-2
ePub: 978-1-4742-6225-5

Library of Congress Cataloging-in-Publication Data
Names: Levent, Nina Sobol, 1971- editor. | Mihalache, Irina D., editor.
Title: Food and museums / edited by Nina Levent and Irina D. Mihalache.
Description: London ; New York, NY : Bloomsbury Academic, an imprint of
Bloomsbury Publishing, Plc, [2017] | Includes bibliographical references
and index.
Identifiers: LCCN 2016019625 (print) | LCCN 2016028631 (ebook) |
ISBN 9781474262248 (hardback : alk. paper) | ISBN 9781474262262 (ePDF) |
ISBN 9781474262255 (ePub)
Subjects: LCSH: Food habits–Exhibitions. | Food–Exhibitions.
Classification: LCC GT2855 .F65 2016 (print) | LCC GT2855 (ebook) | DDC
394.1/2074–dc23
LC record available at https://lccn.loc.gov/2016019625

Typeset by RefineCatch Limited, Bungay, Suffolk

To find out more about our authors and books visit
www.bloomsbury.com and sign up for our newsletters.

To my children, Edis-Alexander and Isabelle, who accompanied me on many museum trips; they quickly developed an appetite for museums surpassed only by their appetites.

Nina Levent

For my niece, Islay, the perfect omnivore.

Irina D. Mihalache

Contents

List of Figures

Acknowledgments

Over the last two years we have been privileged to work with a fantastic group of scholars, museum professionals, artists and chefs, all of whom have contributed their expertise and time to this volume. We are grateful for their trust and partnership.

We would like to extend special thanks to Joan Muyskens Pursley for her candid advice, wisdom, honesty, and support at every stage of this project; and to Marie Clapot for many lively conversations about food, drinks, and culture. Thanks also to Erika Robertson for her diligence and hard work as Research Assistant.

We would like to thank Juan Maria Arzak and Elena Arzak for an unforgettable tour of their restaurant and the Lab, as well as Ferran Adrià and his team for the tour of the elBulli Foundation.

We thank our publisher, Bloomsbury Academic and our editor, Jennifer Schmidt and her team for their faith in the project.

1

Introduction:

Re-thinking Museums through Food (and Food through Museums)

Nina Levent and Irina D. Mihalache

This book project started from a series of observations: visitors go to museums to look, learn and eat, and often they spend more time in the museum restaurant than in the gallery; museums are looking into their collections for food objects, refocusing institutional mandates and curatorial practice to craft narratives through food; famous chefs find inspiration in museum histories and artifacts, transforming their kitchens into artist laboratories; artists use food to engage with local food issues, challenge global food politics, or involve the viewer into the making or consuming of the artwork. All these observations have at their center **the museum**, one of the most complex and diverse contemporary cultural institutions, and **food**, one of the most ubiquitous materials in a society.

As we began working on this book, the field of food and museums was heating up. Major institutions, such as the Getty Center in Los Angeles, curated exhibits solely based on food-related objects, one of which included a culinary component courtesy of the Getty Salad Garden, an artistic edible installation composed of organic heirloom seeds—some originating in the nineteenth century. Also in Los Angeles, the newly opened Broad museum features *Otium*, a restaurant defined by Chef Timothy Hollingsworth, previously at French Laundry, as a place for artistic expression which embraces sophisticated rusticity. In 2015, Expo Milan was the first international exhibition to be focused entirely on food, under the theme "Feeding the Planet, Energy for Life." New museums entirely dedicated to food were opening up in some of the world's most global cities, New York (Museum of Food and Drink, MOFAD) and London (British Museum of Food, BMoF). In Chicago, a Foodmuseum, highlighting the city's culinary culture, is being currently fundraised on Kickstarter. Examples are diverse and multiple and they extend outside museum walls into non-profit art organizations, such as the Center for Genomic Gastronomy currently based at the Science Gallery in Dublin, an artists-run think tank that is interested in mapping human food systems, and the Delfina Foundation in London, which wrapped up its second season of the Politics of Food program.

Our work was to observe and identify intersections between museums and food so that we could share accounts of shifting museological and artistic practices in light of food's increasing presence in museums. We did this without losing sight of the long history of encounters between the culinary and the museological, aiming to position contemporary practices in a broader context.

Before we move on, how about a historic recipe for macaroni and cheese, from the 1809 edition of *Modern Practical Cookery*? "To dress macaroni, with cheese" was cooked in the historic kitchen of the Campbell House

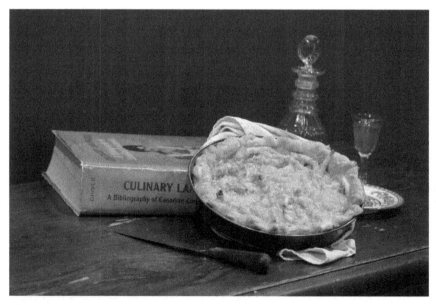

FIGURE 1.1 *Georgian macaroni with cheese in a puff pastry crust, baked by Campbell House Museum curator Liz Driver, waits to be sliced.*
© *Erika R. Robertson.*

Museum in Toronto for *Slow food: Craft macaroni and cheese*, an event where "participants will be introduced to models of food processing and local production that can help us understand issues of sustainability today."[1]

> For a large dish, take half a pound of macaroni; stew it in water, with a little salt, until tender, drain it, return it to the pan, with a little cream, let it stew until it is rich and thick; season with beaten mace, a teaspoonful of made mustard, mixed with two spoonfuls of cream, and the yolks of two raw eggs beat up; add the eggs and cream, give it a toss; have a dish ready lined with puff pastry, pour in the macaroni; grate parmesan or Cheshire cheese over it; bake in a modern oven.

Contextualizing food and museums

This historic recipe is a good place to start our discussion about museums, which we define as interdisciplinary spaces deeply interconnected with external contexts—political, social, cultural, and economic, which "stand at the crossroad of history, high culture and popular culture"[2] and have the "ability to change according to shifting social needs".[3] It is, in fact, the "messy" complexity of the museum, a result of various communicative networks of museum professionals, audiences, objects, discourses, and spaces that produces this change. We engage with the museum as a significant producer of culture, which "actively seeks to share power with the communities it serves"[4] by inviting local audiences to learn about sustainability while cooking an early nineteenth-century recipe for macaroni and cheese in a historic kitchen. For many who believe that museums do not embrace change or lack relevance, we ask them to look closely at the work that museums of all kinds—art, history, food, and agriculture, natural history, science, historic and heritage sites, brand museums, artists' collectives— do with food. Museums' engagement with food allows cafes, restaurants, and food courts, often seen as peripheral and deemed as manifestations of consumerism, to be discussed on the same level as the galleries.

Museums are responding to the current public fascination with food by integrating food displays, programming, and eating in their practices. These new museum practices are convincing more and more audiences that food is worthy of serious museological attention. However, we explore these current developments in museum programming by situating them in a longer history. Further, rather than claiming that food has been coopted by museums in a specific historical context, we believe that food and museums have been borrowing from and informing each other's meanings, structures, and practices. As Constance Classen argued,

One might presume that, as multisensory as the collection experience might have been for early moderns, the sense of taste, at least, would have been excluded from that experience. However, while it is true that visitors to collections did not customarily go around tasting the exhibits, their visit still might be informed by gustatory associations. Just as occurs today, museum visits might be coupled with meals. In early public museums, however, visitors sometimes brought food to eat within the collection space itself. In private collections, the owner, if so inclined, might provide a collation.[5]

The food's flexibility to be studied from multiple perspectives—as a subject of politics, as a form of cultural capital, as gender performance, as global traveler, or as a source of social anxiety—is what facilitates its diverse uses in museum practice. As Roland Barthes wrote, food is "a system of communication, a body of images, a protocol of usages, situations, and behaviors."[6] The public space of the museum reveals food's complexity, making use of its various meanings to support its institutional mandates and strategies for audience engagement.

Take, for example, this recipe for "Creole Jambalaya with Chicken, Sausage, Vine-Ripened Tomatoes," cooked for the "Taste of New Orleans" class at the Southern Food & Beverage Museum in New Orleans.

Ingredients

- 12 medium shrimp, peeled, deveined and chopped
- 4 ounces chicken, diced
- 1 tablespoon Creole seasoning
- 2 tablespoons oil
- 1 cup chopped onion
- 1 cup chopped green bell pepper
- 1 cup chopped celery
- 1/2 cup chopped tomatoes
- 3 bay leaves
- 1 teaspoon hot sauce
- 3 cups rice
- 6 cups chicken stock
- 5 ounces Andouille sausage, sliced
- Salt and pepper

Directions: In a bowl combine shrimp, chicken, and Creole seasoning, and work in seasoning well. In a large saucepan heat oil over high heat with onion, pepper, and celery, 3 minutes. Add garlic, tomatoes, bay leaves, Worcestershire and hot sauces. Stir in rice and slowly add broth. Reduce heat to medium and cook until rice absorbs liquid and becomes tender, stirring occasionally, about 15 minutes. When rice is just tender add shrimp and chicken mixture and sausage. Cook until meat is done, about 10 minutes more. Season to taste with salt, pepper, and Creole seasoning.[7]

Cooked in the museum, this recipe represents what David Howes would call an example of "sensory museology," "the rising tide of sensory experimentation in contemporary curatorial practice."[8] Simply put, the visitor experience of New Orleans history and culture is "sensorialized" through food, inviting the participants to reflect on specific traits of the cuisine, such as hybridity, spiciness, and locality, while cooking and eating the dish. Food here performs the role of immersive museum experience, providing an alternative route to knowledge. However, food consumption in museums, and other intersections between food and museums, require a critical read-through. Echoing Danielle Rice's words, we believe that "we need a practice informed by a broad range of theoretical approaches in art history, criticism, anthropology, cultural and visual studies, as well as visual studies and aesthetic development."[9]

The structure of the volume

We grouped the chapters into five sections, starting with a series of theoretical reflections on food and museums, followed by sections which correspond with the main areas of museums' public presence—collections and exhibitions, interpretation, public programming, and audience engagement. The final two sections are focused on eating in museums and artistic production related to food. We included the perspectives of scholars from disciplines as diverse as neuroscience, anthropology, communication studies, performance studies, sociology, and art history; curators, museum interpreters, educators, museum directors, volunteer historic cooks, activists, artists, and chefs. This volume's chapters come in a diversity of formats, ranging from theoretical reflections on specific aspects of food and museums; case studies from art museums, history and natural history museums, historic homes, heritage sites, science centers, food museums, living history museums, and folk festivals; interviews with chefs, artists, and museum professionals.

It was critical to open with a diversity of intellectual perspectives on food and museums, to show the complexity of food as it intersects with the already intricate museological environment. To do food work in a cultural institution requires more than just an awareness of how "cool" food is or how much food programming might appeal to foodie audiences. To transform culinary engagements in museums into reflective and significant encounters with objects and their histories involves a look at all these theoretical perspectives. We imagined these contributions as forming a "theoretical toolkit" for those doing food work in cultural institutions.

In this volume, we outlined a framework for a new area of research which looks at the complex and layered relationship between food and museums. Others before us have talked about food and museums, but this is the first volume to collect and categorize the existing knowledge on this topic, as well as suggest questions and frameworks for future investigation. When determining our approach it was important for us to be relevant to museum and culinary professionals who work with food in different cultural institutions. Thus, we feature best practices, often developed through trial and error, and practical advice regarding challenges of working with food in museum environments. We also gathered a fascinating collection of recipes, from chefs, historic cooks, and museum curators, that display most vividly the encounters between food, history, and museological spaces. Our volume focuses mainly on North American practices, with contributions from China, Australia, Spain, the Netherlands, Sweden, and the United Kingdom, leaving room for much more research and discussion on similar practices in other cultural contexts. We selected case studies that reflect on food politics, touching on matters of colonialism, globalization, and locality; gender and class relations, as these manifest in museum eating, cooking, and museum objects; ecological activism in urban cosmopolitan areas; issues of authenticity; collective memory and nation-making through institutional mandates.

Interdisciplinary perspectives on food and museums

In her contribution to the volume, anthropologist **Christy Shields-Argelès** puts together a selection of anthropological perspectives on food and taste. She writes specifically for a non-specialist audience to provide some ways in which cultural perspectives on food and taste could aid to re-imagine museum spaces and their practices. To do so, Shields-Argelès discusses a series of foundational concepts and perspectives, such as distinction, place-making, food habits, and cuisine, for the museum professional who wishes to think critically on her food-related practice. For the reflective practitioner, the use of food in museums ought not to be rhetorically empty—much like the add-on of yet another new technology to generate audience engagement—but informed by the rich intellectual contributions of scholars such as Mary Douglas, Claude Fischler, Carolyn Korsmeyer, and David Howes, among many others.

Charlene Elliott shares a similar interest in the museum's participatory attempts to gain audiences through food. In her chapter, Elliott identifies a significant gap in the current museum studies research—literature connecting children, food, and museums is rare, despite the multitude of exhibitions and programs directed to a young audience. With a focus on food, children's and corporate museums, the author crafts a communication and media studies informed framework to analyze the potential of food display and "taste-full" materials targeted at children. Elliott suggests three analytical categories— *fuel, preparation*, and *fun*—that reflect the type of work that institutions such as the Museum of Food and Drink (New York City), Canada Agriculture and Food Museum (Ottawa) and EdVenture Children's Museum (Columbia, South Carolina) do to educate and engage children.

Some of the techniques developed by children's museums, such as emphasis on nutrition or experimentation with flavor profiles, are part of a larger inquiry that brings neuroscience into the museum. **Charles Spence** argues that flavor perception results from the multisensory integration of multiple sensory signals in the human brain. He presents research conducted with his team at Crossmodal Research Laboratory at the University of Oxford on "neurogastronomy," or the scientific study of the brain's perception of flavor. Such research informed the recent Tate Sensorium exhibition at Tate Britain, an exhibit where visitors were encouraged to use touch, taste, smell, and hearing while looking at art. His findings show the significance of context when connecting the work of the brain with that of flavor, emphasizing how naming, labeling and description, price/valuation, and the name of the artist or chef can dramatically influence responses to the evaluation of taste.

Edward Whittall engages in a discussion of food, aesthetics and theatricality in order to understand the relation between food and art, unpacking the connections that have been developed, historically and through the work of chefs, between art and modernist cuisine. The author's explanation for the powerful uses of food in museums—using as example *The Bliss Point*, on display at the Montreal Museum of Contemporary Art during the "Food and Robotics" Festival—rests in observations about food's mutability between the everyday and the exceptional, allowing visitors to transition between multiple roles—to perform, through food. Such experiences confirm for Whittall that rather than comparing food with art to assess its value, food should be allowed its own performative gestures.

From food in museums, **Van Troi Tran** takes his argument on the road to the 2010 Shanghai World Expo, where he explores the mélange between commerce and culture by focusing on the visual cultures that are produced around food by managers, vendors, and restaurateurs, to promote dishes and beverages. Locating the world fair and the museum in the same context of origins—the nineteenth-century colonized world—Tran offers an analysis of the Shanghai World Expo and argues that representations of food on menus, advertising materials, and food packaging encompass a plurality of logistics that serve the interests of multiple communities—vendors, restaurateurs, managers, and visitors. The author's global focus explores the processes of standardization and singularization as characteristic of the foodscapes at an international fair. Food, he finds, escapes its own theorization, to perform a much more complex social and cultural role.

This section concludes with the stories of two chefs, Elena Arzak and Ferran Adrià. **Nina Levent**, who interviewed both chefs in 2015, discusses Arzak's kitchen and Adrià's foundation as laboratories, where the investigation of methods of cooking, culinary history, and creativity results in post-modern recipes, such as the "Pigeon with Guitar Shavings" (Arzak) and the re-writing of food history (Adrià). Both chefs have re-imagined their kitchens to provide a space of experimentation and cultural investigation. And, both of them have collaborated with museums, finding different modes of engaging food and display.

Collecting and exhibiting food

Museums' galleries and storages are full of food-related objects, from agricultural tools to cookbooks and contemporary material culture from celebrity chefs' kitchens. Historic and heritage sites dedicate extensive space to gardens, taverns, mills, and bakeries, inviting visitors to experience history through food. There are dozens of specialized food museums around the world, such as the National Mustard Museum in Middleton, Wisconsin; the Canadian Potato Museum on Prince Edward Island; and the Kimchee Museum of Seoul, South Korea. In this section, we highlight, through four case studies, recent work done by three major North American museums around collecting and displaying food. Each case study highlights a different perspective on food collecting and exhibiting, contextualized in relation to broader institutional mandates.

Most people who love Julia Child know by now that her kitchen is displayed at the National Museum of American History (NMAH) in Washington, DC. **Paula J. Johnson** is the curator lucky enough to have traveled to Child's house in Cambridge, Massachusetts, to inventory her kitchen and take it back to NMAH, where it is now part of FOOD: Transforming the American Table, 1950-2000, an exhibition about changes in American food cultures in the past few decades. The author tells the story of FOOD and of Julia's kitchen in relation to major changes in public programming and audience engagement at the NMAH, which have resulted in the building of a kitchen stage in the museum, the development of food programming, such as the "Food Fridays," and an overall refocus of the museum's research and collecting practice.

Continuing the conversation about NMAH's engagement with food, **L. Stephen Velasquez** zooms in on one aspect: preserving and exhibiting Latino food history, with a focus on Mexican and Mexican American contributions to food production and consumption in the United States. Arguing for a responsible collecting practice, which accounts for differences at the level of community history and background, Velasquez discusses three collecting initiatives at the NMAH: the bracero history collection, the El Chico Tex-Mex collection, and the Mexican winemaker's project. Aspects of these collecting efforts made their way into the *FOOD: Transforming the American Table, 1950-2000* exhibitions, alongside Julia Child's kitchen and examples of food counter-culture in the 1960s.

The cultural specificity of food is something that **Elizabeth M. Williams**, the director of Southern Food and Beverage Museum in New Orleans, considers foundational to the museum's curatorial practice. In her chapter, Williams reflects on the museum's mission and the curatorial practice that celebrates sensory and participatory experience, including the use of nutcrackers, roasted chicory, and coffee tasting to activate visitors' connection with food's history. The author reflects on decisions made throughout the museum's history to increase sensorial engagement, such as the building of a demonstration kitchen and bar, the allowing of eating and drinking inside the museum, and the opening of a restaurant that serves foods that reflect the museum's cultural focus.

One of the challenges for museums collecting and exhibiting food is to consider taste as a generator of knowledge and experience. **Erin Betley** and **Eleanor Sterling** discuss the process of developing *Our Global Kitchen: Food, Nature, Culture*, one of the largest food exhibitions in recent history and the first of its kind at the American Museum of Natural History (New York City). Experimenting with a new curatorial approach, the team decided to focus on how food moves through the global food system from farm to fork and beyond. The display and programming considerations for the exhibition were guided by the main steps of a food system: growing, trading and transporting, cooking, eating and tasting, and celebrating. This approach afforded tasting and eating in the exhibition's galleries, including taste tests, demonstrations of various cooking methods, and guest visits by local farmers and chefs.

These case studies reveal a series of important takeaways for food work in museums that confirm the necessity of in-depth research into food history and knowledge of production and consumption, including understanding of the communities that contribute to national and global food cultures. In addition, food's collecting and display requires an audience engagement component that connects the sense of taste to the political, social, and cultural themes of exhibitions.

Food and audience engagement

There is not a museum in the world that is untouched by the shift in the museum's mandate and self-conception from a focus on collecting and preserving objects and their histories to public space that provides layered multisensory experiences to their diverse audiences. Such experiences include educational, social, sensory, aesthetic, intellectual, or therapeutic experience; experiences that engage audiences in the galleries through online platforms and social media. Museum experiences are becoming more often driven by audience, participatory in nature, and created in real time rather then scripted by museum curators and educators.[10] Museums that recognize the trend have "audience engagement" staff on their education, visitor service, and digital content teams; these museums solicit and feature audience-driven content.

James Deutsch traces the early history of the of Smithsonian Folklife Festival that began in 1967 and included foodways demonstrations along with performing arts and crafts. The importance of this festival's history is in its connections to the Smithsonian museums and its status as a Living Outdoor Museum. During the early years of the event, foodways and food heritage were established as recognized forms of traditional culture. Thus, the festival included cooking demonstrations featuring Native Americans, members of African diaspora, and even "working Americans"; various US states sent representatives of their local Amish, Greek, and Italian communities to prepare distinctive dishes. Blintzes, buffalo meat, Alabama barbequed pork, Haitian grilled fish, Louisiana gumbo, Nigerian fried meat, Senegalese rice, and Trinidadian sweet-potato cakes were among the many cultural attractions that highlighted foodways. Food at the Festival was an instance of cultural encounter, when representatives of various cultural and social groups cooked for the visitors, allowing knowledge to form at the level of taste and multisensory experience of sharing food.

The use of taste to tell history is one of the mandates of the Fort York National Historic Site (Toronto), which holds Canada's largest collection of original War of 1812 buildings. In a conversation with **Elizabeth Baird**, **Rosemary Kovac**, and **Bridget Wranich**, **Irina D. Mihalache** found out about the development of a successful Historic Foodways Programme, the training of a skilled team of volunteer historic cooks and the adaptations of historic recipes for a modern palate. Wranich explains that the Fort's food philosophy is based on rigorous historical research of recipes. While staying authentic to the original recipe as much as possible it is equally important that the recipes are tested before being served to visitors, and adapted to contemporary ingredients and cooking techniques. Making historic desserts such as Little Fine Cakes available to visitors represents a public engagement opportunity as important as historic reenactment or a tour of the site.

The interpretive possibilities of historic foods are further explored by **Scott Hill** and **Jacqui Newling** who explain that passively experienced social history museums are, on their own, no longer enough to engage modern audiences. The authors contribute a case study of food-related programming that unfolded in the twelve historically and geographically diverse Sydney Living Museum (SLM) sites in Australia. *Eat Your History*, an audience-centered food programming initiative, illustrates how food unlocks stories behind SLM's historic collections and gives visitors a sense of ownership about these collections, making historical concepts and past lives more accessible. Hill and Newling point out the limitations and challenges of food-based public programming in historic spaces, such as risk management to collections and controlled environments for perishable produce. One of the outcomes of the expanded conversation about food and cooking is that many of the specialized terms like *terroir* became widely used and often transplanted into new situations. **Jennifer Stratton** and **Ashley Rose Young** tell a story of the application of *terroir* to urban landscapes in the Southern United States, where a sense of place was profoundly shaped by food production. *Terroir Tapestries* is an interactive exploration of the past, rather than academic research, focused on revisiting the *terroir* of street food spaces and markets in New Orleans, through the facilitation of encounters between vendors, consumers, and participants' collective interpretation of previously unfamiliar street foods. Through food wrapper imagery and inscriptions that were later exhibited at the Southern Food and Beverage Museum, participants were able to record their reactions and memories of street food cultures.

The case studies in these sections emphasize how cultural institutions that are not centered on food make cooking and eating integral pillars of their museum practice. Such initiatives were further seconded by projects such as *Terroir Tapestries*, which use urban spaces and markets to connect with place-specific food cultures.

Eating in museums

The contributors to this section discuss various aspects of eating in museums, focusing on serving food in museum galleries or in food service spaces in museums. We take a historical approach in this section to emphasize the long history of food consumption in museums, situating current practice in its proper cultural and social context. Early museum history was rich in sensory encounters: in the late seventeenth and eighteenth century, visitors to the Ashmolean and British Museum would be encouraged to rub, pick up, shake, smell, and even taste the artifacts in the galleries.[11]

Visitors sampled artifacts in museums' galleries and also in various eating spaces. This is the context for **Mark Clintberg**'s investigations into the rhetoric of the museum restaurant through the concepts of "local," "national," and "cosmopolitan". Local diets and national food practices, forged through global connections, influence the menus offered by restaurants in art museums, while many museums also support local art communities and regional cultures. There are, however, challenges inherent in designing museum restaurants that promote institutional mandates. Clintberg takes as an example the V&A Café at the Victoria and Albert Museum (London), tracing the encounters between national and global foods with local and international visitors. Clintberg also problematizes the colonial roots of many local and diasporic foods that made their way onto restaurant menus located in cosmopolitan locations, such as London.

Another cosmopolitan city, Toronto, is witness to the food work of another museum, the Campbell House Museum, a late Georgian-era house, built for Judge William Campbell and his wife Hannah Campbell in 1822. Despite its roots in Georgian culture, the museum's kitchen has created meals based on Russian Jewish recipes, American meatloaf, and a nineteenth-century shrub. An interview with **Liz Driver**, director and curator of the Campbell House Museum, allows us a behind-the-scenes look into a historic kitchen that is not turned into a display but is filled with cooking aromas and warmth from the wood-burning stove. The museum staff host themed events such as *Dinner with Dickens* when the beef is roasted on the open fire in the historic kitchen. Like many other historic homes, the Campbell House was built for entertaining, and this idea is preserved through the programming that includes food service and theater.

A discussion of eating in museums should also reflect on the connection between food and art, a perspective developed by **Marta Arzak** who writes as a museum professional and member of a famous family of Basque chefs. She poses the question of whether cooking could be considered an art form. And what aspects of culinary practice are akin to artistic practice? She answers these questions by tracing her own curatorial and research experience. She begins with her work with Ferran Adrià on his pavilion at *documenta 12,* a significant event for the history of gastronomy as no chef before then was invited to participate on his own terms at a major international art event. Arzak then looks at challenges of curating gastronomy-related projects in art spaces, including working with her sister, chef Elena Arzak, who leads the kitchen at the family's three Michelin star restaurant in the Basque country. Arzak, who works in the Education Department of the Guggenheim Museum in Bilbao, concludes with a look at the restaurant and art experience at the museum. Her prediction is that multisensoriality, especially through food, will play a crucial role in how food is presented and discussed in museums and art spaces.

An unexpected perspective on the artistry of food comes from neuroscientist **Charles Spence**, who looks at the science behind the plating of food, and the aesthetic appreciation of food arrangements and alignment of food elements on the plate. Further, Spence considers the visual depiction of food, informed by food photography and television food imagery, and how it may elicit mental stimulation. In this task, a number of lessons can be taken directly from knowledge of aesthetic responses to paintings. As with all aesthetic judgment, not everyone will adhere to the same norms, such as preference for odd over even numbers or symmetry rather than asymmetry. The author suggests that the interdisciplinary science of aesthetic plating might help to understand whether there are cross-cultural and individual differences in the appreciation of color and the arrangement of food.

Considerations of plating are particularly significant when thinking about the work of chefs who create dishes for museum restaurants. Almost a century and a half after the opening of the first museum restaurant in London, the chefs in museum restaurants around the world are finding ways of connecting with the museum's mission and expanding it. We gave an opportunity to four pioneering chefs to reflect on their culinary styles, their connections with the museums where their restaurants are located and the relation between the restaurant and the museum. These chefs are **Josean Alija**, who runs Nerua, a one Michelin star restaurant, at the Guggenheim Museum, Bilbao; **Petter Nilsson**, whose restaurant is located at Spritmuseum (Stockholm), a museum dedicated to the regional history of alcohol; **Joris Bijdendijk**, an Executive Chef at RIJKS® Restaurant at the Rijksmuseum (Amsterdam); and **Ali Loukzada**, who runs Café Serai at the Rubin Museum of Art in New York City.

In the final chapter of the section, **Josean Alija** shares one of his favorite recipes, "White onion, cod, and green pepper sauce," contextualizing it in the Basque cultural and historic environment. This recipe, yet again, speaks to the complexity of artistic, cultural, political, and geographical forces which make up a recipe. When presented on the menu of a museum restaurant, the recipe is read in the context of its consumption: in the Basque country, in one of the most famous contemporary art museums in the world, in a restaurant led by a chef who has developed his own artistry through food.

Food and art

Since food discourses have become key cultural conversations in the past few decades, art historians and curators have been looking at their museum collections with a new lens for re-interpreting representations of food. Images of produce, game, baked goods, early manufactured foods, cookbooks, as well as utensils, and table arrangements found their way into recent exhibits.[12] This volume includes an article by **Judith A. Barter** who curated *Art and Appetite: American Painting, Culture, and Cuisine* (2014) at the Art Institute of Chicago, an exhibition that revisited iconic mid-century American artworks with a specific focus on the culture of food and dining. The exhibit is important because it was the first attempt to trace American identity through food culture on such scale, using over 100 objects, including paintings, sculptures, decorative arts, works on paper, cookbooks, and menus, from the eighteenth through the twentieth century.

There is no lack of interest in sugar, chocolate, and all things sweet. Sugar is used as a raw material and a symbolic representation of psychological states. A number of now iconic contemporary artworks use sweets to create layers of meanings. Untitled (1993) by Felix Gonzalez-Torres consists of 175 pounds of sweets heaped in the corner. The weight of edible candy is equal to the weight of the artist's partner before he fell sick with AIDS. The candy is a reference to the body, desire, and sacred ritual. A Brazilian artist Vic Muniz known for his chocolate paintings (1997) renders familiar images, such as *The Last Supper, Mona Lisa, Medusa* in chocolate sauce that for him is a psychologically loaded medium that speaks of sex, addiction, luxury, and romance.[13] **Will Cotton** is a figurative painter known for hyper-realistic depictions of cakes, candy canes, ginger bread houses, rivers of molasses, and ice cream floats, reclining nudes covered with ice cream, or floating on a cloud of cotton candy, portraits of pop icon Katie Perry wearing headdress of fantastical edible sugary outfits. Cotton, whose interview with **Nina Levent** is included in this volume, bridges a long tradition of realistic still lifes going back to the seventeenth-century still lifes with the twentieth-century symbolic use of sweets as a complex reference to desire and longing, fantasy, indulgence, and pleasure.

Alcohol, museums, and artist's bars are the subject of **Jim Drobnick**'s article. Drobnick points out an inherent contradiction between a bar and a museum, an institution defined since the nineteenth century as a civilized and sober entertainment alternative. He investigates a phenomenon that defies the separation of drinking and cultural experiences—artists' bars. Drobnick focuses on examples of artists' bars between the 1960s and now, and suggests that they are participatory experiences that invite visitors to consider the aesthetics, social dynamics, and ideologies around the activity of raising a glass or downing a pint. The author also includes artworks that allude to the artist's relationship with alcohol, such as Erwin Wurms' dark artwork, *Drinking Sculptures* (2011), a series of individual mini-bars installations named after artists notorious for their excessive drinking, such as Edvard Munch and Jackson Pollock.

The contemporary tradition of artists feeding the public goes back to the 1970s when artists Gordon Matta-Clark, Carol Goodden, and Tina Giroux opened a restaurant called *Food* in SoHo, New York. From this tradition comes Rirkrit Tiravanija, the first contemporary art practitioner to develop an extensive practice of creating makeshift kitchens in galleries. Jennifer Rubell's practice has exploded into the art scene in 2000s. Rubell's ambitious works are often created as feasts for hundreds of people, and are popular as museum galas, cultural benefits, and art fair openings. In her interview with **Sara Stern**, Rubell reflects on the themes of "tasting, feasting, connecting and providing." Rubell creates grand, witty, and engaging art feasts where participants are invited to touch, smell, break off, and consume edible elements of her large-scale performative food installations. The artist talks about blending performance and sculpture when she piles up bananas or tortillas, drips cheese and honey, arranges donuts or cotton candy in grids, and then allows participants to consume these elements.

The artistic engagement with farming, land, and food production has taken root on many continents where artists live on the land, form communes, and seek a socially engaged alternative creative practice. Such examples include Josef Beuys, Fernando Garcia Dory, Future Farmers collective and many others.[14] A number of important arts events have moved out of urban centers such as Kjerringøy Land Art Biennale in Norway, Mongolia 360° Land Art Biennial, and Echigo-Tsumari Art Triennial in Japan. The chapter on **artists and farmers** includes three case studies from China by **Michael Leung**, **Zhao Kunfang** and **Jay Brown**, representing hyper-local practices involving collaborations between artists and farmers to develop responses to global issues such as mega-cities and land grabbing, global heritage and tourism economies, and the viability of rural economies. Included are the stories of an urban rooftop farm collective, a curator-led rural revival, and an artist residency on a small subsistence farm.

What artists have to offer toward the future of food is not always about activism, it is about creating dialogs, questioning systems, revisiting histories, and re-imagining possibilities.[15] We have included **Nat Muller**'s interview with the **Cooking Sections** (Daniel Fernández Pascual and Alon Schwabe), a duo of artists who "explore the systems that organize the world through food."[16] Using installation, performance, mapping, and video, their research-based practice explores the overlapping boundaries between visual arts, architecture, and geopolitics. Cooking Sections collective uses food, cooking, and feeding to explore geopolitics and ideologies such as colonialism, nationalism, and capitalism. Cooking Sections speaks of "edible cartographies," stories of power relations that are mapped over territories as different as the British Empire and Cold War Europe and Gaza.

Artists engaged with food explore many registers of emotions, interactivity, and politics, embodying in material and edible form ideologies that are often difficult to pin down. Located in art museums, contemporary art galleries, farms and on rooftops, art that involves food is engaging and multisensorial, visceral at times, but powerful overall.

Future avenues of inquiry for food and museums

Just like any other ambitious project, this volume required the constant work of selecting and sorting, identifying the focus of the volume and leaving aside some lines of inquiry and case studies for further investigation. We could not touch on all the different perspectives opened up by this topic. We were able to tell stories of colonialism, gender and class relations, economic inequalities, globalization, urbanization, sustainability, and many others. Other equally fascinating narratives about indigenous heritage, race, and gender politics could not be incorporated into this volume for practical reasons. We wanted to talk to more chefs who cook in museum restaurants around the world and ask more questions about national parks, botanical gardens, and food museums. Likewise, we wished we could talk to visitors who dine in museum restaurants, who line up at a food truck during museum events and volunteers who do gardening in museums.

Notes

1   *Slow food: Craft macaroni and cheese* is one of several events organized by the Textile Museum of Canada (Toronto) under the theme of *Conscious Consumption.* The event took place on February 3, 2016.

2   Danielle Rice, "Museums: Theory, Practice, Illusion," *Art and Its Publics: Museum Studies at the Millennium*, ed. Andrew McClelland (Malden: Blackwell Publishing, 2003), 79.

3   Ibid., 93.

4   Janet Marstine, "Introduction," *New Museum Theory and Practice: An Introduction*, ed. Janet Marstine (Malden: Blackwell Publishing, 2006), 19.

5   Constance Classen, "Museum Manners: The Sensory Life of the Early Museum," *Journal of Social History* 40, no. 4 (2007): 904.

6   Roland Barthes, "Towards a Psychosociology of Cotemporary Food Consumption," *Food and Culture: A Reader*, eds. Carole Counihan and Penny Van Esterik (New York: Routledge, 1997), 29.

7   Courtesy of Elizabeth M. Williams, SoFAB director.

8   David Howes, "Introduction to Sensory Museology," *The Senses and Society*, 9, no. 3 (2014), 259.

9   Rice, 2006, 92

10 Graham Black, *The Engaging Museum: Developing Museums for Visitor Involvement* (London: Routledge, 2005); Nina Simon, *The Participatory Museum* (Santa Cruz: Museum 2.0, 2010); Anne Bergeron and Beth Tuttle, *Magnetic: The Art and Science of Engagement* (Washington DC, AAM Press, 2005); David Anderson, Alex de Cosson, and Lisa McIntosh, eds., *Research Informing the Practice of Museum Educators. Diverse Audiences, Challenging Topics, and Reflective Praxis* (Rotterdam: Sense Publishers, 2015).

11 Constance Classen, ed. *The Book of Touch* (Oxford and New York: Berg, 2005).

12 Donna R. Barnes, and Peter G. Rose. *Matters of Taste: Food and Drink in Seventeenth-Century Dutch Art and Life* (Albany: Syracuse University Press, 2002); Kenneth Bendiner, *Food in Painting: From the Renaissance to the Present* (London: Reaktion, 2004).

13 Al Seckel, *Masters of Deception: Escher, Dalí & the Artists of Optical Illusion.* (New York: Sterling. 2007), 200.

14 Hans Ulrich Obrist, "The Artist as Farmer," *Arts & Foods*, ed. Germano Celant (Milan: Mondadori, 2015), 690–700.

15 Futurefarmers, a collective of artists, designers, architects, soil scientists, and farmers, founded by artist Amy Franceschini, is an example of this approach. It works to deconstruct food, farming, and transportation systems, poses open questions and considers possibilities.

16 "Cooking Sections," http://www.cooking-sections.com/ [accessed February 25, 2016].

PART ONE

Interdisciplinary Perspectives on Food and Museums

2

Anthropology on the Menu: Cultural Perspectives on Food and Taste in Museums

Christy Shields-Argelès

Anthropology is a social science dedicated to exploring the world's diversity from a cross-cultural and comparative perspective. Participant-observation, the discipline's key qualitative methodology, involves participating in the lives of a group of people for an extended period of time in order to understand a given topic from their lived perspective. Anthropologists therefore learn through the careful observation of objects, spaces, practices, and words, but also through the embodied experiences of cuisines, sauces, flavors, and smells. Anthropologists generally write in-depth descriptions, referred to as "ethnographies," of the different life ways and worldviews they encounter. In so doing, they draw from, and continue to elaborate upon, a rich body of social theory that connects culturally and historically situated human experiences to larger questions of universal import.

While anthropologists have long recognized the importance of food to our social relations and cultural worlds, it is only within the past fifty years or so that it has become a focus of study within the discipline. Moreover, a sustained interest in the sense of taste specifically is even more recent, surfacing only within the last decade or two. In the Anglophone world, these developments have taken place in tandem with the rise of "food studies," an interdisciplinary field that places food and eating at the heart of its critical inquires. And, of course, all of these developments have taken place within a wider societal context characterized by vast and profound changes in our food systems and habits.

This article presents a selection of anthropological perspectives on food and taste. It is written for a non-specialist audience, and particularly one interested in thinking about the ways in which cultural perspectives on food and taste might contribute to rethinking museum environments and practices. Its author, however, is not a museum scholar or professional, but a food anthropologist. The article therefore does not necessarily offer pre-digested, ready-to-apply concepts, but a series of terms and perspectives from this particular disciplinary perspective aimed at offering food for thought, so to speak, to a professional world interested in integrating food or eating, taste or tasting more explicitly into a transitioning museum[1] that seeks, among other things, to integrate more participatory processes into its spaces and practices.[2] I therefore suggest that the reader approach this article as an invitation to explore a conceptual "tool-kit" that offers a number of ideas for elaborating critical and reflexive experiences of museum content through food. My central assertion is that the realm of food and taste—which contains (edible) material objects and (thus deeply) interactive processes—fits well with a cultural communication approach to the museum that privileges the agency of objects and audiences.[3]

The article is organized into three sections. The first section provides an overview of foundational texts. The second section presents a selection of early works that explore food and foodways as prime signifiers of identity and belonging. The third and final section examines recent publications that approach food and taste as multisensory engagements and interactive processes. In the conclusions to each of these sections I formulate a series of suggestions, or clear a few reflective pathways, for linking the section's perspectives to the museum experience.

Foundations

As part of a recent ethnographic research project, I have been participating in a monthly cheese tasting panel. Very early on in this experience, I realized that in order to understand and eventually join in the conversations of this taste community, I needed to first be able to identify single aromas—like roasted hazelnut, fresh cream, or lemon peel—before finding them or sensing them in a cheese. In other words, I needed to share basic reference points with the group. To some extent joining an intellectual community, or at least being able to join in its conversations, is a similar endeavor in that it requires some familiarity with basic terms and perspectives in the field. In the following section, I introduce key foundational texts in the anthropology of food and the senses. They are interesting to us here, first, for the variety of terms and perspectives they offer, which are already interesting in and of themselves, and, second, because they are built upon in later works, and thus in the following two sections of this paper.

To begin, it was not until the structural analyzes of the postwar period that food, and to a lesser extent taste, became, in the words of Claude Levi-Strauss, "good to think." Led largely by European scholars writing from a continent where industrial agriculture, mass consumption, and modern advertising were taking hold in dramatic ways, structuralism demonstrated that far from mere necessity, foods and their component parts, "signify," and thus are pertinent objects for social analysis. Drawing inspiration from linguistics, structuralists approach culture as a language. In regard to foods and their taste, this means identifying basic flavors and other sensory properties (e.g., texture, temperature) as sets of binary pairs that transmit information about social structures. In *Structural Anthropology*, Levi-Strauss writes: "Like a language (. . .) the cuisine of a society may be analyzed into constituent elements, which (. . .) we might call 'gustemes,' and which may be organized according to certain structures of opposition and correlation."[4] In other words, just as phonemes function in language, "gustemes" are the minimal gustatory units that every cuisine distinguishes in order to make significant combinations. As the above citation also indicates, "cuisine" is among Levi-Strauss' choice objects of study. In "The Culinary Triangle," he considers the rules and conventions that govern the ways in which foods are prepared and argues that culinary rules are manifestations of underlying universal structures of human thought.[5] While Levi-Strauss' search for such structures has largely been abandoned, his reflections continue to serve in interesting ways; Dylan Clark's analysis of punk cuisine using the "culinary triangle" is one example.[6]

English anthropologist Mary Douglas applies the structuralist method to the study of meals and dietary taboos. She is specifically interested in the ways that food categories encode and maintain social boundaries. In her influential article "Deciphering a Meal," she argues that, in her household, the meal (characterized by hot and solid foods for example) signals intimate social relations, as opposed to drinks (characterized by cold foods and liquid beverages, for example), which encode social distance. She also considers Jewish dietary taboos, showing that a structuralist approach can be applied not only to the foods we eat, but also to those we avoid.[7] For Douglas, taboos are anomalous to larger classificatory systems, and as such can tell us much about said structures.

While not cited as often in the anthropological literature, Roland Barthes also makes use of binary pairs to explore food as a "system of communication."[8] Barthes' article is interesting for its readability (as opposed to the work of Levi-Strauss and Douglas) and for his focus on "contemporary food consumption." Barthes explores a variety of sensory-based binary pairs (e.g., white and brown bread, sweet and bitter) and concludes his article with an insightful look at

French food advertisements, identifying themes that will be widely explored in the decades to follow, namely: commemoration and tradition, gender and sexuality, and health and "nutritional consciousness." While the structuralists' treatment of food and taste is not based on fieldwork and is criticized for its static nature, their work brings into view the cross-cultural variability of tastes and distastes and identifies them as an insightful area of critical inquiry.

In the United States, structuralist thought is challenged by the cultural ecology school, which sought material and functional explanations for food habits.[9] American anthropologist Sidney Mintz, in his pivotal work *Sweetness and Power: The Place of Sugar in Modern History*, combines a material focus on sugar production in the Caribbean with a cultural analysis of British sugar consumption.[10] Clearly differentiating between "sweetness," as a taste, and the various substances that provide it (e.g., sugar, honey), Mintz spans disciplinary and theoretical borders to consider production and consumption, the past and the present, and use and meaning. Moreover, at a moment when anthropology is in the throes of a profound identity crisis, Mintz explicitly calls for the discipline to apply its unique perspective and methodologies to critically examining historical transformation, especially in the realm of food and eating. In the final chapter of his work he urges readers to recognize the parallels between colonial capitalism and contemporary political-economic structures, especially as they shape our food preferences. He picks up this thread of analysis in a later work written for a general audience entitled *Tasting Food, Tasting Freedom*.[11] While Mintz's work is not based on participant-observation (as he himself recognizes), and often only evokes a number of analytical claims (as many of these early works do), it remains an extremely important body of work in the Anglo-American tradition of food anthropology, inspiring later generations to use historical approaches, focus on single foods or flavors, and pay heed to the ways in which political-economic structures and processes shape our food systems and habits. Power, Mintz showed us, is embedded in what we often consider to be only individual taste preferences, even the most innocent and joyful of them all, such as our penchant for sweetness.

Also concerned with questions of power, French sociologist Pierre Bourdieu, though not interested in food and eating per se, influenced the field in important ways. In *Distinction: A Social Critique of the Judgement of Taste*, he identifies and contrasts the taste of necessity and the taste of luxury as a means to explore how distinctions in taste serve to mediate between class and gender on the one hand, and the body on the other.[12] Extremely influential in the 1980s and 1990s as a means to underline the reproduction of social hierarchies through taste preferences, Bourdieu's work has also been criticized for subsuming gustatory taste under the wider category of aesthetic taste.

In contrast to Bourdieu, French sociologist Claude Fischler approached food and taste from the perspective of the modern eater. Extremely influential in France in the 1990s, a small portion of Fischler's work traveled to the Anglophone world, first, through two articles[13] and then through his collaborative research with American psychologist Paul Rozin.[14] Drawing initially from Rozin's work, Fischler begins with humankind's omnivorous nature. As omnivores we are positioned in between neophilia (a tendency to explore, the need for change), on the one hand, and neophobia (prudence, fear and resistance to change), on the other. In the face of food modernity—associated by Fischler with the "destructuration" of our food systems and rules as well as the "trafficking" of our foods' tastes—humans are no longer able to clearly categorize their foods and so are pushed towards the neophobic side of the omnivore's spectrum. Modern eaters are also, for Fischler, robbed of a sense of self because, as the structuralists argued, food integrates us into larger cosmologies and so helps build our collective and individual identities. Fischler argues that "cuisine"—understood as a body of practices, representations, rules, and norms—is a means to respond to the anxiety of the modern eater because as a classificatory system it connects our foods to universes of meaning, making them recognizable and safe. Rozin and Rozin make a similar argument about flavors and flavor combinations.[15] More recently, borrowing from the work of Fischler and Rozin, food journalist Michel Pollan (2006) also explores the "omnivore's dilemma."[16]

Another group of scholars, led by anthropologist David Howes and historian Constance Classen, explore taste from the perspective of the senses. Interested primarily in the cultural life of the senses, this group is "concerned with how the patterning of sense experience varies from one culture to the next" and "the influence such variations have on forms of social organization, conceptions of self and cosmos (. . .) and other domains of cultural expression."[17] Much of this research is organized according to the five canonical senses: sight,[18] touch,[19] sound,[20] smell[21] and aroma,[22] and taste.[23] This body of research was originally founded on a criticism of a Western visual bias and thus structured by the more traditional disciplinary focus on non-Western others within a Western/non-Western binary.

This body of work has been influential in the museum world[24] and scholars working in this tradition have also studied the sensory life of museums. For example, in an article entitled, "The Museum as Sensescape," Classen and Howes examine the sensorial dimensions of indigenous artifacts and the sensory typologies of their European collectors.[25] In another piece, Classen explores museum manners and the sensory life of early museums, which allowed for significant multisensorial participation, including gustatory interactions.[26] Similar themes are also examined in a more recent publication.[27]

While an interest in the taste of food and drink has not necessarily been dominant in this group's work, it has nonetheless been present from the very beginning. An early publication edited by Howes includes three articles on taste.[28] Of particular interest is an article by linguistic anthropologist Joel Kuipers. Drawing from fieldwork among the Weyéwa of the western highlands of Sumba, Kuipers argues that taste vocabulary and taste substances are context dependent. He focuses in particular on the manner in which "taste substances are meaningfully ordered in the context of a 'social visit.'"[29] For Kuipers, taste vocabulary words are best understood as "multifunctional signs." To illustrate this he considers taste terms used in ritual speech. Kuipers draws our attention to the centrality of language to taste and taste practices.

Anthropologist Paul Stoller, though not initially part of this group, shares many of its perspectives. He is also highly critical of a Western visual bias, and calls for anthropologists to know others through their senses.[30] In their article entitled "Thick Sauces: Remarks on the Social Relations of the Songhay," Stoller and Olkes recount a horrible meal served to them during a fieldwork stay in order to explore how the qualities of sauces measure degrees of social proximity.[31] Specific to Stoller's work is the suggestion that anthropological works need to be written sensually, and he integrates a range of creative writing strategies into his ethnographic texts.[32]

Perhaps the most useful volume for those interested in an introduction to taste from the perspective of the senses is an edited volume by philosopher Carolyn Korsmeyer.[33] In it she brings together articles from a variety of time periods and disciplines, including texts by philosopher Emmanuel Kant or gastronome Brillat-Savarin to the work of numerous social scientists such as Mintz and Bourdieu. Korsmeyer also wrote a philosophical investigation of food and taste in which she reflects upon food and art, as well as the relationship between the two. Of particular interest is her examination of food as a symbolic system: "I adapt Nelson Goodman's theory of symbols that operate in art (. . .), for I claim that food (while not art itself) performs many of the same symbol activities as works of art."[34] Similarly, Kirshenblatt-Gimblett is interested in the relationship between food and art. Drawing from numerous kinds of performance art, she examines food as performance: "food, like performance, is alive, fugitive, and sensory."[35]

In conclusion, if the social science literature of any given time can be read as a reflection of that era's most pressing issues, then the first and most obvious remark to be made here is that food—how it is grown, traded, transformed, shared, protected, represented—has become an arena of intense change, public interest, and political debate in the past fifty years. For cultural institutions like the museum, which often strive to guide and propel societal debates, certainly this realm seems an important one today. Second, while the above foundational literature introduces a number of themes that remain important to the field's interests, their diversity also illustrates that food and foodways are, in the words of Marcel Mauss, "total social phenomenon" as they involve simultaneous expressions of religious, political, moral, and economic nature.[36] In other words, any single food, flavor or meal event can provide rich insights into historical processes, power struggles, global flows, cultural values, and identity constructions. As such these works also offer a variety of frames for imagining and elaborating a rich and reflective experience of museum content through food.

Food as signifier of identity and belonging

Many of the ethnographies published in the 1980s and 1990s examine the role of food and foodways in the construction and maintenance of collective identities. National identity, in particular, is a favorite topic. A notable example is Belasco and Scranton's interdisciplinary volume *Food Nations*.[37] As Mintz and Dubois note about this period: "Many studies consider the creation of nation through the invention, standardization or valorization of a national cuisine, often drawing on Anderson's[38] conception of the imagined community and Hobsbawm's[39] concept of invented tradition."[40] While taste (as sense) is largely absent from these works, we do get the feeling that it is perhaps the ubiquitous tastes of sugar and salt in the industrial foods of contemporary America that are propelling them. The foods and foodways of ethnic communities are also a popular topic in the United States. Since American national identity is often understood as being built from an ensemble of ethnic communities and cuisines, we can also see this literature as stemming from a common identity impulse. Within this vein of study, scholars in anthropology, but also adjacent fields such as folklore, explore how foods function—in community festivals, within family meals, in the space of the restaurant—to perform and thereby maintain ethnic identities.[41]

Much of this literature approaches food as symbol, and ritual is frequently included as one of the frames that endow food with additional meaning. Moreover, many scholars produce historical ethnographies, taking an interest in how the symbolic import of particular food items changes over time. Examples of this approach include: Ohnuki-Tierney's nuanced historical ethnography of the symbolic and material significance of rice in Japan and its centrality in the construction of national identity,[42] Boisard's historical study of camembert, in which he traces the manner in which the cheese became a mythic symbol of French national identity,[43] or, Siskind's article on Thanksgiving, which she approaches as a commensal ritual that both expresses national belonging and reproduces cultural ideologies about white privilege.[44]

As this last example suggests, while foods are explored for their power to unite they are also examined for their ability to divide, or reproduce social hierarchies and boundaries.[45] Interestingly, this literature, often drawing on the work of Bourdieu, integrates questions of taste more directly. For example,

Susan Terrio explores the world of high-end, artisanal chocolates in contemporary France, taking an interest in the manner in which new taste standards are produced and disseminated.[46] It is interesting to note that a number of scholars studying France at the time approach taste in a similar fashion, focusing on what we might consider to be the distinction potential of "tasty" French foods and beverages like chocolate and champagne,[47] or Bordeaux wines.[48]

The reinvention and performance of collective identities within consumption spaces, such as bars and restaurants, is also explored. Spradley and Mann examine the symbolic and social construction of gender in an American Midwestern bar using a series of traditional anthropology concepts (kinship, exchange, rites of passage, joking relationships).[49] Wilson brings together a series of articles that explore the production and expression of identity in a variety of drinking sites and practices.[50] Beriss and Sutton approach the restaurant as a "total social phenomenon for our postmodern world," and the volume's articles provide an array of perspectives.[51] Fast food restaurants, and especially McDonald's, are also debated in the 1990s with one set of researchers arguing that "McDonaldization" is rationalization of the highest order[52] and another set of scholars proposing the term "localization" and looking instead to the ways in which McDonald's is shaped by consumer practices and tastes in a wide array of contexts.[53] Rick Fantasia's article on McDonald's in France spans both sides of the debate: he explores the ways in which French consumers use and understand McDonald's as a form of culinary and cultural tourism, but also identifies the potential impact of McDonald's as a political-economic model in which labor is deskilled and rendered expendable.[54]

As the above works also suggest, processes of "Americanization" (integration into the global market dominated by the United States) and "Europeanization" (integration into the European Union) have shaped foods and foodways on the European continent in important ways, from the postwar period to the present day. Europe has therefore been a particularly important context for exploring the relationships between food, memory, and identity, especially in the face of the constant threat of the homogenization of national and regional differences. A number of works are notable here: Letich provides a rich analysis of the politics of memory in regard to *lardo*, a regional Italian food that was among the test cases for the nascent Slow Food movement in the 1990s;[55] Sutton explores the interrelationship of culture, food, and memory on the Greek island of Kalymnos,[56] and Carole Counihan uses food-centered life histories to explore food and memory as a window onto the changes experienced by twentieth-century Florentines.[57] Of special note is the work of Greek anthropologist Nadia Seremetakis who writes in a profoundly moving manner about the erasure of unconscious memory as local varieties of foods are lost through standardization.[58]

Food and memory are also explored in a series of works that consider how immigrant communities reconstruct a sense of home and belonging through multisensory food experiences.[59] A number of these works apply the notion of synaesthesia, which refers to the "union of the senses." Sutton, for example, considers how the use of synesthetic metaphors ("listen to that smell") and multisensory experiences help to make food consumption memorable and thus allow Greeks living in England to "return to the whole," or a sense of relatedness and belonging.[60]

In conclusion, early works in the field generally focus on the symbolic qualities of our foods and foodways as well as their relationship to the construction and maintenance of a range of collective identities. As symbols, foods are revealed in this literature as multilayered, multifunctional, and malleable signs of group belonging and differentiation. A cultural perspective on museum communication also privileges the recognition and use of symbols and symbolic systems because they "shape, express and convey our attitudes and interpretations of our experience" and thus can lead to new ways of conceiving and imagining the relationship between museums and their audiences.[61] Moreover, since museums are often considered to be important regional, national, and global identity markers and makers, these explorations offer frames for connecting foods and foodways in museums to such identity communities and issues in an in-depth manner. While museum professionals and scholars are paying heed to the synesthetic nature of our sensory experience in museums,[62] this literature suggests that additional attention could be given to the manner in which foods are particularly powerful social objects; they can be interesting for their artistic and historical significance, their ability to spark conversation with others and reflect upon the self, but also for their capacity to create a deep sense of connection with others. In other words, their strong tie to identity—and thus to memory, to ritual, to stories, to emotion, to places, times, and people—means that they can play a key role in the elaboration of memorable and transformative experiences inside the museum. It is to this last characteristic that we devote the following, and final, section of this paper.

Taste, agency, and transformation

In recent years, disciplinary focus has shifted from approaching foods as containers of meaning to considering them as objects that exercise agency in their own right; from taste preferences as signs or set of standards that represent or reproduce collective identities to tasting as a reflexive, interactive, and productive activity that has the potential to transform societies and their foods. Phenomenological perspectives shape many of these works, and scholars also paid heed to the body and questions of embodiment.[63] As we will see, some also borrow in interesting ways from theories originally elaborated for the arts. In addition, many of these scholars are testing new research techniques, such as photography and video.

This field of research is still shifting and settling. American anthropologist David Sutton, for example, suggests an integrative approach to its construction: one that combines an "anthropology of food" tradition (as we just explored it) with an "anthropology of the senses" perspective stemming from the work of David Howes and his collaborators. In his review article on food and the senses, Sutton introduces the term "gustemology" to characterize scholarly works that "organize their understanding of a wide spectrum of cultural issues around taste and other sensory aspects of food."[64] British visual anthropologist Sarah Pink takes a more oppositional stance, defining her brand of "sensory ethnography" in opposition to Howes' tradition.[65] In either case, the senses, and taste in particular, are brought center stage. This section offers a brief but informative peek into this literature. Since much of it is focused on forms of "doing" (as "becoming"), we have organized the remainder of the section in regard to the following three actions: place-making, cooking, and restaurant dining.

Place-making

In recent years a number of works have explored food, and its sensory aspects, as an integral part of place-making processes. Several scholars in this area focus on the notion of *terroir*. Amy Trubek is among the first Anglophone researchers to write on the concept, which she proposes to translate into English as the "taste of place."[66] Trubek argues that *terroir* must be understood as a "foodview," or a food-centered worldview, that associates a specific place with a set of practices, actors, and geographies. Trubek begins her exploration with an historical analysis of the social construction of *terroir* in France. She traces the manner in which the concept was produced by taste makers (e.g., journalists, cookbook writers) and taste producers (e.g., wine makers, cheese makers) in order to celebrate and protect an agrarian and rural way of life. In the remainder of the book she contrasts these beginnings with the development of *terroir* in the United States. We certainly get the sense throughout the book—the last chapter is titled "The Next Step: Taste of Place or Brand"– that Trubek is not only telling her audience about *terroir*, but also urging them to further invest it as an alternative to an increasingly industrialized food system.

Based on fieldwork carried out in the Loire region, Wendy Leynse explores the manner in which French children are socialized to become "situated eaters."[67] Leynse defines "situated eaters" as "well-informed consumers whose eating experience is anchored in a culturally specific locale and its associated identities via rich multisensory experiences."[68] Accompanying a fifth grade field trip she demonstrates "how multi-sensory experiences at production sites can connect specific products to particular locales and can multiply and enrich the layers of meaning that children attach to the foods they eat."[69] She also evokes the numerous food fairs and events that take place throughout France as important sites of socialization. Her work clearly shows that the historical construct described by Trubek does not simply perpetuate in France, but is a worldview that is transmitted in specific spaces, through certain events and practices and by using all the senses.

Harry West focuses on cultural transmission among artisan cheese makers in England and France.[70] He draws from Ingold's idea that "the movement of the skilled practitionnner [sic] . . . is continually and fluently responding to perturbations of the perceived environment."[71] He also borrows from and extends Alfred Gell's theory of art.[72] Gell argued that objects can exercise agency, and West agrees: "curd *did* things."[73] However, Gell also argued that the agency of objects is secondary to the primary agency of human actors. West, on the other hand, claims that: "For most of the artisan cheese makers I have worked with the line between the primary agency of people and the secondary agency of objects is considerably blurrier than Gell suggests."[74] Learning to make cheese occurs in interactions between cheese makers and the cheeses themselves. West thereby suggests that foods themselves are central agents in cultural transmission. Similarly, Heather Paxon (2012, especially Chapter 7) suggests that tastings based on a shared vocabulary and a dialogical exchange are an important activity that helps both artisanal cheese makers and their consumers recognize and express the moral value of craft production.[75]

A series of works also explore place-making in urban contexts. Of particular note are the works of Pink[76] and Marte[77] for their innovative methodologies. Pink explores walking and tasting as a means to explore and share a sense of a particular city. Marte, on the other hand, uses various types of mapping (of kitchen spaces, shopping routes, recipes) in order to explore the place experiences (domestic, public, national, and transnational) of Dominicans and Mexicans in New York City.

Cooking

Cooking, too, is being approached as a skilled practice, with a focus on transmission. For example, Sutton examines the role and significance of cooking in the lives of Kalymnians.[78] Like West above, he is interested in objects as agents in transmission processes. He focuses on kitchen tools as a means to see "how the everydayness of cooking is negotiated" and how this everydayness "opens up much larger issues of memory and identity, agency and embodiment."[79] In regard to the second, he divides his exploration into vertical transmission (inter-generational within the family) and horizontal transmission (involving other community members but also the wider Greek society through cooking shows). Central to Sutton's work—and we find this reiterated in other works as well—is a concern with the relationship between objects and humans as co-constructive process; he states, for example: "in transforming materials or ingredients into forms—the cooked dish—one is also engaged in a process of self-transformation, into that of the competent or incompetent cook."[80]

Joy Adapon[81] and Meredith Abarca[82] examine the artistic agency inherent in cooking as a learned skill. Based on fieldwork in Mexico City, Adapon explicitly engages with Gell's theory of the "art nexus," focusing on taste and flavor, as well as cooking (in the home, in the street and in local *fiestas*) as an embodied skill. Abarca draws from a series of oral histories, or *charlas culinarias* (culinary chats), carried out with working-class Mexican and Mexican American women in their kitchens. Both Adapon and Abarca use the concept of *sazón* to examine the cultural value of the sense of taste in Mexico and how in producing taste women project their agency onto the wider world, even when they are marginalized economically or socially.

Restaurant dining

The work of philosopher Lisa Heldke challenges prevailing views of the restaurant, and in particular, what is happening when North Americans dine in ethnic restaurants.[83] Rather than view the ethnic restaurant, and by extension its cuisine and its flavors, as containers of authenticity, she asks us, drawing on Dewey's understanding of art as experiential, to focus instead on the relationship between cook and diner. In this way, Heldke states that "authenticity is understood to be the quality of this exchange"[84] and calls for scholars to attend to the various kinds of transactions that take place in the cross-cultural exchanges involved in eating others' cuisines.

Heldke's work, among others, has inspired scholars to approach the restaurant as a key site of cultural interaction and transformation. For these works, the restaurant, and its cuisine in particular, does not simply reflect meaning or symbolize identity. Instead, restaurants (as well as their menus, foods, and flavors) are understood as active agents in the creation and recreation of meaning. In other words, the restaurant is approached as a site of culinary, cultural, and political agency and negotiation. Articles by cultural studies scholars Karaosmanoglu[85] and Mihalache[86] are both excellent examples. Karaosmanoglu explores the manner in which "the Ottoman past is revived through cooking and eating, smell and taste" in two types of restaurants in contemporary Istanbul: fine-dining restaurants and tradesman diners.[87] She aims to study "the past as/through text and performance by looking at how history is brought back, represented, and performed by food practices in the present."[88] Mihalache focuses her analysis on the restaurant *El Zyriab*, located on the ninth floor of the *Institut du Monde Arabe* (IMA), a French cultural institution dedicated to "the Arab World." Mihalache argues that the eating spaces of cultural institutions "contribute to the overall story that the cultural institutions tells about the objects on display."[89] In the case of *El Zyriab,* she argues that it actually challenges the story told in the rest of the IMA. For an application of some of these ideas to the museum space in particular, readers can consult Mihalache's article entitled "Taste-full Museums."[90]

Other works of note are Klein's exploration of Cantonese restaurant menus.[91] Klein argues that "Cantonese cuisine does not simply reflect any pre-existing or stable community" but should be understood instead as "a medium through which communities and their relation to one another are defined and negotiated."[92] And, in regard to consuming the foods of others in the art world: Bal considers how *glub*, a kind of seed-eating prevalent among immigrants in Berlin, is part of an aesthetic that shapes the Berlin art world, suggesting that it is understood as a cultural habit through which artists "participate in other people's memories."[93]

In conclusion, this group of works offers ideas and frames for reaching beyond food as historical or cultural artifact, or as mere identity symbol. Instead, this group of literature focuses on forms of making and doing, which in the realm of food also involves skill-building, incorporation, and embodiment, making them potentially transformational as well. If contemporary museums aim at further elaborating participation and interaction, the realm of food seems to offer enormous potential. In this way, cooking, gardening, making cheese, or dining are not only windows into others' worlds, but also a means of participating in those worlds, to a certain degree, of course. The literature also helps us to think of food as social object that possesses agency and voice, and remind us that food practices are particularly immersive. Approached from this angle, these works offer a series of ideas for elaborating new museum spaces and activities. New spaces could include restaurants or cafés, though we could also imagine gardens and kitchens. Indeed, if the focus is on forms of doing and the skill experience or development they provide, I do not see any reason why the museum or some small portion of it, could not be loaded into a truck now and then in order to take the show on the road, so to speak, and join audiences in their communities. In other words, a focus on activity might also allow for a certain freedom of movement that has not yet been fully explored.

Conclusions

This article began with an introduction to foundational works in the subfields of the anthropology of food and the anthropology of the senses. In the second section, I introduced readers to a selection of early ethnographies that tend to approach food as symbol, and thus as vehicle for the expression and maintenance of collective identities. In the article's final section, I provide an overview of works from the last decade, which generally share an interest in the agency of flavors, cuisines, foods, eaters, and alimentary texts (such as menus). Concluding remarks in each of these sections offer a few suggestions for applying the literature to the museum context. These suggestions fit with a cultural communications approach to the museum space (Hooper-Greenhill), itself built upon what scholar James Carey calls a "ritual communication" perspective.[94] In contrast to transmission communication, which aims at sending or relaying information to a passive audience, ritual communication is defined by terms such as participation, association, or even, communion, and understood as "sacred ceremony that draws people together in fellowship and commonality."[95]

In this regard, I will offer one final set of thoughts: the museum (like the liberal arts college, which is an institution with which I am perhaps experientially more familiar) has been in the throes of a profound identity crisis in recent years as it is called upon to both question its fundamental mission and methods, but also to project a strong and seductive identity to the world. Despite the difficulties this crisis has engendered, I feel, as many do I believe, that the museum still has an enormously important educational and civic role to play in contemporary societies, which involves, among other things, creating spaces of debate and dialogue, discovery and reflection. The museum's ability to do this so well lies, in part, in its liminal nature. Foucault suggests that museums are heterotopic spaces: both outside the mundane time and spaces of the world and yet integrally connected to them.[96] From an anthropological perspective, such liminal spaces, precisely because they are "betwixt and between", do not simply provide knowledge or access, they also possess the power to emotionally stir, incite critical social and self-reflection, transcend boundaries, and potentially transform individuals.[97] I hope that I have, if nothing else, convinced the reader that the realm of food and foodways lends itself particularly well to such an environment because they are intricately bound to social and symbolic processes that are central to the construction of meaning and identity in human societies and thus involve multiple forms of doing and becoming that can be used to frame both museum objects and audiences as active agents in a dialogical process.

Notes

1 Hilde S. Hein, *The Museum in Transition: A Philosophical Perspective* (Washington DC: Smithsonian Institution, 2014).

2 Nina Simon, *The Participatory Museum* (Museum 2.0, 2010).

3 Eilean Hooper-Greenhill, "Changing Values in the Art Museum: Rethinking Communication and Learning," *International Journal of Heritage Studies* 6, no. 1 (2010): 9–31.

4 Claude Lévi-Strauss, *Structural Anthropology* (New York: Basic Books, 2008), 86.

5 Claude Lévi-Strauss, "The Culinary Triangle," in *Food and Culture: A Reader* (2nd Edition), ed. by Carole Counihan and Penny Van Esterik (London and New York: Routledge, 2008).

6 Dylan Clark, "The Raw and the Rotten: Punk Cuisine," *Ethnology* 43, no. 1 (2004): 19–31.

7 Mary Douglas, "Deciphering a Meal," *Daedalus* 101, no. 1 (1972): 61–81. See also: Mary Douglas, ed. *Food in the Social Order: Studies of Food and Festivities in Three American Communities* (New York: Russell Sage, 1984).

8 Roland Barthes, "Toward a Psychosociology of Contemporary Food Consumption," in *Food and Culture: A Reader*, ed. by Carole Counihan and Penny Van Esterik (New York and London: Routledge, 2008).

9 Marvin Harris, *Good to Eat: Riddles of Food and Culture* (Prospect Heights: Waveland Press, 1998).

10 Sidney Mintz, *Sweetness and Power: The Place of Sugar in Modern History* (New York: Penguin Books, 1986).

11 Sidney Mintz, *Tasting Food, Tasting Freedom: Excursions into Eating, Culture and the Past.* (Boston: Beacon Press, 1996).

12 Pierre Bourdieu, *Distinction: A Social Critique of the Judgement of Taste.* Translated by Richard Nice (Cambridge: Harvard University Press, 1984).

13 Claude Fischler, "Food Habits, Social Change and the Nature/culture Dilemma," *Social Science Information* 19, no. 6 (1980): 937–953; Claude Fischler, "Food, self and identity," *Social Science Information* 27, no. 2 (1988): 275–292.

14 Paul Rozin, Claude Fischler, Sumio Imada, Allison Sarubin, and Amy Wrzesniewski, "Attitudes to Food and the Role of Food in Life in the USA, Japan, Flemish Belgium and France: Possible Implications for the Diet–Health Debate," *Appetite* 33, no. 2 (1999): 163–180. See also Clause Fischler, *L'Homnivore: Le goût, la cuisine et le corps* (Paris: Odile Jacob, 1990).

15 Elisabeth Rozin and Paul Rozin, "Flavour Principles: Some Applications," in *The Taste Culture Reader: Experiencing Food and Drink*, ed. by Carolyn Korsmeyer (Oxford: Berg, 2005).

16 Michael Pollan, *The Omnivore's Dilemma: A Natural History of Four Meals* (New York: Penguin, 2006).

17 David Howes, ed., *The Varieties of Sensory Experience: A Sourcebook in the Anthropology of the Senses* (Toronto: University of Toronto Press, 1991), 3.

18 Elizabeth Edwards and Kaushik Bhaumik, *Visual Sense: A Cultural Reader* (Oxford: Berg, 2008).

19 Constance Classen, *The Book of Touch* (Oxford: Berg, 2005).

20 Michael Bull and Les Back, eds., *The Auditory Culture Reader* (Oxford: Berg, 2003).

21 Jim Drobnick, ed., *The Smell Culture Reader* (Oxford and New York: Berg, 2006).

22 Constance Classen, David Howes, and Anthony Synnott, *Aroma: The Cultural History of Smell* (New York and London: Routledge, 1994).

23 Carolyn Korsmeyer, *Making Sense of Taste: Food and Philosophy* (Ithaca: Cornell University Press, 1999).

24 Nina Levent and Alvaro Pascual-Leone, eds., *The Multisensory Museum: Cross-Disciplinary Perspectives on Touch, Sound, Smell, Memory, and Space* (Lanham: Rowman & Littlefield, 2014).

25 Constance Classen and David Howes, "The Museum as Sensescape: Western Sensibilities and Indigenous Artifacts," in *Sensible Objects: Colonialism, Museums and Material Culture*, ed. by Elizabeth Edwards, Chris Gosden and Ruth Philips (London and New York: Bloomsbury Academic, 2006), 199–222.

26 Constance Classen, "Museum Manners: The Sensory Life of the Early Museum," *Journal of Social History* 40, no. 4 (2007): 895–914.

27 David Howes and Constance Classen, *Ways of Sensing: Understanding the Senses in Society.* (London and New York: Routledge, 2013).

28 Howes 1991.

29 Joel Kuipers, "Taste Among the Weyewa," in *The Varieties of Sensory Experience: A Sourcebook in the Anthropology of the Senses*, ed. by David Howes (Toronto: University of Toronto Press, 1991), 112.

30 Paul Stoller, *The Taste of Ethnographic Things: The Senses in Anthropology* (Philadelphia: University of Pennsylvania Press, 1989).

31 Paul Stoller and Cheryl Okles, "Thick Sauces: Remarks on the Social Relations of the Songhay," in *The Taste Culture Reader: Experiencing Food and Drink*, ed. by Carolyn Korsmeyer, (Oxford: Berg, 2005), 131–144.

32 Paul Stoller, *Sensuous Scholarship* (Philadelphia: University of Pennsylvania Press, 2010).

33 Carolyn Korsmeyer, ed., *The Taste Culture Reader: Experiencing Food and Drink* (Oxford: Berg, 2005).

34 Korsmeyer, 1999, 7.

35 Barbara Kirshenblatt-Gimblett, "Playing to the Senses: Food as a Performance Medium," *Performance Research* 4, no. 1 (1999): 1

36 Marcel Mauss, "Techniques of the Body," *Economy and Society* 2, no. 1 (1973): 70–88.

37 Warren Belasco and Warren Scranton, eds., *Food Nations: Selling Taste in Consumer Societies* (New York and London: Routledge, 2001).

38 Benedict Anderson, *Imagined Communities: Reflections on the Origin and Spread of Nationalism* (New York: Verso, 1983).

39 Terence O. Ranger and Eric J. Hobsbawm, eds., *The Invention of Tradition* (Cambridge: Cambridge University Press, 1983).

40 Sidney W. Mintz and Christine M. Du Bois, "The Anthropology of Food and Eating," *Annual Review of Anthropology* 31 (2002): 368.

41 Linda Keller Brown and Kay Mussell, *Ethnic and Regional Foodways in the United States: The Performance of Group Identity* (Knoxville: University of Tennessee Press, 1984).

42 Emiko Ohnuki-Tierney, *Rice as Self: Japanese Identities through Time* (Princeton: Princeton University Press, 1993).

43 Pierre Boisard, *Camembert: A National Myth*, trans. Richard Miller (Berkeley: University of California Press, 2003).

44 Janet Siskind, "The Invention of Thanksgiving A Ritual of American Nationality," *Critique of Anthropology* 12, no. 2 (1992): 167–191.

45 Anne Allison, "Japanese mothers and obentōs: The lunch-box as ideological state apparatus," *Anthropological Quarterly* 64, no. 4 (1991): 195–208.

46 Susan J. Terrio, "Crafting Grand Cra Chocolates in Contemporary France," *American Anthropologist* 98, no. 1 (1996): 67–79.

47 Deborah Reed-Danahay, "Champagne and Chocolate: Taste and Inversion in a French Wedding Ritual," *American Anthropologist* 98, no. 4 (1996): 750–761.

48 Robert C. Ulin, "Invention and Representation as Cultural Capital," *American Anthropologist* 97, no. 3 (1995): 519–527.

49 James P. Spradley and Brenda E. Mann, *The Cocktail Waitress: Woman's Work in a Man's World* (Long Grove: Waveland Press, 2008).

50 Thomas M. Wilson, ed., *Drinking Cultures: Alcohol and Identity* (Oxford: Berg, 2005).

51 David Berriss and David Sutton, eds., *The Restaurants Book: Ethnographies of Where We Eat* (Oxford: Berg, 2007), 12.

52 George Ritzer, ed., *McDonaldization: The Reader* (Thousand Oaks: Pine Forge Press, 2009).

53 James, Watson, ed., *Golden Arches East: McDonald's in East Asia*, 2nd edition (Stanford: Stanford University Press, 2006).

54 Rick Fantasia, "Everything and Nothing: The Meaning of Fast-Food and Other American Cultural Goods in France," *The Tocqueville Review* 15, no. 7 (1994): 57–88.

55 Alison Leitch, "The Social Life of Lardo: Slow Food in Fast Times," *The Asia Pacific Journal of Anthropology* 1, no. 1 (2000): 103–118.

56 David Sutton, *Remembrance of Repasts: An Anthropology of Food and Memory* (Oxford: Berg, 2001).

57 Carole Counihan, *Around the Tuscan Table: Food, Family, and Gender in Twentieth-Century Florence* (London and New York: Routledge, 2004).

58 Nadia C. Seremetakis, *The Senses Still* (Chicago: University of Chicago Press, 1996).

59 Efrat, Ben-Ze'ev, "The Politics of Taste and Smell: Palestinian Rites of Return," in *The Politics of Food*, ed. by Marianne Lien and Brigitte Nerlich (Oxford: Berg, 2004), 141–160; Lisa Law, "Home Cooking: Filipino Women and Geographies of the Senses in Hong Kong," *Cultural Geographies* 8, no. 3 (2001): 264–283; David Sutton, "Synesthesia, Memory, and the Taste of Home," in *The Taste Culture Reader: Experiencing Food and Drink*, ed. by Carolyn Korsmeyer (Oxford: Berg, 2005), 304–316.

60 Sutton, 2001, 2005.

61 Hopper-Greenhill, 2010, 21.

62 Levent and Pascual, 2014.

63 Tim Ingold, *The Perception of the Environment: Essays on Livelihood, Dwelling and Skill* (London and New York: Routledge, 2000); Mauss, 1973.

64 David Sutton, "Food and the Senses," *Annual Review of Anthropology* 39 (2010): 215.

65 Sarah Pink, *Doing Sensory Ethnography*. London: Sage, 2009; Sarah Pink and David Howes, "The Future of Sensory Anthropology/The Anthropology of the Senses," *Social Anthropology* 18, no. 3 (2010): 331–333.

66 Amy Trubek, *The Taste of Place: A Cultural Journey into Terroir* (Berkeley: University of California Press, 2008).

67 Wendy Leysne, "Journeys Through 'Ingestible Topography': Socializing the 'Situated Eater' in France," *European Studies: A Journal of European Culture, History and Politics* 22, no. 1 (2006): 129–158.

68 Ibid., 130.

69 Ibid., 131.

70 Harry G. West, "Thinking Like a Cheese: Towards an Ecological Understanding of the Reproduction of Knowledge in Contemporary Artisan Cheesemaking," in *Understanding Cultural Transmission in Anthropology: A Critical Synthesis*, ed. by Roy Ellen, Stephen Lycett and Sarah Johns (Oxford: Berghahn Books, 2013), 320–345.

71 Ingold, 2001, 135 quoted in West, 2013, 329.

72 Alfred Gell, *Art and Agency: An Anthropological Theory* (Oxford: Oxford University Press, 1998).

73 West, 2013, 332.

74 Ibid.

75 Heather Paxson, *The Life of Cheese: Crafting Food and Value in America* (Berkeley: University of California Press, 2012).

76 Sarah Pink, "An Urban Tour: The Sensory Sociality of Ethnographic Place-Making." *Ethnography* 9, no. 2 (2008): 175–196.

77 Linda Marte, "Foodmaps: Tracing Boundaries of 'Home' Through Food Relations," *Food and Foodways* 15, no. 3–4 (2007): 261–289.

78 David Sutton, *Secrets from the Greek Kitchen: Cooking, Skill, and Everyday Life on an Aegean Island* (Berkeley: University of California Press, 2014).

79 Ibid., 49.

80 Ibid., 12.

81 Joy Adapon, *Culinary Art and Anthropology* (Oxford, New York: Berg, 2008).

82 Meredith Abarca, *Voices in the Kitchen: Views of Food and the World from Mexican and Mexican American Working Class Women* (College Station: Texas A & M University Press, 2006).

83 Lisa Heldke, *Exotic Appetites: Ruminations of a Food Adventurer* (London and New York: Routledge: 2003).

84 Ibid., 389.

85 Defne Karaosmanoglu, "Eating the Past: Multiple Spaces, Multiple Times – Performing Ottomanness' in Istanbul," *International Journal of Cultural Studies* 12, no. 4 (2009): 339–358.

86 Irina D. Mihalache, "Museums, Consumption, and the Everyday," in *Food and Everyday Life*, ed. by Thomas Conroy (Lanham: Lexington Books, 2014a), 59–83, 340.

87 Karaosmanoglu, "Eating the Past," 2009, 340.

88 Ibid.

89 Mihalache, 2014, 59.

90 Irina D. Mihalache, "Taste-full Museums," in *The Multisensory Museum: Cross-Disciplinary Perspectives on Touch, Sound, Smell, Memory, and Space*, ed. by Nina Levent and Alvaro Pascual-Leone, (Lanham: Rowman and Littlefield, 2014b), 197–211.

91 Jakob A. Klein, "Redefining Cantonese Cuisine in Post-Mao Guangzhou," *Bulletin of the School of Oriental and African Studies* 70, no. 03 (2007): 511–537.

92 Ibid., 531.

93 Mieke Bal, "Food, Form, and Visibility: Glub and the Aesthetics of Everyday Life," *Postcolonial Studies* 8, no. 1 (2005): 51–73.

94 James Carey, *Communication as Culture: Essays on Media and Society.* New York and London: Routledge, 1992.

95 Ibid., 18.

96 Michel Foucault, "Of Other Spaces: Utopias and Heterotopias," *Lotus* 48–49 (1985/6): 9–17.

97 Victor Turner, *The Ritual Process: Structure and Anti-Structure* (Ithaca: Cornell University Press, 1969).

3

Curating for Children:

Critical Reflections on Food, Taste and Food Literacy in Museums

Charlene D. Elliott

In November 2014, *The Senses & Society* published a themed issue on *sensory museology*—a "dynamic new field of inquiry" focused on the "rising tide of sensory experimentation in contemporary curatorial practice."[1] Journal editor David Howes observed the increasing significance of multimodal approaches to learning in museums, and how interactive experiences can transform museums, in some cases, into a type of "sensory gymnasium."[2] The special issue explored how contemporary museums have upended the idea of the museum as a "site of pure spectatorship"[3] and joins a growing body of literature that explores the multisensory potential of museum experiences[4]: that is, how contemporary museums may forgo the "role of transmitter of knowledge to the public" to instead create environments that encourage people to actively create their own learning experiences.[5] Sensory museology, in short, rejects the nineteenth-century idea of "learning at a glance"[6] to revivify the practices of early modern museums—which invited participants to touch, handle, smell, and sometimes taste within the collection space.[7]

I begin this chapter on *children and food in museums* with a nod to sensory museology for two reasons. First, in many respects, its call to return to the senses and to solicit interactivity is a call to engage with the museum as one would as a child—that is, *before* learning the etiquette and rules (often in the form of an imperative) for attending museums (i.e., "don't touch!", "stand back!", "speak softly", "walk slowly", "stay off!", "don't eat here"). Sensory museology is both a childlike engagement and a call for museums to engage the child in us—*not* in a juvenile or intellectually hollow fashion; rather, in the way that young children climb, touch, taste, and use other forms of interaction that historically would be considered disruptive in museums. References to sensory *gymnasiums*, storytelling, and discovery all evoke the tumbles, tales, and hidden treasures of childhood. And yet, not one article in the *Sensory Museology* themed issue or one chapter in *The Multisensory Museum* focuses on children.[8] This is particularly ironic since children's museums and science museums were among "the first public museums to reverse the hands-off trend,"[9] forming part of the push toward making museums more interactive.[10] Second, a call to sensory museology is not only a call to engage— and to be engaged—as a child might. Sensory museology also implicitly embraces the notion of food and taste, interrelated concepts that can be used to intensify participation in the museum experience.[11] While visual representations of edibles in art works have a long history and artists have engaged with food as a "powerful performance medium" for decades,[12] the fact that food is an object of everyday life, easily accessible and relatable, makes it ideal for engaging children. Many museums recognize this: a growing number of museums have gardens or some sort of food-related grass roots initiative, while exhibits about food in science centers especially deal with nutrition, what we eat, and why. Museums entirely devoted to food and drink are increasingly common, with institutions such as Alimentarium (the world's first food museum opened in Switzerland in 1985), the British Museum of Food (London), the Southern Food & Beverage Museum (New Orleans), the Pacific Food & Beverage Museum (Los Angeles), the Canada Agriculture and Food Museum (Ottawa), and Museum of Food and Drink (New York) as representative examples. Such food museums stand alongside a host of commercially-oriented, "brand" and single object museums such as the Hershey Story Museum (Hershey, PA), Dr. Pepper Museum (Waco, Texas), Jell-O Gallery (LeRoy, New York), Canadian Potato Museum (Prince Edward Island), and National Mustard Museum (Wisconsin).

Despite the growing interest in both *food and museums* and *engaging children in museums*, very little literature connects the topics of children, food, and museums. This chapter attempts such a connection. It is both a commentary on the meaning and significance of food-related museum exhibits aimed at children, and an interrogation of how we might understand food in light of the child audience. Here, I sidestep looking at the food sold in museum cafés and restaurants to instead explore the ways that museum displays, programming, and exhibits related to food speak to the child audience—and what this means. Creating and tasting a chocolate "secret" sauce at the Museum of Food and Drink must be understood differently from learning the function of nutrients in the body; and to this end, I look at food museums, children's museums, and a corporate museum to explore how the categories of *fuel, preparation,* and *fun* can broaden our understanding of the potential of food display and "taste-full" materials targeted at children.

Food and children: in and out of the museum

As noted, literature connecting children, food, and museums is rare. Sharon Shaffer's *Engaging Young Children in Museums*[13] makes no mention of food or nutrition, while Graham Black's *Transforming Museums in the Twenty-First Century* restricts discussion on food and children to the restaurant, where special dishes related to the collection (such as a "brainteaser soup in the toy museum and a Picasso sandwich in the museum of modern art"[14]) might be used to generate discussion with children. In stark contrast, Graeme Talboys' *Using Museums as an Educational Resource* views food and eating as disconnected from, and even distracting to, the actual museum and learning experience.[15] Rule 21 of his 26 Rules for "a smooth running day when pupils visit a museum"[16] dictates that lunch must be confined to the designated lunch room, and that food or drink must not leave "under any circumstances."[17]

Some literature that directly engages with children and food exhibits, perhaps oddly, describes them as a type of "intervention" for prompting behavior change. For example, Freedman discusses a school visit to a small children's museum and science center that offered both a nutrition class on the food groups and making healthful meals and a hands-on "Healthy Pizza Kitchen."[18] Here, children "make" pizza with plastic props (e.g., plastic cheese, peppers, mushrooms, chicken, and "sauce" represented by a red vinyl disc) on a silicone pizza crust. This "intervention" was not about learning about food history, context or symbolic meaning. Instead, children's choices of toppings for their plastic pizza became a proxy for determining whether children could identify the right ingredients to make pizza a "healthful, balanced meal."[19] Similarly, a review of the highly popular "Big Food: Health, Culture and the Evolution of Eating" exhibit, housed for 10 months at the Yale Peabody Museum of Natural History, focused solely on Big Food as a "public health intervention"—using pre- and post-visit survey data of 510 students (aged 8 to 18) in order to provide some "metric of impact" by documenting whether they intended to drink fewer sugar-sweetened beverages or drink more water after visiting the exhibit.[20] One key limitation of this focus on "intervention" is that it constrains the museum's function to being an agent of behavior change in children while disregarding other aspects of learning and engagement. Indeed, "Big Food" was not simply about calories and sugar levels in soda, but also covered cultural and environmental aspects of food, food marketing, and the evolution of eating.

Art-full food and taste-full identity

For more compelling literature on children and food, one must look beyond the museum context, and I now turn to some material that is instructive in thinking about, or illuminating, child-targeted food exhibits. In a time where food is increasingly positioned as an object of display and engagement in museums, an insightful piece by Ni Chang problematizes the idea of using food as raw materials for art.[21] Chang observes that in elementary schools it is "common practice" to use food as art materials:

> When a weekly theme is "Fall or Harvest," for instance, potatoes may be chosen as media to assist this theme learning because potatoes are harvested in the fall. Children may make potato prints by dipping half potatoes into paint. Or they may be asked to glue corn on a piece of paper because corn is harvested in Fall.[22]

Chang questions the value and purpose of such activities. Gluing corn on a piece of paper or using potatoes as stamps, she argues, does not teach respect for or understanding of food. Chang questions how much children actually learn about such foods: how much do they "grasp about a tortilla, for instance, when they are asked to use it to make Indian Teepees."[23] Do they learn what a tortilla is made of, where corn is grown or produced? "Likewise, how much can children get to know about yellow, red, and green apples by getting involved in making apple prints when the theme is 'Apples'?"[24]

Chang further laments that using food as an art medium bewilders young children. Pasting cereals onto a paper plate or using pudding as paint, for instance, sends mixed messages: is food to eat or to be played with? This mixed message is compounded by teachers' instructions, as in the case where children were given cereal and a paper plate and told, "Don't eat the food. Glue the food on the plate."[25] Food, however, is *meant* to eat; why, then, is it being taught to be an object for play and an object to waste—especially when many people are food insecure? Chang finds no purpose in using food as art materials, especially when non-food items can be used to accomplish the same goal. Her argument is as instructive for museums as it is for teachers planning art activities. Namely, food-related exhibits should have a purpose *relevant* to the food when it is used as raw materials for art. Food use should be appropriate and its value (whether cultural, economic, social) clearly established. This perspective provides a reproach to food exhibits designed predominately as entertainment and suggests the need to instead discuss broader issues of origin, production, or cultural context. While there are practical (cost) reasons involved, certain irony resides in the fact that the museum with the "Healthy Pizza Kitchen" uses food simulacra (i.e., plastic props) to teach about "real" pizza and what children *should* eat while lessons in the school classroom use real food to create art that children *should not* eat. The ability to taste in each learning space should be switched.

Pasting cereal on plates or "learning" about balanced meals using plastic pizza toppings: neither activity is especially tasteful, in the sense of allowing children to either enjoy the sensation of flavor (i.e., tasting food) or use it to express preferences, identity, or status as children. Both activities also pivot on what *adults* ask children to do with food. And when it comes to adults, a robust literature documents how food and taste function in social relations. Taste, as a sense, is intimate and subjective: yet taste is also profoundly symbolic. It marks status, constructs identity, and confirms difference.[26] French sociologist Pierre Bourdieu, in his widely cited study *Distinction: A Social Critique of the Judgement of Taste* documented how consumption practices work to communicate and legitimate class dispositions.[27] "Taste classifies, and it classifies the classifier," he affirmed, referring to the ways that people distinguish themselves (and others) by their consumption preferences.[28] For Bourdieu, food is filled with social meanings: the amount one spends on food (necessity versus luxury), the preferences for different foods and meals (light and delicate foods versus rich or heavy ones), and the manners and rituals of mealtimes (formal versus informal, plating dinner versus serving oneself at the table) all work to express "distinction." But what about children's tastes and *what children do with food*? Are these important aspects to consider when approaching museum programming and exhibits about food? Absolutely.

Successful displays will take into account whether children identify with food in a unique way or find relevancy in certain elements over others. Although Bourdieu's discussion of food barely mentions children,[29] children certainly use food to signal their own sense of identity—and, in particular, to establish difference from the adult world. For instance, edibles such as penny candy are seen as desirable to children partly because they are "an antithesis of the adult conception of 'real' food and are a rejection of the adult world."[30] Penny candy is not the only edible children use in establishing difference: they use everyday food as well.[31] Children classify junk food, sugary cereals, and uniquely shaped/colorful foods as "kids food", and fruits, vegetables and meat as "adult food"[32]; they describe children's food as "interactive" and "fun"[33] and adult fare as "healthy" or "boring."[34] Children also see the transgressive elements of "kids food" (i.e., "junky," sugary, colorful, fun, "bad" for you) as part of what it means to be a child. Nutrition and health, in contrast, are viewed as adult preoccupations.[35] Beyond this, children use food play to resist the power of adults. When children blow bubbles in milk or shape their mashed potatoes and gravy into a volcano, they are often chastised by adults for transgressing appropriate rules of eating. "Don't play with your food!", they are told—which immediately creates a power struggle over whatever the child was doing to prompt the injunction.[36] Adults' insistence on manners and "rules of eating" aim to bring order to the activity of eating, but playing with food is "one of the few ways children can have any power over adults."[37] Simply put, the literature on children's taste and food underscores that children cannot simply be viewed as "little adults" when it comes to taste. Their perspectives on food are different. Food "play" and fun food are ways that children can have conversations with each other (as children) and/or demonstrate to adults their separateness from the adult order (by rejecting it). The fact that children identify candy, sugar, fun, and junk as uniquely "for them" and health, nutrition (and unprocessed fare) as "for others"—and boring!—means that museum programming focused on food and nutrition must strike a creative balance (between "fun"/interaction and nutrition/health) in order to engage children.

The kids menu: food on display

Food—sensory, relatable, and an object of everyday life—is ideal for engaging children in the museum. Despite this, some museums miss out on the opportunity to include food-related themes or only deal with them in a cursory way. Other museums entirely devoted to food may overlook children (or fail to recognize the importance of curating for them).[38] Yet for the museums that *do* recognize food as vehicle for participation and engagement, certain themes are evident. As earlier noted, I will focus on museum exhibits and programming for children related to the themes of *food as fuel, food as preparation,* and *food as fun.* These categories are permeable and sometimes overlapping—however one theme (i.e., fuel or fun, etc.) typically dominates. Each category serves a different purpose and invites the child to look at food through a different lens (as somatic being, as chef, or as consumer). I briefly examine each category, and then detail what this "kids menu" of *fuel, preparation,* and *fun* contributes to an understanding of food and children in museums, as well as the possibilities for museums in fostering a unique form of food literacy in children.

Food as fuel

Perhaps the most prevalent theme, *food as fuel* focuses on nutrition, health, and the body. Exhibits like *Food For Health* (Canada Agriculture and Food Museum), *Healthy Fun* (Mississippi Children's Museum) and *Healthyville* (Stepping Stones Museum for Children, Norwalk, CT)[39] represent a few of the numerous displays for children that emphasize how to make healthy food choices and the connection between food and health. *Food For Health* includes an online (downloadable) educational program designed for grade 1 to 3 classes, with lessons that instruct children "how to use *Canada's Food Guide* to make healthy food choices," about the various food groups (including serving sizes and what counts as an orange vegetable or fruit or a dark green vegetable), and that "some foods are less nutritious than others and should be eaten in moderation."[40] *Healthy Fun* teaches similar concepts by means of playfully named and designed interactive sections such as "Healthy Helpings," "Boney You," and "Little Cook's Corner." Healthy Helpings pictures a "healthy portion guide" and children are asked to choose six wooden pieces (representing different vegetables, fruits, grains, and protein options) out of a range of options to make a meal. A display panel counsels; "Be careful not to choose **too much** or **too little** of each type of food!" Boney You teaches about the importance of the skeleton, including the high calcium foods important for "Bone Building Fun," while the Little Cook's Corner play kitchen aims to familiarize children with healthy ingredients (through play boxes labeled "oatmeal," "flour," "fruit juice," etc.—not unlike the Healthy Pizza Kitchen discussed earlier). Beyond this, the Gastro Climber display allows children to crawl through tunnels that represent a journey through the digestive system (e.g., from the mouth to the esophagus to the stomach and so forth, ultimately exiting as waste). Finally, the *Healthyville* exhibit, like the *Healthy Fun* exhibit, promises to provide children with hands-on opportunities to explore nutrition and to understand the importance of making healthy choices to fuel the body in a fun, play-based manner. Food-related aspects of this exhibit invite children to scan a variety of foods for their nutrition facts, to learn about "Go, Slow and Whoa foods," to "play sugar or salt detective" or to learn how to stay hydrated (through water, 100 percent fruit juice or from food like grapes, watermelon, and lettuce). Promotional materials explain that *Healthyville* features "engaging content about how the body works and the effects of our positive or negative health choices"; they also underscore that the exhibit "grew out of the knowledge that early intervention and prevention are critical for establishing healthy lifestyles."[41]

As a whole, exhibits in the *food as fuel* category provide a disciplinary approach to food. *Food as fuel* displays insist on their "fun" approach to nutrition and health, but are fundamentally about imposing rules on eating. Imposing rules, as earlier noted, is what adults do when it comes to food. Go, Slow and Whoa foods, teaching proper portion sizes and the imperative to make "smart choices," are all undeniably important. Yet they also disregard the pleasure of food (as well as its symbolic function), and implicitly transform eating into a series of "right and wrong choices."[42] Describing such exhibits as an "intervention" works to underscore this fact. *Food as fuel* is also a functional approach to food, and one which often becomes a numbers game (e.g., how many vegetable servings per day, how many milligrams of calcium in this cheese, how many calories, how much sugar, etc.). Given their proclivity to detail the role of nutrients in the body, such exhibits also communicate what Scrinis[43] calls the ideology of nutritionism—the tendency to look at, and value, foods in terms of their component parts—although the message to eat whole foods (such as fruits and vegetables) is equally dominant. Such exhibits are highly interactive, but not especially sensory in terms of taste. They ask children to value food for *somatic, not sensory, reasons.* Equally they ask children to think of themselves as somatic beings: food, primarily, is about nutrients and health. It is not about identity, pleasure, celebration—or childhood.

Food as preparation

Food as preparation shifts the focus away from food elements, food groups, and nutrient functions within the body. It instead refers to the mixing and combining of foods (now reframed as ingredients, not food elements or nutrients) to create something new. *TasteBuds,* a permanent cooking and nutrition lab at EdVenture Children's Museum (Columbia, South Carolina), *Kids in the Kitchen* hosted at Southern Food & Beverage Museum (SoFAB, New Orleans, LA) and *Kids in the Kitchen* at the Museum of Food and Drink (MOFAD, Brooklyn, NY) illustrate the ways that some museums bring the sensory elements of food to the foreground.

Nutrition may be important in these cooking "labs" and programs but the relationship between food and somatic well-being is a minor chord (and sometimes completely absent). *TasteBuds* promises a fun learning experience "whether you're creating healthy snacks or learning to measure, make and bake."[44] Sometimes this cooking lab has the children make a craft out of a food along with preparing a dish with it (i.e., squash can transform into both stamp and soufflé). Although *TasteBuds* is promoted as "fun," the seriousness of *food as preparation* is equally evident since the program specifically notes that children learn under the "guidance of a real chef."[45] Expertise, provided by the chef, ensures that the food preparation is done correctly.

SoFAB's *Kids in the Kitchen* program takes developing children's food expertise equally seriously. It centers on building culinary skills and techniques as children mature. Lessons encompass cooking, process, science, and design: a session on eggs promises to teach children "how to cook the breakfast staple and explore the types of heat used in cooking."[46] Whisking, boiling, and flipping are some of the culinary techniques taught in the lesson. But the nod to science moves this beyond mere cooking instruction: "At each station, your kids will learn some of the mechanics and science behind cooking eggs and take turns practicing themselves."[47] Another lesson on pies shows children how to cook a healthy filling, make a "fancy" pie crust, seal the dough, and add venting holes. And a session called *Edible Art!* instructs on how to turn a variety of fruits into flowers. Children are invited to bring their imaginations and "let the artist in you come out as we chop, decorate, and design food to not only taste great, but look great!"[48]

Like the *food as fuel* category, the *food as preparation* approach is interactive—but its focus on technique, transformation, and building culinary skills makes the experience more sensory and indisputably more creative than learning food groups or nutrient profiles. Moreover, the tactile elements of, say, rolling out, filling, and sealing a pastry crust, the sizzle and scent of a frying egg and the ultimate tasting of all creations make the experience richly sensory. Inviting children to become "artists" and designers of *edible* art avoids Chang's critique[49] about the wastefulness of using food as materials for art (a critique that applies to the *TasteBuds* craft activity with food as well) because SoFAB's *edible art* is consumed.[50]

The question arises, though: does holding cooking classes in a museum setting "count" as sensory museology? I would suggest it does. There is, of course, the expanded definition of what counts as an exhibition or performance to consider. Several artists have shown that food can prompt us to rethink our ideas about what constitutes art[51]—and like performance art, the kids' cooking activities are temporal, multisensory, and live events. Or one might point to the ongoing programming of both *TasteBuds* and *Kids in the Kitchen,* playfully observing that the different themes (eggs, pie, food art) are not unlike different curations. Yet both ideas—children's engagement with food in cooking classes as performance art, or the idea of food preparation as curation—are debatable. I suggest holding cooking classes in the museum "counts" as sensory museology for a more basic reason: sensory museology is about moving away from the visual to engage the other senses—touch, taste, sound, smell—in the museum. *TasteBuds* and *Kids in the Kitchen* absolutely do this. Treating such programs as sensory museology also aligns with recent scholarship that argues that non-exhibit spaces (such as museum restaurants) and programming can be as important to the meaning making of the visitors as the exhibitions themselves.[52]

The final example of *food as preparation* is MOFAD's *Kids in the Kitchen,* which takes a different approach from both EdVenture and SoFAB. Instead of regular programming, MOFAD offers special events for children, including a "Chocolate 'Secret' Sauce" session and a "Cool Cooking" event recommended for ages 7 to 9. These events are interesting insomuch as they add another component of taste—culinary cultural capital (which I shall address shortly)—to the mix. Chef Dominique Ansel led the "Chocolate 'Secret' Sauce" session for children: detailing "why chocolate makes the perfect base to explore new flavors"; allowing children to taste "some of his favorite combinations"; and guiding children in creating their "own custom-flavored concoction to take home."[53] Chef Wylie Dufresne headlined the "Cool Cooking" event, which was promoted as a "fascinating journey through food science" that results in ice cream. Its promotional materials explain:

> Chef Wylie will demonstrate how chefs use the super-cooling properties of liquid nitrogen to achieve spectacular results in the kitchen. He'll explain the science behind this incredibly cold material (it's under −300 degrees Fahrenheit — colder than Jupiter's moon Europa!). You'll also learn how to use liquid nitrogen to make instant ice cream. This is definitely the coolest physics class you've ever taken![54]

Notable about both sessions are the artistic, technical, and sensory components addressed in this "kids kitchen." Tasting food is the culmination of a rich learning experience, which is framed as exploration, creation, and science. The food science detailed in "Cool Cooking" is a radically different form of knowledge than the nutritionism found in the *food as fuel* displays. Borrowing the techniques, equipment, and substances from a laboratory to produce "instant ice cream" is also an entirely different form of artistic culinary creation: it dissociates eating from nutrition, and is designed to surprise, provoke, and to make children think of ice cream in an entirely new way.

For the purposes of this chapter, even more notable about MOFAD's events is the headlining of celebrity chefs—which implicitly makes a good part of the *Kids Kitchen* event about adults. Chef Dominique Ansel is an acclaimed New York pastry chef, famous for popularizing and trademarking the Cronut. Chef Wylie Dufresne is the leading American champion for molecular gastronomy, winner of the 2013 James Beard Award for Best Chef, and known for his frequent appearances on televised cooking shows (as a judge on Bravo's *Top Chef,* and appearances on The Food Network's *Iron Chef America,* the BBC's *MasterChef,* and HBO's *Treme*). The purpose of headlining celebrity chefs is not to engage children: the average 7-year-old would not know who Ansel and Dufresne are. Instead, profiling celebrity chefs is a strategy to capture media attention and a wide audience of parents, given that celebrity chefs (especially televised ones) enjoy exceptional popularity amongst diverse audiences.[55] With these *Kids Kitchen* sessions, children learn culinary knowledge (how to make chocolate sauce) and "food science" knowledge (the transformations of ingredients that occur in cooking, including the use of nitrogen for "instant" ice cream). Yet both the culinary knowledge and food science knowledge are enveloped by the cultural knowledge that Ansel and Dufresne are leading arbiters of taste. Adults would recognize this; children, likely not. Attending these sessions allows parents and children to engage in what De Solier, drawing from Bourdieu, calls "a form of productive leisure"— namely, investing free time to acquire "culinary cultural capital, as a means of improving the self through food knowledge."[56]

With *food as preparation,* children view food through the lens of a chef, learning the techniques, skills, and often science of cooking. "Rules" in this category are less about rules of eating (as per *food as fuel*) and more about techniques for cooking. Children are given the opportunity to engage with food in a more sensory manner, since smells, tastes, sounds, and textures lie at the heart of cooking. But the programming is not always uniquely child oriented—just as the adult concerns of "health" and nutrition underpin the *food as fuel* category, adult interests in culinary cultural capital can emerge in the *food as preparation* category.

Food as fun

Food as fun uses fun and entertainment as the guiding principles for presenting information to children. Interactive and sensory elements are foregrounded, although (in the example that follows) children look through the lens of "consumer" instead of "chef" or "somatic being." Cadbury World (Birmingham, UK) opened in 1990 and over the past quarter century has grown to become a major leisure destination and popular site for school visits: it hosts over 2,000 school groups visit each year (Cadbury World 2016). Cadbury World is not a proper museum; it is more of a theme park. However, its corporate approach provides some unique insight into sensory museology, food, and children—and given the number of commercially-oriented/brand museums around food (e.g., the Hershey Story Museum, Dr. Pepper Museum, Jell-O Gallery), this corporate approach should be acknowledged.

Cadbury World fits the criteria of a "company museum,"[57] has been categorized as a "specialty museum"[58] and has been examined in conjunction with other museums.[59] Details on Cadbury World's website, in some respects, resemble what you might find in a public museum's description of an exceptional exhibit on chocolate: the website describes Cadbury World as "a self-guided exhibition tour" with education talks and resources that "showcase our history and chocolate making." Under the *Primary School Visits* link, the site explains that Cadbury World offers interactive and curriculum-linked educational talks (in themed education rooms) to complement school visits. Topics include, among other things, "how cocoa originated from ancient civilizations to Cadbury heritage," "the origins of the cocoa tree and sourcing of beans from Ghana," the Mayan empire (myths and legends, counting system, and cocoa pods), design and technology (identifying target markets, the functions of packaging and design), and how Cadbury manufactures popular products.[60] Such educational talks, focused as they are on origins, context, culture, and markets, redress Chang's (earlier noted) critique[61] about how educators miss opportunities to teach children about these critically important aspects of food.

The educational talks for children are also bolstered by interactive, multisensory exhibits such as *Aztec Jungle* (children walk through a tropical rainforest, complete with waterfalls, to discover the cocoa tree and learn about the Aztec civilization) and *Journey to Europe* (a mini theater presentation about the arrival of chocolate to Europe, and its integration into European society).

Cadbury World's educational aspects, however, are muted by a commercial imperative and a focus on fun. This "specialty" museum was created to communicate one key message to the public: "*Cadbury means chocolate, means fun*," which explains why marketing permeates the museum concept.[62] Along with *Aztec Jungle*, Cadbury World offers:

- *Advertising Avenue* (profiles Cadbury advertisements)

- *Manufacturing* (video stations show "how popular Cadbury brands are made")

- *Purple Planet* (children can chase Cadbury Crème Eggs or play in chocolate rain against a digital background)

- *Green Screen* (children can get pictures of themselves against various backdrops, such as riding the Crunchie rollercoaster or surfing on a Cadbury Dairy Milk bar)

- *Chocolate Making* (children can watch "talented Cadbury World chocolatiers" at work, and taste "a delicious pot of warm liquid Cadbury Dairy Milk")

- *4D Chocolate Adventure Zone* cinema experience (viewers can "Dive into a bowl of liquid Cadbury Dairy Milk, ride the Crunchie Rollercoaster, and take to the skies in a Cadbury Crème Egg airship piloted by the Caramel Bunny").[63]

This "*Cadbury means chocolate, means fun*" experience culminates in the Cadbury retail store. In fact, the *School Trip Guide* available on Cadbury World's website specifically reminds to "PLEASE ALLOW TIME FOR: Shopping" since "We have the World's Largest Cadbury Shop" that sells products "for all kinds of budgets."[64] The upshot of the intense promotional activity is that educational contributions become buried within the larger brand experience. More *brandseum* than museum, Cadbury World is interesting in that it addresses children in the very terms they relate to: recall that children identify fun, sugar, candy, and food play with childhood and children's culture. Playing in chocolate rain and (virtually) diving "into a bowl of liquid Cadbury Dairy Milk" certainly represents such food play and transgresses normal rules of eating! "Adult" concerns of nutrition and health are entirely absent—as are the techniques and skills of cooking food in *food as preparation*. Since the *brandseum* exists solely to promote Cadbury, the "food" education is narrowly framed (limited to chocolate, and specifically Cadbury chocolate). The purpose of all activities—as wonderfully sensory and interactive as they may be—is to ultimately create brand loyalty and to sell products. Here, children learn all about Cadbury history, advertising, manufacturing, and product lines in order to create a taste for the brand as consumers.

Curating food literacy: combining experience and education

Fuel, preparation, and *fun.* All three categories can broaden our understanding of the potential of food displays and "taste-full" materials targeted at children. Mihalache (2014) suggests that we should "consider the ability of taste to perform a pedagogical role" in the museum,[65] and the sensory, symbolic, interactive, and accessible nature of food makes it ideal for engaging children. Pedagogically, framing food as *fuel, preparation,* and *fun* results in different types of understanding. Both *food as fuel* and *food as preparation* offer what could be understood as a type of *functional food* literacy,[66] which covers knowing about food groups, nutrients, and its connection to health (i.e., fuel), as well as cooking skills and techniques (i.e., preparation). This functional food literacy is critically important, and potential exists for museums to strengthen it by treating the *food as fuel* category less as "intervention" (and about "rules" of eating) while adding a component of "embrace"—that is, asking children what they think of different foods, why they choose the foods they do, how and why they classify it (as adult food or child food), (as adult or child food) and recognizing the pleasure of food. Doing so communicates to children that food is not just somatic, is not just about feeding the body, but has other roles to play as well. Integrating *food as preparation* programming with *food as fuel* exhibits (i.e., allowing children to interact with real food, not plastic props) would make the "healthy eating" lessons more sensory and memorable.

Food as fun speaks to a different potential of museums; namely, to engage with children in the fun, playful, sensory way that forms part of children's self-identification as children. Cadbury World's focus on the history, sourcing, and development of chocolate, the business of identifying target markets and the history of (Cadbury) advertising could be used to foster *critical food literacy* in children—the ability to understand and decipher the messages around food (how food is represented, promoted, and how it works to persuade). The challenge is that the "*Cadbury . . . means fun*" mandate can transform the sensory experience into a kind of commodified interactivity, where the child plays the role of the consumer instead of the critic. Indeed, *critical food literacy* is necessary when the specialty museum is about a brand, and a confectionary brand at that. The ideal situation would be to build on the taste-full potential of food to offer children the sensory experience of both *functional* and *critical food literacy*.

Taken as a whole, exploring the ways that food is positioned as *fuel, preparation*, and *fun* in the museum reveals new possibilities for sensory museology and children. While Howes (2014) suggested that the museum might be transformed into a type of "sensory gymnasium" through interactive experiences, the food-related exhibits and experiences discussed here might be better understood as a type of sensory kitchen or, perhaps, a sensory buffet—and one that has potential to richly nourish the type of learning available to children in the museum.

Notes

1   David Howes, "Introduction to Sensory Museology," *The Senses & Society*, 9, no. 3(2014): 259.

2   Ibid., 265.

3   Ibid., 260.

4   Nina Levent and Alvaro Pascual-Leone, eds., *The Multisensory Museum: Cross-Disciplinary Perspectives on Touch, Sounds, Smell, Memory, and Space* (Lanham: Rowman & Littlefield, 2014).

5   Vaike Fors, "Teenagers' Multisensory Routes for Learning in the Museum," *The Senses & Society*, 8, no. 3 (2013): 272.

6   Eilean Hooper-Greenhill, *Museums and Education: Purpose, Pedagogy, Performance* (London: Routledge, 2007), 13.

7   Constance Classen, "Museum Manners: The Sensory Life of the Early Museum," *The Senses & Society*, 40, no. 4 (2007): 895–914.

8   In the special issue on sensory museology in The *Senses & Society,* one article by Sandra Dudley notes that children were "especially animated by the excitement of opening and closing drawers" (2014: 304). In *The Multisensory Museum,* one chapter, Andreas Keller's 'Scented Museum,' briefly mentions the Children's Museum of Indianapolis. In both cases, the reference to children is only in passing, found in one line on one page.

9   Howes, 2014, 262.

10   If we turn to the literature on engaging *children* in museums, the strategies for engagement echo those of sensory museology. There is the same call for active interaction (Shaffer 2014; 2011, see note 13), active learning (Black 2012, see note 14), hands-on exhibits and engagement (J. Norris, *Children's Museums: An American Guidebook (2nd Edition)* (Jefferson, NC: McFarland & Company, 2009); E.A. Jant, Catherine A. Haden, David H. Uttal, and E. Babcock, "Conversation and Object Manipulation Influence Children's Learning in a Museum", *Child Development* 85 no. 5 (2014): 2029–2045; multisensory appeals (B. Lord, ed., *The Manual of Museum Learning*

(New York: Altamira Press (2007)), and immersive experience (Hooper-Greenhill 2007).

11 Irina D. Mihalache, "Taste-full Museums: Educating the Senses One Plate at a Time," in *The Multisensory Museum: Cross-Disciplinary Perspectives on Touch, Sounds, Smell, Memory, and Space*, ed. by Nina Levent and Alvaro Pascual-Leone (Lanham: Rowman & Littlefield, 2014), 197–213.

12 Mihalache, 2014, 200.

13 Sharon Shaffer, *Engaging Young Children in Museums* (Walnut Creek: Left Coast Press, 2014).

14 Graham Black, *Transforming Museums in the Twenty-First Century* (London: Routledge, 2012), 173.

15 Graeme K. Talboys, *Using Museums as an Educational Resource (2nd Edition),* (Farnham: Ashgate Publishing Group, 2010).

16 Ibid., 83.

17 Ibid., 87.

18 Marjorie R. Freedman, "A 'Healthy Pizza Kitchen' Nutrition Education Program at a Children's Health Museum," *Journal of Nutrition Education and Behavior*, 42, no. 5 (2010): 353–354.

19 Ibid., 354; Freedman's reframing of a 90-minute field trip to the museum into an "intervention" transforms the experiential learning advocated by sensory museology into something far more clinical.

20 Jeannette R. Ickovics, "Exhibiting Health: Museums as a Venue for Public Health Intervention," *American Journal of Public Health* 103 no. 12(2013): 2204.

21 Ni Chang, "Rethinking Food Utilized as Materials for Art," *Journal of Early Childhood Teacher Education* 19, no. 1 (1998): 25–29.

22 Ibid., 25.

23 Ibid., 26.

24 Ibid.

25 Ibid., 27.

26 Thorstein Veblen, *Theory of the Leisure Class* (New York: Penguin Books, (1994 [1899]).

27 Pierre Bourdieu, *Distinction: A Social Critique of the Judgement of Taste* (Cambridge: Harvard University Press, 1984).

28 Ibid., 6.

29 Children are tangential to Bourdieu's discussion of food. For instance, Bourdieu mentions that, for working classes, fish is viewed as an unsuitable food for men because it is light and not filling (and best reserved for children and invalids), and must be consumed in a fashion that compromises masculinity (i.e., one must chew carefully and daintily, to ensure there are no bones) (190).

30 Allison James, "Confections, Concoctions, and Conceptions," in *The Children's Culture Reader,* ed. by Henry Jenkins (New York: New York University Press, 1998), 402.

31 Anna Ludvigsen and Sarah Scott, "Real Kids Don't Eat Quiche," *Food, Culture and Society* 12, no. 4 (2009): 418–436.

32 Charlene Elliott, "'It's Junk Food and Chicken Nuggets': Children's Perspectives on 'Kids' Food' and the Question of Food Classification," *Journal of Consumer Behaviour* 10, no. 3 (2011): 133–140.

33 Ibid., 136.

34 Ibid., 137.

35 Ibid.

36 Jay Mechling, "Don't Play With Your Food," *Children's Folklore Review* 23, no. 1 (2000): 10.

37 Ibid., 20.

38 The British Museum of Food, for example, positions itself as "the world's first cultural institution entirely devoted to the history, evolution, science, sociology and art of food"; its stated vision is to "celebrate the glories of food, in all its forms" (BMOF 2015). But children are not mentioned anywhere on its site and its profiled exhibits do not cater to children.

39 *Healthyville* is a travelling exhibit, which debuted at Stepping Stones Museum for Children in Norwalk, CT, in February 2014, then travelled to the Boston Children's Museum, the Minnesota Children's Museum, the Children's Discovery Museum of San Jose, and the Bay Area Discovery Museum. At the time of writing (January 2016), it was at Long Island Children's Museum.

40 CAFM, "Healthy: Kids Quest: Food for Health," accessed Jan. 16, 2016, http://cafmuseum.techno-science.ca/en/education/healthy-kids-quest.php

41 This comes from (template) promotional material for the travelling exhibit.

42 Here, I am reminded of a research project in which I held focus groups with Canadian children, including a separate focus group with overweight children, to get their perspectives on children's food. The overweight children were recruited from an intervention-based program with a strong emphasis on healthy eating for weight management. As part of the icebreaker to all focus groups, we asked the children to name their favorite food or meal and why they liked it. Children in the "regular" focus groups enthusiastically named items like pizza, spaghetti, their mom's special casserole, ice cream, and chocolate. Some children from the weight management program appeared concerned about getting the "right" answer, responding: "um. . . a protein?" (girls group, grade 3), "there is the fruit group, the vegetable group, the milk group . . . and I forget the other one" (boys group, grade 4), or "vegetables are really healthy" (girls group, grade 4). That these were all responses to the question *what is your favourite food or meal?* reveals how the pleasure of food for these children was transformed into a list of dietary components and a preoccupation with getting the right answer.

43 Gyorgy Scrinis, "On the Ideology of Nutritionism," *Gastronomica* 8, no. 1(2008): 39–48.

44 EdVenture, "Exhibits: The Cooking Lab," accessed Jan. 16, 2016 http://edventure.org/exhibits/the-cooking-lab/

45 Ibid.

46 SoFAB, "Kids in the Kitchen: All about Eggs," accessed Jan. 16, 2016, http://www.nola.com/events/event/kids-in-the-kitchen-all-about-eggs/185301/

47 Macaroni Kid, "Kids in the Kitchen: All of Eggs at SoFAB," accessed Jan. 16, 2016. http://new-orleans.macaronikid.com/calendar/event/kids-in-the-kitchen-all-of-eggs-at-sofab/2015-10-24/c4442995/

48 SoFAB, "Kids in the Kitchen: Edible Art!" accessed Jan. 16, 2016, http://www.neworleans.me/events/detail/25009/Kids-in-the-Kitchen-Edible-Art-SoFAB

49 Chang, 1998.

50 This said, Chang's point about the missed opportunities to discuss food origins, production, and cultural context still applies.

51 For example, B. Kirshenblatt-Gimblett, "Playing to the Senses: Food as Performance Medium", *Performance Research* 4 no. 1 (1999): 1–30, draws attention to how food can be a powerful performance medium, and conceptual artist Rirkrit Tiravanija is well known for his art that involves cooking a meal and serving it to gallery goers. In April 2012, Tiravanija also transformed the main nave of the Grand Palais in Paris into a 12-hour "banquet" that consisted of preparing and serving one item—*Tom Ka* (Thai soup). The art project was named *Soup/No Soup*.

52 Mihalache, 2014.

53 MOFAD, "Kids in the Kitchen: Chocolate 'Secret' Sauce with Dominique Ansel," accessed Jan. 16, 2016, http://www.eater.com/sponsored/9215143/events-programming

54 MOFAD, "Kids in the Kitchen: Cool Cooking with Wylie Dufresne", accessed Jan. 16, 2016, http://www.eater.com/sponsored/9215143/events-programming

55 Isabel De Solier, "TV Dinners: Culinary television, education and distinction," *Journal of Media & Cultural Studies* 19, no. 4 (2005): 265.

56 Ibid., 245.

57 Mark A. Mitchell and Robert A. Orwig, "Consumer Experience Tourism and Brand Bonding", *Journal of Product & Brand Management* 11, no. 1 (2002): 30–41.

58 Both TripAdvisor (the world's largest travel site) and Yelp (the crowd-sourced review site) list Cadbury World as a specialty museum.

59 Eilean Hooper-Greenhill, *Museums and Their Visitors* (London: Routledge, 1994), 32.

60 Cadbury World, "Cadbury World: Choc-full of fun", accessed Jan. 16, 2016, http://cadburyworld.co.uk/

61 Chang, 1998.

62 Cadbury, "Cadbury World, A Case Study: An Overview of Cadbury World, its Origins, History and Operations," accessed Jan. 16, 2016, https://www.cadburyworld.co.uk/~/media/cadburyworld2015/en/images/content/press/cadburyworldcasestudy.pdf.

63 Cadbury World.

64 Cadbury.

65 Mihalache, 2014, 197.

66 I am grateful to Dr. Emily Truman for her insight on this topic.

4

The Neuroscience of Flavor

Charles Spence

It is intuitive to believe that since we experience the taste of food and drink in the mouth, our understanding of flavor perception would be advanced greatly by knowing about the different classes of receptors that can be found on the tongue and elsewhere in the oral cavity. It turns out, though, that what most people have in mind when they talk about "taste" is really "flavor"; that is, the result of the integration of inputs from several different senses.[1] By themselves, the gustatory receptors on the human tongue only provide information about the so-called "basic" tastes, such as sweet, salty, bitter, sour, and umami. In fact, according to one oft-quoted suggestion, as much as 75 to 95 percent of what most people commonly describe as the "taste" of food actually comes from inputs detected at the olfactory epithelium in the nose.[2] So, for example, the fruity, floral, meaty, fishy, citrus, and burnt notes etc. that we enjoy when eating and drinking all derive from the detection of volatile compounds at the olfactory epithelium. That such inputs are referred to the mouth in our everyday experience of flavor is known as "oral referral." As Bartoshuk and Duffy note, "'Taste' is often used as a synonym for 'flavour'. This usage of 'taste' probably arose because the blend of true taste and retronasal olfaction is perceptually localized to the mouth via touch."[3]

Trigeminal inputs (i.e., coded by the trigeminal facial nerve) also contribute to our perception of food and drink, giving rise to hot, cold, tingling, burning, and electric sensations. According to the International Standards Organization, flavor can be defined as a: "Complex combination of the olfactory, gustatory and trigeminal sensations perceived during tasting. The flavour may be influenced by tactile, thermal, painful and/or kinaesthetic effects."[4] Researchers disagree about the role of the other senses, such as audition, vision, and oral-somatosensation (basically the tactile component of in-mouth sensations) in flavor perception. Some scientists and philosophers believe that while such sensory inputs can certainly modulate multisensory flavor perception they should not be considered as constitutive of it. Others have even suggested that flavor could be considered as a distinct sensory or perceptual modality! Certainly, the sounds we hear when biting into crispy, crunchy, and crackly foods contribute to our overall enjoyment.[5] What is more, many studies published over the past eighty years or so have demonstrated that changing the color of a food or drink can change people's perception of flavor identity, as well as the perceived intensity of both taste and flavor.[6] According to classic psychophysical research, the addition of food coloring influences the thresholds for detecting the basic tastes in solution. And although it is much more difficult to study experimentally, there is now a growing body of scientific evidence showing the important role played by the oral-somatosensory attributes of foods (e.g., viscosity).

However, regardless of one's position on the question of which senses should be considered as constitutive of flavor, the key point to note here is that most people now agree that flavor perception results from the multisensory integration of multiple sensory signals in the human brain. As if to emphasize this point, Dana Small (2012) boldly titled one of her recent review papers "Flavor is in the brain." Along similar lines, Gordon Shepherd (2012) states that: "A common misconception is that the foods contain the flavours. Foods do contain the flavour *molecules*, but the *flavours* of those molecules are actually created by our brains" (p. ix, emphasis in original). Shepherd continues: "It is important to realize that flavor doesn't reside in a flavorful food any more than color resides in a colorful object" (p. 5). Hence, if you really want to know why foods and drinks taste the way they do, then you need to understand something about the underlying neuroscience governing multisensory flavor perception, an area of research that some researchers refer to as "*neurogastronomy*."[7]

One of the striking aspects of multisensory flavor perception is the profound individual differences that exist in terms of the foods that we like/dislike: Why, so the question goes, should it be that the foods you love I hate, and vice versa? It has long been known that we live in different taste worlds.[8] And while some of these individual differences are genetic in origin,[9] others are based on our prior experiences with foods. Indeed, it is interesting to note how many of our food dislikes are linked to specific food textures rather than to particular tastes or flavors. Of course, individuals also vary in terms of how neophilic versus neophobic they are—that is, how willing they are to try new foods and flavors.[10] Neophiles are open to new taste experiences whereas neophobes tend to be afraid of them.

Neuroscientists have demonstrated some marked individual differences in the way in which the brains of different groups of individuals respond to one and the same food. So, for example, one study highlighted increased activity in the orbitofrontal cortex (OFC) amongst a group of supertasters in response to the delivery of a series of emulsions of increasing fat concentration as compared to a group of non-tasters exposed to exactly the same set of stimuli.[11] A nascent field of neuroimaging research has also started to compare the network of brain regions that are recruited by experts and regular consumers (e.g., comparing sommeliers vs social wine drinkers).

Flavor expectations and flavor experiences

When thinking about flavor perception, it is important to draw a distinction between flavor expectations and flavor experiences. Different combinations of senses are involved in the generation of flavor expectations as compared to flavor experiences: Vision and orthonasal olfaction tend to be dominant in the former case (though audition and touch can also play a role), whereas gustatory, retronasal olfactory, and oral-somatosensory/trigeminal inputs tend to dominate the latter. The *orthonasal* system is associated with the inhalation of external odors, as when we sniff. The *retronasal* system, involving the posterior nares, is associated with the detection of the olfactory stimuli emanating from the food we consume, as odors are periodically forced out of the nasal cavity when we chew or swallow food or drink. There are important differences between these two senses of smell (or better said, ways of smelling) at both the subjective/perceptual level, and in terms of the brain areas that are engaged. The everyday experience of this difference that most people are familiar with relates to coffee, which often smells great, but can often be disappointing when we come to taste it. In this case, the orthonasal smell of the coffee is much better than the retronasal olfactory component. As an example of the reverse pattern, i.e., where the taste (retronasal olfaction) can be very pleasing while the orthonasal smell is less so, just think of an Epoissé cheese.

Crucially, our expectations concerning the likely taste and flavor of those foods and beverages that we put in our mouth play an important role in determining the final experience. Our brains generate expectations concerning both the sensory-discriminative aspects of what a food will likely taste of, and hedonic expectations concerning how much we think we are going to like the experience. If our experience on actually tasting a food is not too different from the expectation (in either the sensory-discriminative or hedonic domains) then we will likely end up experiencing what we expected to experience. If, however, the experience is very different from the expectation then a negatively-valenced disconfirmation of expectation response is often seen.[12]

While our response to the disconfirmation of expectation is normally negatively valenced, it should be remembered that this is very much context dependent. So, for example, if one finds oneself sitting at the table in a modernist restaurant, one may actually be positively expecting to be surprised, that is, to have one's expectations disconfirmed.[13] Here, one need only take the example of the "Beetroot and orange jelly" that used to be served at Heston Blumenthal's The Fat Duck restaurant in Bray. The dish would come to the table consisting of an orange-colored and a purple-colored square of jelly. If the waiter suggested to the diner that the chef recommended starting with the beetroot, most diners would dive straight in and taste the purple jelly. However, in this case, the dish was made with golden beetroots and blood-red oranges so the diner is tricked into eating by eye and a positively-valenced disconfirmed of expectation response follows when the waiter tells the diner about the error of their ways. Try exactly the same trick at a dinner party at home and the result may not be quite so successful. You have been warned!

Neural circuits underlying multisensory flavor perception

The last few years have seen a rapid growth in our understanding of the neural networks that give rise to the multisensory perception of flavor.[14] The early cortical representation of visual, auditory, and somatosensory information (e.g., "primary" and "secondary" areas) occurs in the so-called unisensory cortex. By contrast, the cortical representations of the chemical senses (e.g., of smell and taste) are seen in the limbic and paralimbic cortex. Gustatory inputs project from the tongue to the primary taste cortex, whereas olfactory stimuli project directly to the primary olfactory, or piriform, cortex. From there, gustatory and olfactory inputs project to different parts of the OFC, a small part of the brain, located just behind the eyes. The latter structure plays a central role in representing the pleasantness (and reward value) of food and drink. The oral-somatosensory attributes of which are initially represented in the oral/primary somatosensory cortex, but thereafter project throughout the primary gustatory cortex. Oral-somatosensory inputs modulate neural activity in the OFC.

But what are the rules governing the integration of the various sensory signals that give rise to multisensory flavor perception? Certainly, the congruency between the component signals would seem to be one of the key factors here.[15] So, for example, the participants in one influential neuroimaging study had to rate the pleasantness and congruency of various different pairings of orthonasal olfactory and gustatory stimuli. The olfactory stimuli in this case consisted of the aroma of strawberry and methianol (the latter smelling of chicken broth). The taste solutions consisted of sucrose and monosodium glutamate (MSG). The participants received both congruent (e.g., strawberry odor and sucrose) and incongruent (e.g., chicken broth odor and sucrose) combinations of stimuli. Intriguingly, increased OFC activity correlated with increased ratings of the pleasantness and congruency of the combined olfactory and gustatory inputs that the participants were evaluating. Thus, it would appear that the presentation of familiar, or congruent, combinations of olfactory and gustatory stimuli leads to an enhanced neural response in those parts of the brain that code for the hedonic (i.e., pleasantness) and reward value of food.[16] Similar results have also been reported following the presentation of congruent combinations of visual and olfactory stimuli—think only of the smell of strawberries and the color red.

While some researchers have presented their olfactory stimuli orthonasally, others have demonstrated similar results (both behaviorally and neurally) following the presentation of retronasal olfactory stimuli. For example, in one such study, familiar/unfamiliar combinations of retronasal olfactory and gustatory stimuli were presented to participants.[17] Superadditive neural interactions (that is, neural responses that were significantly larger than would have been expected merely by considering the brain's response to the individual sensory signals) were observed in the OFC in response to familiar (or congruent, e.g., a sweet taste and a vanilla aroma), but not to unfamiliar (or incongruent) combinations of stimuli (such as for the combination of a salty taste with a vanilla aroma). Several other brain areas also lit up, perhaps constituting the bare bones of the brain's "flavor network."

In summary, congruent combinations of olfactory (both orthonasal and retronasal), gustatory, visual, and presumably also tactile/auditory stimuli give rise to increased activity in the brain's reward areas, such as the OFC. By contrast, incongruent combinations of sensory stimuli can lead to a sub-additive neural response in those regions that correlates with the participant's subjective response. One obvious question to ask at this point is what determines which combinations of sensory cues will be treated by the brain as congruent, and which incongruent, or familiar and less familiar. This is likely determined by an individual's prior exposure, which starts while we are still in the womb.[18] By six months of age, infants are already sensitive to the pairing of color of a cup and the taste of the contents. While some researchers have, on occasion, argued for the existence of innate correspondences, little convincing evidence in support of such an account has, as yet, been provided.

Sensory dominance

One might ask why it should be that color cues typically exert such a dramatic effect over taste/flavor perception. At one level though this is not so surprising: In particular, in terms of "cortical real estate," far more of the brain (in excess of fifty percent) is given over to processing what we see than to processing either gustatory or olfactory information (roughly one to two percent cent each). That said, it is worth noting how, if a food smells off, most people will not touch it, no matter how beautiful it looks. A similarly strong aversive response is normally seen when people are presented with meat that has been colored blue. Results such as these can be taken to suggest that the processing of multisensory cues concerning off-flavors (i.e., foods that may be potentially poisonous) may be different from the processing of the pleasant or neutral stimuli that have been presented to the participants in the majority of laboratory research.

The hungry brain

More generally, our desire for a given food changes as a function of how hungry we are. Some years ago, Dana Small and her colleagues investigated the changes in neural activity that occurred when participants were fed chocolate to satiety.[19] As the reward value of the food decreased, activity in the insula was seen to decrease on both sides of the brain. Intriguingly, some of the most profound increases in cerebral blood flow that have been reported in neuroimaging studies have been in hungry participants viewing images of appetizing foods and talking about them.[20]

The obese brain

Given the current obesity epidemic, there is obviously great interest in trying to understand how the brains of obese individuals, and the neural responses that appetitive food stimuli elicit in them, differ from what is seen in normal weight individuals. Obesity is certainly a topic that has been addressed in a number of museum exhibits on food and health issues, as well as numerous museum education programs. Of interest is a recent meta-analysis of sixty neuroimaging studies that had assessed the neural response to visual food cues as a function of the weight of their participants.[21] Obese individuals exhibited a greater increase in neural activation in response to food as compared to non-food images (especially for high-calorie foods), in those brain regions that are known to be associated with reward processing. Increased activation was also observed in those brain areas that are involved in reinforcement and adaptive learning, emotional processing, recollective and working memory, executive functioning, decision making, visual processing, and motor learning and coordination, such as hand-to-mouth movements and swallowing. At the other end of the weight spectrum, those individuals suffering from binge-eating disorder and bulimia tend to experience greater reward sensitivity, brain activation, and arousal, in response to viewing images of pleasant foods.[22]

Branding and pricing

Outside of the psychology, or food science, laboratory, we rarely taste a food or beverage without knowing something about what it is that we are eating or drinking, such as, for example, the brand name and/or perhaps the price (or approximate price range). On many occasions, of course, the food will also have some form of label or description attached. It has been known for years that such information can change what people say about the taste, flavor, and/or aroma of a food and how much they like it, not to mention how much they are willing to pay for it. Until recently, though, it has always been unclear just how early in human information processing such effects occurred. Over the last decade or so, a number of neuroimaging studies have demonstrated the sometimes profound changes in brain activity (both in terms of the network of brain areas that are activated and the amount of activation that is seen) that can result from the provision of such product-extrinsic information to the participants who are normally to be found lying prone in the brain scanner. What is more, the effects of such product extrinsic cues have, on occasion, been shown to influence the neural activity at some of the earliest (i.e., primary sensory) areas in the human brain.

Branding and flavor perception

In what has now become the classic experiment on the neural substrates of branding, participants had their brains scanned while one of two famous brands of cola was periodically squirted in their mouth and different visual information concerning the brand that they were apparently tasting was projected on a screen. Under blind tasting conditions, ventromedial prefrontal cortex activity correlated with the participants' behavioral preference. Qualitatively different patterns of brain activation were observed depending on which brand the participants believed themselves to be tasting.[23] In a follow-up, greater activation was observed in the left ventral striatum when participants believed that the cola that they were tasting was a strong rather than a weak brand (e.g., Coke or Pepsi versus a national or fictitious brand). Intriguingly, this effect was stronger in those individuals who drank cola infrequently, possibly pointing to a greater reliance on brand cues in less experienced consumers.[24]

Pricing and flavor perception

A few years ago, neuroscientists over in California investigated what would happen in the brain of social wine drinkers (students) when they were given different (and sometimes misleading) information about the price of a red wine.[25] A $5 bottle of wine could either be correctly described or else mislabelled as a wine that cost $45 a bottle. Another bottle of wine actually cost $90 and was either presented as a $10 or $90 wine. The third wine in this classic study was correctly referred to as costing $35 a bottle. The price was displayed on a computer monitor whenever a small amount of wine was squirted into the participant's mouth. On some trials, the participants had to rate the intensity of the wine's taste on a six-point scale, whilst on others they rated its pleasantness. Participants reported liking the expensive wine more than the cheap wine. Crucially, analysis of the brain scans revealed increases in blood flow in the medial OFC. By contrast, no change in blood flow was observed in the primary taste cortex. This null result is, however, not so surprising given that this part of the brain is more interested with deciphering the sensory-discriminative attributes of a wine's taste (e.g., how sweet, sour, etc. a wine is).

When the same wines were presented eight weeks later, now without any indication as to their price (and away from the confines of the brain scanner), no significant differences in pleasantness were reported. While such results are undoubtedly fascinating, it is perhaps worth bearing in mind here just how unnatural the experimental situation in which the participants found themselves really was. For example, just imagine yourself lying flat on your back, inserted several feet down a narrow tube, with your head clamped still (in order to minimize any motion artefacts that can make it difficult to analyse the brain imaging data), and with a tube held between your teeth as wine is periodically squirted into your mouth. You are told to hold the wine in your mouth and evaluate its taste, without swallowing, before finally having your mouth washed out with artificial saliva before the whole process starts again.

Labelling of food and flavor perception

Researchers conducted a study in which participants were sometimes informed that they would be receiving a very bitter tastant, while on other trials, they were told that they would taste something much less bitter. The neural changes that were observed took place at some of the earliest sites in the brain after the taste and smell signals are initially coded. In particular, activity in the middle and posterior insula was modulated by the verbal description that the participants had been given regarding the intensity of the to-be-delivered tastant. The OFC response also changed systematically as a function of the participants' expectations concerning the bitterness of the solutions that they were given to taste.[26] Along similar lines, researchers have used fMRI to demonstrate that expecting a very sweet drink, while tasting a drink that was not as sweet as expected, led to increased reports of sweetness, and bolstered activity in the primary taste cortex, relative to the same drink when such an expectation was not present.[27]

Elsewhere, researchers have investigated whether people's response to ambiguous (i.e., bivalent) odors would be influenced by the label that was provided. So, for example verbally describing an odor as "smelly cheese" results in people rating an ambiguous aroma as more pleasant than when exactly the same odor happens to be labelled as "sweaty socks." When researchers conducted a version of this experiment in the brain scanner, changing the label was actually shown to change the part of the OFC that was activated in their participants while sniffing. The researchers in one study delivered a savory solution to participants lying in the brain scanner who were provided with one of several different labels designed to vary their expectations concerning the pleasantness, rather than the intensity, of that which they were about to taste. The descriptors included terms such as "rich and delicious taste" versus "monosodium glutamate" for an umami solution. Meanwhile, a solution to which a vegetable aroma had been added was described as "rich and delicious flavor," "boiled vegetable water," or "monosodium glutamate." On the basis of such results, Grabenhorst et al. (2008, p. 1549) concluded that "top-down language-level cognitive effects reach far down into the earliest cortical areas that represent the appetite value of taste and flavour."[28] Meanwhile, elsewhere, researchers have demonstrated that labeling food as organic can give rise to increased activity in the ventral striatum, a part of the brain that is involved in controlling our motivation to acquire and eat food.[29]

In fact, even reading the word salt has been shown to activate many of the same brain areas as when a salty taste is actually experienced in the mouth. Indeed, it is fascinating to note that more of our brain lights up when we merely think about (or anticipate) food than when we actually get to taste it.[30] Finally, the participants in another intriguing neuroimaging study were asked whether they would like the taste of certain unusual combinations of ingredients.[31] Just think, would you, for example, like the taste of a raspberry and avocado smoothie, or how about beetroot custard? Participants exhibited increased neural activation in a part of the brain known as the medial prefrontal cortex (mPFC) while performing just such a task.

In summary, neuroimaging studies have enabled researchers to understand a little more about what happens in the brain when people say that a drink tastes better after having been told that it costs more.[32] Neuroimaging research has also highlighted the way in which the provision of branding information can end up recruiting different brain networks. Finally, the way in which a food or beverage is labeled or described also has a significant impact on the way in which taste and flavor information is represented, and responded to, by the brain.

Food in the museum: The Tate Sensorium

Let's take the Tate Sensorium as a representative recent example. The visitors to this prize-winning exhibit we encouraged to view a series of four paintings from Tate Britain's permanent collection while their other senses are simultaneously stimulated.[33] Groups of four visitors we escorted through the exhibit at roughly 15-minute intervals. Most relevant in the present context, for one of the paintings (Francis Bacon's 1945 *Figure in a Landscape*), the visitors we encouraged to taste a specially designed chocolate while viewing the painting (see Figure 4.1).

While not designed to taste especially pleasant, the idea was that the deep smoky scent that rises from the chocolate will bring something extra out from

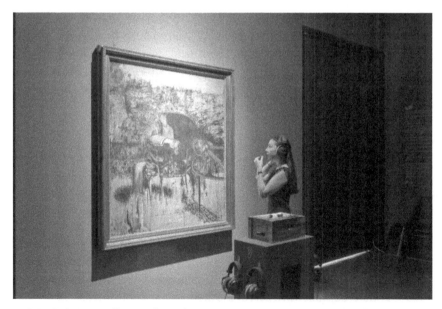

FIGURE 4.1 *Installation shot of UK Prize 2015: Tate Sensorium at Tate Britain with Francis Bacon's* Figure in a Landscape, *1945.*

© Tate. Photography by Joe Humphrys/Tate Photography. Courtesy of Tony Guillan.

the painting that wouldn't have been achieved simply by viewing the painting using only one's visual sense. Biometric data was collected from the visitors by means of a wrist band. The hope of the team behind this exhibit (Flying Objects) was that this data, collected in a naturalistic museum environment, and involving food (and the other senses), will, on subsequent analysis (together with researchers working at the University of Sussex), provide some useful insights about the brain's response to the various multisensory exhibits that they have put together. This is perhaps as close to ecologically valid testing conditions as one can hope to get.

It will be interesting to see what, if anything, such data really does reveal from the c. 2,500 people who we expected to visit the exhibit. Undoubtedly, whatever comes out will likely be very different from what might have been observed with participants lying in a brain scanner tasting, but not swallowing, the chocolate while viewing a computerized rendition of the painting projected on a screen or mirror. As this very recent example hopefully illustrates, though difficult, it is possible to collect data concerning the neuroscience, or better said biophysics, of taste in an actual museum context. It is my hope that we will see many more such exhibits in the years ahead. If anything, the chances of success in this space will likely be enhanced by the growing trend toward "Sensploration" that has apparently gripped many consumers recently.[34]

What museums need to know about flavor perception

Flavor perception is one of the most multisensory of our everyday experiences involving as it does gustation (taste) and olfaction (retronasal smell) together with (possibly) trigeminal inputs. As the world famous modernist chef Heston Blumenthal once put it: "Eating is the only thing we do that involves all the senses. I don't think that we realize just how much influence the senses actually have on the way that we process information from mouth to brain."[35] A large body of empirical research over the last century or so has unequivocally demonstrated that the other senses, e.g., oral-somatosensation, audition, and even vision, can profoundly influence flavor perception, though the jury is still out when it comes to the question of whether they are constitutive of flavor perception or merely modulate it. Nevertheless, regardless of where one stands on this debate, three key rules have been shown to explain the integration of signals from different sensory modalities that give rise to flavor experiences: these rules are sensory dominance, superadditivity, and sub-additivity. Put simply, one cannot hope to understand the multisensory perception of flavor (or, by extension, art) simply by studying what each of the senses does individually.

As the present review has hopefully made clear, the neuroscientific study of multisensory flavor perception, and the factors that modulate it, has made great strides over the last decade or so. However, that said, it is nevertheless important not to lose sight of the fact that the situation in the brain scanner is far removed from the conditions of everyday life, and, more importantly, of everyday consumption. One just needs to consider, for example, the participant lying passively with their head clamped still, unable to swallow until instructed to do so, as small amounts of liquid or liquified food are squirted into their mouth. Note here that the scanning environment is typically extremely noisy, such that the participant likely has to wear noise-canceling headphones, as bits of information (or visual images) are presented via mirror reflection on a computer screen, perhaps pertaining to the suggested price or brand of that which they are about to taste. Ultimately, dining is a fundamentally social activity and, as such, this is another aspect of our everyday experience of food and drink that is simply not captured by the neuroimaging approach to the study of flavor perception. The problems in trying to gain a fuller neuroscientific understanding of flavor are, then, in some ways equivalent to the difficulty of capturing the viewer's aesthetic response to the arts. No matter whether one is talking about the visual or culinary arts, context turns out to be very important. Furthermore, naming, labeling and description, price/valuation, the name of the artist or chef, all of these factors can dramatically influence our response to what we see or what we taste, and yet can be difficult to capture in the neuroscience laboratory.

Notes

1   Spence, C. (2015). Multisensory flavour perception. *Cell*, 161, 24–35.

2   Spence, C. (2015a). Just how much of what we taste derives from the sense of smell? *Flavour*, 4:30.

3   Bartoshuk, L. M., & Duffy, V. B. (2005). Chemical senses: Taste and smell. In C. Korsmeyer (Ed.), *The Taste Culture Reader: Experiencing food and drink* (pp. 25–33). Oxford: Berg.

4   ISO (2008). *Standard 5492: Terms relating to sensory analysis*. International Organization for Standardization. Vienna: Austrian Standards Institute.

5   Spence, C. (2015). Eating with our ears: Assessing the importance of the sounds of consumption to our perception and enjoyment of multisensory flavour experiences. *Flavour*, 4:3.

6   Spence, C. (2015). On the psychological impact of food colour. *Flavour*, 4:21.

7   Shepherd, G. M. (2012). *Neurogastronomy: How the brain creates flavor and why it matters*. New York, NY: Columbia University Press. Though see also Spence, C. (2012). Book review: "Neurogastronomy: How the brain creates flavor and why it matters" by Gordon M. Shepherd. *Flavour,* 1**:**21.

8   Bartoshuk, L. (1980). Separate worlds of taste. *Psychology Today*, 14, 48–49, 51, 54–56, 63.

9   Bartoshuk, L. M. (2000). Comparing sensory experiences across individuals: Recent psychophysical advances illuminate genetic variation in taste perception. *Chemical Senses*, 25, 447–460; Mauer, L., & El-Sohemy, A. (2012). Prevalence of cilantro (*Coriandrum sativum*) disliking among different ethnocultural groups. *Flavour*, 1:8.

10 Veeck, A. (2010). Encounters with extreme foods: Neophilic/neophobic tendencies and novel foods. *Journal of Food Products Marketing*, 16, 246–260.

11 Eldeghaidy, S., Marciani, L., McGlone, F., Hollowood, T., Hort, J., Head, K., et al. (2011). The cortical response to the oral perception of fat emulsions and the effect of taster status. *Journal of Neurophysiology*, 105, 2572–2581.

12 Piqueras-Fiszman, B., & Spence, C. (2015). Sensory expectations based on product-extrinsic food cues: An interdisciplinary review of the empirical evidence and theoretical accounts. *Food Quality & Preference*, 40, 165–179.

13 Piqueras-Fiszman, B., & Spence, C. (2012). Sensory incongruity in the food and beverage sector: Art, science, and commercialization. *Petits Propos Culinaires*, 95, 74–118.

14 Small, D. M. (2012). Flavor is in the brain. *Physiology and Behavior*, 107, 540–552.

15 Dalton, P., Doolittle, N., Nagata, H., & Breslin, P. A. S. (2000). The merging of the senses: Integration of subthreshold taste and smell. *Nature Neuroscience*, 3, 431–432.

16 De Araujo, I. E. T., Rolls, E. T., Kringelbach, M. L., McGlone, F., & Phillips, N. (2003). Taste-olfactory convergence, and the representation of the pleasantness of flavour, in the human brain. *European Journal of Neuroscience*, 18, 2059–2068.

17 Small, D. M., Voss, J., Mak, Y. E., Simmons, K. B., Parrish, T., & Gitelman, D. (2004). Experience-dependent neural integration of taste and smell in the human brain. *Journal of Neurophysiology*, 92, 1892–1903.

18 Schaal, B., & Durand, K. (2012). The role of olfaction in human multisensory development. In A. J. Bremner, D. Lewkowicz, & C. Spence (Eds.), *Multisensory development* (pp. 29–62). Oxford, UK: Oxford University Press.

19 Small, D. M., Zatorre, R. J., Dagher, A., Evans, A. C., & Jones-Gotman, M. (2001). Changes in brain activity related to eating chocolate: From pleasure to aversion. *Brain*, 124, 1720–1733.

20 Spence, C., Okajima, K. Cheok, A. D., Petit, O., & Michel, C. (in press). Eating with our eyes: From visual hunger to digital satiation. *Brain & Cognition*.

21 Pursey, K. M., Stanwell, P., Callister, R. J., Brain, K., Collins, C. E., & Burrows, T. L. (2014). Neural responses to visual food cues according to

weight status: A systematic review of functional magnetic resonance imaging studies. *Frontiers in Nutrition*, 1, 7.

22 Schienle, A., Schäfer, A., Hermann, A., & Vaitl, D. (2009). Binge-eating disorder: Reward sensitivity and brain activation to images of food. *Biological Psychiatry*, 65, 654–661.

23 McClure, S. M., Li, J., Tomlin, D., Cypert, K. S., Montague, L. M., & Montague, P. R. (2004). Neural correlates of behavioral preference for culturally familiar drinks. *Neuron*, 44, 379–387.

24 Kühn, S., & Gallinat, J. (2013). Does taste matter? How anticipation of cola brands influences gustatory processing in the brain. *PLoS ONE*, 8:4, e61569.

25 Plassmann, H., O'Doherty, J., Shiv, B., & Rangel, A. (2008). Marketing actions can modulate neural representations of experienced pleasantness. *Proceedings of the National Academy of Sciences USA*, 105, 1050–1054.

26 Nitschke, J. B., Dixon, G. E., Sarinopoulos, I., Short, S. J., Cohen, J. D., Smith, E. E., Kosslyn, S. M., Rose, R. M., & Davidson, R. J. (2006). Altering expectancy dampens neural response to aversive taste in primary taste cortex. *Nature Neuroscience*, 9, 435–442.

27 Woods, A. T., Lloyd, D. M., Kuenzel, J., Poliakoff, E., Dijksterhuis, G. B., & Thomas, A. (2011). Expected taste intensity affects response to sweet drinks in primary taste cortex. *Neuroreport*, 22, 365–369.

28 Grabenhorst, F., Rolls, E. T., & Bilderbeck, A. (2008). How cognition modulates affective responses to taste and flavor: Top-down influences on the orbitofrontal and pregenul cortices. *Cerebral Cortex*, 18, 1549–1559.

29 Linder, N. S., Uhl, G., Fliessbach, K., Trautner, P., Elger, C. E., et al. (2010). Organic labeling influences food valuation and choice. *NeuroImage*, 53, 215–220.

30 O'Doherty, J., Deichmann, R., Critchley, H. D., & Dolan, R. J. (2002). Neural responses during anticipation of a primary taste reward. *Neuron*, 33, 815–826.

31 Barron, H. C., Dolan, R. J., & Behrens, T. E. J. (2013). Online evaluation of novel choices by simultaneous representation of multiple memories. *Nature Neuroscience*, 16, 1492–1498.

32 Spence, C. (2010). The price of everything—the value of nothing? *The World of Fine Wine*, 30, 114–120.

33 Davis, N. (2015). Welcome to the Tate Sensorium, where the paintings come with chocolates. *The Guardian*, 22 August. Downloaded from http://www.theguardian.com/artanddesign/video/2015/aug/25/welcome-tate-sensorium-taste-touch-smell-art-video accessed on 13/09/2015.

34 Leow, H. C. (2015). Never heard of Sensploration? Time to study up on epicure's biggest high-end pattern. *The Veox*, 22 December. Downloaded from http://www.theveox.com/never-heard-of-sensploration-time-to-study-up-on-epicures-biggest-high-end-pattern/ accessed on 31/01/2016.

35 This quote appeared on the front of the Tasting menu from The Fat Duck restaurant, Bray, UK).

5

Food and Objecthood:
Food, Museums, and
Anti-Theatricality

Edward Whittall

In a *New York Times* opinion piece, cultural critic William Deresiewicz argues that despite its cultural prominence, "food, for all that, is not art. Both begin by addressing the senses, but that is where food stops [. . .] Food is highly developed as a system of sensations, extremely crude as a system of symbols. Proust on the madeleine is art; the madeleine itself is not art."[1] Indeed, recent popular and academic criticism has turned (again) toward the question of whether food can be art. Much of this discourse engages in comparisons between food and different art forms like sculpture, music, literature, and painting, and inevitably finds food falling short of being "art." The most conciliatory stance emerges from philosopher Aaron Meskin, who offers that food might be seen as an "emerging hybrid art form that combines haute cuisine, sculpture, various chemical technologies and, *arguably*, one or more of the performing arts."[2] Food as art, in this formulation, exists between art, food, and theater. But there is little mention in this story of the institutions that might contribute to such distinctions.

This chapter draws out institutional tensions between the museum, the theater, and the restaurant by unpacking Meskin's assertion, exploring how current iterations of the food-as-art debate are mired in the older issue of anti-theatricality. Theatricality is often taken to relate, of course, to that which takes place in a theater, or worse, to that which, in everyday life, is marked by the unreal, the excessive, or the fictional. Anti-theatricality, then, is a critique of theatricality that, from Plato onwards, has defined the gap between reality and representation, known as mimesis. Mimesis is suspect because, through its showiness and excess, it "masks an inner emptiness, a deficiency or absence of that to which it refers."[3]

Recently, performance theorist Josette Féral argued that theatricality is "a *process* that has to do with a 'gaze' that postulates and creates a distinct, virtual space belonging to the other, from which fiction can emerge."[4]

> If the notion of theatricality goes beyond the theater, it is because it is not a "property" belonging to the subjects/things that are its vehicles. It belongs neither to the objects, the space, nor the actor himself, although each can become its vehicle. Rather, theatricality is the result of a perceptual dynamics linking the onlooker with someone or something that is looked at.[5]

Theatricality, then, requires an encounter between the object (performer) and the subject (spectator) grounded in space and time. Indeed, it is the relationship between the act (the art object) and the engagement with it upon which I base my case for theatricality's importance in understanding the relationship between food, art, and the museum. Food, crossing the line between the everyday and the representational, the real and the imaginary, is a fervent site for the process of theatricality. So too is the museum.

This chapter first brings recent work on food and aesthetics into conversation in order to propose that the critical language of performance and the theater, rather than philosophical aesthetics, might be more illuminating in discussing food as an art. Then, I argue that performance and its operative forces of theatricality and performativity lie at the heart of food's cultural power, and at its inclusion in the museum. Moreover, tracing food's institutional history, I suggest, reveals that food has long been a "hybrid" form. I unpack Meskin's allusion to chef/author/entrepreneur Nathan Myhrvold, whose neologism "Modernist Cuisine" has become a definitive term in propelling food as art into the public imaginary, linking molecular cuisine to modernist art in an easy-to-grasp term. Myhrvold's assertion that molecular cuisine derives its lineage from modernist art relates to the well-known essay "Art and Objecthood" where art critic Michael Fried argues that art is threatened by an "encroaching theatrical sensibility."[6] Theatricality, for Fried, brings the objecthood of the art object into view. Reading Myhrvold and Fried together affords a critique of the food discourse that dismisses food's artistic potential. In light of these frameworks, I suggest that the museum, rather than the restaurant or the theater, is a lucrative site for observing food's intersections with art.

Finally, this chapter examines an exhibit by Natalie Doonan and Ken Gregory, two Canadian artists whose collaborative work draws on critical intersections between food and contemporary art practice, and whose installation, *The Bliss Point*, was part of the *Hedonistika* "Food and Robotics" Festival exhibit at the Montreal Museum of Contemporary Art which was held under the umbrella of the International Digital Arts Biennial (May, 2014). *The Bliss Point*, which sought to explore the boundaries between food and technology, engages in the process of theatricality inside the museum to challenge the power of sugar as an economic and cultural force. The artists invoke the power of the museum to create fiction from an everyday food staple, making the interpretation of the art installation dependent on its presence in the museum, which confers "authority" onto the subject matter. Rather than asking whether food can be art, I am interested in what the museum can teach us about food and ourselves that we might not learn elsewhere.

Food and art

Yael Raviv argues that food requires a critical language that exceeds the gastronomic, replaces the aesthetic, and can account for both changes in the art world and in the restaurant world.[7] These two worlds, she points out, are collapsing into each other and demand the ability to think and speak critically about food across genres and then narrate these experiences into the history of art. "The stakes for developing a vocabulary for interpreting food-work is not restricted to a greater understanding of art, but also to a greater understanding of some of the work within the culinary world," she writes.[8] For Raviv, performance is key to this critical language. Other scholars have provided input into this discussion.

Lisa Heldke, Carolyn Korsmeyer, and Aaron Meskin have found in food a way to trouble aesthetic theories that displace the senses and specifically the gustatory as valid and vital ways of knowing and experiencing the world. Korsmeyer, in particular, interrogates arguments against food's representational and symbolic power. Countering the downgrading of sensual taste as a category of aesthetic value by arguing for food's expressive and representational abilities, she still finds food quite different, when compared to *fine arts,* like sculpture and painting. She writes that "foods seems to be heavily dependent on either ceremonial context or personal or cultural narrative to attain cognitive and aesthetic significance."[9] However, she adds that food should not be asked the same questions as are asked of art, "because eating is a repetitive and transient experience, because food does not last but spoils, because it not only nourishes but poisons, eating is a small exercise in mortality. Rather than transcend time, as romantic ideas of art suggest is the goal of masterworks, food succumbs to time—as we do ourselves."[10]

Aaron Meskin cites from Korsmeyer's robust analysis, but cautions against generalizations that ask all art forms to work as mimetic, representational, symbolic, or expressive forms. Not all do, and not all arts fit neatly into categorical forms. He sees food, like prose poetry, as a hybrid art form. This conciliatory gesture is encouraging, but somewhat incomplete. Food is contingent, transient, and processual. It seems sculptural and painterly, but these aspects of food's presentation, unlike sculpture and painting, cannot withstand their exposure to time and consumption. That food is a hybrid art form also depends upon claims of historical lineage. Rosalind Kraus, in *The Originality of the Avant-Garde and Other Modernist Myths* argues that this kind of historicism is laden with contradictions: art at once is eternal and trans-historical, and yet its formal lineage must always be reinforced through constant renewal.[11] The danger in this thinking, she claims, lies in the critic becoming instrumental in assessing the value of art without regard for the methods: "It is in this declaration of the ontic status of art, of its unbreathable, seamless continuity, that led [Clement] Greenberg vigorously to deny that it is in method rather than the content of the judgments that the interest of criticism lies."[12] Post-structuralism demands a challenging of historicism through, among other tools, material analysis. What material and discursive conditions make something "art" and something else "food"? And who decides and names them as such? These questions are especially fundamental to the issue of food as art. Simply put, to attribute food's hybridity only to its relationship to haute cuisine and sculpture is to ignore both food and art's institutional history, and equally, the role of the theater in shaping them.

The museum, the restaurant, and the theater

Food, art, and performance, along with the histories of their supporting institutions, the restaurant, the museum, and the theater are entangled. This overlap is visible when observing forms of cultural expression such as the banquet or the festival. Barbara Kirshenblatt-Gimblett asks what theater history might look like "if it were written backward from the Futurist Banquets and Dali dinners and performance art."[13] Might we then also ask what the history of food as an art might look like if we trace it back to the feast and the Renaissance garden? Denise E. Cole describes the feast as a fused form of theater in which "food did not just accompany a performance; food was a performance."[14] In the Tudor feast, "to be 'entertained' meant not only hearing and seeing performance but also tasting, touching, and smelling it. Consumption was not only visual but also tactile and gastronomic. An audience member's involvement was complete and active, not fragmentary and passive, because every one of his or her five senses participated in hospitality's revelry."[15]

Food, in banquets and festivals, was certainly sculptural. Kirshenblatt-Gimblett describes "edible monuments" as "an edible world where sausages, cheese and pastries grow on trees" where fountains flowed with wine rather than water. "Large, free-standing and edible, such festival architecture and sculpture enacted its own ephemerality," she writes.[16] According to Cole, food and human performances at Tudor banquets were subject to the same theatrical conventions. For example, food and human performers entered and exited from the kitchen. Disguise was employed through masks and costumes on the humans, and through spicing and *trompe l'oeil* on the food. The human performances were the interlude between courses, a distraction from the clearing of one course and the setting of another. "The feast was really the catalyst for theatrical productions at court. Usually given at the end of a meal, human performance was as much a dessert as the edible productions were."[17]

Modernity, Kirshenblatt-Gimblett claims, saw the dissolution of the hybrid arts and its sites. "It has taken considerable cultural work to isolate the senses, create genres of art specific to each, insist on their autonomy, and cultivate modes of attentiveness that give some senses priority over others," she writes.[18] In this observation the institutional garden, the banquet, and the feast transformed into the restaurant, the theater, and the museum. But I suggest that these institutinal boundaries were porous and that the connection between them can be found in the process of theatricality. Early nineteenth century gastronome Grimod de la Reynière wrote that "the table is a hub around which all reputations are formed; it is a theatre where there never is a flop; and without a doubt, plays would never fail if, on opening night, their authors could give a dinner in the orchestra."[19] The theater is more than simply a metaphor used to describe the modern restaurant. Barbara Kirshenblatt-Gimblett traces the staging of cuisine within the restaurant that emerged as a "dedicated space of food theatre," uncovering the dramaturgy of the dining room and the emergence of the kitchen as display of artisanal labor.[20] The open kitchen, she writes, "converts performance, in the sense of doing, into theatre, that is, into an exhibition of itself."[21] Rebecca Spang draws a more pointed comparison between the theater and the restaurant when she writes that "the restaurant, like the theatre, was a privileged locus of ephemerality."[22]

While the restaurant embraced its theatricality, the theater formed a tense relationship with food. Kirshenblatt-Gimblett outlines the various "fused" forms of performance that lasted beyond the formation of the theater as an autonomous art form, such as the banquet, the *opera gastronomica*, the Hassidic *Tish* and the *repas en ambigus*, all of which existed parallel to, but not integrated into, the Western theater as a place to *see* plays. Laurence Senelick exposes a trend in the Western theater at the *fin-de-siècle* that Brecht deridingly referred to as "culinary theatre."[23] The use of real food and the naturalistic replication of meals and feasts on stage, in France, England, and the United States, mirrored the rise of haute cuisine.

The proliferation of stage meals reflected the rise of dining out, or the public performance of gastronomy. The development of a complex cuisine, based on well-provisioned markets and the affluence of money and leisure, was dependent on the growth of cities. So was the eventual evolution of the restaurant and, for that matter, the permanent playhouse. Urban culture nurtured phantasms of luxury and sensual pleasure in both sites.

SENELICK 2005: 45

However, food threatens theatricality by disrupting the gaze of the spectator with the promise of eating. When staged, food becomes difficult to contain and the codes of theatricality threaten to decay. Smell permeates the fourth wall. Distinctions between spaces are troubled by the presence of something "real," something that moves our bodies toward a consumptive inquiry. Smell produces salivation, hunger, and excitement.

Prior to moments of absorption, food draws attention to its own life, its own presence, and in so doing, highlights the "liveness" of the theatre by forcing the acknowledgement of its permeability. Theatre is a leaky place whose artificial borders are crossed easily by the smells that waft into the audience. The sensory transgression of boundaries goes unacknowledged in key models of the conventional theatrical frame.[24]

On the surface, the restaurant space seems to negate this idea. The restaurant makes the promise of eating not just palpable, but central to theatricality. However, rather than resting solely on Kirshenblatt-Gimblett's dramaturgy of the restaurant—which refers to its content—I suggest that it is the distinction between the outside and the inside of the restaurant that draws on the tensions between food and theatricality. As Spang explains, "the nineteenth century's restaurant fantasy implicitly required the presence of someone outside: some poor devil with his nose pressed to the window."[25] For Spang, restaurants, unlike the streets outside, "were places of daydream and fantasy," and "by placing the pleasures of the wealthy before the eyes [and noses] of the poor, restaurants aroused insatiable and dangerous desires."[26]

Kirshenblatt-Gimblett suggests that "while we eat to satisfy hunger and nourish our bodies, some of the most radical effects occur precisely when food is dissociated from eating and eating from nourishment. Such dissociations produce eating disorders, religious experiences, culinary feats, sensory epiphanies, and art".[27] In the same vein, Iball argues that food is traditionally present as art in the museum in the form of the still life, which fixes food's boundaries within a frame.[28] Must food be dissociated from eating (and nourishment) to be considered art? This seems to me to reify Deresiewicz's stance that eating is simply too basic a mode of perception to allow for art to happen at the same time. This belief reaffirms Fried's argument that "theatre is the negation of art."[29]

It is the museum that brings out the forces of theatricality in food when it incorporates desire, consumption, and ephemerality into the museological space. Much of the debate surrounding food-as-art suffers from an underlying reliance on anti-theatricality. Anti-theatricality is not new to the discourse of art and the museum. However, it is a new thread in food studies. Indeed, to reiterate Korsmeyer's problematic: how can food be art if its objecthood is compromised by its dependence on the social? I suspect that Meskin's temptation to separate the context in which food is served from the actual food on the plate is what is at play in his assertion that food is only "arguably" connected to the performing arts. In order to qualify as art, food must stand alone as an object proper. The key to Meskin's caution, I believe, is linked to his unproblematic acceptance of Myhrvold's neologism "modernist cuisine." Unpacking Myhrvold's claim, then, is a good place to start.

Myhrvold, Fried, and perspectives on anti-theatricality

Myhrvold, a polymath who has made his name and fortune in high tech, has turned his attention to the world of gastronomy. He co-authored and self-published a five-part tome called "Modernist Cuisine," which *Forbes Magazine* claims is the world's most influential and profitable cookbook.[30] His intellectual and practical work asks "one of the great intellectual questions for gastronomy in the twenty-first century . . . can food be art?"[31], but also argues that Ferran Adrià's cuisine represents a long-awaited modernist revolution in gastronomy, akin to the revolution of thought that carried the Impressionists and the Bauhaus school to the heights of the art world in the early twentieth century. It is a revolution, he claims, that somehow managed to by-pass the culinary arts. He argues that some of the more noticeable actors in the history of cuisine failed to revolutionize gastronomy to the same extent that modernist painting and sculpture revolutionized the arts.

About Escoffier and his creation of the brigade system, he writes "he was an artisan striving to run a factory rather than be an artist."[32] Further, Myhrvold dismisses the Futurists and their multi-sensual culinary events by claiming that "[their] posturing succeeded in attracting attention but failed to create a genuine gastronomic aesthetic."[33] And of the inventors of Nouvelle Cuisine, he argues that they were "all about techniques and ingredients."[34] Through this perspective, Adrià and his contemporaries, such as Grant Achatz, Heston Blumenthal, and Joan Roca are modernist chefs, unable to enter postmodernity with their craft. By reducing "Modernism" to two simple categories—that it must be both revolutionary, representing a total break from "tradition," and concerned with the thoughts and emotions it provokes, rather than the mere process of making food—Myhrvold denies the possibility of Postmodernism, which he aligns with the rather thinly defined term "deconstruction," a term whose use, he states, "owes more to simple appropriation of a name than what is really at play."[35]

Myhrvold's argument is built upon the logic that Modernism and Postmodernism are delineated by definitive time periods which cuisine simply missed. In this frame, he argues that chefs, having not engaged with Modernism, are now enacting modernist sensibilities. Ann-Britt Gran and Diane Oatley suggest that these two periods do not represent literal time, "rather that they express something of a period's self-perception (its mythology) . . . the modern self-perception understands 'the modern' as non-theatrical, while postmodern self-perception views 'the postmodern' through theatrical metaphors."[36] It seems productive then to ask what the self-perception of "modernist cuisine" might be and why it has become a signal phrase in popular food culture. The roots to this question lie in the art and museum world.

In tone, Myhrvold's essay is similar to Michael Fried's "Art and Objecthood." Like Fried, Myhrvold seems intent on arguing for a rigid definition of what is and is not art. Despite his statement that "impact, or reception, is key to the Modernist project in art and literature,"[37] there is a deeply felt vein of anti-theatricality that runs through Myhrvold's arguments, as though an admission of theatricality will delegitimize food's potential as an art form. By aligning the discourse of gastronomy with those of modernist painting and literature, Myhrvold is asserting the autonomy of food as a product of artistic labor. Myhrvold's construct of cuisine as Modernist Art, and of the chef as a modernist artist relies on the autonomy of the art form as distinct from other creative forms, of the chef as author, and of the object, food. I argue, simply, that these elements defy the conditions necessary to declare them Modernist.

Myhrvold begins his quest by arguing that the difference between art and craft is that the focus of craft "is on the process of manufacture, or on the food itself, with less emphasis on the thoughts and emotions triggered by the food. Food is deeply constrained by rules and traditions."[38] Moreover, Myhrvold insists that "the Modernist project in art and literature . . . posits art as a dialogue between artist and audience."[39] These claims are curious in relation to Fried's similar claim that "modernist painting's self-imposed imperative [is] that it defeats or suspends its own objecthood."[40] Auslander shows that "what Fried calls 'objecthood' is equivalent to what he . . . calls 'theatre,'"[41] and so Fried argues that the encroaching theatrical sensibility of minimalism—

or what has come to be known as postmodernism[42]—is insistent on the presence of the object and the viewer's encounter with that object in space and time. Fried argues that modernist painting only exists as art if its objecthood is suspended, if the viewer and artist form a communion despite the objecthood of the canvas. For Fried, this means that painting must engage with, rather than deny, its physical qualities that make it a unique art form—in this case, its flatness—while suppressing its support structures, techniques, and spaces of reception.

Myhrvold, I believe, means the same thing. For the diner and chef to have a "dialogue," the food must transcend its own materiality, its own objecthood. Food becomes the passive conduit for the conversation. The space (the restaurant) and the support (the waiters, cooks, plates, forks, etc.) must be sublimated along with the food, so "craft" becomes invisible, leaving "art" in its place. I am not arguing that Myhrvold is either right or wrong in asserting that cuisine should do this in order to be Modernist, but rather that it is an inert category unless it can be shown that Modernist cuisine actually behaves this way. I turn now to Fried to think through this argument. The first pillar of Fried's opposition to theatricality lies in its "presence." "Something is said to have presence," he writes, "when it demands that the beholder takes it into account, that he takes it seriously."[43] "Presence" is problematic to Fried because, as Auslander explains, "it depends for its completion and fulfillment as an aesthetic object on the presence of a spectator—it is not self-sufficient and self-referential in the way Fried believes modernist art to be."[44] In other words, modernist art, according to Fried, exists with or without the spectator. It transcends not only the canvas upon which it is painted, but also the circumstances in which it is viewed.

The fundamental difference for the spectator between art and theater, Fried argues, lies in the difference between "interest" and "conviction," where "interest implies temporality in the form of continuing attention directed at the object whereas the concept of conviction does not."[45] In the theater, the spectator's interest must be held over time and contained in a space of reception for the work to be experienced. The same is true of food. In cuisine, timing is everything, from cooking to delivering the plate to the table. A timing misfire results in a ruined dish. When museums close, the lights go off and the painting is still a painting.

Myhrvold never explicitly describes where the "art" is in food. While he argues that "chefs have been strangely absent" from engaging in the discourse of art, he leaves us to intuit that the "art," in cuisine, is the food on the plate.[46] Regardless of the presentation of the actual dish, it does not exist as a dish until the diner interrupts the visual and sculptural aspects of the food. A dish is not a dish until someone digs in, until the food is literally consumed. Molecular cuisine then, in Fried's formulation, is not a Modernist art object because it insists on the objecthood or the theatricality of food, and thus, relies on the various social, historical, and aesthetic layers that construct it as "cuisine" and the diner as a subject. Theatricality is a result of a series of cleavages between everyday space and representational space, and between reality and fiction. "Without this division of space, theatricality cannot arise, much less theatre, because the Other would be in my space."[47] The space between the spectator and object/performer is vital to the formation of theatricality. As we have seen above, Fried and Myhrvold require that the space and the object must be transcended in order to have the experience of art that modernism requires. Clearly, then, Meskin's assertion that food is descended from sculpture, painting, or anything else that forms its hybrid ontology is inconsistent with the possibility of Myhrvold's modernist cuisine. Josette Féral reminds us that "the beholder is fundamental to the definition of theatricality."[48] Performance has its audience, minimalist sculpture has its spectator, and restaurant food has its diner. However, in the museum, food can have all three.

The Bliss Point: Food, museums, and theatricality

Natalie Doonan and Ken Gregory's *The Bliss Point* was rooted in a series of observations about the production and consumption of sugar. When the food industry faced growing concern over the amount of sugar being consumed in American diets, it sponsored research that found that infants had an immediate, "innate" response to the taste of sugar. This "enabled companies to argue, at least, that sugar was not something 'artificial' they were thrusting upon an unsuspecting public. Rather, sugar was sinless, if not entirely wholesome."[49] But sugar hardly qualifies as a tough sell. Sidney Mintz explained that "few are the world's peoples who respond negatively to sugar, whatever their prior experience, and countless those who have reacted to it with intensified craving and enthusiasm."[50] But that craving has limits to which the food industry pays careful attention. The "bliss point" is a food science term for the combination of flavor enhancers—sugar, salt, or fat—that, according to Moss, makes food and drink most enjoyable.[51]

This was the inspiration for Natalie Doonan and Ken Gregory, whose installation *The Bliss Point* is described by Doonan:

> Part love affair with all things sweet and part critique, *The Bliss Point* explores food technology with an emphasis on the production and consumption of sugar in its various forms. The specific site of investigation is the human body and its manipulation by major corporations, marketing, government and other institutions. The tension between medical issues

such as diabetes and obesity and the idea of a fun and colourful candy mountain sugar party drives this multimedia installation.[52]

Doonan and Gregory were also interested in the way money made from sugar production has supported museums, notably the Redpath Museum in Montreal, commissioned as a museum of natural science by Peter Redpath, whose family fortune was derived from the Redpath Sugar company, and Tate Modern, in London, named for the art patron Henry Tate, whose wealth arose from patenting the sugar cube. And so, the exhibit staged what Doonan described as a "critique of museology."[53] Using old display cases obtained from the Montreal Museum of Fine Arts, the artists presented sugar "artefacts." Modern items such as gummy bears, licorice babies, and coke cans were placed alongside teacups, postcards, and shards of sugar cane. Sugar crystal formations of different size, color, and texture were found either standing alone or on delicate, antique servers inside the display cases. A book featuring a depiction of an old map of the Belgian Congo was left open under the display glass along with didactic panels that twisted "factual" information about sugar. For instance, a marzipan pyramid was accompanied by a didactic panel which claimed that marzipan was a preserved "subtlety" that was created by La Toundra restaurant and served to patrons of Expo '67 in Montreal. While the restaurant did indeed exist at Expo '67 and marzipan is a well-known ingredient, the rest of the "facts" are a fabrication.

Another didactic panel entitled "Queen Elizabeth II and Prince Philip attend the opening of the Redpath Sugar Refinery in Toronto, June 29, 1959, City of Toronto Archives, Fonds 1257, Series 1057, Item 4986," accompanied displays of teacups, history books, and postcards depicting a young Queen Elizabeth waving to a crowd from the sunroof of a limousine as it passes along a city street. The evidence purports to "document" Queen Elizabeth signing a guestbook at the Redpath Sugar refinery in Montreal. She is described giving a speech about the ancient European associations between "whiteness and purity." "Emphasized as a luxury good in the early days of its import to England," the didactic reads, "refined sugar became less so as it trickled down to the poor." The separation of display space from the spectator, enforced by the glass cases, divides the space in exactly the manner Féral suggests is vital to theatricality. The artefacts, though "real," create a fiction: The postcard photo of Queen Elizabeth might have been taken in any number of cities, while the proximity of the teacups might suggest they were used by the Queen herself. The critiques of class and race were masked in the playful illusion constructed by Doonan and Gregory. More work was required of the spectator than simply met their eye.

The deception is both appealing and appalling in its proximity to fact and the nonchalance with which it distorts reality. Despite sugar's everyday presence,

Mintz described how sugar's spread through the West was one of the most economically and culturally significant phenomena since the seventeenth century. Likewise, sugar, along with coffee and tea were "the first luxuries to become regarded as necessities by vast masses of people who had not produced them, and they were probably the first substances to become the basis of advertising campaigns to increase consumption."[54] In other words, sugar has long been associated with the very kinds of themes that *The Bliss Point* was employing, supported by the museum's institutional context.

According to Doonan, patrons asked questions and expressed surprise at not having known these "facts" about sugar before. Doonan, dressed in a white lab coat, was present during the exhibit to interact with spectators. In addressing questions about the displays, she embodied the role of a curator, who, David Balzer argues, has become recognized as an "imparter of value" in museums and galleries.[55] But the lab coats did more than simply position Doonan and Gregory as caretakers of the objects as they also signified them as researchers. Doonan and Gregory installed a scanner and custom-fit 3D printer, which produced sugar masks of patrons who sat to have their faces scanned. Computers and MRI scans paired with didactics explaining that 3D sugar scanning had been used to create molds for "enhancing organs" support the

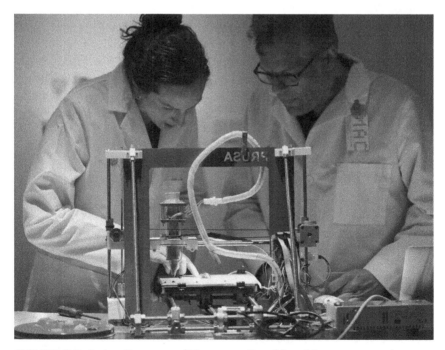

FIGURE 5.1 *Artists Gregory and Doonan at "work" making a sugar mask.*
© *Erik de Leon.*

fiction of research that was performed in the installation. The "scientists" were seen at work on their scanner or circulating among the crowd. Doonan reports that several spectators asked her whether she was a food scientist, only to be surprised when she informed them that she was an artist. Indeed, spectators became complicit in supporting Doonan's claim to artistic authorship. They did so by providing an audience to the art-making process, but also by transforming themselves into performers either by sitting for a "sugar portrait" or by becoming interlocutors and investigating the theatrical codes.

The lab coats, reinforced by the scenography of the display cases, the technology, and the artist-and-model trope of classical painting, served to remove Doonan and Gregory's bodies from their everyday contexts by marking them as curators, researchers, and artists at work. The two artists allowed spectators to look at them freely, only answering questions if they were asked. What I would point out, however, is that these performances did not take place on the street, or in a theater, a lab, or, for that matter, in a restaurant, but in a museum of contemporary art. That Doonan and Gregory were granted all or a combination of artistic, curatorial, and scientific authority by the spectators, speaks to the range of expectations that the museum-going public have, pre-formed, of the institution. I suggest that the museum's hybridity is created not by the artistic medium, but by the specific relationship formed between the artists, the spectators, and the objects, and by the processes that mediate interactions with the space.

Duration was also vital to the audience's perception. Anyone who sat for a "portrait" would have to wait up to three hours for the mask to be printed. Also on display, literally, is the dissonance between the museum's articulation of the past through the curation of archives, and performance's immersion in the present and unrepeatable moment. This temporal dimension forces performance into a realm of aesthetic experience that removes it from modernist projections of timelessness, and exposes the museum as complicit in constructing that very category of art. Moreover, the production of unique, temporally unstable, and tasty sugar masks overturns technology as a signifier of mass production and speed by making it complicit in the process of art making. This inversion of the role of technology in our lives and on our diets constitutes a performative critique of food production and consumption that can only be realized by sitting for a "portrait" and waiting for the mask to print.

But what does food bring into the museum that performance does not do on its own? After all, duration, transformation, and fiction are all components of performance, but taste, touch, and smell also show up in *The Bliss Point*. For Doonan, the smell of candy cooking as patrons enter the space evokes memories of fairgrounds, play, and childhood. The stickiness of the lollipops and masks and the brightly colored sugar creates invitations to "improper" behavior in the museum, touching and tasting. Constance Classen writes that "artefacts for the most part are only to be seen, not felt, smelt, sounded and certainly not tasted."[56] But touching artefacts was common in the time of the cabinet of curiosities before the rise of the aesthetic moved patrons away from objects. "By the end of the nineteenth century, in fact, the use of the proximity senses of smell, taste, and touch, had been generally relegated to the realm of the nursery and the 'savage' [. . .] The important thing in modernity was to *see*."[57]

Classen demonstrates how clearly gendered and classed the issue of touch became in the museum. Connoisseurs, generally male, formed impressions through sight, as it was believed that the "common visitor" touched and otherwise profaned the exhibit.[58] *The Bliss Point* recreates this class partition by preventing patrons from touching the authoritative artefacts, while being able to smell, taste, and participate in making of sweets. These visceral reactions and playful behaviors engage visitors, denying them the opportunity to form aesthetic judgment in a manner that frustrates modernist aesthetics. But that very immediacy allows the artist to engage participants, sometimes unwittingly, in critique. For Doonan and Gregory, the critique that was available for their audience to discover was in the relationship between sugar, colonialism, and slavery. Little licorice babies were consumed by museumgoers who only later might become aware of the invocation of slavery, undermining the appreciation of the familiar candy. These webs of signification, technology, and sensual pleasure take on new meanings when supported by the theatrical structures of museum display that are also being raised to consciousness by the viscerality of the medium itself—food.

The complex social and spatial dynamics of the museum suggest that food is at once an object and a process; it is equally given to and threatening of theatricality. It demands serious contemplation and permits openings for play that challenge social and spatial norms. Touching artifacts, Classen argues, was not only a way to verify what the eye sees, but also to transfer power and social prestige. In this sense, then, "eating a museum piece was, perhaps, the ultimate act of ownership."[59] I suggest that food in the museum, like Fried's "theater," threatens to democratize connoisseurship by challenging the boundaries of the object and the spatial and social processes that makes art "Art." The museum is more accessible and more people can afford to play with their food. Reservations for a table at one of the temples of modernist cuisine are difficult to get and exorbitantly expensive for those who do manage.

Conclusions

The intent of this chapter is not to undo or counter critique of food as art. As Korsmeyer, Meskin, and others point out, it is difficult to imagine that food cannot provide an aesthetic experience. Meskin insists that modernist cuisine has affinities with sculpture, but that it is not necessarily sculpture itself. For Meskin, food's centrality in our lives makes its appreciation of vital importance, but he wonders whether interest in food makes individuals "just self-indulgent and misguided hedonists, or does food have some sort of significant value over and above nutrition and the provision of gustatory pleasure."[60] For Meskin, there is no value in comparing food to art so "let's make the case for the value of food as food and not worry so much about its aesthetic and artistic status."[61] But what is that value?

The Bliss Point reveals that there is no simple answer to the question. Food, cleaved from the everyday and ushered into the museum as an object that is not quite an object, as a process that demands attention to itself, and as a performative critique of the theatrical codes that produce both cuisine and art, extends minimalist sculpture and performance while providing a challenge to the limits of both. People who engaged with The Bliss Point were one or all of spectators, audience, diners, and performers. Food's hybridity lies not in its relationship to other arts, but in its mutability between the everyday and the exceptional, the banal and the sublime, the nutrient and the object of contemplation. Helen Iball argues that there is a "moment before" food is consumed in theatrical settings where food "melts all other thought."[62] She calls this moment a "Poohvian" moment, referring to Winnie the Pooh, who enjoyed soliloquizing the honey on his hand the moment before getting his head stuck in the jar, smearing honey all over his face. It is tempting to imagine that it is in this moment, where time stands still and thought is absent, that food can become art in the modernist sense. But, I suggest, it is one of several moments in a process that simply cannot be divided, and which adds up to the value of "food as food."

The museum, as it does with art objects, offers an intensified experience of food. Yael Raviv describes this heightened encounter with food, both in art and dining, as humans being made to stop and think. "Food artists . . . wish to make us stop and think; they try not only to create delicious food, but also to do so in a way that alters our perception, confounds our existing notions, and expands the way we view the world."[63] The Bliss Point suggests that it is art that fails to make the case for food, and not food that fails as art. For Raviv, the epistemologies and practices of performance are necessary: "the slippage between food as artistic medium and food as culinary medium is most pronounced in live performance, particularly performances involving actual consumption."[64] Food, like performance, is transient and repetitive and it succumbs to time in the same way the body does. The value of the museum, and not just the theater or the restaurant, is that it is a dynamic site not only to witness food and performance, but also to question its boundaries, and the boundaries of our bodies and our social lives.

Notes

1   William. Deresiewicz, "A Matter of Taste?" *The New York Times*, Oct. 28, 2012, http://www.nytimes.com/2012/10/28/opinion/sunday/how-food-replaced-art-as-high-culture.html?_r=0 [accessed April 22, 2016].

2   Aaron Meskin, "The Art of Food," *The Philosophers' Magazine* no. 61 (2013): 81–86, italics added.

3   Tracy C. Davis and Thomas Postlewait, "Theatricality: An Introduction," in *Theatricality*, edited by Tracy C. Davis and Thomas Postlewait (Cambridge: Cambridge University Press, 2003).

4   Josette Féral, "Foreword," *SubStance* 31, no. 2 (2002a): 3–13.

5   Josette Féral, "Theatricality: The Specificity of Theatrical Language," *SubStance* 31, no. 98/99 (2002b): 105.

6   Michael Fried, *Art and Objecthood: Essays and Reviews* (Chicago: University of Chicago Press, 1998).

7   Yael Raviv, "Eating My Words: Talking About Food in Performance," *Invisible Culture: An Electronic Journal*, no. 14 (2010): 8–31.

8   Ibid., 30.

9   Carolyn Korsmeyer, *Making Sense of Taste: Food and Philosophy* (Ithaca: Cornell University Press, 1999), 141.

10 Ibid., 145.

11 Rosalind E. Krauss, *The Originality of the Avant-garde and Other Modernist Myths* (Cambridge: MIT Press, 1986).

12 Ibid, 1.

13 Barbara Kirshenblatt-Gimblett, "Making Sense of Food in Performance: The Table and the Stage," in *The Senses in Performance*, ed. by Sally Banes and André Lepecki (New York: Routledge, 2007), 71.

14 Denise E. Cole, "Edible Performance: Feasting and Festivity In Early Tudor Entertainment," in *The Senses in Performance*, ed. by Sally Banes and André Lepecki (New York: Routledge, 2007), 92.

15 Ibid., 93.

16 Barbara Kirshenblatt-Gimblett, "Playing To the Senses: Food as a Performance Medium," *Performance Research: On Cooking* 4, no. 1 (1999): 4.

17 Cole, 2007, 101.

18 Kirshenblatt-Gimblett, 2007, 71.

19 Denise Gigante and Michael D, Garval, *Gusto: Essential Writings in Nineteenth-Century Gastronomy* (New York: Routledge, 2005).

20 Kirshenblatt-Gimblett, 2007, 75.

21 Kirshenblatt-Gimblett, 2007, 77.

22 Rebecca L. Spang, *The Invention of the Restaurant: Paris and Modern Gastronomic Culture* (Cambridge: Harvard University Press, 2000), 236.

23 Laurence Senelick, "Consuming Passions: Eating and the Stage at the Fin De Siècle," *Gastronomica* 5, no. 2 (2005): 43–49.

24 Helen Iball, "Melting Moments: Bodies Upstaged by the Foodie Gaze," *Performance Research: On Cooking* 4, no. 1(1999): 70.

25 Spang, 2000, 245.

26 Ibid.

27 Kirshenblatt-Gimblett, 1999, 3.

28 Iball, 1999, 71.

29 Fried, 1998, 153.

30 Randall Lane, "How Nathan Myhrvold's Modernist Cuisine Became the World's Most Influential – and Profitable – Cookbook," *Forbes,* June 10, 2013, http://onforb.es/10mQDIO [accessed April 22, 2016].

31 Nathan Myhrvold, "The Art in Gastronomy: A Modernist Perspective," *Gastronomica* 11 (2011): 13.

32 Ibid., 15.

33 Ibid., 14.

34 Ibid., 16.

35 Ibid., 20.

36 Anne-Britt Gran and Diane Oatley, "The Fall of Theatricality in the Age of Modernity," *SubStance* 31, no. 2 (2002): 251–5.

37 Myhrvold, 2001, 17.

38 Ibid., 13.

39 Ibid. 17.

40 Fried, 1998, 153.

41 Philip Auslander, *From Acting to Performance: Essays in Modernism and Postmodernism* (London, New York: Routledge, 1997), 50.

42 Ibid., 52.

43 Fried, 1998, 155.

44 Auslander, 1997, 50.

45 Fried 1998, 167.

46 Myhrvold, 2011, 13.

47 Gran and Oatley, 2002, 255.

48 Féral, 2002, 3.

49 Michael Moss, *Salt, Sugar, Fat: How the Food Giants Hooked Us.* McClelland & Stewart. (New York: Random House, 2014).

50 Sidney W. Mintz, "Time, Sugar, and Sweetness", in *Food and Culture: A Reader,* ed. by Carole Counihan and Penny Van Esterik (New York: Routledge, 2012), 96.

51 Moss, 2014.

52 Natalie Doonan. *Hedonistika* Food and Robotics Festival. *Natalie Doonan,* n.d. http://nataliedoonan.blogspot.ca/2014/03/hedonistika-food-and-robotics-festival.html [accessed April 22, 2016].

53 Natalie Doonan, artist, in discussion with the author, June 2015.

54 Mintz, 2012, 93.

55 David Balzer, *Curationism: How Curating Took Over the Art World and Everything Else* (Toronto: Coach House Books, 2014), 9.

56 Constance Classen, "Museum Manners: The Sensory Life of the Early Museum," *Journal of Social History* 40, no. (2007): 895.

57 Ibid., 907.

58 Ibid., 908.

59 Ibid., 905.

60 Meskin, 2013, 86.

61 Ibid.

62 Iball 1999, 75.

63 Raviv, 2010, 30.

64 Ibid., 8.

6

On the Life of Culinary Images at the 2010 Shanghai World Expo

Van Troi Tran

As announced, Shanghai 2010 was a gigantic World Expo of unprecedented magnitude. It was the largest in history so far, with over 73 million visitors, 192 participating countries, and dozens of international organizations that exhibited on an area of 528 hectares distributed on both banks of the Huangpu River in the southern part of the city. In an age where universal exhibitions tend to be perceived, at least in the Western world, as lavish industrial carnivals of a bygone era, the Shanghai World Expo was a surprisingly successful event.

During the three months that I spent in Shanghai for my research on food at the 2010 World Expo, tourism and ethnography intersected to a great extent. I did try, as one can imagine, to visit quite a number of restaurants on the Expo site, from the fancier to the comfier, and I also interviewed a number of international managers about their experience of operating a venue inside the World Expo. What interested me specifically about this topic was how the management and organization of these restaurants involved the entanglement of various facets of globalization: cultural globalization—the promotion of national or regional culinary heritage; economic globalization—hitting the Chinese market with the introduction of new products; and political globalization—implementing international standards of food safety in a country rife with adulteration scandals. In some respects, these facets reinforced each other, but in many cases they also came at odds. Food safety measures entailed the prohibition of some typical products, such as saffron or raw meat. It also implied a logistical centralization in the management and the infrastructure of food distribution on the site in order to ease the inspection process, which disadvantaged some restaurants over others, depending on their connections with the distribution firms. And for some national restaurants, more than others, there were compromises to be made between culinary authenticity and the demands of the Chinese public. If globalization does imply a great amount of unifying and standardizing processes, it also creates fragmentation between different globalities,[1] and even in the case of world's fairs, universalism often comes in various guises.[2]

It the context of a collection on *Food and Museums*, a contribution on the case of world's fairs might come across as a bit off topic, as, despite many similarities, international exhibitions and traditional museums do differ in many significant ways. World's fairs historian Robert Rydell thus asserts that "World fairs seem like ephemeral theme parks from another time; museums seem like pillars of both community and nation."[3] They convey a sense of ephemerality and transitoriness whereas traditional museums may tend to express groundedness and historical continuity. But on the other hand, universal exhibitions can also be treated as "exhibitionary complexes" that, just like modern museums, took form in the nineteenth century as "vehicles for inscribing and broadcasting the messages of power [. . .] throughout society."[4] Food, in this regard, is a very interesting point of entry. According to geographer Kevin Hetherington, in today's era of museumified cities and commodified culture, the frontier between spaces of exhibition and spaces of consumption tends to blur, and thereby: "[t]he culinary experience in the restaurant can be as important to a visit as the artistic experience to be found in the gallery."[5] This is not untrue, and the point could certainly apply to a host of institutions, from the MoMA to the Institut du Monde Arabe.[6] But it also begs the question of the actual processes taking place in this "culturalization of the economy" and "economization of culture."[7] World Expo constitutes thereby a fascinating case study insofar as national delegations who included a restaurant, bar, or café within their pavilions operated along different cultural and commercial logics.

I would like, however, to insist on something else, precisely at the intersection of commerce and culture. In this chapter on the visual culture of food at the Shanghai World Expo, I will address the role played by both *images* of food and *environmental* contingencies in the context of an international event.[8] A striking element of the different catering places on the site of the Shanghai World Expo of 2010 was the widespread use of images for the promotion of dishes and drinks. This exaltation of a consumerist visual culture in the context of a universal exhibition is far from surprising, the mass production and consumption of culinary images in menus, screens, and advertisements at the Shanghai World Expo was nevertheless peculiar: large photos of beer bottles at the Belgian pavilion, icy desserts at the Cambodia pavilion, colorful drinks at the Latvian pavilion, grilled steaks at the Uruguayan restaurant, or a whole smoked sterlet at the Russian restaurant. Visual renditions of dishes, delicacies, cooks, and cuisines played the role of universal translators and swift mediators of culinary globalization in a transnational context. However, whereas studies on world's fairs often emphasize *reductions*, and how the world is reduced in representations (or reduced to representations), in the second part of this chapter, I will insist conversely on how images, representations, and visual devices at the World Expo also attest for a plurality of logics in the exhibition and promotion of food.

The air-conditioned foodie field trip

Around the world

Expo Weekly was a magazine edited by the *Beijing Review* during the Shanghai World Expo. Its issues featured short pieces on a variety of themes related to the Expo, visiting tips, and accounts from visitors. In the fifth issue, the main topic was the variety of food at the World Expo. It featured on the cover the omnipresent blue mascot Haibao wearing a toque while awaiting visitors for

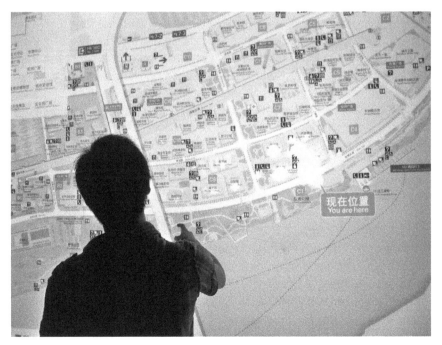

FIGURE 6.1 *A plan of the World Expo, 2010.*
© *Van Troi Tran.*

a "Foodie field trip" across the Expo. The magazine coverage presented, as stated on the cover, short notes on the "Exotic and Unique Food from Africa, South America and Oceania" available at the World Expo, the "classic European delicacies" from Belgium, Switzerland, Germany, and France, the "Asian delicacies" from Singapore, Thailand, India, and Pakistan, as well as short notes on the various Chinese restaurants which featured cuisines from Jiangsu, Zhejiang, Anhui, Sichuan, Guangdong, and Hunan, among others.[9]

For any outside observer trained (or even just acquainted) with basic notions of cultural theory, postcolonial studies, and cultural studies, the advertisement of this "field trip" that advertises a typical form of cosmopolitan culinary tourism, where one can appropriate other cultures through immersion albeit in an enclosed sanitized space, would most probably draw chuckles and smiles. To be sure, universal exhibitions, perhaps more than other "modern" phenomena, have historically participated in the construction of this touristic outlook of a world to be appropriated and domesticated though sampling, consumption, and experiences.[10] This goes back to the nineteenth century universal and colonial exhibitions, where it was possible for visitors to taste food from exotic countries or French and British colonies, such as Tunisian pastries or Ceylonese tea.[11]

Urban exotic restaurants have indeed already been analyzed as places of postcolonial encounters, where the client can symbolically discover and appropriate another culture through consumption,[12] and therefore use this experience as a means of cosmopolitan social distinction.[13] The pervasiveness of this culinary colonialism was noted by Lisa Heldke,[14] who further remarked that: "just by eating 'ethnic' we adventurers don't have a claim on another culture. Neither can we pretend to understand it because we think we know how the natives eat. Good intentions aside, that is simply impossible."[15] Heldke's doubts are perhaps all the more accurate in the context of the universal exhibitions, where objects and commodities deemed typical are integrated within exhibitionary narratives that produce metonymies of nations and cultures for things through processes of museological detachment and recontextualization in an overarching narrative.[16]

But with these caveats in mind, I would like to take the image of the "foodie field trip" a little bit more seriously, if only because, as I and most of the people I interviewed would attest, even if the World Expo portrays a utopian and pacified version of a cosmopolitan world, the experience of visiting is nonetheless carnal, that is: often tiring and overwhelming for the legs and for the senses. For reasons ranging from the scale of the site to the number of restaurants and catering places available, even the most dedicated visitor would not have had the physical and mental capacities to see and taste everything that was offered at the Expo. The five areas of the Expo site featured no fewer than 128 restaurants, including national restaurants, bars or cafée annexed to the country pavilions, fast foods, cafeterias, Chinese restaurants, and other venues of various sorts with different price ranges.

In her tips for "gourmet travel" on the site, the *Expo Weekly* journalist testified that: "Like most Expo visitors, I felt like a drop in the ocean during my first day. The official claim that a restaurant is always just a five-minute-walk from anyplace at the Expo seemed impossible to me. I couldn't even find one!" She further added that it took her "a few days of exploring the Expo Park to figure out where the restaurants were" (Jing 2010b: 23), something that most visitors could not indulge in.[17] Her other recommendations to visitors for their field trip included other concerns of bodily comfort: not wearing high heels, keep an eye on toilets, rest areas, and places providing services for the disabled. While these tips may certainly sound as commonsensical, they also indicate that the Shanghai Expo was almost a city in itself, and that the enjoyment of a visit was dependent on a series of material factors to be correctly assessed by the visitor.

Eating fast

In my previous research on the Paris *Expositions universelles* at the end of the nineteenth century, I was precisely interested in identifying these discrepancies between the abstract nature of the globalizing, modernizing, nationalistic narratives broadcasted at world's fairs, and the mundane down-to-earth concerns of the millions of fragile and finite bodies that had to eat, drink, and rest.[18] And unsurprisingly, from conversations I had with restaurant staff and managers, a great proportion of visitors at the Shanghai World Expo did not necessarily put that much importance on the discovery of exotic food and foreign culinary cultures (a perhaps rather Western and postcolonial outlook on things). The public rather chose to buy either take-away meals at fast foods like KFC or prepared snacks at stalls or convenience stores like Lawson on the Expo site, and have an express picnic on public benches or under the cool shadow of the elevated walkways. At noon, the fairgrounds and the alleys were indeed much more crowded than the restaurants, an understandable state of affairs in the context of a massive global event with hundreds of pavilions to see.

According to Quan and Wang, eating and drinking in tourist studies can be construed as either a "peak experience," a new experience that is conspicuously different from daily life, or a "supporting experience": they can either be at the front stage or constitute the backdrop of the touristic experience.[19] The range of different catering venues available to the Expo visitor is itself a reflection of the variety of meanings that food can have, at the threshold of "nature" and "culture." As Cohen and Avieli put it: "Any study of the place of food in tourism will indeed have to analyze its role as an attraction. But it is at least equally important to deal with its other face, as a basic necessity on the trip, a crucial precondition for other touristic activities, as well as for the tourists' well-being and satisfaction."[20] As it happens, at the World Expo, national restaurants had many uses that overflew their official function of promoting national cuisines. With the exceptionally long waiting lines for some pavilions (up to 9 hours in the case of Saudi Arabia) combined with extreme temperatures during summer, the Expo restaurants could then fill some very pragmatic functions: they could be air-conditioned resting areas where visitors could escape from the crowd or the weather, from extreme heat in August to heavy rain in October. Also, in some other cases, national restaurants had doors leading into the exhibits of the pavilions so that customers could actually enter the building without having to follow the queue. These down-to-earth concerns are not directly related to issues of taste, culinary appreciations, cultural discoveries, and how nations exhibit their cuisine, but in my own experience they nevertheless played a significant role on how visitors experienced restaurants at the Shanghai World Expo, and more generally how the public ultimately performed and occupied the site.

Crafting the global

With these carnal and sensory elements taken into account, notions of globalization and international tourism can therefore be tackled from a more materialist perspective of engineered atmospheres[21] that are crafted, built, and sustained through practices of construction, repair, and maintenance.[22] If "mega-events," as Maurice Roche categorizes universal exhibitions and Olympic Games, have been for over a century "important and influential forces in the history of modern international culture in general" and have "important attitudinal effects in terms of the cultivation of mass interest in consumer culture and tourism culture,"[23] this environmental focus allows, though ethnographic descriptions, to uncover an assemblage of immanent practices that are needed for the enactment of these larger processes. Garbage trucks emptying containers when closing time was coming, security guards organizing the serpentines of waiting lines, sweepers, volunteers, translators, and plenty of other actors were working on a daily basis in order to clean and sustain the "world image" or the world made image.[24]

Food, as Fischler has shown, also has both an alleviating and a disruptive potential (poisoning, disgust, etc.),[25] which is why some international restaurant managers used a diversity of cultural and *atmospheric* attunements[26] in order to facilitate the intercultural culinary mediation, such as testing the reception of some dishes and ingredients with the local public, such as "smelly" cheese, or adapting the order of meals according to the customers' request. Food can be "an attraction and an impediment," despite the fact that "the problem of producing nutritious, hygienic, accessible, and culturally acceptable food to tourists is more complicated than what might be assumed from promotional brochures or magazines."[27] Therefore, cultural variations in the visceral reactions to edibility had to be taken into account by restaurant managers in the transnational situation of the Expo, and attuning the restaurant to the public involved a host of local adjustments in the craft ad presentation of meals. Thus, whereas Tony Bennett described the exhibition as "exhibitionary" complex and complementary to the Foucaldian "disciplinary complex": "a power made manifest not in its ability to inflict pain but by its ability to organize and co-ordinate an order of things and to produce a place for the people in relation to that order,"[28] from the perspective of the culinary products themselves, the Expo is indeed a disciplinary space where food is pacified for the public gaze.

Enacting spaces of culinary globalization

Visions of food

For this reason, images and visual depictions of food played an essential role in precisely domesticating the potentially disruptive encounter between consumers and edible substances. According to John Urry, "Gazes organize the encounters of visitors with the 'other', providing some sense of competence, pleasure, and structure to those experiences. [. . .] It is the gaze that orders and regulates the relationships between the various sensuous experiences while away, identifying what is visually out-of-ordinary, what are

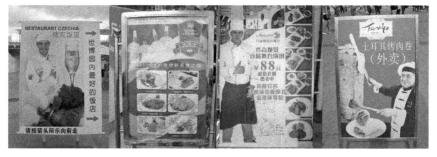

FIGURE 6.2 *Advertisements for restaurants at the Austrian, Czech, Romanian, and Turkish pavilions, 2010.*

© *Van Troi Tran.*

the relevant differences and what is 'other'."[29] Urry's emphasis on the sense of vision has been criticized, albeit rightfully, for not taking into account the corporeal and sensuous dimension of tourism,[30] but here again, the World Expo offers a particular context where visual devices are crowding the landscape thus providing "affordances,"[31] that is, surfaces and objects that frame, open, and also limit opportunities for action.

A prevalent feature of the Expo was thus the overwhelming sea of images and advertisements for national pavilions, multinational brands, and, of course, nations branded through symbols and snappy slogans for the international public. The various restaurant chains partnering in the World Expo like (the American) Starbucks, KFC, and Burger King or (the Chinese) South Beauty, Kungfu, and Bi Feng Tang were occupying the visual landscape with their logos and the easily recognizable design of their respective dining rooms and furniture. As standardized affordances for the global public, the trademark logos and furniture of Starbucks or KFC can certainly inject a sense of instant familiarity in an otherwise potentially disorienting environment.[32] But what was striking and perhaps more interesting was the use of images for the advertisement of some national restaurants in the European zone of the World Expo. What caught my attention on my first visit at the Expo, was how advertisements for national restaurants displayed in the open alleys were standardized to a great extent in both form and content. The posters were all of comparable size, they were using roughly the same palette of colors (red, gold, and white) and they were featuring vignettes of typical dishes next to a chef in uniform.

To be sure, for the foodie interested in tasting and comparing samples from the world's culinary traditions, many of the Expo's national restaurants exhibited the trademark dishes of their cuisines on their menu: smoked salmon in Norway, *paella* and *ensalada de jamon* in the Spanish pavilion, waffles, fries, chocolate, and beer in Belgium, reindeer meatball in Finland, beef and wine in Argentina, quesadillas in Mexico, wiener schnitzel in Austria, Bavarian sausages and sauerkraut in Germany, pasta and tiramisu in Italy, curry in India, sushi in Japan, poutine, bacon, and maple syrup in Canada, cheese fondue and chocolate in Switzerland, rum in Cuba, wine and ceviche in Chile, and so on. Much like the collection of country stamps on "Expo passports" could stand as an ersatz for travel around the world, it was possible to eat the world by a *dégustation* of various international dishes, preferably advertised in pictorial evidences through various social media sites, with the same logic of accumulation of experiences that is actually advocated by the design of the event itself. But, as one can easily observe in these advertisements above for the Czech, Turkish, Austrian, and Romanian pavilions, this production of culinary differences was coextensive with a general process of standardization.

Engineering the universal

To that effect, material contingencies such as the spatial organization of the kitchens, the shape and size of the counters, the cooking and refrigeration devices, the control of ambient temperature through air-conditioning, and the disposal of trash, were all subjected to the regulations imposed by the Expo administration.[33] In other words, the international traffic of cultural objects on the Expo site had to be constrained through a host of constant infrastructural interventions that allowed for the situations of intercultural mediation to function smoothly and without risk. But in the context of the World Expo, this dual logic of infrastructural standardization and "superstructural" differentiation was also at work in the use of promotional images for national dishes and delicacies. On one hand, they assembled and homogenized visually the variety of cultural goods and assets under both the encyclopedic logic of the universal exhibition and the market economy where different restaurants compete. But on the other hand, visual depictions of food also participated in processes of singularization for the valuing of typical dishes and specific culinary heritages. This mobilization of visibility as a source of value (and cultural capital) was all the more evident in the most gastronomic restaurants, such as the 6SENS operated by the Pourcel brothers at the French pavilion, or the Essence restaurant at the Belgian pavilion, where the kitchen was exhibited to the public (through closed circuit cameras at the French pavilion, and behind glass windows at the Belgium pavilion) as part of the performance.

At the World Expo, these dual practices of standardization and singularization could be related to what Yves Citton (2014b) calls the economy of attention, which refers to a context of massive circulation of images and information where it is the attention of the consumer that becomes a resource for competing stakeholders.[34] For a visitor drawn into the ocean of stimuli at the world's fair and inundated with information asking for attention, the pictures were "capitation" devices. Images participated in the fabric of globalization as mediators for the swift communication of information on exotic dishes and products that would be otherwise opaque for a large portion of the public, a public that was all the more pressed with time constraints, considering the width of the Expo area and the amount of attractions to visit, and had to quickly choose among a wide variety of venues without necessarily having sufficient culinary knowledge in order to make an enlightened selection. Thus, for the operation of foreign restaurants at the World Expo, the use of visual renditions of dishes was crucial in the production of an ideal landscape for the consumer to make choices and judgments, something Barrey, Cochoy, and Dubuisson-Quellier have studied in the case of supermarkets.[35] Pictures of food were precisely what Karpik[36] calls judgment devices in his criticism of neoclassical models of consumer behavior: tools that produce easily digestible information about goods so that customers can swiftly acquire sufficient knowledge about multidimensional goods (such as dishes, irreducible to a bundle of finite quantifiable properties) in order to orient their choices.[37]

Of course, the engineering of cultural globalization on the Expo site was not necessarily much different from more general tendencies affecting the cultural development of global metropolises around the world where, as Sharon Zukin puts it: "[c]ompetition among corporations and cities has led to a multiplicity of standardized attractions that reduce the uniqueness of urban identities even while claims of uniqueness grow more intense."[38] The Expo is indeed on these set apart contexts, much like airports, hotel lobbys, or other "non-places"[39] that seem to characterize the "supermodern" world, globally connected but locally disconnected. But, as stated earlier, globalization in Shanghai, just as everywhere else, has to be crafted in daily material practices, devices, routines, and negotiations.[40] If images can be mobilized as efficient tools for international communication because they are "abstractable, mobile, and dynamic,"[41] and thereby taming some of the uncertainties associated with food and especially *exotic* food, their social life in the public sphere can also highlight logics of distinction and differentiation.

In Shanghai 2010, there were different discourses on authenticity and hence different regimes of value in the promotion of national cuisine, between a cultural display and a commercial operation.[42] Not that these two logics are necessarily contradictory, but in the context of the Expo, there were nation states who had different regimes of value regarding food cultures. France featured (as expected) a gastronomic restaurant, the United States (as expected) a fast food restaurant, Japan (as expected) a sushi bar, and Latvia a refreshment bar serving mojitos and iced teas because apparently, according to the informant, "people don't care about Latvian cuisine." They would therefore rather capitalize on the massive demand for ice cream and cold drinks rather than promote national dishes. Moreover, as other international caterers testified, it was simply not worth the cost and the effort to propose a high-priced gastronomic restaurant with celebrated chefs or top notch delicacies, as in France or Norway, that would only reach a tiny portion of the public.

Hence, despite the rather homogenized formula imposed by the Expo format, narratives of culinary identity at the Shanghai World Expo were hardly homogenous with some restaurant managers emphasizing the origin of products, others the cooking techniques, and others speaking only in commercial terms. Moreover, the confrontation between the different regimes of value for the *image* of food could even lead to controversies. Despite the fact that a World Expo could be to some extent described indeed as a celebration of the world as it is, a microcosm of the world that has been domesticated, cleaned, and air-conditioned in order to construct a pacified version of the world, it also appears that the images produced within the event can also be controversial. In one case, a restaurant manager installed a not too fancy but otherwise immensely popular ice cream stand in the courtyard of the national pavilion, an initiative that was not met with great enthusiasm by the delegation, fearing it would disfigure the pavilion.[43] The stand was ultimately kept because of its popularity, but the example showed that the fusion of the logics of culture and commerce, an idea that has been present since the world's fairs of the nineteenth century,[44] could lead in certain cases to a confrontation of different conceptions of the role of consumption within the exhibition.

Conclusion

I came across this stand of coconut juice located in the European sector of the World Expo. It was one of the many unglamorous stalls selling refreshments on the site, along with the stands of Coca-Cola or the ice cream booths of the Chinese dairy provider Yili. This one, however, felt perhaps even more "out of place" in the context of the World Expo, especially with the pile of cardboard

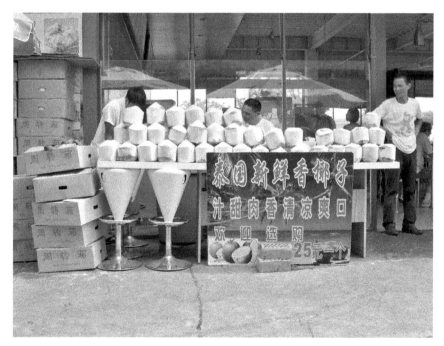

FIGURE 6.3 *A stall of coconut juice, 2010.*
© *Van Troi Tran.*

boxes on the left, the apparently improvised table made of bar stools and a Formica desk, and the advertisement poster held in place by two bricks.

This curious stand was certainly not representative of the meta-narrative of the World Expo, but its presence illustrates well how an attention to food and consumption practices can lead to alternative versions of the event. To be sure, the presentation of culinary specialties and delicacies in the context of a universal exhibition does tend to follow the encyclopedic logic that inherits from the Enlightenment values of the nineteenth century, which led to the invention of the modern museum.[45] That logic implied a selection of objects based on their typicity for their smooth integration into a broader narrative of progress, imperialism, or nation-building. Another oft-repeated argument, along the lines of Walter Benjamin,[46] identifies universal exhibitions as spectacles of capitalism where the world is commodified and thus standardized under the universal criterion of exchange value.[47] However, as this example shows, food also unveils other narratives, less concerned with abstract notions of national identities, culinary authenticity, cultural heritage, and exchange value, and more in tone with the daily vicissitudes of visitors looking for a minute of comfort between two pavilions. As a carnal and commercial object integrated in museographic spaces, one for which visitors have to pay and consume, food also produces other images of the world, images that overflow the slick scenography of the exposition.

Notes

1   Michel-Rolph Trouillot, *Global Transformations: Anthropology and the Modern World* (New York: Palgrave Macmillan, 2003).

2   Sophie Houdart, *L'universel à vue d'oeil* (Paris: Éditions Petra, 2013).

3   Robert Rydell, "World's Fairs and Museums," in *A Companion to Museum Studies*, ed. by Sharon Macdonald (New York: Routledge, 2006), 135.

4   Tony Bennett, *The Birth of the Museum: History, Theory, Politics* (London: Routledge, 1995).

5   Kevin Hetherington, "Museum," *Theory, Culture & Society*, 23, no. 2–3 (2006): 602.

6   Irina D. Mihalache, "Museums, Consumption, and the Everyday," in *Food and Everyday Life*, ed. by Thomas Conroy (Lanham: Lexington Books, 2014a), 59–83, 340; I personally love the espresso at the newly renovated Fogg Museum.

7   Scott M. Lash and John Urry, *Economies of Signs and Space* (London: Sage, 1995); Andrew Sayer, "For a Critical Political Economy," *Antipode*, 33, no. 4 (2001): 687–708.

8   My perspective is greatly informed by the environmental anthropology proposed by Ingold (1999). See: Tim Ingold, *The Perception of the*

Environment. Essays on Livelihood, Dwelling and Skill (London: Routledge, 1999).

9 Shi Ran, "Classic European Delicacies," *Expo Weekly* 5 (2010a), 20; Shi Ran, "Integrated Asian Delicacies," *Expo Weekly* 5 (2010b), 21; Shi Ran, "Exotic and Unique Food from Africa, South America and Oceania," *Expo Weekly,* 5 (2010c), 22.

10 Dean MacCannell, *Empty Meeting Grounds: The Tourist Papers* (London: Routledge, 1992).

11 Van Troi Tran, "Sensing the Colonies at the 1889 and 1900 Universal Exhibitions," in *A Taste of Progress: Food at International and World Exhibitions in the Nineteenth and Twentieth Centuries*, ed. by Nelleke Teughels and Peter Scholliers (London: Ashgate, 2015).

12 Laurier Turgeon and Madeleine Pastinelli, " 'Eat the World': Postcolonial Encounters in Quebec City's Ethnic Restaurants," *Journal of American Folklore*, 115, no. 456 (2001): 247–268.

13 Jon May, " 'A Little Taste of Something More Exotic: The Imaginative Geographies of Everyday Life," *Geography*, 81, no. 1 (1996): 57–64.

14 Lisa Heldke, *Exotic Appetites: Ruminations of a Food Adventurer* (London: Routledge, 2003).

15 Lisa Heldke, "Let's Eat Chinese!: Reflections on Cultural Food Colonialism," *Gastronomica: The Journal of Food and Culture* 1, no. 2 (2001), 79.

16 Mieke Bal, *Double Exposures: The Subject of Cultural Analysis* (London: Routledge, 1996). See also: Barbara Kirschenblatt-Gimblett, *Destination Culture: Tourism, Museums, and Heritage* (Berkeley: University of California Press, 1998).

17 H. Jing, "Reporter's Note: Tips for Gourmet Travel," *Expo Weekly*, 5 (2010b): 23.

18 Van Troi Tran, *Manger et boire aux Expositions universelles. Paris: 1889, 1900* (Rennes and Tours: PUR and PUFR, 2012). In a way, I did follow the very common paradigm shift along the noughties, from an attention to discourse and representation to a focus on materiality and presence. See Ewa Domanska, "Beyond Anthropocentrism in Historical Studies," *Historein*, 10 (2010): 118–130.

19 Shuai Quan and Ning Wang, "Towards a structural model of the tourist experience: an illustration from food experiences in tourism," *Tourism Management*, 25 (2004): 297–305.

20 Eric Cohen and Nir Avieli, "Food in Tourism: Attraction and Impediment," *Annals of Tourism Research*, 31, no. 4 (2004): 755–778.

21 Interestingly, in his idiosyncratic theory of mediation, Vilem Flusser refers to air as a "medium" between a transmitter and a receiver just like language, only one is "thermodynamic" and the other is "cultural"; see Vilem Flusser *Writings*, edited by Andreas Ströhl (Minneapolis: University of Minnesota Press, 2002), 8–9.

22 Peter Sloterdijk, *In the World Interior of Capital: Towards a Philosophical Theory of Globalization* (Cambridge: Polity Press, 2013); Peter Sloterdijk, *Écumes* (Paris: Hachette, 2005).

23   Maurice Roche, *Mega-events and Modernity: Olympics and Expos in the Growth of Global Culture* (London: Routledge, 2000), 6.

24   Although, as Marazzi puts it: "we cannot take for granted the predominance of the visual in the present world by simply adopting the common opinion that we are all immersed in a global 'culture of the image'" (Marazzi 1999, 391), thus the relevance of adopting an "ecological" angle (Citton 2014a) on this "hypermediatic" setting that takes into account surfaces, objects and atmospheres. See: Antonio Marazzi, "Visual Anthropology in World of Images," *Visual Anthropology* 12, no. 4 (1999): 391–403; Yves Citton, *Pour une écologie de l'attention* (Paris: Seuil, 2014a).

25   Claude Fischler, *L'Homnivore: le goût, la cuisine, le corps* (Paris: Odile Jacob, 2001).

26   Kathleen Stewart, "Atmospheric Attunements," *Environment and Planning D: Society and Space* 29, no. 3 (2010): 445–453.

27   Cohen and Avieli, 2004.

28   Bennett, 1995.

29   John Urry, *The Tourist Gaze*, Second edition (London: Sage, 2002), 149.

30   Soile Veijola and Eeva Jokinen, "The Body in Tourism," *Theory, Culture & Society*, no. 11 (1994): 125–151.

31   James J. Gibson, *The Ecological Approach to Visual Perception* (Boston: Houghton Mifflin, 1979).

32   Although, as Watson's study (2006) shows, the standardization of space in fast food restaurants through design and architecture by no means implies a homogenization of foodways across different countries and cultures. On the importance of brands for the global economy, see Lury (2004) and my own research on brands at the Shanghai Expo in Tran (2015). See: James Watson, *Golden Arches East: McDonald's in East Asia* (Stanford: Stanford University Press, 2006); Celia Lury *Brands: The Logos of Global Economy* (London: Routledge, 2004); Tran, 2015.

33   Van Troi Tran, "Les restaurants à l'Exposition universelle de Shanghai: Utopie cosmopolite sous contrainte," *Ethnologie française*, 44 (2014): 149–156.

34   Yves Citton, "Introduction" in *L'économie de l'attention: nouvel horizon du capitalisme?*, ed. by Yves Citton (Paris: La Découverte, 2014b).

35   Sandrine Barrey, Franck Cochoy, and Sophie Dubuisson-Quellier, "Designer, packager et merchandiser: trois professionnels pour une même scène marchande," *Sociologie du travail*, 42 (2000): 457–482.

36   Lucien Karpik, *L'économie des singularités* (Paris: Gallimard, 2007).

37   Charlene Elliott, "Consuming the Other: Packaged Representations of Foreignness in *President's Choice*," in *Edible Ideologies Representing Food and Meaning*, ed. by Kathleen LeBesco and Peter Naccarato (Albany: State University of New York Press, 2008), 179–198.

38   Sharon Zukin, "Urban Lifestyles: Diversity and Standardisation in Spaces of Consumption," *Urban Studies* 35, no. 5–6 (1998): 837.

39 Marc Augé, *Non-Places: An Introduction to Supermodernity* (New York: Verso, 2009).

40 Aihwa Ong, *Neoliberalism as Exception: Mutations in Citizenship and Sovereignty* (Durham: Duke University Press, 2006).

41 Stephen J. Collier and Aihwa Ong, "Global Assemblanges, Anthropological Problems," in *Global Assemblages: Technology, Politics, and Ethics as anthropological problems*" ed. by Aihwa Ong and Stephen J. Collier (London: Blackwell, 2005), 4.

42 On the various narratives of authenticity at the Seville World Expo in 1992, see Penelope Harvey, "Culture and Context: The Effects of Visibility', in *The Problem of Context*, ed. by Roy Dilley (New York: Berghahn, 1999), 213–235.

43 I treat these controversies in Tran, 2014.

44 Paul Greenhalgh, "Education, Entertainment and Politics: Lessons from the Great International Exhibitions," in *The New Museology*, ed. by Peter Vergo (London: Reaktion Books, 1997), 74–98.

45 Dominique Poulot, *Musée et muséologie* (Paris, Editions La Découverte), 2005.

46 Walter Benjamin, *The Arcades Project* (Cambridge: Harvard University Press, 2002).

47 Curtis M. Hinsley, "The World as Marketplace: Commodification of the Exotic at the World's Columbian Exposition, Chicago, 1893," in *Exhibiting Cultures: The Poetics and Politics of Museum Display*, ed. by Ivan Karp and Steven D. Lavine (Washington: Smithsonian Institution Press, 1991), 344–365.

7

Chefs as Content Creators:

Arzak Kitchen and elBulli Foundation[1]

Nina Levent

Elena Arzak

The Arzak restaurant in San Sebastian, Spain was put on the *haute cuisine* world map by Juan Mari Arzak, a legendary Basque chef and one of the founders of the New Basque Cuisine. This three Michelin star restaurant has been in the vanguard of Spanish cuisine for many years. Juan Mari's daughter, Elena Arzak, started working in the kitchen at the age of eleven and began developing new recipes with her father when she was nineteen. Today, the pair run the kitchen at Arzak. Elena was named Best Female Chef in the World in 2012 by Veuve Clicquot. Although she insists she is a chef, rather than an artist, the parallels between creative cooking and contemporary artistic practices are many.

Arzak's test kitchen, or Laboratorio, opened in 2000. Recently renovated, it is located on the second floor of an old brick building that also houses the Arzak restaurant. It is the incubator for new ideas, methods, and recipes. It is where the Arzaks and their team, Xabi Gutiérrez and Igor Zalakain, keep their bank of over 1,500 ingredients or the "bank of ideas," as Elena refers to them. Along the wall, there are rows and rows of transparent containers with seeds, dry fruit, mushrooms, nuts, and grains from all over the world. Often, these exotic and familiar ingredients serve as initial inspiration for a dish.

When a restaurant patron from Iran gave a dried black lemon to Elena, it inspired a marvelous dessert. Iranian dried black lemons are used commonly

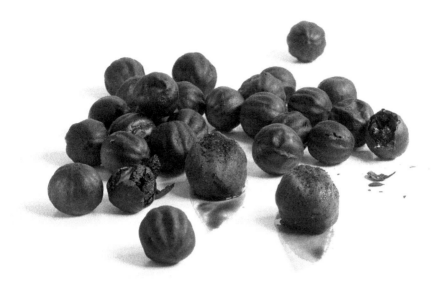

FIGURE 7.1 *Black lemon dessert.*
© *Juan Maria Arzak Arrabitel and Elena Arzak Espina.*

for rich meat dishes and soups in the Middle East. Elena liked the shape and smell of these lemons, and used them as an inspiration for a **Black Lemon Dessert**, in which she recreated their look with a crispy chocolate cover filled with a sweat citrus cream and sprinkled with lemon.

The idea for **Big Truffle Dessert** came to Arzak's chefs when they saw a video of melting glaciers. This dynamic visual image inspired another dessert, a large cacao and sugar truffle with a creamy chocolate and carob filling that melts dramatically right in front of the customer's eye when a syrup is poured over it.

Sometimes a chance encounter is turned into a discovery. A conversation with a noted Spanish guitar maker led to the creation of another dish, **Pigeon with Guitar Shavings**. The guitar maker spoke of the rare precious wood that he used in his work, and Arzak asked him for the aromatic wood shavings from his studio, which they then used to roast pigeon breast. Circular "guitar" wood shavings carrying light cypress aroma are placed on top of the lid that covers the dish to add aroma.

When a recipe is formulated in the test kitchen, the first version of the recipe is written by hand, cooked, and tasted by the team and the patrons, and then revised again and again. There are many thick binders of handwritten recipes with drawings and notes by the chefs that very much resemble artists' notebooks. About ten percent of the recipes tried in this test kitchen end up on Arzak's menu, but the process of trying out new ideas is ongoing. Not

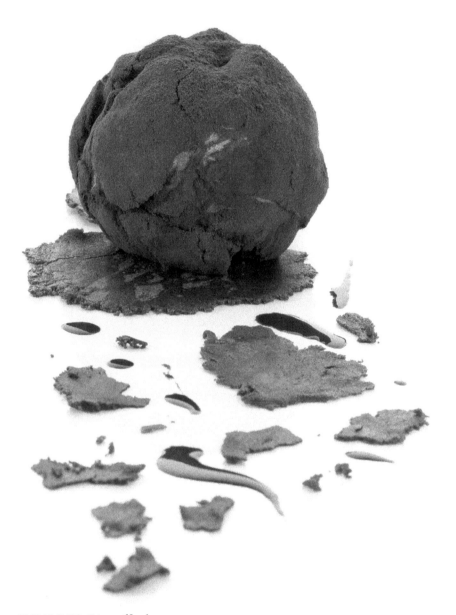

FIGURE 7.2 *Big truffle dessert.*
© *Juan Maria Arzak Arrabitel and Elena Arzak Espina.*

unlike many art and design studios, the Arzak test kitchen has a system and a process of perfecting the final product, but mistakes are also often embraced and turned into discoveries. For example, when Elena and her father were working on a carrot-juice-based sauce, they wanted to add salt but grabbed some coconut by mistake. The result was surprisingly good, and coconut was incorporated in the recipe. Another time, a trainee put a fish dish into a steamer instead of an oven as he was instructed. When the dish was ready, Arzak recognized that the flavor was superior to that of the original recipe.

Like many contemporary arts practitioners, Elena works with many disciplines and draws on expertise and inspiration from them. She approached

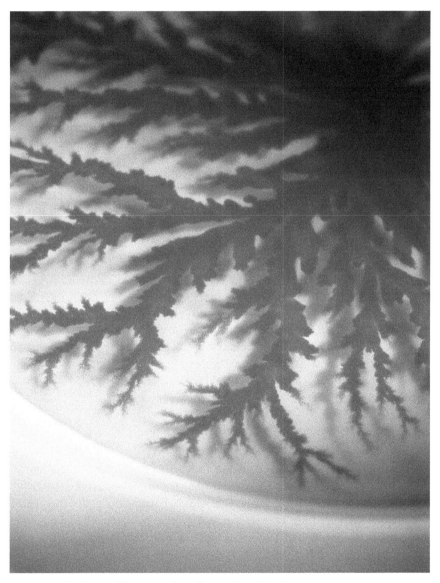

FIGURE 7.3 *Soup of honey with vodka and cochineal*
© *Juan Maria Arzak Arrabitel and Elena Arzak Espina.*

Professor J. J. Iruin, a chemist-physicist from Basque University, to help her with the **Soup of Honey with Vodka and Cochineal** recipe, a transparent soup with an intricate coral-like fractal design. The fractal design was generated by the white mead, based on water and honey, and the red is vodka and cochineal. However the chefs could not control the fractals design in the soup; sometimes the design turned out great but most times not. They were advised to look at the process of the formation of fractals in liquid and then control for the right combination of temperature and density. Another time they wanted to have a color change in a soup and the scientists helped them to work with pH and achieve this in a cabbage and lemon soup.

Elena Arzak is often approached by museums, such as Chillida Leku in Gipuzkoa, Spain and the San Francisco Museum of Modern Art, for talks, recipes, and presentations. She values museums as increasingly important public spaces that are also democratic, and open to people of different backgrounds. For chefs, museums pose a challenge and an opportunity. It is an opportunity to present one's cooking and creative process to a wider audience, but the challenge is to communicate one's cuisine. "It is very difficult for chefs to describe their work. Now we describe our cuisine as signature cuisine, Basque, research-based, evolving, and cutting edge, but it took us a long time to be able to formulate our approach to cooking and find the right words to describe it," says Arzak. Museums can play an important role in helping chefs communicate their craft and process. "When we were first asked to showcase our processes in an art and museum setting, we were very open about the fact that we need help."[2] When asked about how she would design a museum of food, Elena Arzak said that she would like a museum that provides insights into the chef's creative process. "I would want people to see how we work and what is the result."[3] As for the final dining experience, however, it will only be possible in a restaurant rather than a museum gallery.

Ferran Adrià

Ferran Adrià, who might be one of the most important chefs of our time, and definitely one who has reinvented gastronomy, closed his legendary restaurant elBulli in 2011. He now leads elBulli Foundation and elBulli Lab, two creative hubs that are actively involved in food research, education, and exhibit development. Adrià has plans to open a residency for top chefs in the former space of the elBulli restaurant in the holiday village at Cala Montjoi in Spain. In a recent interview, Adrià pointed out that there is no comprehensive museum of food and that the research on cooking and gastronomy has a long way to go.

Adrià also seconded Elena Arzak's opinion that the full gastronomic experience might not be possible outside of a restaurant, the same way as the full dance experience will transform a museum into a dance theater. He sees the role of museums in knowledge dissemination, especially knowledge pertaining to global food and the history of cooking, including ingredients, methods, and utensils, starting from prehistoric times to today. Some of the research and exhibition development work Adrià has begun at the elBulli Foundation, and he hopes to collaborate with museums around the world in the future.

When I visited in August of 2015 the elBulli Foundation—located in a big warehouse loosely divided into sections that house different "research" teams—the teams and the divisions were constantly in motion. Adrià brought his creative approach from his kitchen into this new start-up. The flexibility and openness with which the team approaches their work is reflected in the layout of the space that is open and allows for constant movement of partitions, desks, exhibits, so much so that the layout changes almost weekly. Several teams intersect in this space: business development that worked on creative collaborations and product development with commercial food, beverage, and appliance companies. The elBulli teams work with local artisans and designers in creating new tableware and other products. An exhibition part of the warehouse at the moment of the tour featured an exhibit on the history of food. At the time of my visit, another team was working on the history of drinks and beverages, putting together a database of drinks, from milk to tequila. Another group is working on reorganizing the traditional knowledge related to cooking, which typically focuses on the history of modern gastronomy by bringing in knowledge from the Neolithic period. The latter is the subject of a volume the elBulli team was preparing in 2015. One of the important lines of inquiry at the elBulli Foundation is an attempt to catalog produce and other ingredients, and determine a qualification system that reflects a chef's point of view, as opposed to a botanist's or an agricultural scientist's perspectives. One of the team members shared with me their expansive vision: the method of creative inquiry and sensory investigation that is being developed here can be applied to gastronomy, but has a relationship with other disciplines, venturing even into multiple theoretical domains.

Notes

1 The material for this chapter was collected by the author during her site visits to Arzak restaurant and Laboratorio and elBulli Foundation in August and September of 2015.

2 Interview with Elena Arzak, August 30, 2015.

3 Interview with Elena Arzak, August 30, 2015.FIGURE **7.3** Soup of honey with vodka and cochineal

PART TWO

Collecting and Exhibiting Food

8

Growing Food History on a National Stage:

A Case Study from the Smithsonian's National Museum of American History[1]

Paula J. Johnson

The National Museum of American History (NMAH) is one of nineteen museums and research bureaus that make up the Smithsonian Institution. As a major museum on the National Mall in Washington, DC, the NMAH welcomes about five million visitors annually and many millions more online. Known for its icons of American history, the museum also maintains significant collections reflecting the experiences of everyday Americans. Food history was not a formal area of interest when the museum opened in 1964. Yet because important aspects of food production, distribution, and consumption are threaded throughout American history, it is possible to revisit the NMAH's early days and find significant strands of food history in many areas of inquiry and research. Some of these past efforts have helped influence the more recent, formalized food history initiative.

A survey of objects within disparate curatorial divisions reveals an astonishing array of food-related material culture—from cooking vessels and kitchen appliances to tractors and equipment used in fast-food restaurants— and documents from government and industry, political campaign materials, and ephemera.[2] Likewise, a look back at several exhibitions produced at the NMAH reveals bits of food history embedded in many other topics. "A More

Perfect Union," the groundbreaking exhibition on the internment of Japanese Americans during the Second World War, included a stark look at a camp's mess halls and meals. "American Encounters" featured a Pueblo feast day table as part of its compelling exploration of five hundred years of encounters between Native, Hispanic, and Anglo people in New Mexico. "America on the Move" depicts the impact of new transportation systems on agriculture around Watsonville, California, beginning in the 1880s, and "On the Water" examines the link between sugar production in the Caribbean and the transatlantic slave trade.[3] The museum also produced several important public programs organized around food-related topics, notably two symposia in the 1990s cosponsored with the National Museum of Natural History. "Good as Gold: Foods the Americas Gave the World" (1991) and "What's the Catch?: Fish, Shellfish, and Fisheries in America" (1994) brought together scholars and the public to explore the history and culture of these complex subjects.[4]

This chapter touches upon the history of food-related activity at the NMAH, and explores in-depth the recent acceleration and expansion of work in food history. It addresses changing perspectives on the role of food in American history and how those changes have influenced research and collecting, as well as exhibitions, programs, and the reimagining of the museum's public spaces. The chapter will specifically address the acquisition and display of Julia Child's home kitchen; the creation of the major exhibition, "FOOD: Transforming the American Table, 1950–2000"; and the development of new programming initiatives, particularly those that utilize the museum's demonstration kitchen, which opened in 2015.

Food at the NMAH: New directions in food research and collecting

Motivated by diverse research interests—from native foodways to fishing technologies, to agriculture and business history—several staff members formed a team in 1996 to focus on the topic of American wine and winemaking. After fielding an intriguing public inquiry about whether the museum planned to mark the twentieth anniversary of the "Judgment of Paris," the group began reviewing the collections relating to wine in America.[5] Discovering a paucity of winemaking artifacts in the collections, the group organized a symposium, "Red, White, and American," on the history of winemaking in America as a first step toward building the collections, and developed a small exhibition featuring bottles of winning vintages from the tasting. Inspired by the symposium, and with new funding for wine-history research, the group launched an oral history and documentation project on winemaking in

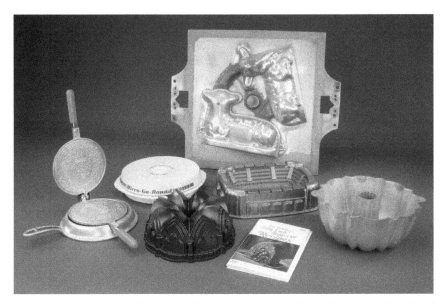

FIGURE 8.1 *In 2006 the NMAH food history team collected objects and archival records from Nordic Ware, makers of the Bundt pan and other items of cookware.*
© *Smithsonian Institution.*

twentieth-century America—and formed the "American Food and Wine History Project."[6]

The kitchen that changed everything

In August of 2001, America's beloved cookbook author and television cook Julia Child announced she was leaving her home in Cambridge, Massachusetts, to return to her home state of California. Upon hearing this news, the team contacted Julia to discuss a possible donation of objects. While we did not know exactly what that might be—balloon whisks, copper cookware, i.e., the tools associated with her in the popular imagination—we arrived in Cambridge full of questions.[7] As Julia welcomed us into her kitchen, we experienced something of a curatorial mind meld—recognizing that the entire kitchen as created and organized by Julia was the real artifact, not a few disassociated bits. Here was a serious working environment designed and used by a serious cook—tools and equipment were arranged in work zones, and, contrary to modern gourmet kitchen designs, almost everything was visible and ready to be used. The place also looked like home; the warmth of the central table and the well-used utensils evoked familiarity and comfort. Even before Julia told us, we could sense that this kitchen was "the beating heart of the home."[8]

Securing appropriate space to process a large collection is often a challenge, which was certainly the case with the kitchen. Because the acquisition happened so quickly, we had to scramble to find space, to say nothing of equipment and staff to do the work. We lobbied to use a small, empty gallery with a wall of windows facing into a wide corridor, and decided to make ourselves into an exhibition, essentially processing the collection in front of the public. Over the course of seven months, we worked with interns and volunteers to unpack, survey, catalog, photograph, and house the 1,200 objects in Julia's kitchen. Members of the team would often step outside of the gallery to speak with visitors informally, an exercise that helped us understand the tremendous reach of Julia's influence. We listened to testimonials from many people, "I grew up watching Julia on TV and she made me love cooking!" and also noticed that visitors kept asking, "When will the kitchen be on view?" That question, coupled with many visitors' stated desire to see just how Julia arranged her kitchen, bolstered our case: rather than display individual objects in a traditional exhibition presentation, the kitchen should be rebuilt right in the gallery. On August 19, 2002, less than a year from our first visit in Cambridge, we opened "Bon Appétit! Julia Child's Kitchen at the Smithsonian."[9] Julia, who had just turned 90, came to take part in the opening, and, as she stepped inside the kitchen (not generally allowed) she exclaimed, "It makes me feel like turning something on and starting to cook!" We took this as proof that everything was in its proper place.

Originally scheduled to be on view for six months, the exhibition was a hit. The gallery, while admittedly small, was always full, even during slower seasons. Visitors took their time and lingered in the space. They gazed into viewports, noticing such details as Julia's much-used copies of *The Joy of Cooking* and remarking on tools they had in their own home kitchens. Many people stood or sat, rapt, in front of the monitor showing clips from Julia's many cooking shows.[10] Visitors who were complete strangers when they entered the gallery left having had a conversation about a recipe, a cooking technique, a piece of kitchen equipment, or a memory of Julia. The atmosphere in "Bon Appétit!" was friendly in a way we had not experienced before, one we chalked up to the warmth people felt toward Julia and the connective power of food. This reinforced the conviction that food could be a serious, and seriously engaging, subject for the museum to be exploring on its own, not just as an aspect of other topics in American history.

As six months turned into a year, then five years and more, Julia's kitchen remained on display and continued to draw crowds. With the success of "Bon Appétit!" the team kept imagining an exhibition that would take a broader view of Julia and her influence, essentially to place her in the larger context of American food history. Our decision also made perfect sense at a time when scholars, journalists, policy makers, nutritionists, and the public were taking a closer look at food in America and globally. At the same time, renewed interest in American regional cuisine, in the foods and flavors brought by migrants from different parts of the world, and in the explosion of celebrity chef culture and televised cooking competitions, helped shift the topic of food to the front burner. Within this milieu, the team continued to explore how the NMAH could contribute to the conversation by creating a more vigorous food history program on its national stage.

A new food exhibition

Our opportunity came when the museum announced plans to close all three public floors in the building's west end for much-needed renovations. Packing away the kitchen was an untenable prospect to the team (and, we believed, to the public), so in 2009 we undertook a feasibility study to explore some options. The study stated our vision for the future, which combined four elements: Julia's kitchen, a new kitchen stage for programming, a changing gallery for food-related exhibitions, and a revenue-generating component. Over a nine-month period, the team researched existing models for food history programming in museums; met with potential partners to gage their interest in collaborating on different aspects of the proposal; and examined the challenges, including the financial realities inherent in such a project. While the team's hybrid idea was not adopted, some of the key elements came to fruition.[11]

In 2010, the team proposed a new exhibition for a 3,500-square-foot gallery on the building's east end. Originally called "Food for Thought," the new exhibition would place Julia Child's kitchen within a larger context of food history and look more broadly at the complexities of food in twentieth-century America. As we began developing the exhibition, we were aware that we were not alone: several other museums and organizations were also working on food-related projects.[12] To learn more about the public's interest in food history, we surveyed people attending the annual Smithsonian Folklife Festival. The survey revealed broad interest in regional and ethnic food traditions, and a desire to know more about where our food comes from and "food people—chefs, growers, winemakers, and cooks."[13] While many respondents acknowledged that nutrition and health were important, some pointed out there were other places besides the museum to access such information. The survey results, together with our sense of the new food studies scholarship, and the general heightened awareness about food safety, security, and sustainability, formed the foundation for "FOOD: Transforming the American Table, 1950–2000," which opened in 2012.

At the NMAH, as in many other museums, developing an exhibition is an intensely collaborative process. As the project got underway, the core team expanded to include a designer, an educator, a curatorial/graphics assistant, and various specialists for media, business, and fundraising. We also identified a panel of food historians who advised on particular stories and provided comments on the script, messaging, and overall layout and flow.[14] Two related issues dominated our earliest discussions: the time frame to be covered, and the placement of Julia's kitchen within the exhibition's storyline and layout. While our first impulse was to take a long view of American food history—perhaps including Thomas Jefferson's well-known interest in American agriculture, winemaking, and culinary pursuits—as we considered the gallery's size and visitor feedback, we ultimately narrowed the scope to 1950–2000. After all, this half-century was a period of tremendous change, when an explosion of new technologies and major social and cultural shifts transformed American life.

We ultimately agreed that the organizing concept would be the transformed American table, and that one of the show's major sections, "New and Improved!" would explore how innovative technologies influenced the production, distribution, and preparation of food. Another major section, "Resetting the Table," would focus on the range of demographic, social, and cultural factors that helped expand the American palate and called into question basic notions of meals and mealtime. Another major section, "Wine for the Table," would draw on our extensive field research and collecting to explore the revolution in American winemaking between 1950 and 2000. This fifty-year period proved an excellent fit for the gallery and for the main object that comprises another of the exhibition's main sections: Julia Child's home kitchen.

Integrating Julia's Kitchen into "FOOD"

As we studied the gallery footprint, we debated where to place Julia's eleven-by-fourteen-foot kitchen—at the entrance or further inside? One perspective argued for placing it deep within the gallery, using its popularity to draw visitors through the rest of the content. Others argued for giving the kitchen pilgrims what they wanted right up front. In the end, we looked to the kitchen for guidance and recognized that its contents represented a healthy slice of the 1950–2000 period. The kitchen contains tools Julia bought while studying at Le Cordon Bleu in Paris in 1948, as well as items acquired shortly before her 2001 move. Yet the color scheme and layout had not changed since 1961, making it an effective introduction to the period. Julia's story also dovetailed beautifully with the theme of change and transformation.

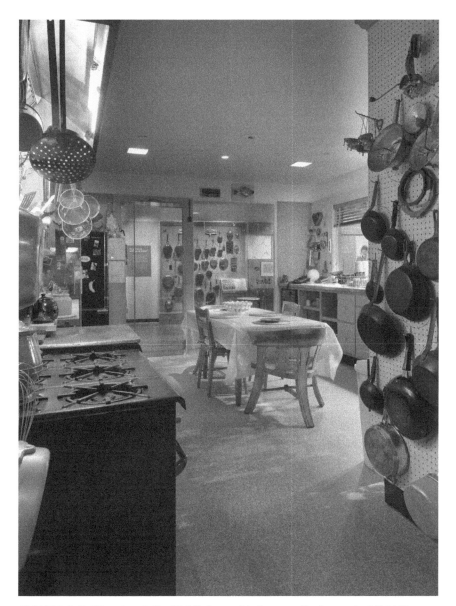

FIGURE 8.2 *View into Julia Child's home kitchen, on display at the NMAH.*
© *Smithsonian Institution.*

While the material culture in Julia's kitchen spans the time period, her story introduces the concept of conflicting perspectives on food in general and cooking in particular. Although influential, Julia's message was at odds with other views rampant in American culture in the early 1960s that promoted new convenience foods and kitchen shortcuts, and encouraged women to abandon what was portrayed as the drudgery of cooking, or to swap out the family dinner table for the fast-food drive-thru.[15] The gallery is set up to allow these and other contradictions to coexist, much as they do in contemporary American life.

The time frame and thematic statement for the exhibition: "Between 1950 and 2000, new technologies and cultural changes transformed how and what we eat" guided the selection of objects and stories. Despite the wealth of existing collections at the museum, we discovered we needed to do some targeted collecting to reflect and represent food and change in the postwar period. The team grappled with, for example, how to depict the rise of centralized, industrial agriculture? How to address both the early embrace and the unintended consequences of an abundant, affordable, highly processed food supply? How to convey the tremendous changes and resulting inequalities in food distribution and accessibility? How to show that despite an array of "new and improved" devices for the kitchen and changing roles within families, women remained the primary cooks at home, yet struggled to become professional chefs?

The team developed a series of touchstone objects and case studies that quickly communicated the essence of some of the changes in American food. The "New and Improved!" section, for example, opens with the story of lettuce. From iceberg's dominance in 1950 to bagged, organic micro-greens grown on an industrial scale by the 2000s, this story of change is conveyed with a simple short-handled hoe and lettuce hump used by Mexican guest workers in the 1960s, imagery of fields and an ad touting the freshness of iceberg lettuce delivered by refrigerated rail cars, protest posters and buttons from the lettuce boycotts over labor practices in the 1970s, and a large graphic of modern precision-harvesting of organic greens for the bagged-lettuce market. An adjacent video offers a view of the scale of industrial lettuce production: vast fields of organic lettuce and the machinery used to wash, bag, and ship it. A thought bubble asks: "Bagged lettuce—the best thing since sliced bread?" to encourage visitors to think about the trade-offs of this fresh convenience food. The team's intent was to provide the framework for exploring the pros and cons of centralized, large-scale food production, a place to begin a discussion or spark further inquiry.

Another case study in "New and Improved!" traces some of the big changes in food distribution in the 1950 to 2000 time period. As highway construction increased in the postwar period and as suburbs expanded, so did the development of supermarkets. Food produced in one area of the country could be trucked to suburban stores or distribution centers elsewhere, while customers were delighted to find spacious aisles filled with an astonishing array of cleverly marketed foods and food products. The touchstone objects that help focus attention on this big story of transformation include side-by-side shopping carts—two small carts from 1948 sit beside a warehouse shopping cart from the 2000s that can accommodate loads of packaged goods and two small children. The visual contrast between the carts makes clear the point about increased size and scale; the more nuanced aspects of the story—rising concerns about the environmental impacts of food transportation systems, growing interest in supporting local agriculture and farmers' markets, and questions about equal access to abundant food supplies—are addressed through graphics, text, and video.[16]

Counterpoints to the mainstream stories in the "New and Improved!" section of the exhibition are raised in "Resetting the Table," a large section that stretches along the opposite wall of the gallery. Here, we explore some of the country's social and cultural shifts through case studies, including the expansion of Mexican foods and flavors throughout the country; the counterculture movement and its rejection of industrial foods and supermarkets; the growing interest in foods and cooking techniques from around the world; and the seeds of the local, fresh, and organic movement and farmers' markets.

An open table

The team discussed the importance of maintaining the relaxed and engaged atmosphere of the "Bon Appétit!" exhibition in the new gallery. Would the larger space and expanded content quash the intimate, friendly feeling that had been so successful in the past? We felt it was important to create an inviting, comfortable space that would welcome conversation and interaction, along with content that visitors could easily access. Our designer, who had been advocating the inclusion of tables and chairs throughout the gallery, proposed an idea that clicked: create one long, open table down the center of the space. An exhibition about changes in the American table needed a big table, she argued, and the "open table" became one of the exhibition's signature elements. We envisioned visitors taking a seat, speaking with each other, and accessing content that would change on a regular basis—also an opportunity for us to keep the exhibition current. After debating ways of conveying content, we decided on four huge Lazy-Susan-like disks embedded in the table's surface to contain graphic content on topics that would expand the themes and stories in the exhibition. At opening in 2012, the four disks contained twenty-four different versions of food advice pyramids ranging from 1948 to 2011. A subsequent set of content revealed changes in school lunches in America from the 1950s to the 2010s.

The team explored ways to provide a forum for discussions with small groups of visitors and we hoped the big, open table might work for that purpose. Mindful of the contemporary food-related issues that our public might wish to discuss, we imagined inviting experts with different perspectives in food policy, innovation, health, and culture to participate in regularly scheduled conversations around the open table. Starting with book signings, we found that visitors did appreciate the chance to sit at the table with the author/expert for a brief conversation. Our attempts to hold discussions with students around the table were less successful, however: the table was not conducive to conversations involving more than a handful of people, largely because of the noise and general level of activity in the gallery. So, while the open table worked well for small family groups and school children, it did not provide the perfect venue for discussions or programs. Clearly, we needed a larger, more flexible space to do the kind of programming the topics warranted and the public wanted.

Seven months after opening, the Smithsonian's Office of Policy and Analysis (OP&A) conducted an evaluation of "FOOD." After meeting with the museum's head of interpretation and the project director to determine the exhibition's goals, the OP&A staff developed a survey tool and conducted the evaluation. The results were generally positive. We learned, for example, that the exhibition evoked strong personal and family memories and that a majority of visitors learned something new about food history.[17] Julia's kitchen remained a highlight. The formal OP&A evaluation considered our visitors' different "experience preferences," and we learned that for visitors who have an orientation toward physical preferences ("an attraction to physical sensations, including movement, touch, sound, taste, lights, and smells"), the exhibition fell short.[18] In essence, these visitors wanted more interaction and a closer experience with actual food. It was an understood critique: the team had been advocating for a demonstration kitchen that would permit the museum to develop more interactive and sensory experiences around food, and allow staff to expand programming in concert with diverse partners and for new audiences.

A place at the table for everyone: Connecting through food programming

Imagine you're the new director of the NMAH. It's your third week on the job and you're about to make your first public remarks at an event marking the preview opening of a new exhibition on food history. Your staff has provided you with briefing documents and a walkthrough of the event, which they estimate will last about five minutes tops. Piece of cake? Well, make that a huge and exquisitely decorated cake, three thousand cookies, dozens of green and blue balloons held by fidgety summer campers, 499 chef's hats balanced on as many bobbing heads, and jazz musicians dressed in chef's whites, more or less directed by an irrepressible young intern wielding a giant balloon whisk. Oh, and thousands of visitors from all over the country ready to participate in whatever happens on the stage you're approaching. That's what John Gray faced on August 15, 2012, when the museum celebrated what would have been Julia Child's 100th birthday.[19] Moments before the appointed hour, Gray appeared with a huge smile that carried a hint of concern: "Where's my chef's hat?" he asked. The 500th hat had found a home and the event began.

Julia Child's birthday bash ushered in a new era of programming for food history at the NMAH. Recognizing that food could serve as a powerful lens through which the museum—and the public—could explore different facets of American history, Gray identified food as one of three "portals" for museum-wide programming. Essentially, every exhibition would now develop dynamic programming involving food, music, and theater under a new Office of Programs and Strategic Initiatives. A new director of the "food portal" was appointed in 2013 and the former American Food and Wine History team and the food portal initiative merged to become the American Food History Project. Within the first year, the project organized the Kitchen Cabinet, an advisory group representing various sectors of the food world—from scholars to chefs, industry executives to business owners, writers to community educators—to help the museum shape the future of food history programming.[20]

Since 2013, the agenda for food history programming has taken shape and, fittingly, it can best be understood by invoking the familiar food pyramid. As the pyramid graphic shows, all of the museum's food programs are supported by a solid foundation of research and collections.[21] The dual tracks of traditional outreach and digital media are shown as framing the different types of programs under development for the museum's diverse audiences.

Within the pyramid, the largest layer represents the museum's responsibility to its daily visitors and includes such offerings as "Ask a Farmer," a program that connects visitors to farmers nationwide via a streaming live conversation. Developed with the curators of "American Enterprise," a new business history exhibition, the conversation is also available to museum partners around the country, allowing greater numbers of people to interact with someone who grows food for a living.[22] Daily food-related programming also includes scheduled chocolate-making demonstrations, opportunities for curators to bring objects out of storage, and cooking demonstrations. As of July 2015, these and other programs are held at the museum's new demonstration kitchen on the Wallace H. Coulter Performance Plaza, one of many new features of the museum's renovated first floor in the west end. The multiyear renovation project resulted in a new, highly interactive experience for visitors, and food-related conversations, demonstrations, and

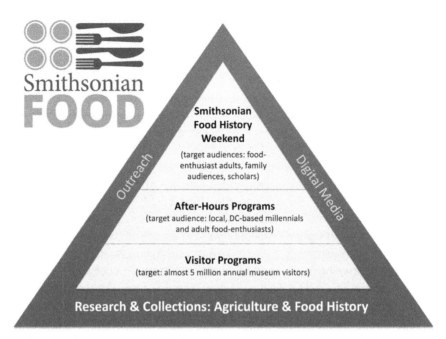

FIGURE 8.3 The NMAH food history project's programming pyramid.

© *Smithsonian Institution.*

events are among the dynamic new offerings. The stage is designed to allow for a variety of non-food-related activities, as the kitchen's cooking island can be safely moved out of sight.

From July through December 2015, the food history team conducted a trial phase for a "Food Fridays" series. With two forty-five-minute cooking demonstrations scheduled every Friday, a chef from one of our four partner organizations appeared on stage to prepare a dish that related to a theme determined by the museum.[23] The kitchen stage is equipped with professional cooking appliances, an enormous vent and fire-suppression system, and donated cookware and equipment.[24] The stage and plaza are also outfitted with cameras and large screens to allow all visitors seated in the plaza to see what's going on. A staffer hosted the demonstrations, and was also responsible for linking them to museum content—objects on display, topics within exhibitions, and historical events. While health department regulations prohibit the museum from serving food cooked on the stage, the team arranged with the chef from the museum's food service contractor to prepare dishes inspired by the demonstration for purchase in the museum's café that day. In addition, all recipes for dishes prepared on the stage were posted on the museum's website. The public responded enthusiastically to the program and our partner chefs were eager to continue creating experiences that combined food history, American history, and culinary history. Off to a promising start, evaluation of the inaugural model for "Food Fridays" is ongoing.

Envisioned many years ago, the kitchen stage is now a reality and a unique facility at the Smithsonian. It allows the museum to provide a sensory and experiential dimension to food history not possible in the "FOOD" exhibition. During the "Food Fridays" trial period, the team developed demonstrations that linked directly to stories in the exhibition, including foods of the counterculture and the 1969 Woodstock music festival; the influence of Julia Child on American culinary history; and the expansion of Mexican foods and flavors throughout the United States. While the team started out with professional chefs from partner organizations, the intention is to welcome home cooks and gardeners, fishermen and farmers, brewers and winemakers, and others to broaden the scope of food programs and vary the voices of authority. The team is envisioning the stage as a space that will make connections—among local and national audiences, and people who will share their knowledge of culinary history as well as food-related social, technological, political, environmental, and cultural history in America.

Food programs after hours

"FOOD in the Garden" is a collaborative effort with staff from Smithsonian Gardens, a pan-institutional unit. Eager to work with the NMAH staff, Smithsonian horticulturists volunteered to co-develop a program in the museum's Second World War-inspired Victory Garden. One important goal was to attract a new audience to the museum—the much-sought-after millennials, seasonal interns, and an after-work crowd of all ages—by combining creatively delivered food history with great food and drink in a meaningful setting. Organized around the theme "Growing Local," the first season of "FOOD in the Garden" ambitiously stretched over five consecutive Thursdays in July and August, 2013. Each week explored a different subtheme, from heirlooms to foraging to soil nutrients, around which the team created a panel discussion, demonstrations, and a unique menu. Because this was a new program with new partners and a new venue, we viewed the first season as a prototyping period, which allowed some risk-taking and adjustments as the series progressed. As a ticketed event, we could follow up with attendees for feedback, which helped shape subsequent programs.

In a city filled with talks, tastings, and tours, the museum continues to ask: what is our niche as the NMAH and how can we engage more successfully with our diverse local communities? Instead of grabbing onto the latest trend or food fad, or duplicating programs that could be done in any venue, the team continues to develop programs that remain true to the Smithsonian's mission and values, that are based in research and collections, are educational and balanced, and also incorporate elements of style and surprise. Mirroring the structure of "FOOD in the Garden," the "After Hours" programs are held inside the museum, permitting an "objects-out-of-storage" component. Feedback from guests revealed that this element—the chance to see some of the museum's hidden collections and to speak with curators about them—was one of the highlights of a memorable (and always food-centric) evening.

At the top of the NMAH food history pyramid sits a new initiative—the first annual Smithsonian Food History Weekend. The weekend grows out of requests from our local audience to expand the museum's food-related programming for families, as well as inquiries from professors interested in exploring how we can enrich food course offerings for their students. The first weekend (2015) included a day of roundtable discussions, a family festival day, and an evening gala—a fundraiser for the project—at which the first annual Julia Child Award was presented to Chef Jacques Pépin.[25] The NMAH is well situated to convene discussions of large topics among diverse participants, and the weekend aims to bring together scholars, inventors, practitioners, chefs, policy makers, and the public to explore and experience the history of innovation in food in America.

Key ingredients for food history in museums

History museums can play a significant role in bringing visitors together to explore and understand the complex and sometimes contradictory threads of history that illuminate how and why we eat what we eat. Food is a fundamental, accessible topic for all ages that often leads to conversations about family, fun, and memories—and to discussions about access, justice, health and safety, and sustainability. While there is no single recipe for creating a dynamic, food-related program in museums, there are several key ingredients that are worth sharing from the NMAH experience.

First, without a solid foundation of research and collections, food exhibitions and programs can be like empty calories. With an abundance of food events in non-museum venues, it is more important than ever to take the time to integrate research and collecting activities into the programming plan to create memorable, educational, and potentially transformative experiences for and with our diverse audiences. In addition, committing to a view that includes, for example, agriculture and horticulture, business and environmental history, technology and innovation, food and politics, as well as the culinary arts makes solid strategic sense. It puts the museum in touch with academics, policy makers, educators, and practitioners who can help inform and shape the program, but also help it grow. Partnerships and collaborations are essential to expanding value and attracting new audiences and resources. Likewise, developing a work culture that values experimentation and inclusive discussions helps deliver better results for the public. Finally, as we all need food, we all need each other. Strong, interdisciplinary, and multi-functional teams are essential. And having support from the museum's management also makes a world of difference.

The NMAH is committed to sharpening its focus on food and helping to facilitate conversations on food history within the museum and around the country. What we have gained over many years of building a food history program is a shot at sustainability. By seeking and maintaining strong relationships with people and organizations representing diverse parts of the food world, by building a new infrastructure for an integrated approach to food history and public history, by creating a context where food studies can flourish, and by committing to an inclusive and diverse future, food history stands a strong chance of long-term viability. Within the context of the current and seemingly unquenchable public interest in all things food, we are working strategically to focus on what the Smithsonian can do best through research and collecting while welcoming new audiences through creative, robust, sensory, and experience-based programming. We stand ready to be part of the conversation among museum colleagues, scholars, practitioners, policy makers, and the public, since food is what ultimately brings everyone to the table.

Notes

1 The author gratefully acknowledges the assistance of colleagues who commented on earlier drafts of this chapter: Jessica Carbone, Nanci Edwards, Susan Evans, Rayna Green, Melissa McLoud, and Steve Velasquez. Any errors or omissions are the author's alone.

2 The Archives Center houses the papers of many food-related businesses, including Goya Foods, Whitman's Chocolate, Krispy Kreme Doughnut Corp., Hills Bros. Coffee, Good Humor, Earl S. Tupper, Nordic Ware, and many more.

3 "A More Perfect Union" (1987–2004) http://amhistory.si.edu/perfectunion/experience/; "American Encounters" (1992–2004); "America on the Move" (opened 2003) http://americanhistory.si.edu/onthemove; "On the Water" (opened 2009) http://americanhistory.si.edu/onthewater.

4 Conference proceedings for "Good as Gold: Foods the Americas Gave the World" (1991) and "What's the Catch: Fish, Shellfish, and Fisheries in America" (1994) were printed and bound by the museum's Office of Public Services.

5 The Judgment of Paris was a blind tasting of French and new California wines in 1976 that resulted in American wines placing first, ahead of the

French, and is widely acknowledged as the impetus for accelerating worldwide interest in American wine.

6   The symposium "Red, White and American: Wine in American History and Culture" was held at the NMAH on May 10–11, 1996. The accompanying case exhibition, "Doubtless as Good," featured the 1973 Chateau Montelena Chardonnay donated by James Barrett and the 1973 Cabernet Sauvignon made and donated by Warren Winiarski. While the museum doesn't ordinarily collect organic material, an exception was made for these bottles.

7   Rayna Green, Nanci Edwards, and the author traveled to Cambridge to meet with Julia Child in August 2001. See our project diaries at: http://americanhistory.si.edu/kitchen/diary01_01.htm

8   Julia Child interview with Smithsonian staff, September 11, 2001.

9   See the "Bon Appétit!" website: http://amhistory.si.edu/juliachild

10 "Julia Child's Kitchen Wisdom," Geoffrey Drummond and A La Carte Productions, 2000.

11 "Interim Report, Feasibility Study for Julia Child's Kitchen," Report to NMAH Management by Nanci Edwards, Rayna Green, Paula Johnson, and Steve Velasquez, May 2010.

12 E.g., "What's Cooking Uncle Sam?" (National Archives, Washington, DC); "Big Food: Health, Culture and the Evolution of Eating" (Yale Peabody Museum of Natural History); "Lunch Hour NYC" (New York Public Library).

13 "Food and Wine Survey Summary," internal document, July 20, 2010.

14 Advisors for the "FOOD" exhibition included food historians and authors Warren Belasco, Amy Bentley, Melissa McLoud, and Laura Shapiro.

15 See imagery associated with the "Shortcuts for Home Cooks" section of the "FOOD" exhibition at http://americanhistory.si.edu/food/new-and-improved/help-home-cook and http://americanhistory.si.edu/food/new-and-improved/no-work-no-dishes (accessed May 24, 2015).

16 It is beyond the scope of this chapter to discuss in depth the complete content of the exhibition. See the exhibition online at http://americanhistory.si.edu/food.

17 Office of Policy and Analysis, *A Study of Visitors to* FOOD: Transforming the American Table 1950–2000 *at the National Museum of American History* (August 2013).

18 Ibid., p. 6. The IPOP theory considers four experience preferences: Ideas, People, Objects, and Physical.

19 Julia Child died on August 13, 2004.

20 Susan Evans became the new director of the food portal. Members of the Kitchen Cabinet can be found at http://americanhistory.si.edu/press/releases/national-museum-american-history-convenes-kitchen-cabinet (accessed May 24, 2015).

21 The NMAH Food Programming Pyramid was created by Susan Evans in 2014.

22 "American Enterprise" opened on July 1, 2015, in the newly renovated first floor, west end.

23 For the trial phase the museum partnered with L'Academie de Cuisine, Restaurant Associates, Sur La Table, and Wegmans. Partners are essential to the museum's food history programming.

24 Developing the special museum requirements for the kitchen and plaza involved staff and consultants. The team will share lessons learned with other organizations desiring greater detail.

25 The Julia Child Award was inaugurated in 2015 and is presented to an individual who has had a significant impact on cooking, eating, and drinking in America http://www.juliachildaward.com (accessed September 24, 2015).

9

Tortillas, Tacos, and Berries:

Reflections on Collecting Latino Food History at the National Museum of American History

L. Stephen Velasquez

Standing in the kitchen of Amelia Moran Ceja, I watch as Amelia stirs a large bubbling pot of *caldo*, or chicken soup. We are talking about Ceja Vineyards, the winery she owns and the work she did as a child with her father in the Napa, California vineyards. Sitting in front of the bowl of *caldo*, I am not only reminded of the influence of family and tradition, but also the power of food to reveal stories about migration, identity, labor, and national history. As I look out over the California countryside with Amelia, I ask myself, what are some of the contributions of Latinos to the changing food landscape? How can food collections tell us about Latino and about national history? What does the National Museum of American History (NMAH) collect to illustrate Latino contributions to the changing food landscape? What is the NMAH's approach to collecting and displaying Latino history in a food exhibit?

At the NMAH, why we collect, what we collect, and how we collect informs our approach to preserving and exhibiting Latino food history. This chapter looks at three case studies that help illustrate Mexican and Mexican American contributions to food history, food production, and food culture. I will highlight how these collections inform and shape our food history exhibit *FOOD: Transforming the American Table*. As a curator for Latino collections at the NMAH, I am responsible for collecting a community history that is broad in scope and that shows the differences among and between these histories.

The Mexican American experience is different from the Cuban American experience, which is different from a Mexican American experience in Michigan which is different in California, and so on. Our collecting reflects this diversity of experiences.

I focus on three different Latino collections that illustrate our curatorial approaches to collecting and presenting Latino history which tells a broader food history within the nation. First, the bracero history collection is a nationwide collaborative collecting initiative assembles and tells the story of Mexican agricultural guest workers and their cultural impact. The El Chico Tex-Mex collection is a private donation that tells strands of business and cultural history. Finally, the Mexican winemaker's project is a collecting initiative looking at how Mexicans and Mexican Americans in Napa, California have not only been instrumental in working in an industry but are now shaping an industry. These three collections illustrate changes in the American cultural landscape from the role immigration had on changing communities, to growth and access to different foods, to the diversity within the Mexican American community, as well as the role of memory, tradition, and politics in food history.

Collecting Latino history

The Smithsonian Institution has been collecting for over one hundred and fifty years.[1] In the area of food, we have a wide range of agricultural implements, domestic and industrial food prep and serving items, gadgets, business records, and oral histories.[2] For years, the Smithsonian struggled with Latino representation in exhibits and programs. A 1994 internal report criticized the Smithsonian for lack of Latino representation in staffing, exhibits and programing and it recommended that NMAH "should become an important vehicle for research, study, and presentation of the Hispanic role in the history of the United States."[3] In this context, the need and desire to address lack of representation created opportunities to illustrate diverse Latino histories through food. Two goals drove us forward: the desire to collect more Latino experiences, especially stories and objects representing everyday life; and the opportunity to contribute a more targeted approach focused on agriculture, food production, and food distribution of post Second World War food history. My work makes visible the role Latinos have in transforming the American table and shaping what, why, and how we eat.

Objects, oral histories, archives, and research inform museums exhibits and enable us to highlight important events and make meaning of social and cultural changes.[4] Public historians and museum curators engage with diverse and often unacknowledged, voices and bring them to light.[5] We use food to help visitors understand cultural and social changes through everyday objects.[6] Collecting oral histories like those of Amelia and food-related objects—a short-handled hoe, a tortilla press, or restaurant menus—enables the interpretation of history. With so few Latino food history holdings and such a broad scope to follow, we knew we had to create a more targeted public representation of Latino communities and in so doing broaden our educational and collecting goals.[7]

The food exhibit

The desire to represent Latino communities informed parts of NMAH's exhibit *FOOD: Transforming the American Table, 1950–2000*. Covering fifty years and more than just Latino history, the exhibit explores some of the significant changes in what Americans eat and how they eat. The exhibition is arranged in five thematic sections: "New and Improved" which emphasizes the impact of new technologies in food production, distribution, and consumption highlighting the progress we make but also questioning long-term effects; "Resetting the Table" which explores major social and cultural changes in American life that have influenced foods and foodways; "Wine for the Table" which highlights wine and wine production bringing in technological and social changes together; "Julia Child's Kitchen" and the impact and influence of television personalities, which includes Julia Child's kitchen; and a large kitchen table with rotating content as an exhibition interactive.[8]

We want to create opportunities for visitors to reflect on the political, cultural, and social changes Latinos have brought to the US food landscape. To this end, we incorporate throughout the exhibition various strands of Latino history that illustrate contributions of Mexicans and Mexican Americans to food production, distribution, and consumption, helping us tell broader stories of immigration, politics, and economics.

Work, lettuce, marriage, and oral history of the bracero program

Food has social, economic, and cultural meanings as well as political significations that must simultaneously be made visible. One collection that informs the *FOOD* exhibition and illustrates production, labor, and social change, is the Bracero History Project (BHP), a nationwide collaborative project we undertook between 2005 and 2009.

The BHP documents the Second World War Mexican Agricultural Workers Program, commonly known as the bracero program. The program brought an estimated two million Mexican men, called braceros, to the United States to work in fields on temporary guest worker contracts. The men planted, tended irrigation systems, picked crops, packed produce and in these roles had a significant impact on the agribusiness landscape.[9] Some of these men eventually married American women or settled in the US, contributing to demographic shifts in small towns, large cities, and changing community dynamics. Although originally intended to fill labor shortages caused by the Second World War, the program lasted twenty-two years, making it the largest guest worker program in US history. The stories of the men, women, families, and communities touched by the bracero program are a little known chapter of both American and Mexican history.[10] Often invisible yet fundamental in agriculture fields, this central yet forgotten story of the bracero is what NMAH is interested in preserving and presenting. [11]

To undertake this extensive collecting project, the BHP created a national consortium of museums, universities, and cultural institutions to focus on this critical piece of history.[12] Our project is informed and shaped by The Leonard Nadel Collection, a collection of 1,730 photographic prints from 1956 and 1957 that the museum purchased in 1999. To bring these images to life, we recorded oral histories of ex-braceros and family members, growers, merchants, nurses, and others. Through oral histories, we portrayed their journey to the US, the contracting process, medical examinations, work, and

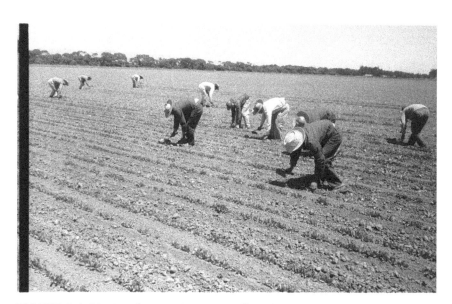

FIGURE 9.1 *Mexican braceros in Watsonville, CA, 1956.*

© *Leonard Nadel Collection, Archives Center, National Museum of American History, Smithsonian Institution.*

their daily life. Additionally, we collected artifacts, photos, and letters depicting work and daily life. We created a centralized website and online digital archive of this material.[13] Finally, we developed a traveling exhibition, *Bittersweet Harvest: The Bracero Program 1942–1964.*[14]

Our oral history and collecting project adds a historical framework to the personal and familial experiences of the many bracero men who were central to change in food production. The merging of personal and historical adds dimension and voice, producing an unofficial history, which expands far beyond labor and into social and cultural spheres. The BHP used the Nadel images and oral histories to tell the story of the agricultural workers through their own perspectives. For example, Jose Natividad Alva Medina talks about backbreaking fieldwork, "in the Imperial Valley . . . That is where we met *el cortito* or what they call a short-handled hoe. And for sure, that is where I shed my tears."[15] We include the short-handled hoe, a hat worn by a former bracero, and lettuce hump wheelbarrow to explicitly connect the everyday objects to the history of the bracero program and to technological and political changes. Another ex-bracero, Pedro del Real Perez reflects on his experience and the importance of a bracero ". . . we came here to get work that those here couldn't do. They were at war, they were doing whatever they were doing, we were the ones that came here to do the work . . . some on the railroad, others harvesting crops in camps."[16] Antonia Duran talks about marrying a bracero, pointing to some of the broader effects agricultural workers had on cultural and family

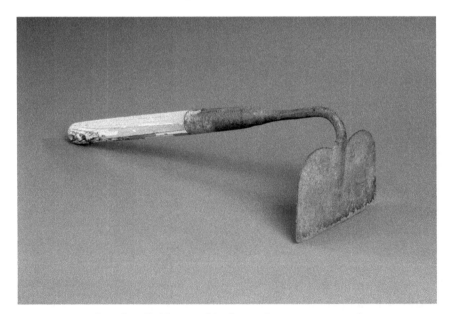

FIGURE 9.2 *Short-handled hoe used by former bracero Diaz Savala.*
© *Archives Center, National Museum of American History, Smithsonian Institution.*

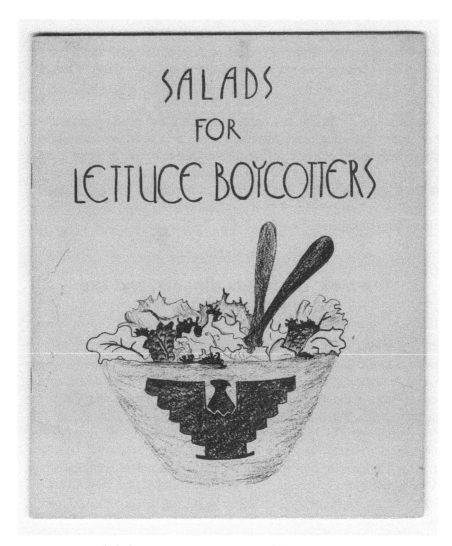

FIGURE 9.3 *Salads for Lettuce Boycotters pamphlet, United Farm Workers.*
© *Division of Home and Community Life, National Museum of American History, Smithsonian Institution.*

issues: "I always prayed that if I married this person that he could stay here, that I would pray that he would like California and he wouldn't go back."[17] The project collected hundreds of oral histories and artifacts for researchers, curators, and others to draw upon. Our objective is to create a broad picture of the bracero experiences as well as collect examples of these experiences.

Large-scale agriculture and shifting cultural and political awareness acted as a catalyst for agricultural unions and activism, which we explore in the *FOOD* exhibit. The United Farm Workers (UFW) union, started in 1966 by

Cesar Chavez and Dolores Huerta, fought to reclaim rights and power for domestic agricultural workers, many of whom were overlooked for work in favor of the Mexican guest workers, who tolerated a lower wage.[18] The UFW used food boycotts as a means to reach out to a largely unaware consuming public to rally behind fixing the problems of farm labor.[19]

Some of the most effective nationwide consumer boycotts and strikes, often lasting for years, were against big fruit and vegetable growers and bulk wine producers. These two stories, the guest worker program and the agriculture union, inform our "New and Improved, Field Work" and "Resetting the Table, Voting with Your Fork" sections of our exhibit. Using a pamphlet, "Salads for Lettuce Boycotters," we connect the social everyday act of eating with political action.

Tex-Mex, enchilada dinners, and the China Poblana

Sitting at a long conference table in a large room in Dallas, TX, I met John Cuellar, Carmen Summers, and other members of the Cuellar family, whose matriarch, Adelaida, left Mexico and settled with her husband in Kaufman County, Texas in the 1920s. Adelaida began selling tamales and chili at the Kaufman County Fair in 1926 and opened a small café soon after. In 1940, her sons moved with her to Dallas and established the first El Chico Tex-Mex Restaurant chain that can now be found in Texas, Oklahoma, Louisiana, Arkansas, Florida, and other southern states.[20] Boxes and albums detailing the business operations, marketing, and direction of the El Chico chain from the 1960s through the 1990s were displayed for us. The boxes contained menus, original packaging for canned tortillas, frozen tacos, enchilada sauce, as well as listings identifying head cooks that went on to start their own restaurants. This material offers a snapshot of the explosion of post Second World War Tex-Mex food restaurant businesses and the rise of what Robb Walsh calls "America's oldest regional cuisine."[21] Jeffery Pilcher describes this change as "novel cooking styles [that] combined North American ingredients with Mexican sensibilities."[22]

Carmen pulled out a glittering China Poblana dress with sequin images of the Mexican eagle and the Aztec calendar, symbols connecting the dress to the cultural traditions of Mexico.[23] At first, I was not sure how the dress would connect to the broader themes of the exhibit. We had similar dresses from the 1930s that were sold as tourist items. Would we use the dress in an exhibit? Could it be read as a stereotypical or appropriated image? The dress was worn by Carmen at trade shows and special events for the El Chico restaurants.

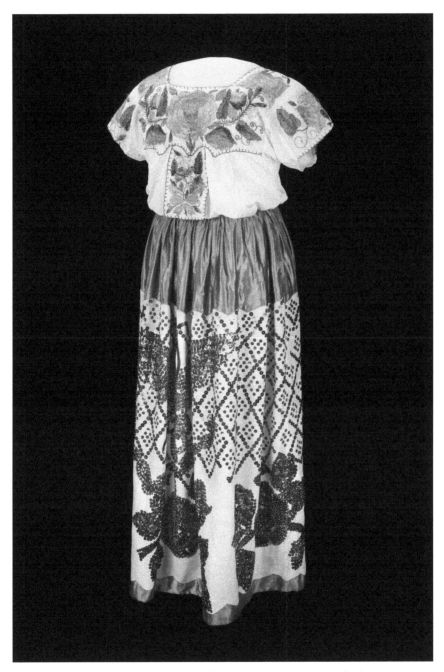

FIGURE 9.4 *China Poblana dress used by Carmen Summers in El Chico restaurant promotions.*

© *National Museum of American History, Smithsonian Institution.*

Although El Chico did not invent the use of the China Poblana folkloric imagery in marketing, they certainly drew upon these cultural markers to identify their restaurant as a particular genre which connects Mexican cultural history to Texas-Mexican business.[24] The dress was used during the 1960s and 1970s when Mexican ethnic cultural awareness was at its height within the Mexican American community.[25]

Mexican Americans experienced a Mexican consciousness renaissance where the Chicano Mexican cultural identity, drawing from signs and symbols of Mexico's past, claimed social and political rights and spaces for their community.[26] The dress speaks to Mexican Americans by referencing these signs and symbols. At the same time, the El Chico chain was aiming to make its food and culture accessible to everyone. Walsh describes this as an adaptation of the bi-cultural existence, serving "Mexican dishes" but actually serving food white Anglos might prefer.[27] As the dress references a Mexican identity it also, evokes an image of "authenticity" and ethnicity to a white Anglo customer. As David Beriss and David Sutton explain, restaurants are places where the interplay of identity and food defines and separates people.[28] Food businesses and restaurants are powerful cultural brokers that help define a neighborhood and keep tradition alive but are simultaneously sites of both appropriation and homogenization. Tex-Mex restaurants like El Chico acted as a cultural bridge bringing Anglos and Latinos together.[29] The El Chico restaurant helped usher in the Tex-Mex food revolution, shaping how we perceive "Mexican" food while also popularizing Tex-Mex food across the globe.[30]

The El Chico story and the collections we acquired show how changes in distribution, marketing, access, and cultural consciousness enable Tex-Mex expand across the country.[31] The story of Tex-Mex and El Chico emphasize the role of entrepreneurs, competition, industrial production, distribution, and marketing that provided food to people of diverse backgrounds.[32] These collections sit with other business-related collections in the FOOD exhibit, in the section "Resetting the Table, Tex-Mex Revolution" which highlights packaging, promotional material, the dress, menus, even the first frozen margarita machine. The display is set in the context of immigration and social change and emphasizes how multiple traditions and identities shape the American foodscape.

Grapes, wine, family, and tradition

Back in the Ceja kitchen near Napa, California, Juanita Ceja, Amelia's mother-in-law walks in. Juanita is the wife of Pablo Ceja, a former bracero who came to California in the 1950s to work in the fields on a temporary guest contract. He worked along the west coast in various jobs until getting a sponsor in 1967.

He then moved his family from Aquila, Michoacán, Mexico to Napa. Juanita tells me her story of the journey with the kids to California, finding housing, and the difficulties with language and schools.[33]

Families like the Cejas and others like the Robledo Family Winery make their culture and family tradition the center of their winery business. The Robledo Family Winery, also started by Mexican migrants, draws from their Mexican rancho culture to decorate their tasting room with lush hand-carved chairs and tables, awards, and family images of Reynaldo Robledo in his younger days. Like many businesses, it is a family affair where several brothers run the tasting room, distribution, and winemaking. Even the extended family is involved in cultivating vineyards. Similarly, Amelia Ceja uses her cooking skills to pair traditional Mexican food with their wines. A 2001 poster for the Macy's Cellar Kitchen cooking demonstration and class indicates "you will learn first hand about the Mexican culture and the art of Wine pairing," most likely the first time a wine pairing with Mexican food was highlighted in a public space like Macy's.[34] Amelia uses this knowledge and tradition to promote food and wines, physically and digitally.[35]

The Ceja and Robledo family stories, like other stories from Napa, are common experiences of Mexican migrants coming to work in the vineyards. Some arrivals found success while others continue to struggle with housing, wage, and safety issues. The Robledo and Ceja families, for instance, used their knowledge and skill to buy land, plant grapes, and make wine. The dozen items which we collected, such as vineyard tools, tasting room menus, advertising posters, and the interviews we have conducted with Mexican and Mexican American vineyard workers, winery owners, and winemakers make up the "Wine for the Table" section of the *FOOD* exhibit where we explore technological and social changes in the wine industry. These Mexican American families are represented not just as wine workers, but as shaping an industry where they used to be invisible. These families, and many like them, take their own traditions and explicitly make them part of the American experience.

Latino food history is national history

NMAH's efforts to collect Latino history and food history are ongoing. As curators and public historians, we connect our visitors with everyday objects and stories. By collecting stories and objects of everyday life, about industrial food, consumption, and production, we expand ways that explore complex American experiences. Further, we include multiple and diverse voices to tell stories of food history and Latino contributions to the American cultural and food landscapes. NMAH narrates the national history while being mindful of regional and community history, innovations, policies, and the everyday lives of people who are shaping and negotiating the national food landscapes. *FOOD: Transforming the American Table* and other NMAH efforts on immigration, innovation, politics, medicine and health, and cultural history give the visitor multiple entry points for thinking about Latino history in an American context. As museum professionals, our goal is to constantly expand what it means to collect food history and use the multiple tools at our disposal, such as archives, oral histories, and material culture to help tell the contributions of Latinos to national history.

Notes

1   For more about Smithsonian collecting see Steven Lubar and Kathleen M. Kendrick, *Legacies: Collecting America's History at the Smithsonian* (Washington and London: Smithsonian Institution Press, 2001).

2   For a sampling of material throughout every collecting unit at NMAH see "Food," American History, accessed May 28, 2015, http://americanhistory. si.edu/collections/subjects/food

3   Raul Yzaguirre and Mari C. Aponte, *Willful Neglect: The Smithsonian Institution and U.S. Latinos, Report of the Smithsonian Institution Task Force on Latino Issues* (Washington, D.C.: The Smithsonian Institution, 1994).

4   James B. Gardner, "Contested Terrain: History, Museums, and the Public," *The Public Historian* 26, no. 4 (2004): 11–21.

5   David Glassberg, "Public History and the Study of Memory," *The Public Historian*. 18, 2 (1996): 14

6   Kristin L. Ahlberg, "Introduction," *The Public Historian*, 34, No. 2 (Spring 2012): 9–12 and Megan Elias, "Summoning the Food Ghosts: Food History as Public History", *The Public Historian*, 34, No. 2 (Spring 2012), 14

7   The Goya Foods collection being the large expectation. Food preparation and serving items from Puerto Rico exist in the Vidal collection.

8   See http://americanhistory.si.edu/food.

9   Don Mitchell, *They Saved the Crops: Labor, Landscape, and the Struggle Over Industrial Farming in Bracero-Era California* (Athens: University of Georgia Press, 2012).

10 The literature on bracero history is extensive. See Erasmo Gamboa, Barbara Driscoll, and Gilbert González. In addition, Ernesto Galarza's *Merchants of Labor* (see next note) was published during the final year of the program. Three other scholars, Mae Ngai, Stephen Pitti and Matt Garcia have written about the program within larger books about Mexican immigration, labor, and culture. (For Matt Garcia's work see n. 19 below.) Manuel Garcia y Griego's article remains the most authoritative and focused study of the politics and the management of the bilateral agreement. For a more social and personal history of the bracero program see Maria Herrera Sobek (n. 25 below), Ronald Mize, Deborah Cohen, and Ana Rosas.

11 For more about the role of braceros in agribusiness see Mitchell, *They Saved the Crops: 2* and Ernesto Galarza, *Merchants of Labor: The Mexican Bracero Story: an Account of the Managed Migration of Mexican Farm Workers in California 1942–1960* (Charlotte: McNally and Loftin, 1964), 86.

12 The Bracero History Project, with the aid of funds from the Smithsonian Latino Center, Latino Pool partnered with the University of Texas, El Paso, Brown University, and George Mason University. Some partner institutions that hosted events and collecting were Californian State University Channel Islands, San Jose Heritage Plaza, and other small libraries and community organizations.

13 Bracero History Archive, accessed September 30, 2015, http://braceroarchive.org/

14 The exhibit opened in September of 2009 at NMAH and travelled around the country. It has been extended several times and has been to more than thirty venues such as San Jose Heritage Plaza, Kansas City Public Library, California State University at Channel Islands and encouraged the venues to supplement the exhibit with local oral histories and objects of their own.

15 Méndez, Ivonne, "José Natividad Alva Medina," in Bracero History Archive, Item #658, http://braceroarchive.org/items/show/658 (accessed May 28, 2015).

16 Loza, Mireya, "Pedro del Real Pérez," in Bracero History Archive, Item #152, http://braceroarchive.org/items/show/152 (accessed May 28, 2015).

17 Antonia Duran, interviewed by Steve Velasquez, September 18, 2007.

18 Susan Ferriss and Ricardo Sandoval, *The Fight in the Fields: Cesar Chavez and the Farmworkers Movement* (San Diego; New York: Harcourt Brace, 1997).

19 Matt Garcia, *From the Jaws of Victory: The Triumph and Tragedy of Cesar Chavez and the Farm Worker Movement* (Berkeley: University of California Press, 2012).

20 Robb Walsh, *The Tex-Mex Cookbook: A History in Recipes and Photos* (New York: Random House, 2004). For more on the El Chico chain see "El Chico," Funding Universe, http://www.fundinguniverse.com/company-histories/el-chico-restaurants-inc-history/accessed May 28, 2015.

21 Walsh, *The Tex-Mex Cookbook*, xix.

22 Jeffery Pilcher, *Planet Taco: A Global History of Mexican Food* (Oxford and New York: Oxford University Press, 2012), 131

23 For a history of the China Poblana dress see Kimberly Randall, "The Traveler's Eye: Chinas Poblanas and the European-Inspired Costume in Postcolonial Mexico," in *The Latin American Fashion Reader*, ed. Regina A. Root (Oxford and New York: Berg 2005), 44–65.

24 Walsh acknowledges, "The rise of the small, inexpensive restaurant in the post WWII era coincided with the emergence of a new cultural identity for Texas Mexicans" Walsh, *The Tex-Mex Cookbook*, 157.

25 Maria Herrera-Sobek, *Chicano Folklore: A Handbook* (Connecticut, Greenwood Press, 2006).

26 Rodolfo Acuña, *Occupied America: A History of Chicanos* (New York: Harper and Row, 1988), 320.

27 Walsh, *The Tex-Mex Cookbook,* 157–160.

28 David Beriss and David E. Sutton, *The Restaurants Book: Ethnographies of Where We Eat* (Oxford and New York: Berg, 2007).

29 Walsh, *The Tex-Mex Cookbook*, 160.

30 Pilcher, *Planet Taco*, 131.

31 Ibid.

32 Ibid.

33 Juanita Ceja interviewed by Steve Velasquez, Oct. 24, 2011.

34 Cellar Kitchen, "Colores de Mexico, Welcome Ceja Vineyards" (poster, National Museum of American History, 2004).

35 See "Recipes," Ceja Vineyards, https://www.cejavineyards.com/recipes accessed May 28, 2015.

10

Telling Cultural Stories through Food and Drink at the Southern Food and Beverage Museum

Elizabeth M. Williams

There aren't food museums everywhere. Unlike art museums, which can be found in most large communities, food museums are rare commodities. The Southern Food and Beverage Museum (SoFAB)[1] set out to create a museum that concentrates on the intersection of culture, food, and drink. The museum opened in 2008 in the Riverwalk Marketplace and, in 2013, moved to its current location in the Dryades Street Market, which was one of more than thirty public markets in New Orleans' once bustling market system. The goals were to create an educational and engaging museum that offered several experiences to visitors: interactivity, sensorial connection with museum content, and historical and cultural awareness through objects and stories about food and drink.

What is a food museum?

First, it is a cultural institution that self-identifies as a food or beverage museum. Second, it specializes in artifacts that are used in producing, gathering, preparing, eating, or disposing of food or drink; and, third, it focuses on cultural and social implications of food, such as hunger, tracing trade routes through evidence of food, or the growth of cities in relation to changing food supplies. Of course, many museums may certainly contain aspects of these purposes. And in fact there is evidence of increasing numbers of exhibits that focus on food and drink. The requirement to actually serve food and allow for the experience of tasting is not essential to a food museum. No one would expect to paint or sculpt in an art museum. But eating and drinking are essential to connecting with the museum's subject matter, so having tastings and other sensual contacts within the museum can definitely contribute to the visitors' experience and enjoyment of the visit.

Many visitors asked "What is Southern food?" SoFAB defines Southern food as the food eaten in the South. That means that Southern food is not only made up of the traditional foods associated with the historical South, like pork, corn, bourbon, cornbread, grits, and pecan pie, but also the food of recent immigrants trying to replicate the foods of home in their new Southern kitchens. This definition allows for the broadest exploration of Southern food, while at the same time recognizing that Southern food is continuously changing as new peoples move to the South and as American trends in food are adopted in the South. SoFAB's mission reflects this scope: "dedicated to the discovery, understanding and celebration of food, drink, and its related culture in America and the world."[2] This exploration of mission led the museum to decide that it would focus on the food and drink in the context of everyday culture. And that meant finding artifacts that illustrated that intersection, as well as planning culinary events and building new spaces for cooking and eating.

Sensory experience as curatorial practice

Although most museums do not encourage people to eat or drink inside the galleries, SoFAB celebrates eating and drinking. For example, an exhibit about nutcracker technology is greatly enhanced not only by looking at various nutcrackers, but by allowing the patrons to try different nutcrackers by cracking nuts that are supplied on a table in the exhibition. Seeing and smelling roasted chicory in a coffee exhibit was very popular, as was the ongoing vote on whether pure coffee or a coffee and chicory mixture was better. Samples are available for tasting.

The museum space provides an open floor plan with only four exterior walls to provide space for hanging. The building's history as a market lent a theme to the materials used in creating exhibits. The wall that was created to partially separate the kitchen from the museum was paneled with charred wood to evoke the inside of a barrel. Inside the museum are several barrels used to age bourbon, and even a used bourbon barrel where hot sauce is aged. And the overall organizational structure of the museum also reflects the building's market history. Large cans, wooden crates, and milk cartons are used throughout the museum as platforms for object display. The barriers between objects and visitors are subtle and do not feel like barriers. And

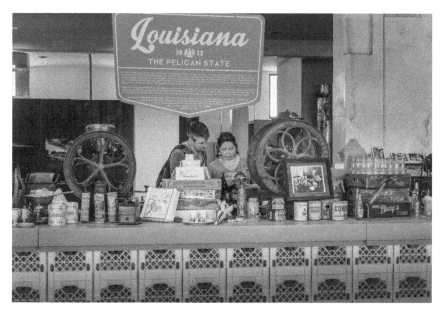

FIGURE 10.1 *The Louisiana Gallery, Southern Food and Beverage Museum.*
© *Stephen Binns.*

where possible, visitors can touch and actually manipulate cast iron pots, crank grinders and mills, and pick up objects to read labels and packaging.

One gallery section is dedicated to the development of the cocktail, featuring antique bottles, rare books and menus, and antique cocktail equipment. To protect artifacts without taking away the sense of intimacy with the objects, the museum staff placed bar highboys in front of the exhibit. The tops of the highboys were used to display additional artifacts, such as menus, napkins, and coasters, all covered with glass. Standing at the highboys, a visitor might feel as though this is a visit to a bar instead of a barrier to touching. Connecting the visitor with the object as opposed to presenting the object as an isolated subject of contemplation is a constant curatorial goal.

The demonstration kitchen and food programming

Before the construction of the demo kitchen, there were two categories of demonstrations at the museum. One type focused on cocktails and was held at Brunings Restaurant's nineteenth-century bar, the only furniture which survived Hurricane Katrina.[3] Some demonstrations, such as programming around absinthe, were related to changing exhibits, while others were merely seasonal or based on some other theme. They were conducted by bartenders, who usually emphasized techniques and flavor profiles, or by historians, who discussed the history of spirits or historical contexts, such as Prohibition. The bar was not functional so pitchers of water and containers of ice had to be placed on or around the bar, which was reminiscent of the limited conditions of nineteenth-century bars. From an interpretive perspective, this made the connection between the bar and the demonstrations "real," but it made using modern equipment quite difficult.

The other type of demonstrations involved cooking. In order to set up the cooking demonstrations, the museum created a custom demonstration table. The table was raised using castors—which also made it easier to move around— to approximately counter height. A large mirror was mounted on posts on either side of the table, in such a way that its tilt could be adjusted, making it possible for those sitting in the audience to see the action happening on the surface of the table. It also allowed the audience to see what was happening inside of the pots that were sitting on small propane burners and placed on the table. In these weekly demonstrations, the presenters were cookbook authors, local chefs, or staff members presenting a "how to" demonstration for cheese or homemade pasta. Sometimes, the demonstrations were related to an ongoing

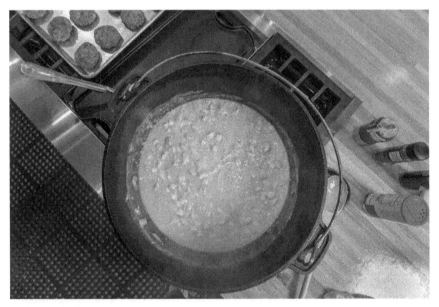

FIGURE 10.2 *Crawfish etouffee cooked in the demonstration kitchen, Rouses Culinary Innovation Center by Jenn-Air.*

© *Stephen Binns.*

exhibit, and sometimes they were seasonal or part of the educational program of the museum.

SoFAB spotlights various US states throughout the year. For example, in 2015, March was Mississippi month, so every demonstration was related to Mississippi and the Mississippi exhibit. In this context, chefs from Mississippi restaurants demonstrated dishes from their menus. For example, from Natchez, Regina Charboneau made her famous biscuits. In addition, a standing demonstration, "Taste of New Orleans," was featured every Monday, including New Orleans food, such as remoulade salad, jambalaya, and bananas Foster. While the food is cooking, the group is taken on a guided tour of the museum. When the tour is complete, the group sits down to eat jambalaya and bananas Foster before leaving. The success of the kitchen and demonstration area has raised the bar on the museum's ambitions. It is now clear that an outdoor kitchen with areas designated for eating, crawfish boils, turkey frying, barbecue, smoking, and outdoor bread baking is needed. Demonstrating historic techniques, introducing patrons to new flavors and food experiences, allowing patrons to learn more about how food is grown and prepared, making food science accessible and helping to make nutritional literacy more than just theoretical are all part of the museum's mission.

The museum's restaurant: Purloo

In the new museum building, a space was carved out for a restaurant and bar, Purloo, which would operate in support of the museum, under the guidance of Chef Ryan Hughes, who worked with the museum to develop a menu that reflected the food of the states represented in the museum. The menu was sophisticated and not traditional, featuring dishes such as "ancho glazed meatloaf with buttermilk mash, collard greens, red eye gravy," "fried catfish pistolette: slaw, tomato, pickles, Mississippi comeback sauce, petite salad," and "individual Alabama lane cakes: w/bourbon soaked pecans, raisins, coconut, chocolate sauce, coconut ice cream,"[4] and the food is presented in a modern style. This modern style manifests itself in plated food that is garnished with thinly sliced pickled okra and presented in a polished style—grits molded in a ring mold, for example.

The restaurant's bar is outfitted to function as a modern bar. As people enter the museum, they are encouraged to get a drink at the bar and to walk around with it. They are often offered food to nibble while they peruse the museum. And they can also eat when there is a demonstration in the demonstration kitchen. When there is a special exhibit or an opening, the chef produces a special menu. For example, when the permanent absinthe gallery opened in the museum, which reflects the history of absinthe drinking, in addition to serving absinthe in several ways for tasting in the gallery, the restaurant prepared a menu that included absinthe in each course.

Conclusions

The Southern Food and Beverage Museum is a museum with little precedent, which means that creating goals and solving problems are products of ongoing invention. It also means that the goals and procedures of the museum are in constant flux as visitor experiences are incorporated into the everyday practice of the institution. By displaying objects with care while allowing interaction in the gallery, it has been possible to allow eating and drinking in the museum without damaging the museum collection. Creating dishes with different local or regional ingredients, introducing historical equipment, and planning food demonstrations are as much a part of the educational mission of SoFAB as are the exhibits. Connecting the food and drink with the artifacts, and allowing visitors to eat in the museum makes the experience not only visual but also sensorial. Learning through experience makes the mechanics of tools, their materials, and their functionality manifest. Thus, SoFAB has come to realize that its best path in creating a meaningful visitor experience is to allow eating and drinking, controlled touching and interaction with the artifacts, and to present demonstrations that also create educational experiences.

Notes

1 The SoFAB has been recently renamed as the National Food and Beverage Foundation.
2 "About National Food and Beverage Foundation," *National Food and Beverage Foundation*, accessed January 28, 2016, http://natfab.org/southern-food-and-beverage/
3 For the background story, see "Bruning's Restaurant Bar Restored at the Southern Food and Beverage Museum," *New Orleans WWOZ*, accessed on January 28, 2016, http://www.wwoz.org/programs/new-orleans-all-way-live/brunings-restaurant-bar
4 "Menu," Puraloo, accessed on January 28, 2016, http://www.nolapurloo.com/menu/

11

Exhibiting the Food System at the American Museum of Natural History in New York City

Erin Betley and Eleanor Sterling

At the American Museum of Natural History (AMNH) in New York City, our mission is "to discover, interpret, and disseminate—through scientific research and education—knowledge about human cultures, the natural world, and the universe." As part of this mission, we explore topics of critical importance to contemporary society, recognizing the role of museums in informed engagement of visitors through exhibitions and public programs. Over the past several decades, the museum has taken on a series of exhibition topics of concern for society ranging from endangered species and genomics to water stewardship, energy use, and most recently, global food systems. In this chapter, we examine how the AMNH researched, developed, and displayed the content for *Our Global Kitchen: Food, Nature, Culture*, an exhibition which traces the complex and intricate food systems that bring what we eat from farm and fishhook to fork.

Developing a food exhibition: making choices and creating content

Our Global Kitchen[1] is a wide-ranging exhibition exploring issues related to food systems. Led by the curatorial team,[2] we conducted an expansive and in-depth research program, starting years in advance, on the six key themes of the exhibition: What is the role of human ingenuity in shaping food past, present, and future? How does food reflect and influence culture and identity?

What is the environmental impact of the food we eat? What is the role of food in human health? How does our sense of taste and flavor affect our food choices? And why is diversity in food important?

In the early planning stages, the scope for the exhibition was global and extended from deep time to the future of food. We considered developing a structure that followed the topic of food chronologically through time, certainly apt for a natural history museum, starting with a look at evidence for what human ancestors ate all the way through to what we will eat in the future. However, we realized that since visitors may be expecting this approach, it might not have the same ability to spur people to think deeply about the issues that an unconventional approach might engender. We therefore chose an unexpected route for a natural history museum, deciding to examine how food moves through the global food system from farm and fishhook to fork and beyond.

Drawing from the body of research we had assembled on the topic, we developed the framework of the exhibition by interweaving our six key themes through the major steps of many food systems: growing, trading and transporting, cooking, tasting, eating, and celebrating. Each of these six steps, along with an introductory section, translated into a separate area within the 8,300-square-foot (770-square-meters) exhibition space, to reinforce the architecture of food systems as visitors journeyed from section to section. We designed an immersive exhibition consisting of a range of objects, from historical artifacts from the museum's collection to cutting-edge kitchen tools, and interpretive approaches such as text and graphics, dioramas, interactive audiovisual content, and physical experiences such as food samples and scent-generating stations.

An exhibition tour: themes, objects, and experiences

Visitors enter the exhibition space through an introductory media section where iconic words, each reflecting the six key themes, along with lush photographs are projected onto five oversized five-foot (1.6-meters) radius circular screens. Visitors then turn a corner into a large narrated theater experience, anchored by whimsical seating of oversized fruits and vegetables, and designed to embed visitors in the steps of a food system and echo the six key themes of the exhibition. They are presented with information on the global challenge of feeding a projected nine billion people by 2050[3] and asked some deceptively simple questions: "What did you eat today, where does your food come from, and why does it matter?" The sections that follow provide visitors with clues as to why these basic questions matter ecologically, politically, socially, and culturally.

Growing food

The section on growing food traces food back to its origin, including themes such as raw ingredients, methods for growing food, diversity in food and food systems, and the future of growing. For this section, we wanted the visitors to think about the complexity of the food they eat every day, so we designed "Reshaping Our Foods: Where did our crops and farm animals come from?" Here, we explore the mechanics of natural and artificial selection and the ingenuity of countless farmers before us which resulted in foods that are easier to harvest and store, more resistant to pests and disease, and diverse in shapes, sizes, flavors, and nutritional content.

Here and in the following sections, we use engaging stories to communicate messages on many complex topics, such as the costs and benefits of modern crop breeding techniques, genetic engineering, the Green Revolution, and the consequences of overfishing on fish populations. For example, a display of models of varied and colorful Andean potato varieties pinpoints the origin of the familiar plant and aligns with the story of Parque de la Papa (Potato Park). The Park, comprising 22,000 acres (8.9 hectores) and six villages in the Peruvian Andes, aims to conserve the native habitats—and traditional growing methods—for about 900 varieties of potato.[4] This exhibition element also explores the trade-off of monoculture as exemplified by the Irish potato famine, which was triggered in part because potatoes grown in Ireland were mostly all one variety that was therefore vulnerable to diseases.

In addition, we also wanted to raise awareness about the diversity of ways of producing foods, often dependent on climate, geography, and human innovation. Mini-dioramas showcase how people in several places in the world have tackled the challenge of producing foods in diverse conditions. Through the stories of subsistence rice agriculture in Vietnam, oyster aquaculture in France, urban agriculture in Brazil, and multi-scale corn agriculture in Kenya and in the United States, visitors navigate the complexity of food production. We brought living organisms into the exhibition through a display of hydroponic plants[5] to anchor a section on "Conserving Diversity." Here visitors learn that humans have domesticated some 2,500 crops for human use but only use a small fraction for most of consumed food; and that 40 percent of the world's calories come from just three grains—wheat, rice, and corn—which make up 40 percent of our cropland.[6] While there are countless varieties of each of these species, the key to a resilient food system is diversity and a broad base from which we draw our food. Finally, visitors look to the future of growing, where we reinforce the message that we need a network of solutions and approaches to deal with the challenges of procuring food for a growing and urbanizing population, with a mix of tried and true systems with technology and innovations.

Trading and transporting food

All around the world, humans have been creative in coming up with ways to exchange, trade, and transport food. In the "Trading and transporting" section of the exhibition, visitors consider some of the unexpected ways that our global food economy operates as we follow food from the farm into the massive global distribution system. A diorama of a sixteenth-century Aztec market reinforces that the global food trade is ancient. Visitors see many foods that are familiar, such as tomatoes and corn, and note the absence of many foods such as chicken, wheat, and dairy products, that only made their introduction through the massive changes wrought by trade between the Old and New Worlds, beginning in the late fifteenth century.

Today, the movement of food is more complex than ever, and policy, economics, and culture collide to help determine who eats what. Visitors explore modern trade stories on a large wall map and trace four food items around the world through an interactive audiovisual kiosk, "Food Ships," where they discover how bananas travel from Central and South America to far away markets, and why apples from Washington State are so prevalent in New York City markets. A critical and often-overlooked externality is the pervasive issue of food loss and waste. This theme is explored in depth in a display that

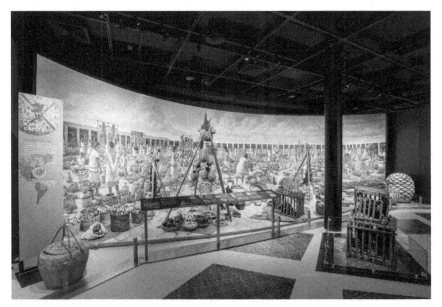

FIGURE 11.1 *Diorama of Tlatelolco market serving the capital city of the thriving Aztec Empire in the early sixteenth century.*

Photograph by D. Finnin © American Museum of Natural History, 2012.

includes a text and graphics panel examining various causes for waste and loss in high and lower income countries, along with a sculpture that illustrates the over three-quarters of a ton (750 kg) of food wasted by a typical family of four in the United States every year.[7] This amount represents just consumer waste—even more food is lost on farms and in processing and transportation. The accompanying panel explores solutions, such as improving food storage and distribution systems in lower income countries and the development of secondary markets and food recovery programs in higher income countries.

Engaging visitors: cooking, eating, and celebrating foods in the museum

In the next section of the exhibition, visitors explore cooking as a dynamic expression of human creativity. Through wall-mounted exhibits, we feature tools, techniques, and cookbooks involved in all types of cooking, from fermentation and preservation to molecular gastronomy. We explore the culture of cooking through five exhibits drawn from AMNH collections representing different places and moments in time. We highlight the following: China's Han Dynasty, where, 2,000 years ago, people developed cooking tools that are still in use—pots made of earthenware, bronze, and even cast iron; the central role of corn in the Americas hundreds of years ago; Korea and the longstanding tradition of kimchi making; and Morocco, where we explore the influence of African, European, and Arabic cultural traditions. In addition, a six-foot (1.8-meter) backdrop depicts the kitchen in the Chenonceau castle in France's Loire Valley, where copper pots were used to create classic French dishes. For each display, custom scent-generating stations produce the smells of ginger, lemons, and garlic, among other scents chosen to reflect the content of the exhibition, to immerse visitors in a multisensory experience. In the center of the section is a one-of-a-kind interactive audiovisual display, a projected table where visitors "cook" four virtual meals from around the world: groundnut soup in Africa, tamales in the Americas, poached eggs and hollandaise sauce in France, and grilled salmon with peaches in the US. As visitors proceed through each recipe step by step, they learn about the science and chemistry of cooking and about the culture that created the dish.

The exhibition's section on "Tasting food" comprises a working kitchen, a first for the AMNH, where staff distributed food samples as part of a comprehensive programming schedule with rotating themes,[8] including activities such as taste tests, demonstrations of various cooking methods, and guest visits by local farmers and chefs. For example, during the Chinese New Year, Grace Young used the kitchen to demonstrate stir fry techniques to visitors,

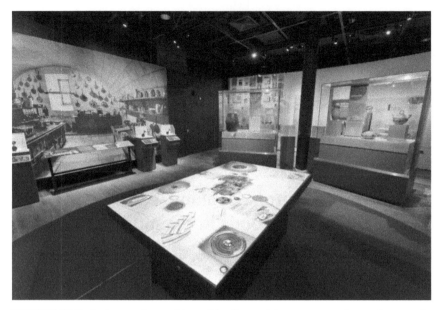

FIGURE 11.2 *An interactive cooking table allows visitors to create four unique meals. Photograph by D. Finnin © American Museum of Natural History, 2012.*

while during the week focused on honey, chef Jason Wood and apiary expert Rodney Dow from Glynwood Farm in New York State talked about the wonders of bees and honey in the kitchen, while distributing samples of local honey.

As visitors are experiencing food, they can learn more about their own bodies through two taste experiments. In one experiment, visitors are asked to identify the flavor of a jellybean while pinching their nose closed. They find the task to be impossible because unlike the five basic *tastes* detected by the tongue, the *flavor* of a food is detected by receptors in the nasal cavity. Once visitors released their nose, the flavor of strawberry or cherry immediately registered, prompting many expressions of surprise and delight. In the second experiment, visitors performed a diagnostic genetic test by tasting a piece of paper treated with a safe chemical that activates one of the twenty-five different bitter receptors in humans. Finally, in a series of eight exhibits set along the outside walls of the kitchen, we explore the influence of biology, cultural context, prior experience with food, and evolution on perception of foods.

As they move into the "Eating" section, visitors explore the intersection between food, health, and culture. "Iconic Meals" features three life-sized dioramas, where visitors can sit down with noted personalities, past and present, to simulate sharing opulent appetizers with the first empress of ancient Rome, Livia Drusilla, explore the ancient fusion cuisine of the court of Kublai

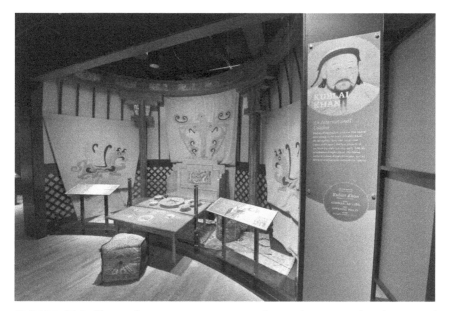

FIGURE 11.3 *Flavors from eastern, western, and central Asia mixed at the court of Kublai Khan, the Mongolian ruler who conquered China and became the first emperor of the Yuan Dynasty (AD 1271–1368). No menus survive from Khan's court, so this meal was pieced together from an imperial cookbook published not long after his reign, titled* Proper and Essential Things for the Emperor's Food and Drink *(Buell and Andersen 2010).*

Photo by D. Finnin © American Museum of Natural History, 2012.

Khan, and enjoy ice cream with Jane Austen before the age of refrigeration. Smaller exhibits tell other stories, including the interplay between eating and exercise through to Michael Phelps' famous Olympic-sized breakfast, Ötzi the iceman's last meal from 5000 years ago, Gandhi's favorite vegetarian foods, and the home cooking of Kenyan Nobel Peace Prize recipient Wangari Maathai.

A wall-mounted graphic panel titled "Too Much/Too Little" explores the twin challenges of undernourishment and overweight and obesity around the world. A video display, "Thoughts on the Future of Food," features the perspectives of various experts[9] on key issues relating to industrial food systems, including the impact of climate change, technology in agriculture, and sustainable food production for a growing population. Visitors also had a chance to add their own content to this section, through an interactive kiosk called "What Does Food Mean to You?" highlighting visitor photos submitted through Instagram, celebrating the moments in life marked with food. Finally, a graphic panel explores some underutilized foods that may figure more prominently in our future diets, including some 2,000 species of insects as high protein options that require less land, water, and food than animals raised for meat.

In the final section of the exhibition on "Celebrating food," we explore food's role in how we celebrate with friends, family, and even with complete strangers. Cases of artifacts tell vivid stories of "Feeding the Spirit," through harvest celebrations and artifacts of death and rebirth. The highlight of this section is the "Celebrations Theater," where visitors feel immersed in the sights and sounds of celebrations projected on a large, rectangular screen. Filmed specifically for this exhibition, the featured celebrations focus on the many significant roles that food plays in cultural events including the Hindu festival celebrating the birthday of the deity Ganesh Chathurthi; Oktoberfest in Munich; and the Chinese New Year and the secular holiday of Thanksgiving in the US as seen through the eyes of a local multi-cultural family.

Conclusion

Our Global Kitchen: Food, Nature, Culture was an ambitious exhibition, presented during a time of tremendous interest in the topic of food in general. The curatorial team, working in conjunction with numerous departments from across the museum, succeeded, through the exhibition and supporting programming,[10] in creating an immersive visitor experience that traces the complex and intricate food systems that bring what we eat from farm and fishhook to fork and beyond. Through sections on growing, trading and transporting, cooking, tasting, eating, and celebrating food, visitors considered key themes relating to human ingenuity in shaping food past, present, and future; food's relationship with culture and identity; the environmental impact of the food we eat; the role of food in human health; the impact of our sense of taste and flavor on our food choices; and the diversity of food. The integration of rigorous content vetting and interactive and compelling design elements resulted in an exhibition that was at times whimsical, surprising, reflective, and impactful, and we hope that this exploration of our experience will be useful for professionals developing food-related content in museums and other cultural institutions.

Notes

1   The exhibition was open at the AMNH from November 2012 until August 2013, and has traveled around the US, at the Museum of Science (Boston, MA), the History Colorado Center (Denver, CO), the National Geographic Museum (Washington, DC), and the Bullock Museum (Austin, TX).

2 *Our Global Kitchen: Food, Nature, Culture* was curated by Dr. Eleanor Sterling and Dr. Mark Norell.

3 United Nations Department of Economic and Social Affairs, "World Population Prospects: The 2012 Revision," *United Nations,* http://esa.un.org/wpp/index.htm accessed June 12, 2015.

4 Alejandro Argumendo, "The Potato Park, Peru: Conserving agrobiodiversity in an Andean Indigenous Biocultural Heritage Area," in *Values of Protected Landscapes and Seascapes*, edited by Thora Amend, Jessica Brown, Ashish Kothari, Adrian Phillips, and Sue Stolton (Heidelberg: Kaspareg Verlag, BTZ & IUCN), 45–58.

5 In conjunction with the exhibition, the entrance to the American Museum of Natural History's Judy and Josh Weston Pavilion featured an 18-foot-tall (5.5 meter) hydroponic vertical growing system designed and maintained by Windowfarms. The 280-plant installation and a smaller unit in the exhibition gallery grew a variety of fruits, vegetables, and herbs to showcase sustainable growing techniques and agricultural biodiversity in increasingly urban habitats.

6 Food and Agriculture Organization of the United Nations Statistics Division, "FAOSTAT," *Food and Agriculture Organization of the United Nations,* http://faostat3.fao.org/home accessed June 12, 2015.

7 Jean C. Buzby, Jeffrey Hyman, Hayden Stewart, and Hodan F. Wells, "The Value of Retail- and Consumer-Level Fruit and Vegetable Losses in the United States," *Journal of Consumer Affairs* 45, no. 3 (2011): 492–515.

8 Rotating themes included: apples; bread making; cookies, gingerbread houses, and holiday treats; healthy eating for children and adults; chocolate; coffee; cheese; pasta and noodles; teas, grains and granolas; international cooking, Aztec market; bees and honey, jams and jellies; ice cream and frozen treats; pickling; five borough tasting with seasonal foods from each NYC borough; and gazpacho.

9 Experts included Robert Lawrence (Center for a Livable Future, Johns Hopkins School of Public Health) Roseline Remans (Columbia University), and Amy Bentley (New York University), among others.

10 Given the tremendous scope of *Our Global Kitchen*, the AMNH exhibition development team worked to supplement the exhibition material with a comprehensive portfolio of digital assets, educational materials including an Educator's Guide, and educational programming. The curatorial team worked with the AMNH Education Department to create a series of public programs targeted to diverse audiences of adults, youth, teachers, and families to extend and complement the content of the exhibition with high impact programming that was hailed as innovative, dynamic, and informative.

PART THREE

Food and Audience Engagement

12

People's Genius and Creativity:

Folklife Festival Foodways at a Living, Outdoor Museum

James I. Deutsch

When Ralph Rinzler and James Morris produced the first Festival of American Folklife (FAF) in July 1967, they deliberately sought to expand the scope and repertoire of existing folk festivals in the United States. The FAF's predecessors, such as the Mountain Dance and Folk Festival (established in 1928), National Folk Festival (1934), and Newport Folk Festival (1959), focused primarily on music and performance. And although music and performance have always been important components of the FAF—which changed its name in 1998 to the Smithsonian Folklife Festival—it differentiated itself from similar events in several significant ways: 1) it used the term *folklife*, rather than *folk* or *folklore*, to underscore its presentation of not simply verbal or oral traditions, but rather "the total folk-culture as seen in all of its ramifications and expressions, verbal, material, and spiritual";[1] 2) it highlighted crafts traditions and foodways as vital signifiers of every group's material culture and cultural identity; and 3) it regarded itself as a living, outdoor museum without walls, which would complement the more static, indoor museums of the Smithsonian Institution that circumscribed the Festival's location on the National Mall of the United States. Following the original mission of the Smithsonian Institution, which was established in 1846 "to promote the increase and diffusion of knowledge," the Festival (in the words of a former director of the Center for Folklife and Cultural Heritage, which produces the annual event) has been "an optimistic exercise of cultural democracy," which allows "the voices of the people who gather each summer—in all their diversity—to celebrate and understand their cultural heritage. The Festival embodies a very powerful cultural dialogue that benefits the public and participants alike."[2]

The FAF's creation in 1967 began with S. Dillon Ripley (the Smithsonian Secretary from 1964 to 1984) wanting to make not only the Smithsonian Institution more relevant (a key word in the 1960s), but also the National Mall more lively. Ripley and James Morris, head of what was then the Smithsonian Division of Performing Arts and formerly director of the short-lived American Folk Festival in North Carolina, hired Ralph Rinzler to help produce the FAF. As the Newport Folk Festival's director of field research, Rinzler had conducted fieldwork in many traditional communities and knew that their crafts and food traditions were as important as musical performances in conveying the folklife and identities of those communities. Rinzler himself played the banjo and mandolin, but had tremendous appreciation for the cultural significance of food. As he explained in one of the early Festival program books, "the preparation of food is frequently the most persistent of cultural traits, lasting among the descendants of immigrants long after language, song, dance, religious and secular rituals have been eradicated or thoroughly diluted ... Just as folk communities have had their blacksmiths, basket-makers, bards, and professional musicians to play for weddings and feast days, medicine shows, and juke joints, they also have their culinary specialists. The techniques involved in the preparation of food, like those of craftsmen and instrumentalists, are passed on from one generation to another by word of mouth and simple imitation."[3]

Rinzler became director of the FAF in 1968 and remained active in the production of every Festival thereafter until his death in 1994. His legacy continues in the sense that a foodways component is now taken for granted at each year's Folklife Festival, even to the point of a specific program devoted entirely to food culture in 2005. Festival organizers support the notion that traditional food customs (i.e., what people eat, how they prepare it, how they present it, and how they consume it) are important signifiers of community culture and identity. This case study explores the presentation and interpretation of foodways for the FAF's first ten years, culminating in the unprecedented (and never again equaled) twelve-week Festival to mark the bicentennial of the United States in 1976. During these years the Festival has demonstrated that the presentation of foodways is one of the best multisensory means not only for engaging audiences, but also for demonstrating in a tangible (and tasty) way a traditional community's identity, heritage, and contemporary relevance.

The Folklife Festival as a living, outdoor museum

The Smithsonian Folklife Festival is the most prominent and popular event taking place each year within the borders of the National Mall of the United

States in Washington, D.C. The Mall is administered by the US National Park Service—the same federal agency that maintains and preserves national parks, monuments, historic sites, and recreation areas in the United States. It is where Martin Luther King Jr. declared his dream in 1963, where large protest marches and demonstrations regularly take place, and where millions of people stood in below-freezing temperatures to watch the presidential inauguration of Barack Obama in 2009. With the US Capitol on the eastern end, the Lincoln Memorial on the western end, the Washington Monument and National World War II Memorial in the center, and several museums of the Smithsonian Institution on both north and south, the National Mall is arguably the nation's most important civic space. The Folklife Festival almost always takes place during the days just before and after the Fourth of July, which is the nation's most important civic holiday.

Because of its strategic location on the National Mall, the Festival is often seen as an extension of the Smithsonian museums; and in several instances exhibitions and programs inside the museums have complemented the programs at the Festival. However, *festival* and *museum* have different connotations. According to Smithsonian legend, Secretary Ripley told Rinzler to "take the instruments out of their cases and let them sing"—meaning that the Folklife Festival should not only demonstrate the utility and vitality of the Smithsonian's collections of musical instruments (most of which were locked lifelessly and soundlessly inside museum exhibition cases and vitrines), but should also present the sights and sounds of diverse living musicians, crafts demonstrators, and cooks—and thus the relevance of their cultural heritage. According to one interpretation, "Museum is a noun, the Festival is a verb," which thus contrasts the Festival's vitality and dynamism with the static nature of museums, where permanent exhibitions may remain on display for twenty years.[4] The programs at the Folklife Festival are never static, but rather change from year to year. For instance, the 1971 Festival featured the occupational traditions of bakery and confectionery workers, meat cutters and butchers, glass bottle blowers, and iron workers; the performance traditions of Cajun music, Caribbean music and dance, country music, Puerto Rican music and dance, blues, jubilees, ragtime, rock and roll, rhythm and blues, shouts, work songs, and old-time banjo and fiddle music; and the folklife of Ohioans and Native Americans from the Northwest Coast. In 1972, a completely different set of participants came to Washington, including the occupational traditions of carpenters, molders, joiners, lithographers, and photoengravers; the performance traditions of Chicago blues, old-time country blues, gospel, and fiddlers; and the folklife of Native Americans from the Southwest. Each and every year, one of the key goals is to promote mutual understanding between Festival participants and Festival visitors through "cultural conversations," in which the two groups speak directly to each other in their own voices. The objective is to promote cooperative learning, rather than to rely exclusively on the expertise of Smithsonian curators, which is much more the norm for the exhibitions displayed inside the Smithsonian's four-walled museums.

Foodways at the Festival

The very first FAF in 1967 did not feature foodways demonstrations, but this omission was quickly corrected. As Rinzler later explained, "Food traditions were incorporated into the Festival of American Folklife in 1968. In each year's planning, we invariably went to community leaders to discuss how they would like to design this component of their cultural program. This question always provoked thought and often involved complex problem solving."[5] Thus in 1968, there were daily demonstrations of butter churning, candy making, sorghum making, and Mexican-style cooking from southern Texas. In 1969, the FAF featured "Corn Culture" as one of its themes, which meant that there was corn milling by machine from North Carolina, corn milling by hand from Texas, and the demonstration of a corn whiskey still from North Carolina. The program book for the 1970 Festival—which featured the state of Arkansas—was the first to include entire articles focusing on foodways. For instance, in Robert "Mack" McCormick's impressionistic report on one night of fieldwork in Hughes, Arkansas, local residents tell him about wild watercress and the scuppernong wine that is made from wild grapes growing in a thicket. McCormick is advised, "If you come back in the right time of year I could carry you out in the bottoms and show you how to find some of the best food you'd ever put in your mouth."[6] And on the following pages, Ruth Moore Malone's guide to "appetizing traditions" provided recipes for stack cake, roast wild duck, Arkansas rice dressing, catfish and hushpuppies, strawberry shortcake, Ozark fried chicken, Ozark apple pudding, sorghum gingerbread, country cured ham with red-eye gravy, hominy grits, Brunswick stew, corn pudding, and persimmon pudding.[7] A critic for the *Washington Post* that year reported enthusiastically on the ways in which Festival visitors learned about culture through foodways: "Blintzes, buffalo meat and black-eyed peas tell the food story of the three cultural attractions represented at the [1970 FAF]. A food tour through the festival provides the opportunity to taste authentic American Indian dishes, Southern cooking from Arkansas and dairy products involving such things as milking cows, churning, cheesemaking and baking. The three areas are separated, giving one the opportunity of walking off the calories and digesting one cuisine, while heading off to try another."[8]

Over the next several years of Folklife Festivals, the presentation of food traditions continued to increase. In 1971, the state of Ohio sent members of

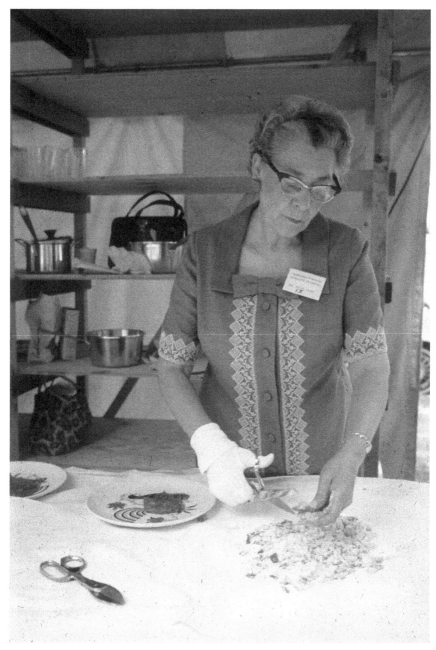

FIGURE 12.1 *Mrs. Russell Cartee of Kentucky prepares sassafras candy at the 1968 Festival of American Folklife.*

Courtesy of Ralph Rinzler Folklife Archives and Collections, Smithsonian Institution.

Amish, Greek, Italian, and Serbian communities to prepare distinctive dishes, as well as makers of apple butter, bagels, cheese, soul food, sourdough, and maple-sugar candies. In 1972, Greek food and Southwest cooking vied with Apache piki and Isleta bread. Kentucky was the featured state in 1973, which brought traditional recipes for foods prepared "at family reunions, community picnics, and dinners-on-the-ground observed by many rural Kentucky church groups. The butter, home-butchered meats, deviled eggs, pastries, and home-produced vegetables cooked according to time-honored recipes, are as much a part of the folk process as the Nine Patch quilt or the handmade comfort."[9] The 1974 FAF brought foodways of Americans with roots in Finland, Ghana, Greece, Norway, Sweden, Trinidad and Tobago, and Tunisia, as well as cookers of catfish and fried chicken from Mississippi, which was that year's featured state. In 1975, with the Festival looking ahead to a massive celebration of the 1976 bicentennial, the presentation of foodways was even more elaborate. From the Northern Plains came blood pudding, sauerkraut, and fruit preserves. From Japanese Americans came sushi and *mocha-tsuki*. Italian Americans demonstrated the preparation of pasta, polenta, pastries, and sausages. In the area of the Festival devoted to the African Diaspora, there was a garden where okra, turnips, and other root vegetables were growing. The Native American area had demonstrations of fry bread, corn, and sassafras tea.

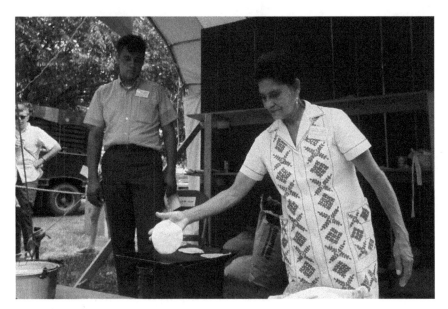

FIGURE 12.2 *Maria Luisa Ochoa from the Navajo Nation of Arizona demonstrates cooking techniques at the 1969 Festival of American Folklife.*

Photograph by Diana Davies, courtesy of Ralph Rinzler Folklife Archives and Collections, Smithsonian Institution.

The 1976 FAF lasted all summer—opening on June 16 and closing on September 6—with participants rotating in and out for two weeks at a time. Much like the 1975 Festival, there were five distinct cultural presentations— Native Americans, African Diaspora, Old Ways in the New World, Regional Americans, and Working Americans—each with their own foodways traditions. A corn field formed a circle around the Native American location, with beans and squash sharing the area to demonstrate the "three sisters" of many Native groups. The African Diaspora area brought Alabama barbequed pork, Haitian grilled fish, Louisiana gumbo, Nigerian fried meat, Senegalese rice, and Trinidadian sweet-potato cakes. Old Ways in the New World and Regional Americans featured bagels and knishes, falafel and baklava, bratwurst and *schenkeli*, jambalaya and tourtière, corn beef and cabbage, gazpacho and sangria. And Working Americans highlighted the occupational cultures of bakers, bartenders, dairy farmers, ice carvers, meat cutters, produce workers, ranchers, waiters, and waitresses.

Reviewing the 1976 FAF was Marian Burros, soon to become the influential cookbook author and columnist for the *New York Times*, but then a food writer at the *Washington Post*. "The festival is a gourmand's paradise," Burros proclaimed. "Food at the festival is America the Melting Pot at its best—a little bit of a lot of things, all of them interesting." She even described the way in which the Festival attracted two types of eaters: "Those who are fearful of tasting something new and eat hot dogs and hamburgers no matter what, and those who come especially for the ethnic food." Burros's sympathies were clearly with the latter group, but she noted that both groups "go away happy" because "[t]here is something for everyone to eat . . . and if you don't find what you want one week, wait; there will be something new the week after." [10]

Similar observations were expressed by Festival staff members—including Rinzler and several of his program coordinators—who gathered ten days after the 1974 FAF closed. According to notes found in the Smithsonian Archives, "The meeting started with comments from Sue [Roschwalb] about what she found was the public's reaction towards the food on the Mall. The ethnic foods had a very favorable reaction. People like to eat the foods and they come to sample the foods. Foods can be an important item, through recepies [sic] placed in food magazines we can reach an audience not otherwise available. When Sue had VIP tours and someone wanted to try some food, there was always a line." [11]

More than forty years have passed since that staff meeting, but Folklife Festival planners today still share many of those same concerns. They seek to uphold the Smithsonian's mission "to promote the increase and diffusion of knowledge" by educating the public about community identity, tradition, and diversity. Moreover, they have learned that members of the public are regularly

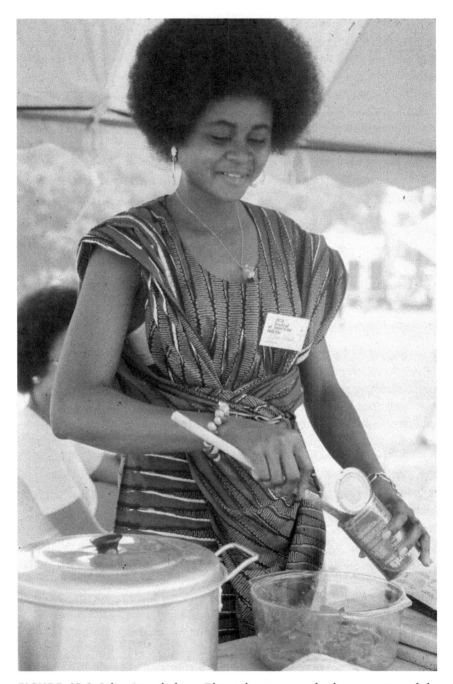

FIGURE 12.3 *Juliet Amoah from Ghana demonstrates foodways as part of the African Diaspora program at the 1974 Festival of American Folklife.*

Photograph by Reed and Susan Erskine, courtesy of Ralph Rinzler Folklife Archives and Collections, Smithsonian Institution.

fascinated with foodways, in part because eating (if not also cooking) are daily activities with which everyone has firsthand experience.

The Smithsonian's experience suggests that foodways can help make the exotic familiar, thereby strengthening cross-cultural connections and dialogue. One anecdote from the African Diaspora program at the 1975 FAF nicely demonstrates this principle. As described in a *Washington Post* article: "Out in the marketplace, two pots of black-eyed peas are being ladled out to the public. One of the recipes is Ghanaian and includes pieces of fish, palm oil and red peppers. 'It tastes just like the stuff I've been eating all my life,' says a surprised black American. A woman peers curiously at the cup of Afro-American beans she has just been handed. 'What is it?' she asks Lynn Whitfield. 'Black-eyed peas,' says Mrs. Whitfield. 'What do you call it?' the woman insists, expecting an exotic name. 'Black-eyed peas, ma'am,' is the patient response. 'Oh,' says the startled black woman. 'Black-eyed peas.'"[12] In other words, black-eyed peas in Ghana taste just like black-eyed peas in the United States.

Promoting this type of mutual understanding through direct "cultural conversations" has been one of the great strengths of the Smithsonian's Folklife Festival. But it is also the type of experience that can be replicated at other outdoor festivals, as well as at historic homes, historic farms, and history museums. Making these sorts of personal connections does not require digital interactivity or any form of technological mediation. Rather it is simply bringing people together face-to-face to learn from one another in ways that education has worked for centuries, if not millennia.

The words of the FAF's first director continue to resonate. Speaking to a reporter from the *Washington Post* shortly before the 1973 Festival, Rinzler reflected, "When people think of national celebrations like the Bicentennial, they usually think in terms of things like world fairs . . . They think of politics, hardware, buildings, projects, parks, incredible constructions." But we at the Smithsonian Institution are "trying to say it's people, their passions and loves: making a pot, cooking a bit of food. We're talking about people's genius and creativity."[13] That's some serious food for thought.

Notes

1   Don Yoder, "Folklore and Folklife," in *Festival of American Folklife 1968*, ed. Ruri Sakai (Washington: Smithsonian Institution, 1968), 9.

2   Richard Kurin, *Smithsonian Folklife Festival: Culture Of, By, and For the People* (Washington: Smithsonian Institution, 1998), 3.

3   Ralph Rinzler, "Bagel-Making in Ohio," in *1971 Festival of American Folklife*, ed. Peter Greenwood (New York: Music Sales Corp., 1971), 8.

4   Kurin, *Smithsonian Folklife Festival*, 30.

5   Ralph Rinzler, "Foreword," in Katherine S. Kirlin and Thomas M. Kirlin, *Smithsonian Folklife Cookbook* (Washington: Smithsonian Institution Press, 1991), viii–ix.

6   Mack McCormick, "Mister, Can You Tell Me Where This Road Goes?" in *1970 Festival of American Folklife*, ed. William O. Craig (Washington: Smithsonian Institution, 1970), 8.

7   Ruth Moore Malone, "Appetizing Traditions of Arkansas," in *1970 Festival of American Folklife*, 10–13.

8   Vicki Ostrolenk, "Blintzes and Buffalo Meat," *Washington Post*, 5 July 1970, H2.

9   Lynwood Montell, "Folklife in Kentucky," in *1973 Festival of American Folklife*, ed. Gerald L. Davis and Ralph Rinzler (Washington: Smithsonian Institution, 1973), 11.

10   Marian Burros, "The Food at the Folklife Festival: Something for Everyone," *Washington Post*, 22 July 1976, F6.

11   Minutes, Food Meeting, 24 July 1974. Post '74 Festival. African Diaspora Site Plans, Key Meeting. Smithsonian Institution Archives, Washington, DC.

12   Joel Dreyfuss, "Cultural Parallels at the Diaspora," *Washington Post*, 4 July 1975, D3.

13   Tom Zito, "Their Passions, Genius, Creativity," *Washington Post*, 24 June 1973, K1.

13

Feasting on History in Toronto's Fort York National Historic Site

Irina D. Mihalache in conversation with
Elizabeth Baird, Rosemary Kovac
and Bridget Wranich[1]

Historian Carl Benn calls Fort York National Historic Site "Toronto's most important historic site. It is the spot where the British founded urban Toronto in 1793 ... Today, its defensive walls enclose Canada's largest collection of original War of 1812 buildings."[2] The Fort was named a historic site museum in 1934, to celebrate the centennial of the 1834 incorporation of Toronto, opening to the public in the same year, on Victoria Day.[3] Currently, the Fort and its 17 hectares are part of a heritage conservation district, located in the midst of downtown Toronto, surrounded by new condominium buildings, the Gardiner Expressway[4] and the CN Tower. At Fort York, visitors can find a richness of public programming, ranging from artillery firing and battle tactics performed by the Fort York Guard, hands-on living history experiences for students, conferences, and exhibitions. One type of programming that makes the Fort unique in the Toronto region is the Foodways Programme, coordinated by Bridget Wranich and ran entirely by a group of volunteer historic cooks, among which are Elizabeth Baird and Rosemary Kovac. Every week, volunteers get together in the Fort's kitchen to research, test, and prepare recipes for culinary workshops, cooking demonstrations, ceremonies, and for the two annual events, *Queen Charlotte's Ball* and *Mad for Marmalade*. The team of volunteers has developed a line of historic baked goods and preserves which visitors can purchase in the Fort's gift store, the Canteen.

Developing a historic foodways programme

Irina D. Mihalache (IDM)　*How did the Foodways Programme start and how has it changed?*

Bridget Wranich (BW)　The program was developed in mid-1980s based on the American foodways programs that were in existence, in particular Colonial Williamsburg but we wanted to get away from "oatmeal cookies and brown bread"[5] to tell a well-researched story. Around that time, everybody started making what they thought was old fashioned, but they weren't really doing the research. I think one of the things that changed was the availability of cookbooks. Truly, our research was limited but the development of Google Books and libraries going online, opened up a plethora of new recipes and new information for us. Programming changed as well. We began to do more specific research projects, in particular a Georgian Dinner as a fundraiser for The Friends of Fort York. We started to get a little more focused in what we did, so we did not just operate a general and broad program. That still happened, but on a smaller scale, as we started to get more specialized, is the best way to put it. Then, we started to develop some special events that were more specific as well. So *Queen Charlotte's Ball*, which has a Georgian supper, and then *Mad for Marmalade*, which took us a little further out of our historic realm. So, to sum up, the new volunteer corps, the availability of cookbooks, more specific programming has brought the program out of the four walls of the historic kitchen and it developed into multiple ways of telling the story of the Fort. The story is still there. It's just we've learned to tell it through different forms.

Elizabeth Baird (EB)　I think what was happening in the historic kitchen has evolved, especially as we started to make baking available for special occasions within the Fort, such as citizenship ceremonies, festivals, and symposiums. But also, more important, is that we've added our products to the Canteen. So, people can taste for example, a Little Fine Cake in the historic kitchen, and then on their way out, they can buy some Little Fine Cakes that we have made in our kitchens. And, if they really like the Little Fine Cakes, the Shrewsbury Cakes or the Strawberry Jam or the other things that we make from Georgian recipes, they can buy our cookbook.[6] And that was the other way in which we've expanded the Fort beyond its walls. We decided on a defined area of expertise, which was what was served in terms of sweets, drinks, and preserves at the Fort in the nineteenth century. And all this knowledge became "Setting a Fine Table," because we wanted visitors to know that there was a "fine table" that was created here for the officers.

A community of volunteers

IDM *What does the training involve and how does one become a volunteer? I'd be interested to know what keeps your volunteers here.*

BW I think it's the site itself. I think a lot of them fall in love with the site. They feel protected, they feel it's theirs. They want to tell the story, they feel it's very important. I know most of the volunteers have a strong emotional connection to the site. And that's what keeps them. The training itself is long and tedious: It means a lot of reading, it means getting familiar with the cookbooks of the era, getting familiar with how to test a recipe. Some people are not as interested in some parts as others and we've allowed that to happen as I think people have their abilities and their expertise.

IDM *So you get to know them, know what they're best at.*

BW I get to know them, what they're best at, what they like and what they don't. Some people prefer being in the historic kitchen setting, with the open hearth fire and the historic equipment, making the recipes and serving them to people as they come through the kitchen. And there's a lot of training involved: How to cook over the open fire; what recipes work in order to make and serve right away to the public. Not all recipes are conducive to that. So through our testing, which takes time, we know what things work. The next ingredient is familiarity with the cookbooks, techniques, how to test, how to fill out testing sheets, and how to work together. We work very hard to make a team. There are always individuals who want to do their thing and we let them do that but we do in the end still pull them back to the team. So when we're working on a recipe, we encourage discussion. Why didn't this work? "Well, I thought I did this, but maybe I did this." The other important part of the training is knowing the site and understanding the overall Toronto history and context. So, where do we fit in, why are we here, and why are we doing this? They need to understand the broader story as well.

Rosemary Kovac (RK) Lots of people say "well, I love to cook." That's not the point here. You've got to be a historian as well.

EB The training, the quality. That struck me as well, you're expected to know how to do these things. And people like Rosemary have been very helpful in keeping up that quality.

BW Quality is important and visible in how you animate in the kitchen, how you talk to the public, how you cook the food that you serve. If the food that you serve is not the best, then you're not giving the opportunity to the visitor to experience the food as it should be. Yes, you can make something and it burns or it scorches, but you can't serve that. You can talk about it. We will talk to the public about our mistakes, that's all part of the evolution of the recipe. We sometimes even show them the burnt pie or the scorched cake, but you can't serve that because they'll remember that. In the modern kitchen, quality matters as well. Because of this, we even taking the modern food handling courses through the City of Toronto. We are a kitchen that is inspected by food inspectors. You have to be professional. We run the kitchen like a commercial kitchen but with historic food research as our objective.

Historic recipes, adaptation and authenticity

EB   I just want to say something about the recipes that we make. There has to be sometimes a bit of tweaking in order to work with current ingredients. But the recipes that are cooked, sold in the Canteen or served at events like the Georgian Dinner or in the historic kitchen are not compromised by "oh, I think it would taste better if we added a little more of this" or "why don't we use raisins instead of currants." That was one of the things that impressed me.

IDM   *Have you developed an instinct for recipes that might not work?*

RK   When you listen to people saying "it doesn't work" we say, "well, your ingredients are not going to be the same as fifty or a hundred years ago. Your flour won't be the same." The ingredients don't work. The milling is different; it's quite fascinating.

IDM   *If you don't have access to that flour, do you decide not to put that recipe out?*

RK   Yes, sometimes we don't put the recipe out but sometimes we just have to go with what we have at hand.

BW   Sometimes, we'll decide to try a softer flour if it's a British recipe. We know, for example, that their flour was softer, so we'll try a cake and pastry flour. We'll experiment as much as we can with what we have available today. But as Elizabeth and Rosemary will agree, not all recipes are created equal. Some recipes are just bad. They may be in a cookbook but just because they're in a cookbook doesn't mean they're good recipes. And I think there have been times when we've all beaten ourselves up because we could not get a recipe to work because we really wanted to include it. Shortbread's a perfect example. We wanted to have a Georgian shortbread. Not possible. Too stodgy, too much flour, not enough butter. We tried multiple recipes.

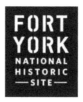

Canadian War Cake

Cookbook:
Clergue, Gertrude, Clergue Harrison, Grace, Allied Cookery: British, French, Italian, Belgian, Russian. (New York: G. P. Putnam's Sons, The Knickerbocker Press, 1916), pg. 92.

Original recipe:
Two cups brown sugar, 2 cups hot water, 2 tablespoons lard, 1lb. raisins, cut once, 1 teaspoon salt, 1 teaspoon cinnamon, 1 teaspoon cloves.
Boil these ingredients for 5 minutes after they begin to bubble. When cold add 1 teaspoon soda dissolved in 1 teaspoon hot water, add 3 cups of flour. Bake in 2 loaves, for 45 minutes in a slow oven.

Modern Equivalent:
2 ¾ cups (685 mL) (1 lb) raisins
2 cups (500 mL) packed brown sugar
2 tbsp (30 mL) butter
1 tsp (5 mL) ground cinnamon
1 tsp (5mL) salt
½ tsp (2 mL) ground cloves
2 cups (500 mL) boiling water
1 tsp (5 mL) baking soda
1 tsp (5mL) hot water
3 cups (750 mL) all-purpose flour

Line two 8" x 4" inch loaf pans with parchment paper or grease; set aside.

Chop raisins coarsely. In a medium saucepan, combine the raisins, sugar, butter, cinnamon, salt, cloves and boiling water. Bring to the boil; reduce heat to simmer the raisin mixture for 5 minutes. Transfer to a large bowl and let cool to room temperature. Combine the baking soda with hot water; stir into the raisin mixture.

One-quarter at a time, stir the flour into the raisin mixture. Pour half into each prepared pan; smooth tops. Bake in centre of preheated 325°F oven until golden brown on top, firm to a light touch and a tester inserted into the centre comes out clean, about 50 minutes to 1 hour. Let cool in pans for 10 minutes; turn out onto racks to cool right-side up. (Make-ahead: Wrap and store at room temperature for up to 4 days or freeze for up to 1 month.)

Makes 10 slices, easily cut in halves or thirds.

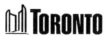

FIGURE 13.1 Recipe for Canadian War Cake, Fort York National Historic Site.
Copyright and courtesy of Fort York National Historic Site.

Some words of advice

IDM   *Lastly, what suggestions do you have for other museum professionals who use food to tell history?*

BW   My advice would be to always pursue a foodways program. They can be at various levels. Even if you have one or two recipes that help tell the story of your site, whatever aspect that may be, I think that you should have a recipe or a cookbook available. And if you have the facilities, make the food. I think it's an absolute must. Even if it's just for special events.

EB   And have the recipe so people can take it home, get the experience.

RK   It goes back to reading these recipes and getting the historical context correct. Also, let the visitors taste the food! At many museums in the United States and Canada visitors can only look, not taste. Visitors come to the Fort, they are amazed and say "You let people taste the food?" This opportunity to share the food allows the visitors to leave the Fort with a greater appreciation and connection to the food from the various eras that we research.

Notes

1   Elizabeth Baird is author of more than 20 cookbooks, former food editor at *Canadian Living* and Volunteer Historic Cook with the Fort York Foodways Programme; Rosemary Kovac is Volunteer Historic Cook with the Fort York Foodways Programme; and Bridget Wranich, Program Officer, Historic Foodways Programme, Fort York National Historic Site.

2   Carl Benn, *Fort York: A Short History and Guide* (Toronto: City of Toronto Culture), back cover.

3   Victoria Day is a federal Canadian public holiday celebrated on the last Monday before May 25, in honor of Queen Victoria's birthday.

4   The Gardiner Expressway is one of Ontario's major municipal expressways.

5   Comment based on the work of John Summers, "Beyond brown bread and oatmeal cookies: New directions for historic kitchens," *Material Culture Review* 27 (1988), 1–13.

6   *Setting a Fine Table: Historical Desserts and Drinks from the Officers' Kitchens at Fort York*, ed. Elizabeth Baird and Bridget Wranich (Toronto: Whitecap, 2013).

14

Eat Your History at the Sydney Living Museums

Scott Hill and Jacqui Newling

In recent years there has been a significant shift in context for social history museums. Research commissioned by Sydney Living Museums (SLM) has shown that passively experienced house museums, their buildings and grounds, collection and displays, are, on their own, no longer enough to engage modern audiences. SLM manages a portfolio of historic properties, which date from between 1788 and 1950, as well as the contemporary Museum of Sydney, built on the site of Australia's First Government House in 1995. As custodians of historic properties and their collections, it is our task to bring life and meaning to these objects and places, to unlock the stories behind and within them, and to activate the visitor experience to help audiences understand and appreciate them. Given the thematic, geographical, and historical diversity of the institution's properties, this becomes a particularly challenging task.

Food's universality makes it a particularly effective means of connecting, communicating with, and relating to people—past and present. SLM's *Eat Your History* and subsequent SLM food programming have enabled the institution to deliver a veritable banquet of food-related experiences within its museums. The menu has included place-based public programming events, curriculum-based education and children's vacation programming, a regular food history blog, an exhibition and commercially operated cafes and tearooms. While food is a useful mechanism for audience engagement, using food as a means of interpretation in a museum and heritage environment comes with inherent challenges. Here, the authors draw on SLM's *Eat Your History* initiatives, including the exhibition, *Eat Your History: A Shared Table*, which ran at the Museum of Sydney between September 2013 and March 2014 as a case study. As well as identifying the opportunities these projects responded to, we expose the challenges they posed and how these were addressed.

Sydney Living Museums: A snapshot

Sydney Living Museums was established in 1980 as the Historic Houses Trust of New South Wales (HHT). It is a place-based museum and heritage institution principally funded by the New South Wales State Government. The balance of its operating revenue is generated from donations and bequests, corporate partnerships, membership, program ticket sales, and commercial activations including venue hire, leaseholds, and retail leases. SLM opens twelve different sites to the public: the Museum of Sydney, the Sydney Mint, the Caroline Simpson Library and Research Collection, seven house museums, a crime museum, and a UNESCO World Heritage-listed convict barracks. The properties are set within landscapes that feature native bush land, archaeological footprints, Aboriginal rock engravings, formal "pleasure" and productive kitchen gardens, semi-rural farmland and even a harborside beach. Together, they house thousands of collection items and stories.

From 2010 to 2012, the institution underwent a significant restructure, which involved extensive rebranding and a new identity. In 2013, HHT was relaunched as Sydney Living Museums, adopting a more audience- rather than product-focused ethos. Supporting four new brand values—"authentically resourceful", "personally fascinating", "sociable host," and "reviving and revitalizing"—the first major initiative under its new identity, SLM: Food, was a natural fit with this new audience focus.

The role of food

We all eat. Food is fundamental to our survival, but what we eat and how we prepare and consume it is dictated by cultural, societal and personal constructs. Our food reflects our circumstances, heritage, values and identity, on macro and micro scales. This was no different in history, and, as a lens into the past, food provides a means of investigating and understanding our historical "other". Food is also a highly effective "hook", particularly at a time when there is a greatly heightened awareness about food and cooking in the mass media— cooking programs, magazines, celebrity chefs and reality television competitions for example, with their appeal to all ages. With improved culinary literacy, many people understand and appreciate preparation and cooking processes to at least some degree. This awareness offers an invitation for us to compare our own food and eating habits with those of past generations, to appreciate differences and discover direct connections with people in the past through similarities. Coupled with this, period movies and dramas have often placed emphasis on the authenticity of their food and dining scenes: note, for example, the recent debate over the "historically correct" way to eat asparagus in the British series Downton Abbey.[1] This has led to public familiarity with the food and food customs of the past and, for curators, an understanding that recipes, ingredients and customs can provide an "entrée" into past lives.

Both SLM and its predecessor, HHT, have used food as a means of interpretation in a way that extends far beyond the creation of traditional static and "hands-off" displays. Its house museums have kitchens, pantries, dining rooms, and gardens, which curators have interpreted in a holistic, interconnected way to suggest the life and activity that has taken place in each of these spaces at different times. Furnishing a kitchen or dining room with period pieces and items provenanced to families associated with a property allows us to play on a visitor's existing impressions of life in the past; so too does preserving an extant, *in situ* collection. These are not new concepts; elaborate dining settings and displays of kitchenalia have long been a staple of the house museum. A food theme can, however, be used to effectively connect different parts of the museum. At Vaucluse House, for example—a nineteenth-century harborside villa associated with the early Australian historical figure William Charles Wentworth—pineapples can be seen growing in the kitchen garden, crowning an epergne in the dining room and again in the kitchen, where pineapple jam is made, and in the pantry where the jam is stored. In turn, jelly molds in the kitchen relate to a jelly "cooling" in its mold in the larder and a "made" (resin) jelly on the dining table. These subtle associations help to create a cohesive picture of life in a historic house. At the same time, they introduce historical concepts such as cultivation and agriculture, cooking and preservation technologies, gender and class divide, social and cultural change. They can also be more fully explored during a tour or program, serving as the visual prompts that are a fundamental device of house museum interpretation, especially in SLM houses, where signage and labels within spaces are avoided.

Food has also played an important role in SLM's education programs, which have a "then and now" emphasis in programs for primary school children and more abstract or technical applications for secondary-level Food Studies students. Property-based interpretative activities and programming focusing on domestic arts, social and gender division, dining and etiquette have been conducted since the mid-1990s. In this way, institutions are able to counter "pervasive perceptions, here [in Australia] and abroad, that house museums [in particular] are out of touch, boringly academic with recreated interiors that are lifeless, static and soulless".[2] At SLM, larger-scale events such as the Kitchen Garden Festival at Vaucluse House, which is home to a recreated Victorian vegetable garden, and the Festival of the Olive at Elizabeth

Farm, site of Australia's oldest olive tree, have been based on site-specific heirloom produce and cultural and community engagement. These themes were continued when in 2009 "gastronomer" Jacqui Newling introduced the successful series of *Colonial gastronomy* programs that continue today.

Eat Your History

SLM's *Eat Your History* project was initiated in 2011. It responded to consumer demand for immersive, experiential, and interactive involvement rather than didactic delivery. As a multi-faceted concept, it created further opportunities to engage visitors at SLM properties, while uniting various food-related concepts across the institution and reflecting the cultural shift within the institution from a singularly property- or product-driven ethos to one with an audience focus.

Eat Your History's interpretative initiatives are place-based, underpinned by research into SLM properties, the people who lived and worked in them, and their social and historical contexts. In keeping with the institution's rebranding as a suite of *living* museums, they relate to real practices and lived lives. The concept uses food-related buildings and spaces, collection objects, historic references and stories as platforms to introduce wider concepts and ideas, including curricular objectives for students. *Eat Your History* shifts the thinking from objective to subjective, material to personal. It is strengthened by sensorial, experiential, and hands-on activities, and uses food to enliven or activate static spaces and objects, making historical concepts and past lives more accessible to visitors.

While *Eat Your History* concepts draw upon resources and initiatives from many departments across the institution, gastronomer Jacqui Newling was appointed to develop content along with properties portfolio curator, Scott Hill. The exhibition *Eat Your History: A Shared Table* which ran at the Museum of Sydney between September 2013 and March 2014, came as a direct result of this collaboration. The exhibition was, in turn, the catalyst for and "centerpiece" of *SLM: Food*, the first in a series of core, or "pillar" themes, being created under the institution's new brand identity.

Eat Your History: A Shared Table exhibition

Concept development

Long before the *Eat Your History* concept was established, both authors had identified the fact that, collectively, SLM properties formed a wonderful chronology of kitchen technology, food culture and social change, which mirrored evolving political, economic, technological, and cultural influences in Australian society. Each had argued for programs and publications on the strength of the properties' relevance to gastronomy, with an exhibition being conceived of as the ultimate possibility. Scope for content and audience appeal was tested with a blog, *The Cook and the Curator*, launched in 2012.[3] Its authors, Newling (as the Cook) and Hill (as the Curator), wanted an accessible and relaxed form of delivering factual content, delivered with informality in tone and language rather than a didactic approach. By featuring content that may not otherwise be available to museum visitors, such as lengthy cooking processes taking place in historic kitchens, the blog provided an extra dimension to communicate stories that may not be viable in the real-time sense. *The Cook and the Curator* successfully achieved its three key aims: to create an online platform to promote SLM and its properties to a wide audience through food stories; to create an accessible archive of research material for the organization (including being used as a pre-and post-visit resources for education programs); and as a means of assessing the potential and viability of a food-related publication in a market that was perceived to be likely saturated.[4] Significantly, *The Cook and the Curator*'s content and approach to interpreting places, objects, and historical concepts through food, were recognized as having potential to translate into an exhibition format.

Finding form

When first discussed, the concept for a food-based exhibition was centered on a single "long lunch" table that moved through a historical timeline and, potentially, through each of the meals from morning to night. The concept, influenced by the seductive power of table settings, immediately presented the obvious challenges of food itself being central to the visual effect of the show. It also directed the emphasis of the exhibition heavily towards the "table", and away from a more holistic approach which includes food production and practices. The other significant challenge was to find food that would survive in a six-month static display and could be displayed on collection items that cannot come into direct contact with organic matter. As the concept developed, the interpretation formula moved towards using the properties themselves to lead the visitor through what became, conceptually, a place-based "progressive dinner" through time, between European settlement in 1788 and the 1950s—a reflection of the place-based approach fundamental to the institution. The show's narrative began with First Government House, the site on which the venue, the Museum of Sydney is built, and continued with seven

SLM house museums to form a chronological sequence. Each stage featured key social history themes relating to the property, society in general and continuing changes in food culture. How to incorporate food into the show was still a significant concern, but less so than it would have been in a fully realized dining scene.

Audience-focused interpretation of food content

The exhibition set out to give visitors a taste of the individual characters of SLM properties, and offered an idea of what they might experience should they choose to visit them in the real. It was important, therefore, that the exhibition conveyed a genuine sense of people, place, and time for each representation, and delivered content that could be recognized in a real-time visit: a tangible connection with the museums themselves. It was also important to the curators, from a gastronomic perspective, to demonstrate how food was used to convey each site's historical concepts. Indeed, this premise formed the basis of an education program for senior high school history students (aged 17 to 19) in the museum space as part of an all-day learning intensive.

Each display was framed around a key physical element—a kitchen, a dining table, even a summerhouse—that would be recognizable when people visited the property itself (see fig.14.1). Gallery space allowed for six main themes or time periods, two of which would incorporate two properties in tandem. Each theme provided the opportunity to deliver one principal theme and two, perhaps three, sub-themes. Each thematic section was distinguished by a different wall-paint color, and motifs from nineteenth-century cookbooks, sourced from SLM collections, were used as accents to embellish wall space and provide a continuous design signature throughout the gallery. A selection of these motifs was used for retail items to support the exhibition—aprons, shopping bags, and magnets for the kitchen fridge.

The subtitle, "A Shared Table" was chosen to be inclusive; as an institution, we wanted visitors to feel that they could, as the exhibition concept stated, "sit at our tables, peek inside our kitchen cupboards, leaf through our cookbooks and be introduced to our residents."[5] Exhibition designers visited each property to assess the symbolic elements the curators had chosen and integrate them into the layout. Each section had to be inviting, immersive, and, at least to some degree, interactive. And although the exhibition themes focused on the social and cultural aspects of food, food itself had to play a key role in the displays. These essential elements of the exhibition were addressed in a variety of ways.

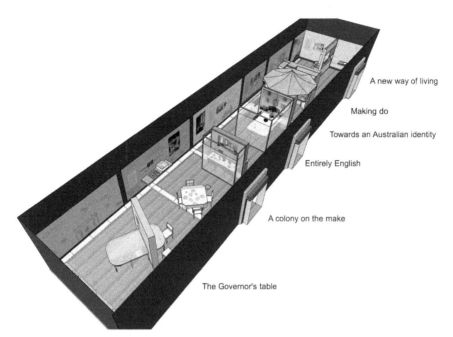

A new way of living

Making do

Towards an Australian identity

Entirely English

A colony on the make

The Governor's table

FIGURE 14.1 *3D exhibition schematic showing the six thematic spaces for* Eat Your History: A Shared Table *exhibition's centerpiece, 2014.*

© *Sydney Living Museums.*

Food content

The biggest challenge remained: how to present food in a static display for six months within a controlled museum space. Faux food, either purchased or custom made, seemed the only choice, but time and budgetary constraints put custom-made options out of reach, and even then, the curators and design team were not satisfied that these would be of suitable quality when seen up close in a well-lit gallery. In the end, faux fruit and foliage were only used for epergne or fruit-bowl displays behind Perspex, and positioned at least half a meter from the visitors' viewing point. These were hand selected from various sources. Subsequent visits by the curators to museums that have commissioned or created their own faux food in the United States and Europe have confirmed that the right decision was made; meat products, and cooked dishes especially, rarely look convincing, and more typically detract from their display. In the section named "Making do", melted paraffin candle wax was used to give a realistic impression of dripping in a dripping tin, and wooden eggs (purchased from a toy shop) were displayed in a bowl inside the ice-chest.

Another drawback of faux food is that it lacks that key association with food: aroma. Our olfactory senses evoke powerful associations and, as Marcel Proust reminds us, food smells especially trigger memories.[6] It was hoped that food and cooking smells could be used to enrich the visitor experience— synthetic smells can be purchased from laboratories in the US and UK—but budget constraints limited these specialized effects. Dried spices and Chinese tea samples were displayed in lidded cups set into a bench in "A colony on the make", which visitors could see and smell as they discovered the story of trade in colonial New South Wales. A cloth-bound "pudding" (containing a pudding bowl stuffed with cloth and sand for bulk and weight) was placed in one of the copper pots on the kitchen dresser in "Entirely English", with cloves and cinnamon inside it to give it fragrance. A tray of smoky lapsang souchong tea was concealed in the bottom of the fuel stove in "Making do", which gave a waft of smokiness when the oven door was opened. The spices and tea were replenished regularly as their effect faded.

Some other real foodstuffs were used. Each was freeze-dried to eliminate the risk of pests inhabiting them before, or after, being installed in their display cases. Examples of the colonists' daily ration in the fledgling colony were displayed under Perspex in "The Governor's table", the first thematic area. The perishability of these foodstuffs is intrinsically low, allowing the use of real food: a portion of aged salted pork, stone-ground flour, dried peas, rice and— the only faux rendition—beeswax to emulate the daily allowance of butter. Similarly, in "A colony on the make", hand-blown and size-appropriate pullet eggs (laid by hens at another SLM property) sat in eggcups next to a basket of bread rolls, hollowed out and freeze-dried to prevent any mold or decay. For that display, the case was also recessed into the table under Perspex, with the captions printed directly onto the white damask tablecloth.[7] As with the "First Fleet rations" display, visitors were then able to pull up a chair and literally "sit at the table". In "Making do", a salt-crust pie top baked in an enamel dish was positioned to surprise anyone who opened the oven door on the fuel stove in the kitchen representing SLM's property Susannah Place—a set of four terrace houses located in Sydney's historic The Rocks. The piecrust had to be remade after a few months, as it became chipped and cracked from handling (a good sign of interactivity).

Visual imagery of food and dining

The exhibition relied on rich imagery, using nineteenth-century line-drawn motifs applied as decals onto the walls, specially commissioned stills photography and video footage. A photography shoot at the historic Elizabeth Farm homestead provided a luscious "hero" image for the exhibition, showing an abundance of fresh produce authentic to the 1820s and arranged on that house's kitchen table, with the lit stove glowing in the background. Greatly enlarged, this photograph was positioned on the wall in direct view of the visitor as they entered the gallery, in outdoor posters on the museum's street boundaries and on postcards and other marketing for the exhibition <http://blogs.hht.net.au/cook/a-spring-in-our-step/>.

Photography was also used to enhance the visitor's sense of "real life" rooms that were featured in the show: the dining room at Elizabeth Bay House ("Entirely English")—home to colonial secretary Alexander Macleay, and once considered the finest house in the colony—and the kitchen from Sydney modernist icon Rose Seidler House ("A new way of living"). A replication of the Macleays' dinner table, set for fourteen using a dinner service from that property's collection, was to be the visual spectacle of the show, the "centerpiece" that visitors carried away in their memories. At its full length, to accommodate the historically accurate fourteen diners, the table would be at least twenty feet long; this was simply not possible and other solutions were considered. Curator Scott Hill initially suggested a mirror be used to reflect a half-length table to achieve the full effect of a table set for fourteen, a device used at Sans Souci Palace at Potsdam, Germany. A mirror this size, however, would confusingly reflect other parts of the exhibition and any people movement in its view. A solution was found in using a photographic image of the other half of the table in the dining room itself, fully set with the same tableware to give the full splendor of the dining space in the house museum (see fig. 14.2). Disappointingly, the narrow breadth of the gallery precluded the hoped-for seamless connection between the table in the image and the one in the show, which was constructed to match the dimensions of the actual table in the house. While the image could have been zoomed out to match the table width, it would have lost the surrounding view of the dining room and, with it, its sense of grandeur and place. Setting the table for the photograph also enabled the process to be filmed. The subsequent time-lapsed sequence of the table being painstakingly set *à la française* by the curators from a dark, shuttered room to a full opulent display awaiting diners was shown on an iPad next to the display and later housed on the blog.[8]

An enlarged historical image of the Rouse family taking tea in their garden at Rouse Hill House and Farm formed the internal walls of the walk-in summerhouse (a feature of the property) in "Towards an Australian identity". This offered a very personal connection between the family's cookbooks and manuscript recipes on display, enabling the visitor to put the names of the original owners in context. Similarly, a life-sized photograph of the kitchen at Rose Seidler House became the northern wall of a walk-in space within the gallery, in similar proportions to the kitchen itself. Visitors could stand in the kitchen and look out into the adjoining space through the three-dimensional

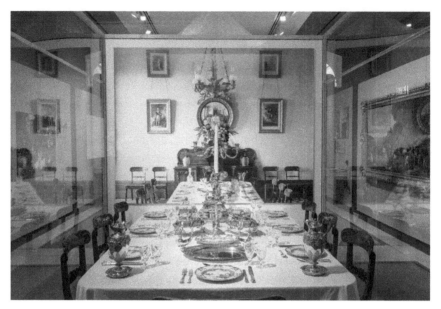

FIGURE 14.2 *The "Macleays' table" recreated as* Eat Your History: A Shared Table *exhibition's centerpiece, 2014.*

© *Jamie North, Sydney Living Museums.*

construction of the kitchen's servery and overhead cupboards, just as you can in the house.

Filmed content

Video was used throughout the exhibition. To demonstrate the point that the first European colonists were not limited to imported salt-provisions in their diets, but had access to a wider range of local produce, a film was made as an "evocation" of an officers' dinner that took place to celebrate King George III's birthday in 1788. Informed by a primary account of the meal, SLM staff volunteers donned period-appropriate shirtsleeves and were filmed dining on authentic food and wine, prepared using eighteenth-century recipes and served *à la française*.[9] As the meal progressed and the brandy flowed, the table became messier and the "huzzahs" more enthusiastic. Footage was filmed from an overhead camera, showing the proceedings of the table itself (only the diners' forearms are shown), and the film was projected from the gallery ceiling onto a viewing screen embedded into the "Governor's table". Replica late eighteenth-century chairs allowed people to sit at the table and engage in the festivities unfolding before them. The table itself, a copy in Perspex of a significant colonial D-end table in the SLM collection, introduced the discussion of the evolution of dedicated dining room furniture through time. Subtle inclusions such as this could then be highlighted on guided tours of the exhibition and on *The Cook and the Curator* blog.

The officers' dinner video, along with one on jelly-making,[10] proved to be the most popular and memorable interpretative components of the exhibition for many visitors—especially the raucous "huzzahs" that rang out through the gallery and museum. Video was also used to market the exhibition via the SLM website, social media, and *The Cook and the Curator* blog.[11] The jelly-making video was filmed in the historic kitchen at Vaucluse House. Highlighting the hidden aspects of food production, Jacqui Newling takes viewers step-by-step through a Mrs Beeton recipe from 1861 to make a jelly base from calf's feet. The feet are shown whole, then cut up and cooked, rendered down to a fatty, murky mass, skimmed then clarified using egg whites and crushed egg shells to finally produce an insipid and unappetizing jelly—a direct contrast to the decorative, fanciful desserts that grace a dessert table. What the video did not show exemplifies the perils of food in the museum environment: the iron pot cracked during the clarification process and the almost-completed stock flooded across the floor in a torrent of hot, sticky liquid. Fortunately, the bulk of the actual cooking was conducted in a modern staff kitchen, removed from the nineteenth-century kitchen space, and another batch was in reserve ("here's one we prepared earlier") to complete the filming.

Visitor interactivity opportunities

Pages from the recipe collections from Rouse Hill and Meroogal, an 1880s property in regional New South Wales, were photographed and displayed as "virtual cookbooks" on iPads throughout the exhibition. Visitors could email recipes and images of food-splattered pages to themselves or friends in PDF format, direct from the screen for future reference. This offered visitors a virtual "take-home" souvenir of the exhibition, and provenanced recipes they could experiment with at home. iPads were also used for the "curio wall" located outside the gallery itself, at the entrance to the exhibition space. This introductory display indicated the exhibition's underlying themes and was filled with all manner of kitchenalia, from a decorative nineteenth-century majolica eel dish to a plastic 1950s donut maker, and a tiny pocket-sized Georgian silver nutmeg grater to a 1930s penny-in-the-slot gas meter. The objects were sourced from SLM collections and personal items from staff and SLM members, following a call-out inviting them to be part of the show. Instead of each item having descriptor labels, visitors were invited to guess each item's use, or tap the image of each item on an iPad mounted next to the display, to access a 30-word caption. The curio wall proved a simple but effective intergenerational interpretation device; it triggered memories for some older audience members as much as puzzlement for younger, and successfully encouraged discussion among visitors of all ages.

iPads were also installed at the exit point of the gallery to introduce visitors to *The Cook and the Curator* blog and invite them to complete feedback surveys. Within a few weeks, the surveys showed that visitors wanted some form of children's activity within the gallery to engage younger visitors in the content, enhance their experience and allow accompanying adults more time in the space. The exhibition had not been pitched to a junior audience, but this feedback was responded to in time for the Christmas holiday period. In consultation with the Children and Families' Audience Engagement Officer and Museum of Sydney staff, an activity card aimed at primary school-aged children was developed, and an activity table and stools were installed in the museum space. Just as people would in their own homes, the exhibition interpretation was also able to respond to seasonal change, with decorations over the Christmas period being added to the displays; festive Regency-style paper flowers, swags and bunting, and a pudding tied up with a festive tartan bow.

To conclude the exhibition experience, visitors were encouraged to add their own flavor to the exhibition using cards printed with "Share your thoughts, fondest food memories, or a favorite recipe". Almost 1,000 cards were contributed by visitors. Taking their cue from that bearer of all household material, the kitchen refrigerator door, the cards could then be stuck onto a large magnetic white board using colorful magnetized tiles or fridge magnets. Several consistent themes emerged with the cards: favorite recipes, reminiscences (often of grandparents' kitchens), national dishes accompanied by pictures of flags left by international visitors, and a score of children's drawings of their favorite foods: pies, pizzas, cakes, and bowls of pasta. Amazingly, some (but not many) of the original 200 fridge magnets were left at the end of the six-month season; no doubt they may still exist on people's fridges as reminders of the exhibition experience. Social media-savvy visitors were encouraged to "snap and share" and post in situ "selfies" on Facebook and Instagram with the hashtag *#eatyourhistory*.

Museum programming around food

While *The Cook and the Curator* blog has scope that relates to many of the *Eat Your History* concepts in the digital space, public programs tap into the "experience economy". SLM's *Colonial gastronomy* programs, for example, take the form of house and garden tours with emphasis on food-related topics, immersive or hands-on experiences in historical kitchens and dining rooms. They can be as simple as an afternoon in the drawing room reading extracts from a resident's personal letters and period-appropriate recipes that demonstrate the food culture of their times, themed "gala" dining events framed around provenance menus, or involve hands-on "masterclass"-style workshops with industry specialists from butchers to chefs. But all generally follow a combination of "talk, tour, taste", drawing on people and place through collection, historical anecdotes and stories—and actual food.

The *Eat Your History: A Shared Table* exhibition launched a new SLM programming strategy, becoming the central point for institution-wide programming. A feast of programs was developed by the Programs team, to be delivered at the Museum of Sydney and at the properties themselves. In many instances, these were realized in partnership with external operators; this was critical to the viability and success of the programming schedule, at a time when the organizational restructure was still being implemented, and several units within the institution were still in flux or regrouping. The associated programs spanned the full six-month period of the exhibition, "[d]esigned to underscore the pleasures and depth of what we regularly offer visitors at all our houses and museums, gardens and cafes" and were marketed under *SLM: Food* in a dedicated booklet.[12] These included one-off dining events and workshops, a series of talks and tours held at various SLM properties, plus initiatives devised with commercial hospitality leaseholders on their sites. This was new ground for SLM and was, for the most part, successful. Working with established food-industry identities who had little or no experience working within heritage sites posed some challenges, at times testing curatorial and administrative boundaries, including building conservation and public health and safety issues. But at the same time, these partnerships helped introduce SLM, its properties and programs, to new audiences—many of them through social media communities untapped at that stage by the institution's marketing strategies. These history-related *SLM: Food* programs attracted over 2,000 visitors; an additional 4,000 attended a Christmas market held at Hyde Park Barracks Museum, which has now become an annual event.

Food for thought

As an institution-wide concept, *Eat Your History* has provided new ways of bringing together the various aspects of food-related activity and initiatives across SLM properties—whether historically interpretative and education-based or contemporary commercial facilities—and has resulted in an ongoing collective offering under *SLM:Food. The Cook and the Curator* blog has received industry awards, and was short-listed for the prestigious New South

Wales Premier's History Award (multimedia) in 2013.[13] Together, the blog, the *Eat Your History: A Shared Table* exhibition, and food-related programming make a strong statement to the public that SLM is a portfolio of museums—individual in nature but similar in character—and support the institution's brand values. Further outcomes from the *Eat Your History* initiative include outreach opportunities to work with complementary cultural organizations and regional communities. An Arts NSW Regional Partnership Grant has enabled SLM to work as a major institutional partner for the Central West region of New South Wales *Villages of the Heart* project, which is designed to preserve and tell rural stories. A community-focused extension of *Eat Your History* through interpretation and public programs is being created for rural and regional museums, many of which are run by volunteers. Following a round-table conference and a full-day intensive masterclass on food-related interpretation and public programming, developed by Jacqui Newling for museums staff, several *Eat Your History* concepts have been adapted in the region including historical dining events and projects reviving heirloom recipes within communities.

Content from *Eat Your History: A Shared Table* is in the process of being developed for an online audience, to be accessed through *The Cook and the Curator* blog and the SLM website. *The Cook and the Curator*, colonial gastronomy programming and a new publication, *Eat Your History: Stories and Recipes from Australian Kitchens* (2015) provide a research resource for staff and secondary and tertiary students and continue to support museums-based interpretation and strengthen the overall SLM: Food offer.

Breaking down barriers

Food in the museum environment presents its own set of issues and challenges, but it is one of the most powerful and immediate interpretative tools with which to captivate modern audiences. While food seems logical in house museums, it also has applications for other types of museums. Food lends itself just as strongly to most social history museums, but also science, ancient or classical history and archaeology museums. The most obvious is risk management to collection, heritage fabric and controlled environments from perishable produce. While faux food has often been the answer, unless expertly (and expensively) crafted, it is unsatisfying for increasingly sophisticated audiences. Synthetic olfactory stimulants are becoming more accessible; they can activate food-related objects to evoke a food memory or experience, revealed when lifting the lid of a pot or opening a biscuit container, for example. Although digital technology applications may be perceived as intrusive in many historic environments, they are also proving to be engaging as audiences become more accepting of digital devices and virtual interaction.

Opportunities for direct sensorial interaction with real food can be part of the museum experience through hands-on components or associated tasting activities. These do not necessarily have to be held in controlled heritage or exhibition spaces, but can be attached to tours or exhibitions in neutral spaces, either within the museum itself or a nearby location, perhaps in partnership with local businesses or councils. Questions of food handling and safety invariably arise in discussions with museums staff as a barrier to "real food" tastings and activities, and while food safety training courses and accreditation may not seem a natural part of a museum professional's job description, they can easily be obtained through local authorities.

While real time, hands-on place-based activities continue to be popular and meet the interactivity that museum visitors now expect, they can be resource heavy. Due to the nature of working in historic sites or necessarily controlled environments, such as gallery-style museums, they can typically only cater to small audiences and are often highly temporal and ephemeral, one-off experiences. A blog can therefore act as a perfect counterpart to place-based interpretative programming and support an exhibition during its season and well after it has closed. *The Cook and the Curator* blog and resulting book, *Eat Your History: Stories and Recipes from Australian Kitchens* complement the suite of programs and other initiatives within the *SLM: Food* brand "pillar", activating museum spaces for audiences and bringing flavor to Sydney Living Museums as an institution.

Notes

1   John Millar, "Downton Abbey's etiquette expert on how TV drama was rocked by asparagus rammy" in *The Daily Record and Sunday Mail*. UK. August 2007.

2   Beth Hise, *A good story gets people in: a new approach to interpretation at the Historic Houses Trust of NSW*. Conference paper presented at Interpretation Australia National Conference, 2012.

3   http://blogs.hht.net.au/cook now in its fourth year, The Cook and the Curator continues to publish weekly posts related to Sydney Living Museums properties and Australian food heritage.

4   This objective has now been realized: *Eat Your History: Stories and recipes from Australian kitchens* was published in December 2015.

5   Hill and Newling, *Eat Your History: a shared table* presentation (internal) Sydney Living Museums, 2012.

7   In *Swann's Way*, volume 1 of Proust's *À la Recherche du temps perdu* ("Remembrance of Things Past," 1913–27), the smell of a madeleine cake triggers a succession of memories from the narrator's childhood.

8   See http://blogs.hht.net.au/cook/tricks-of-the-trade/

9   "Setting the scene" http://blogs.hht.net.au/cook/a-gentlemans-dinner/

10   See http://blogs.hht.net.au/cook/a-behind-the-scenes-peek/

11   "Spoiling the broth?" in "Discover some sneaky secrets," The Cook and The Curator March 6, 2014. http://blogs.hht.net.au/cook/sneaky-secrets/

12   "You're invited to share our table," in The Cook and the Curator. October 3, 2013. http://blogs.hht.net.au/cook/youre-invited-to-share-our-table/

13   Historic Houses Trust of NSW Annual Report 2013–2014. http://sydneylivingmuseums.com.au/sites/default/files/2013-14_Annual_Report_Historic_Houses_Trust.pdf p12

14   See http://www.sl.nsw.gov.au/awards-nsw-premiers-history-awards-multimedia-history-prize/2013-multimedia-history-prize and http://blogs.hht.net.au/cook/blowing-our-trumpet/

15

Terroir Tapestries:

An Interactive Consumption Project

Jennifer Jacqueline Stratton and Ashley Rose Young

Historically, in France, food identified with *goût de terroir* (the taste of place), was associated with the filth of the provinces and the savagery of more distant lands.[1] More recently, *terroir* was reappropriated as a powerful vehicle for regional pride and identity.[2] Foods with a strong taste of place are celebrated for their connections to the local environments that shape their flavors. *Terroir Tapestries* explores the *terroir* of American cities. It highlights the interactions among chefs, vendors, and consumers in the making of urban food cultures, past and present. It expands the domain of *terroir* to historic urban landscapes whose environments and sense of place profoundly shaped the foods produced in cities. Specifically, the project examines how smog, refuse, and dirt influence, historically, the taste of street foods. The project further engages the elasticity of the word *terroir* by applying "taste of place" to urban spaces in order to bridge the gap between rural and urban food cultures. These cultures were connected through the movement of people and goods along inland trade routes. Further, leaving the *terroir* of urban spaces unexamined contributes to a romanticization of rural-based *terroir*.

Problematizing *Terroir* in New Orleans

Terroir Tapestries began with a few seemingly simple questions: What remains after the preparation, gathering, and consumption of a meal? In what ways do our individual interactions with food compose collective culinary histories? *Terroir Tapestries* explores these questions in a tactile, experiential sense as well as through the documentation of specific food cultures and experiences. This exploration led us to use debris left by food consumption: the scraps and residues on plates and placemats. We allowed food debris to soil placemats printed and inscribed with memories of food, featuring the consumers' complex relationship to food before, during, and after a meal. The project looks concurrently at the ephemerality of food and how the memories of a meal can be powerful and lasting. We are not only interested in the decomposition of organic matter, but also in people's shifting opinions of what food remains at the end of a meal. Working with the idea of food in an artistic, anthropological way, food wrappers were custom-designed to bring together visual and literary representations of urban food cultures in a specific city. These food wrappers also serve as canvases for the crumbs, rips, and stains of personal food consumption.

New Orleans, Louisiana served as the pilot city for the *Terroir Tapestries* project. The city's historic Creole food culture is well documented in both writing and imagery, which enabled us to explore the city's culinary history in depth. For the pilot tapestry, a total of three double-sided designs were created to provide historic and cultural context for the foods served at community events tied to the project. These dining events invited the local community to enjoy historic street foods alongside talks and discussions, as well as to share their experience following the meal. Wrappers were sewn together to create a colorful tapestry of this collective experience.

The designs highlight the movement of people and goods in the city's public food markets and out into its streets—a connection that contributed to the development of a vibrant street food culture. One of the wrappers features photographs and artistic renderings of mobile vegetable carts and vendors in New Orleans. The remaining two wrappers trace the 165-year history of the Dryades Market in New Orleans—one of the city's most important commercial centers since its founding in 1849. By creating tapestries that weave together images, experiences, and threads of inquiry we are interested in turning both eye and mouth to often overlooked or discarded aspects of food production, distribution, and consumption.

Looking at the concept of *terroir* in rural and urban contexts further explains how notions of privilege are often embedded into the identification of *terroir*. For example, many haute cuisine restaurants over the past decade have elevated certain Southern culinary traditions typically associated with the rural

South or low-income Southern communities. The dishes they have repurposed include shrimp and grits, pig ear sandwiches, and pickled watermelon rinds. These foods, which often went unnoticed by American consumers in urban areas, are now featured dishes on popular restaurant menus. Recently, the growth of local food movements has revitalized urban areas throughout the South. However, many problems continue to persist in terms of food access. Who is excluded from access to *terroir*? What are the relationships between commerce, identity, and eating, and can historic street foods such as calas[3] still fit into modern food systems? Finally, how can the success of *terroir* in gourmet circles be useful in resolving modern public policy issues brought on by poverty and environmental degradation?

Urban *Terroir* and Subnature

"Subnature" is a term developed by architectural historian David Gissen to categorize what architects have historically referred to as marginalized spaces in buildings and landscapes, but which have been re-appropriated by architects, urban planners, and vendors into aesthetically pleasurable and functional places.[4] *Terroir Tapestries* was created as part of the transdisciplinary Subnature and Culinary Culture Program, a subset of the Emerging Digital Humanities Network at Duke University. In fall 2014, the Subnature Program inaugurated a semester-long series of interdisciplinary talks, experiments, and public humanities initiatives. Scholars engaged with culinary professionals and members of the public to explore the question, "What do subnatures look like when applied to examinations of culinary cultures?" Participants examined flavors, textures, and dishes considered unpalatable by different societies at different times. The list of foods prepared and shared ranged from fermented goods and offal to blemished produce and foraged foods.

New Orleans' subnatural culinary cultures

New Orleans' Creole cuisine drew upon and fused together a wide range of food cultures from throughout the Atlantic World. The mixing of these diverse cultures is apparent in New Orleans' historic street food culture. On a daily basis, vendors originating from communities along the coasts of Europe, West Africa, Latin America, and the Caribbean came together in the municipally-run markets and the surrounding areas. Amidst quotidian interactions of purveying and purchasing foods, vendors and customers exchanged important ideas about food preparation and consumption, creating a hybrid urban food culture.

Although smaller than the market halls in other cities, New Orleans' markets were important economic, social, and cultural spaces.[5] Vendors were integral members of both the local economy and community, influencing their neighbors' taste preferences and consumption habits. Vendors not fortunate enough to occupy stalls in the covered markets clustered on street corners, selling fresh loaves of French bread and steaming bowls of gumbo. These vendors set up itinerant kitchens and food stands along bustling throughways where the particulates of urban life perfumed the air and flavored the dishes they prepared. Their dishes were exemplars of urban *terroir* because they were "seasoned" with the flavors and fragrances of city life. *Terroir Tapestries* addresses the role of vendors in the streets and those in the public markets together, highlighting how these people and their food cultures were inextricably linked.

Terroir Tapestries shares the history of the Dryades Market—one of the longest operating neighborhood markets in the city until its closure in the late 1940s. The Dryades Market was selected for *Terroir Tapestries* because of its relevance to modern New Orleans and also its integral role in the making of New Orleans' street food culture. The market was originally built as an open-air pavilion in 1849 and was intimately connected to the urban *terroir* of the neighborhood. This open design allowed for the easy movement of people and foods from the streets into the market and vice versa. Over the years, the municipal government renovated the Dryades Market to outfit it with modern amenities. These architectural and technological changes largely sought to improve public health, but they also changed interactions among community members. During a series of citywide renovations in the early twentieth century, the market was physically closed off from the streets that had been integral to its food traditions for generations. It was also closed off from the soot and soil that had shaped the flavors of prepared dishes and market foods for generations. New Orleans' market system thus began to resemble those in other American cities as processes of cultural homogenization swept across the United States in the mid-twentieth century. The Second World War marked a critical turning point in American culture and consumption. Cities experienced significant population loss as Americans moved into the suburbs, so vendors in municipal markets and the surrounding streets lost a substantial portion of their customer base. As markets became less profitable, there were fewer attempts to maintain the structures and they ultimately fell into disrepair. The residents that remained in cities came to view the markets as antiquated and unsanitary.

New Orleanians are increasingly interested in reviving their city's historic market and street food traditions, as was the case with the Dryades Market in 2014. In the spring of 2015, another one of New Orleans' neighborhood markets, the St. Roch Market, was historically preserved and re-opened as an artisan

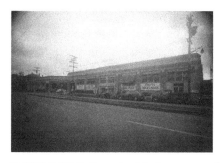 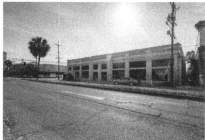

FIGURE 15.1 *Dryades Market past and present.*

Photograph on left: New Orleans, LA 1947 © Charles S. Franck Studio Collection, Historic New Orleans Collections. Photo on right: New Orleans, LA Summer 2014 © Stephen Binns.

food hall. This institution readily embraces the city's cultural ties to food and is using its space to support local farmers while also keeping New Orleans' culinary heritage alive. With more ready access to local foods, community members have the opportunity to familiarize themselves with the distinct tastes of Southeastern Louisiana. These same community members are incorporating regional foods, such as mirliton and crawfish, into their daily consumption. In doing so, they are contributing to the revival of historically important dishes, many of which are deeply informed by the flavors and environmental conditions of Louisiana, such as the subtle brininess of Gulf oysters or the unique texture and crisp crust of New Orleans-style French bread.

Crafting a collective archive of consumption: Engaging through the senses

The *Terroir Tapestries* project is centered on public engagement with historically significant street foods. Many of these dishes and ingredients were unfamiliar or strange to participants and as such could be considered "subnatural." During a community lunch series[6] and a corresponding outreach event with high school students,[7] participants ate New Orleans street food such as po'boys and calas and learned about the history of the city's municipal markets and surrounding street food cultures. By printing landscape imagery and text from street food vendor spaces on food wrappers and place mats, consumers physically peeled away layers of culinary cultures to access historic street foods. These foods were chosen for their potential subnatural qualities. The smoked pigeon prepared for one of these community meals, for example, elicited diverse reactions from consumers who had not considered pigeon meat before. Historically, however, pigeon was consumed in cities across the globe.

Following the sharing of historically significant food items at the community dining events, participants inscribed their own personal "taste reactions" on the food wrappers. Their reactions were drawn and scribbled directly onto the food wrapper imagery dating from the nineteenth to twenty-first centuries, thereby illuminating both continuities and discontinuities in the collective memory of street food cultures in the United States. These taste reactions in combination with the food crumbs and stains create an intimate record of each diner's personal eating experience and her engagement with the past. Through a variety of expressive forms—sketches of produce, animals and people, abstract shapes, even poetic phrases—interactions between personal experiences and the historical foods consumed were concurrently created and recorded. For example: "I didn't like the okra salad because it wasn't slimy enough!"; "Pigeon smelled good, but didn't interest my taste buds"; "Okra—slimy in a good way"; or "Smoked Pigeon—soft, juicy, smooth."

When looking at the wrappers together, a combination of colors, textures, crunches, smells, and tastes emerged in the tapestry. To tell the story of this concurrently collective and individual consumption experience, we decided to present the wrappers together in the form of a large-scale tapestry. Our inspiration comes from the artistic production of the Middle Ages, when tapestries were often commissioned by the clergy or royalty to depict religious stories, coronations, battles, or various historic motifs. Moreover, tapestries were often prominently positioned on display in dining halls during this time. In addition to the used food wrappers, historic and modern maps of inland routes were utilized as a border for the tapestries. Through using these maps, we sought to draw viewers' attention to the movement of foodstuffs from the countryside into the city of New Orleans. Communities located upriver, for example, maintained ties to the city by transporting agricultural products down the Mississippi and taking finished goods back on the return journey. The exchange of ideas, some of which were related to food production and consumption, accompanied this constant circulation of goods along the river, thereby entwining urban and rural cultures together.[8]

Conclusions: Weaving together alternative food futures

Terroir Tapestries lends itself to additional case studies. A long-term project goal is to craft tapestries in and about different cities, which will then be presented together and toured throughout North America. This expansion will allow audiences to engage with both the cultural commonalities and eccentricities of American urban food cultures. New Orleans' food culture, for example, is often viewed as distinct from the rest of the United States. Even within the region of the South, New Orleans is identified as exceptional due to pan-Atlantic influences on its food culture. The city and its food are often labeled as "exotic" and even "foreign." However, as other American city food cultures are examined, such as Baltimore and Philadelphia, commonalities between these seemingly divergent cities can emerge. Both New Orleans and Philadelphia, for example, had important economic and cultural connections to the Caribbean in the eighteenth and nineteenth centuries.[9] In both cities, street foods were either purveyed or influenced by West African and Caribbean migrants' food traditions. One of the more common street foods was okra stew, or gumbo. Philadelphia had its own version of okra gumbo called pepperpot that Caribbean migrants hawked in the early-nineteenth century.[10] Food is therefore a dynamic lens through which to unearth these shared histories.

By weaving together these and other seemingly disparate narrative threads of ever-evolving city food cultures, *Terroir Tapestries* creatively illuminates how historic urban food systems inform our present daily interactions with street food cultures, and provides insight into access to *terroir*. The shared stories and experiences are embodied in the material objects which make up *Terroir Tapestries*, inviting participants to engage in conversations about community, perceptions of taste and textures, and developments of street food and market cultures. The project archives the deeply rooted spirit of cooking and eating that would otherwise be as ephemeral as the foods consumed. That spirit is preserved in a tapestry of food stories, which promotes deep contemplation of our modern food cultures.

Notes

1   For a comprehensive exploration of *terroir*, see Amy B. Trubek, *The Taste of Place: A Cultural Journey into Terroir* (Oakland: University of California Press, 2009).

2   Thomas Parker, *Tasting French Terroir: The History of an Idea* (Oakland: University of California Press, 2015), 18.

3   Creole rice fritters or donuts.

4   David Gissen, *Subnature: Architecture's Other Environments* (New York: Princeton Architectural Press, 2009), 21–22.

5   Between 1791 and 1910, New Orleans developed an expansive food distribution network consisting of the centrally-located wholesale retail market, the French Market, and a set of auxiliary neighborhood markets.

6   Hosted by the Forum for Scholars and Publics at Duke University.

7   Rogers-Herr Middle School in Durham, North Carolina.

8   The tapestries are currently installed as part of the permanent exhibit collection in the Leah Chase Gallery at the Southern Food and Beverage Museum in New Orleans.

9   Emily Clark, *The Strange History of the American Quadroon: Free Women of Color in the Revolutionary Atlantic World* (Chapel Hill: University of North Carolina Press, 2013), 12–15, 37.

10 Jessica Harris, *High on the Hog: A Culinary Journey from Africa to America* (New York: Bloomsbury, 2011), 72–73.

PART FOUR

Eating in Museums

16

Local, National, and Cosmopolitan:

The Rhetoric of the Museum Restaurant[1]

Mark Clintberg

Museums and galleries are multisensory environments that unite many rhetorical details of display, art, design, and architecture in order to communicate institutional attitudes and mandates. The modern restaurant, where food and other objects are put on display and sold in immersive sensory environments, is in dynamic parallel with the design and operation of the museum since it uses similar means to highlight local, national, and international settings. The purpose of this chapter is explore the rhetorical structure of food service sites in museums in order to understand how food cultures interact with and are integrated into museum practices. My aim is to offer a discussion that will be beneficial to museum staff, architects, chefs, curators, and artists (among others) who hope to think critically about the relation between food service sites and their hosting museums.

Specifically, I will focus on rhetorics of locality, nationalism, and cosmopolitanism implemented in the Victoria and Albert Museum (V&A) and its Café. The V&A is a museum of art and design with a collection of more than four million objects and 145 galleries. The Café offers a self-service buffet of hot and cold prepared meals starting at around £10 per person. The V&A's mission and objectives are several, including: "To be the world's leading museum of art and design" suggesting its international scope, and "to provide diverse audiences with the best quality experience and optimum access to our collections, physically and digitally," implying an investment in regional *and* global constituencies.[2] In the context of this book about food and museums, this study of the V&A Café's history, menu, and architecture offers an important perspective on how institutions can develop a meaningful sensorial encounter for visitors, taking into account the communicative value of food cultures and the ideological implications of serving "cosmopolitan" foods inside of museums. Museum professionals can pay more attention to the history of restaurants in museums as well as the rhetorical value of the local and global food cultures to museum visitors, particularly since these rhetorical values are equally at play in collections and programming.

In this chapter, after a brief introduction to a series of significant theoretical concepts, I will lay out a brief genealogy of the restaurant as a social institution, followed by an account of the sensory turn in museum studies and practice. Then, I will present a history and an analysis of food service sites in the V&A and discuss how local and cosmopolitan values are animated in this site. This discussion is also intended to offer practical knowledge about the growing sensory turn in museums in order to frame the museum visitor as an embodied, intellectual, and social being.

Setting some theoretical foundations

I use "rhetorical" borrowing from Roland Barthes in "The Rhetoric of the Image," where he studies the persuasive properties and strategies of a mid-twentieth-century photographic pasta advertisement.[3] He explains the direct communicative value of advertising as rhetorical since "in advertising these signs are full, formed with a view to the optimum reading: the advertising image is *frank*, or at least emphatic."[4] That is to say that the advert attempts to be as rhetorically clear as possible in order to spark desire in its observer. Barthes points out the nationalistic symbolism in his chosen example, which uses the colors of the Italian flag to communicate "Italianicity."[5] Rhetorical claims can be made effectively through art, design, architecture, and food in order to communicate nationalist, regionalist, and cosmopolitan values to museum visitors and therefore make claims about the institution's reach and attitudes. Museum restaurants often use locally harvested foods, national staples, imported ingredients, and cuisines associated with particular geopolitical sites to suggest such associations in the minds of their visitors. Such gastronomic selections have a parallel in terms of the art and design practices exhibited in museums, when cultural objects created by local or national producers are put into conversation with global practices. This dialectic is inherent in a larger contemporary epistemological tone connected to ecological, economic, cultural, and political factors that are outcomes of globalization but such attitudes should not be accepted at face value. Claims for global reach in Western museum collections have been often marked by the legacies of colonialism, since many cultural objects have arrived in these museums via the works of the colonial enterprise. This could also be argued by the impact of global food cultures in the urban centers of former colonizers—such as London, where the V&A Café is found. It is legitimate to question, in the wake of an unresolved history of colonialism, if cosmopolitanism does indeed exist. Food service sites in museums offer an opportunity to address this question.

Tammi Jonas defines cosmopolitanism as "an openness to and willingness to engage with cultural Others"[6] and draws on Ulf Hannerz's belief that "one cannot simultaneously be both nationalist and cosmopolitan, or feel a strong sense of belonging to both the nation state and the world."[7] Starting from Jonas' perspective, I build on the discussion of cosmopolitanism by Sheldon Pollock, Homi K. Bhabha, Carl A. Breckenridge and Dipesh Chakrabarty.[8] They claim that "cosmopolitanism is yet to come, something awaiting realization."[9] The disappointments associated with nationalism in the twentieth century, they argue, must be counterbalanced by the potentially positive values of "promoting territorially based identities" that are local in quality, in contrast to the siteless, sprawling qualities of the cosmopolitan.[10] To be cosmopolitan is sometimes a matter of necessity rather than choice—not a luxury—as in cases of diasporas and refugees, since "cosmopolitans today are often the victims of modernity, failed by capitalism's upward mobility, and bereft of those comforts and customs of national belonging."[11] I propose that it is because of, not in spite of, such complications hinged on modernity that there has been an upswing in rhetorics of locality in recent years, as apparent in the local food movement that has impacted the menus of museum restaurants. In this context the phrase "think global, act local" is potentially ideologically charged and politically vacant. The local is frequently presented as "the good"—that thing which is so obviously praiseworthy (and prideworthy) that it can allow little room for argument. This discussion of museum restaurants is intended to add nuance and trouble emphatic associations with locality, which often takes the form of nationalism, and cosmopolitanism.

As for my use of the key term "local," I am influenced by Miwon Kwon's approach to the legacy of site specificity in artistic production.[12] Site specificity, describing a set of art practices that are motivated by and designed for particular local contexts, is one of the core principles of later twentieth- and early twenty-first-century art practices. In her study of locality, identity, and site specificity in contemporary art, Kwon identifies key qualities of site-specific art practice, some of which inform my reading of museum restaurants: a direct physical connection between work and site; that the meaning of the artwork occurs in interpreting its context, and is not intrinsic to the work itself; and a post-Cartesian approach to the audience that takes into account the visitor's entire body.[13] Further, Hal Foster proposes that identity itself can be a site for the production of site-specific practices.[14] This trend toward site specificity and locality in art contributes to a broader discourse of the local in popular culture—and especially in food. The museum restaurant can fruitfully unite the site-specific, locale-oriented, and identity-focused art practices that Kwon and Foster study.

A brief genealogy of the restaurant: Inns, taverns, and cookshops

Like museums, restaurants have been studied according to their ritual value, especially in terms of their utility for individuals who hope to put their social identity on display.[15] What is today commonly referred to as "the restaurant" is a malleable category that has incorporated several models of hospitality dating back to at least the early modern period. It has frequently been argued that the foundations of the modern restaurant were first established in post-1789 France as a direct result of the French Revolution and the emergence of the bourgeoisie, a group that sought new sites in which to express their social identity, and found that restaurants suited such pursuits.[16] Restaurants continue to fulfill this socially performative role to this day, providing opportunities to reflect on what groups can access museum food service sites.

Although these genesis stories contribute to the legacy of French nationalism, they do not account for other food service sites established inside and outside of France before 1789. Rather than attempting to concretize a period-location that produced the restaurant, it is important to determine the historically particular iterations of food service sites, which include the restaurant, in order to understand the use of such spaces to other institutions, in this case, museums. These early forms of food service sites reveal distinct functions of eating in public spaces that are deliberately engineered through food, cuisine, architecture, and design.

What I refer to as the quasi-restaurant or a precursor of the modern restaurant was established in England and France as early as the eleventh century. Unlike grocers and markets, which generally sell produce and ingredients in a raw state, quasi-restaurants retail ready to eat foods in "cookshops," street stalls, and other mobile food sites. As sociologist Stephen Mennell explains, cookshops were sites where customers could buy hot food or where they could bring a cut of meat to be cooked.[17] Poor housing conditions, a lack of domestic kitchen facilities, and population density figured into the foundation of the quasi-restaurant in Europe. Amy B. Trubek argues that "increasing urbanism" resulted in a spike in the production of prepared foods in France.[18] These details are important since they reveal that the effects of early modernity ushered in the use of food service sites, which coincided with the outsourcing of tasks previously associated with the domestic sphere, as well as the eventual flourishing of other platforms of public life and the civic sphere, such as libraries, museums, and public plazas. This model of food service is especially useful to consider in museums located in dense urban environments, where alternate institutional food service sites such as food stalls and food carts can provide for the alimentary needs of a local population. As with the early quasi-restaurant, when accessible to people of many different class identities, such food service sites are advantageous because they animate public life, and also provide affordable foods to urban citizens.

The proto-restaurant is a term I use to refer to inns and taverns, which emerged concurrently with the quasi-restaurant. Clients of such places were typically travelers. Inns usually catered to lodging guests rather than the general public. Unlike diners in modern restaurants, guests at inns did not order from a menu full of choices, but instead had to be content with whatever the innkeeper cooked for them.[19] At inns, diners shared seating at large tables with other guests, an arrangement called *table d'hôte* that also featured set menus.[20] Taverns are usually thought of as places mainly for drinking and not for dining, with the exception of the English pub. In the eighteenth century, these were "noted eating-places and centers of social life."[21] Sociability and commensality mark the tavern as distinct from the inn, which would be largely used by strangers, while taverns served as social loci for people who were for the most part familiar with one another and lived in the same community. The proto-restaurant is an important precedent for the museum restaurant: by catering to both local and global visitors, museum restaurants similarly have an opportunity to engage and put into conversation relative strangers. Borrowing design elements from the traditional inn, such as the *table d'hôte* which encourages strangers to dine together, can encourage a sense of commensality for museum visitors.

European inns and taverns existed concurrently with another proto-restaurant: a curious food site that served only soup, after which the "restaurant" of today is named. The French term *restaurant* was used as early as the fifteenth century to refer not to an architectural site, but a "semi-medicinal preparation" designed to revive the ailing.[22] It was not for the sake of social eating that clients ostensibly visited these purveyors, but for the purpose of imbibing a remedy designed to tax the client's digestion as little as possible while still providing apparent nutritional value. "*Restaurant*" draws from the French *restauratif*, meaning to restore, and the food served at these sites was itself called *restaurant* since it was intended to restore the strength of clients. Those who maintain restaurants were and still are called *restaurateurs* in reference to these early soup-serving sites.[23] *Restaurateurs* were part chef, and part pharmacist. Such restaurants were designed specifically for artists and intellectuals, and offered a unique feature: small private tables rather than large shared banquet tables, and flexible hours of service.[24] These clients of delicate aesthetic taste, it would seem, also required delicate tasting food because of their real or feigned fragile health, and required a site that could respond to erratic schedules dictated by their impulsive appetites. In this way, we can see that the museum and the restaurant were enfranchised in similar goals: the reform and amelioration of social bodies in public spaces.[25] Because of these connections, it comes as little surprise that museums house restaurants.

The emergence of modern restaurants in France did not immediately result in food sites of equality, fraternity, and liberty. First of all, kitchens in restaurants were notoriously gendered and homosocial spaces, and according to Trubek, in Europe women were never employed as chefs in the nineteenth century or before[26] and often they were not welcome even as clients. Modern restaurants were class-segregated sites catering to individuals who no longer wished to patronize inns and taverns since these latter sites were known for cheaper food and therefore a mixed demographic of clients, including the lower classes.[27] Higher prices at modern restaurants set up a class-filter, effectively barring entry for the lower classes. This tendency toward class-specific dining was unfortunately continued in the V&A's first restaurant. Also, unlike inns and taverns—where a kind of sociability was expected between guests who were potentially strangers to one another and seated around immense tables—modern restaurants offered islands of controlled and contrived social isolation in a sea of public life. The bourgeoisie, it seems, was the ideal client-group for the modern restaurant since they had disposable wealth and were eager to be conspicuously present in the growing public sphere, while also enjoying a degree of privacy. Like the stand alone restaurant, the museum restaurant offers visitors an opportunity to express their class identity, as well as other markers of identity, in a public setting. If museums hope to genuinely engage with diverse demographics in terms of their programming and collections, by the same token their food service sites should be as open to people of divergent classes, ethnicities, genders as their exhibitions—particularly as museum restaurants have become an important route through which hospitality is extended to visitors.

Sensory experiences in museums

Many museums have food service sites built into their function and space. It has become commonplace that museum renovations include the addition or expansion of food service sites. For example, the Musée du Louvre in Paris has been extensively retrofitted with fifteen food service sites; restaurants are scheduled to open in Tokyo's Mori Museum's renovated spaces and in Cape Town's Zeitz Museum of Contemporary African Art. This food turn is motivated by several factors. Not only do restaurants located in museums generate revenue, which can be channeled back to the institution, but food service sites also offer opportunities for visitors to eat without leaving the museum. Beyond this, working in concord with exhibitions and collections, museum restaurants offer opportunities for institutions to realize and to transmit components of their mandates at sensorial levels. These developments are also connected to a surge of sensory programming in museums and galleries today.

While the increase in sensory programming in many museums, such as tours for the blind and partially-sighted, may seem to be an entirely new phenomenon, it is in fact a return to seventeenth-century attitudes about the means by which collections should be experienced. Constance Classen explains that "the first galleries in private houses were employed precisely for walking. Paintings were added to these galleries in order to give people something at which to look as they walked."[28] Her comments alert the reader to the locomotive quality of early galleries and to the fact that a non-visual sensory experience was a vital component to engaging with such collections. Prior to the nineteenth century, members of upper social classes were admitted to and toured collections freely. During their visits, these guests were given the opportunity to encounter objects from collections through several sensory modes.[29] Englishman John Evelyn's diaries from the seventeenth century reveal that he was given license to handle, to smell, and even to shake artifacts in European collections, and this was usual behavior.[30] The attitudes of this period are echoed in the writing of Johann Gottfried Herder in the 1700s, who valued sculpture because of its ability to stimulate the sense of touch. According to Herder's line of thought, prohibiting touch in museums prevents visitors from developing a complete understanding of sculpture and therefore "[denies] them access to art at its highest level."[31]

Once collections were opened to the general public, including the working classes, sight became the principal means by which visitors were expected to encounter exhibitions. As Fiona Candlin writes, "one of the costs of improved public access to museums was the loss of touch as a valid means of engaging with the collections."[32] Later in the twentieth century touch was increasingly taken into account as a means by which visitors could access collections. Since the 1980s and 1990s, many museums have initiated touch tours and included other sensory components into their programming, often in response to federal and provincial legislation requiring equal access to public institutions.[33] This renewed interest in and support of the non-visual senses in collections and museum programming is the context for observing dialogic relations between art, design, architecture and spectrums of locality, nationalism, and cosmopolitanism in institutional food service sites. Museum restaurants exist within this setting, where sensory access is integrated with education and equitable access to collections.

Other studies serve to contextualize the museum restaurant further in terms of its role as site of entertainment and education. In *The Birth of the Museum*, Tony Bennett compares the sociological effects and organizational models evident in early public museums, and American fairs and amusement parks circa the 1890s.[34] Bennett is interested in programs of social reform and rules of comportment that have been implemented in museums. He highlights the pleasurable properties of sites of amusement that are in parallel to museums of the late nineteenth century: early amusement parks used new technologies of entertainment to enact modernity's fixations on progress and to function as populist places.[35] Museums and fairs, he explains, had in common their "concern to devise ways of regulating the conduct of their visitors, and to do so, ideally, in ways that are both unobtrusive and self-perpetuating."[36] He writes,

> The museum [. . .] explicitly targeted the popular body as an object for reform, doing so through a variety of routines and technologies requiring a shift in the norms of bodily comportment. This was accomplished, most obviously, by the direct proscription of those forms of behavior associated with places of popular assembly by, for example, rules forbidding eating and drinking, outlawing the touching of exhibits and, quite frequently, stating—or at least advising—what should be worn and what should not.[37]

Museum restaurants bring eating and drinking into close contact with environments that have, in general, prohibited such practices. The inclusion of food service sites in museums does not necessarily represent a slackening of rules of conduct, since restaurants, too, have a unique set of such deeply encoded regulations and associations. Museums and galleries are highly ritualized settings that invite visitors to "perform." As Carol Duncan claims,

> In art museums, it is the visitors who enact the ritual (presupposing at least a minimal preparation), whether or not they think of themselves as performers. The museum's sequenced spaces and arrangements of objects, its lighting and architectural details constitute a dramatic field—a combination stage set and script—that both structures and invites a performance.[38]

Duncan's model positions the visitor as an actor who is given the opportunity to perform a script. Immersive museum environments are designed to prompt certain behaviors and responses from visitors. Through these actions, visitors recite or reject the rhetorical scripts of the institution. Duncan writes that the "dramatic field" of the museum, which includes the restaurant is engineered, not accidental. In restaurants, these scripts and performances include architecture, codes of hospitality, rules of sociability and table manners, as well as expressions of taste and distinction.

Sensory design is also implemented in other areas of the museum and not always with strictly educational objectives in mind. Jim Drobnick points out that the multisensory qualities of the museum extend beyond exhibitions: gift shops, for instance, have long offered an array of multisensory products.[39] He notes at the Montreal Museum of Fine Arts gift shop the merchandising of scented soaps wrapped in packaging that depicts artworks such as Vincent Van Gogh's *Starry Night* (1889), suggesting both that the image is affiliated with a particular aroma, and that the museum visitor could somehow transport a component of their museum experience back to their home bathtub.[40] This is one example of how sensorial experience is commoditized in the museum, and food service sites extend this development into the comestible realm.

The history of food services at the V&A

The institution now referred to as the V&A was first opened in 1852 with the objective of increasing local British industry's knowledge and skill in the field of design. First called the Museum of Manufactures, and then the Museum of Ornamental Art, it moved to its current location in 1857, when it was known as the South Kensington Museum. Its earliest exhibitions featured "collections of art and science, *foodstuffs* and animal products, mirroring the informal arrangements of international exhibitions."[41] The museum displayed exhibitions on the subject of food to give "lessons in household and health subjects, especially addressed to the working classes."[42] The display of food cultures was one of the earliest priorities of this museum.

Food service and refreshment also figured into the institution's vision: in 1856, a temporary building was designated as the museum's Refreshment Rooms, designed by Francis Fowke. In a history of the V&A, John Physick refers to these Rooms as a "daring innovation" since it was the first museum in the world to have an affiliated food service site. It also had an alcohol license.[43] However, the first manager of the Rooms, one Mr. G. Withers, made a point of reporting that the public evidently preferred to drink coffee and tea rather than gin while visiting the museum, a comment that was perhaps meant to underscore that food and drink service was not at odds with the moral and social improvement agendas of the nineteenth-century museum project.[44] Returning to Tony Bennett's work, this "agenda" involved a series of rules of museum behavior, which usually prohibited eating and drinking. The Refreshment Rooms were a bold departure since they suggested that the museum should take an interest in the bodily cravings of its visitors, implying in turn that museums should be sites of education and hospitality, and perhaps even that they should educate the visitor in matters of gustatory taste.

In 1899, the museum opened a new building, at which time it was renamed the Victoria and Albert Museum.[45] Although elements of the museum's façade might give the impression of uniformity, its interior is heterogeneous and, according to Michael Darby and his co-authors, involves "changes of level, unhappy junctions between galleries and corridors, different constructional materials, and areas decorated with polychrome tiles, enameled tin, or spirit fresco."[46] It is an architecturally complex—some might say muddled—setting that adapts and presents many styles, ornaments, and traditions drawn from several periods, histories, and regions.[47]

The stylistic elements and menus offered in the V&A Café today echo this tendency toward heterogeneity and hybridity, even if the food service in this museum has a history of class stratification. Early in its history, the South Kensington Museum's restaurant had class-specific menus. The "first class" menu included steak pudding, tarts, and jugged hare, while the "second class" menu had stewed rabbit, veal cutlets, and poached egg and spinach. The "third class" menu was designed for "mechanics and all workmen employed at the Museum Buildings and even for the humble working class visitors."[48] Physick points out that the prices for these items "were not cheap but they remained more or less constant at least till the end of the century."[49] This underscores that at the museum the dimensions of social class were also regulated and subjected to "norms of bodily comportment" to borrow Bennett's phrase, according to the ingestion of comestibles.

Today, in terms of floorplan, the V&A Café is comparatively subordinate to the museum's massive galleries. It occupies a handful of rooms situated at the extreme rear of the Cromwell Road entrance to the museum. Nonetheless, I argue that this site is, in some ways, central to the museum experience for many visitors, as they may reflect upon the galleries they have visited while nourishing their bodies. The V&A Café is housed in the Morris, Gamble, and Poynter Rooms on the first floor of the museum, originally referred to as the Green Dining Room, the Refreshment Room, and the Grill Room, respectively. These are well-preserved examples of interior design in their own right, as worthy of the visitor's attention as any other gallery in a museum devoted to art and design.[50] Occasional statuary is exhibited in the dining areas, including Giovanni Maria Benzoni's *The Italic Venus* (c. 1860). In effect, this site permits eating and drinking in an immersive artistic environment.

The Gamble Room (1865–1878) features ceramic columns and tilework designed by Godfrey Sykes and James Gamble. A contemporary viewer might find the pervasiveness of tilework in the space overwhelming—in part because of the echoing acoustic environment it produces—but this was in part due to a requirement that the decorative elements in the space be entirely washable.[51] Philosophies of taste are also put on view in the space. Stained glass windows are decorated with several quotations, including some that relate to cuisine, such as "Hunger is the best sauce," an aphorism famously used by Immanuel Kant to denigrate cooking as a merely agreeable art.[52] Another frieze incorporates a quotation from Ecclesiastes: "There is nothing better for a man than that he should eat and drink, and make his soul enjoy good in his labour—XYZ".[53] The Morris Room (1866–1868) is so named after William Morris, who along with his firm Morris, Marshall, and Faulkner, designed the Room in a style in the tradition of Gothic Revival. Its floor is covered in geometric, crimson tiles, and its windows are filled with colored glass decorated with figures, and green glass in round panes decorated with small animals. The Poynter Room (1876–1881) includes a stove ornamented with Japanese inspired elements, while the walls feature blue and white tilework that draws on Dutch styles of the seventeenth century. Today, these spaces are decorated with chrome and burgundy leather dining chairs surrounding metal pedestal-based tables that can seat four to five people. This brief description gives evidence of the array of aesthetic styles of diverse origin on display in the space.

Locality, nationalism, and cosmopolitanism at the V&A Café

There are compelling parallels between the museum's exhibition program and its food service. The V&A's programming has a global reach, with exhibitions and collections that draw on global cultures. Galleries are devoted to objects from locations including South-East Asia, Korea, Japan, the Middle East, and Europe. These tendencies are also echoed in the cuisine purveyed in its restaurant. The Café's menu is a mix of European cuisines and dishes associated with North African, Middle Eastern, and South-East Asian cultures. The menu includes selections from French and Anglo-Saxon contexts, with dishes such as goat cheese crostini, *pain au chocolat*, butterbean, leek and mushroom casserole served with mash, as well as more internationally oriented dishes like prawn Vietnamese spring rolls, tamarind marinated salmon filet, and meze including tzatziki, beetroot labneh, and harissa butternut squash. The expected British high tea, with scones and clotted cream, is also available. All of these foods are displayed in a series of service stations that the diner can visit at leisure, just like museum galleries. These elements give visitors the sense that they are in an institution rooted in national culture—one can enjoy a ritualistic high tea—but that also has a global reach, reminding the diners that London has large diasporic communities with diverse gastronomic cultures, many of which have arrived in London as a direct or indirect outcome of colonial histories.

The V&A Café's arrangement of service stations encourage visitors to wander and to piece together whatever edible commodities they like to fashion their own cosmopolitan blend of foodstuffs. In this sense, the perambulatory component of the gallery is used advantageously to promote the consumption of commodities *as well as* a sense of internationalism. Although drawing attention to the commoditized components of museum design may seem vulgar, not only does the V&A gift shop commoditize its collection through various objects, from postcards to T-shirts, the V&A Café also commoditizes the experience of dining in historically important Morris, Gamble, and Poynter Rooms. This food service site provides a range of edible commodities associated with national and global cultures, the consumption of which can be rehearsed through dining. These are symbolic acts of consumption that encourage visitors, who are also diners, to consider the V&A as an institution with global and national reach and interests. Through ingestion, the visitors may also be given the impression that they too are cosmopolitans, just like the museum's collections, exhibitions, and overall location. This raises the question of how *local* cultures can be highlighted in such settings, as well as how the complexity of personal identity and food's associative value is at play in museum restaurants.

Arjun Appadurai's theory of gastro-politics influences my approach to locality and the commoditization of food in connection with food's associative value.[54] He emphasizes the ability for food to "bear social messages" and act as a "peculiarly powerful semiotic device" and "cultural system."[55] Building on Appadurai's ideas, the semiotic system of food is remarkably engrained on a cultural level but this system is also malleable according to local context. The V&A eating spaces offer complex, even confused, semiotic chains. At the V&A Café, it is possible to consume a harissa[56] butternut squash seated in a room decorated by William Morris, an English designer, while admiring a sculpture by Benzoni, an Italian sculptor. To understand the complexity of these associations, it is important to point out that Tunisia was a French protectorate, which occasioned the early import of commodities, such as harissa, to the metropole. Encapsulated in the visitor's experience of this site, therefore, is a cosmopolitan encounter between the history of French, and by extension, European, colonialism in North Africa, the legacy of neoclassicism and the Italian Renaissance, the British setting, and the aesthetic philosophies of a British designer. These situations present a kind of sensorial, material, and semiotic *mise-en-abyme* of the national and the global. To that extent, the V&A Café is a hybrid environment.

I use the term hybrid borrowing from Homi K. Bhabha, who argues that there is "overwhelming evidence of a more transnational and translational sense of the hybridity of imagined communities."[57] Bhabha gives many examples of this tendency to demonstrate how narratives dealing with a particular locality are in fact hybridized and give account of other locale-specific narratives. Hybridized food and hospitality practices, which combine ingredients and design elements associated with divergent geopolitical sites, are evident in the V&A Café. When food becomes hybridized, national food cultures are morphed according to locally available ingredients, further reflecting the site-specific qualities of gastronomy. The valuable potential of such food practices is that they bring awareness of embodied experiences, and in particular multisensory and discordant sensory experiences in museum contexts that reflect such locale-specific alterations to national foods. An additional benefit is that these initiatives use food and harness sensory experience to raise debate about how local subjective identities are defined through geographic location, rooting in community, and hybrid cultures.

Taking into account Herder's perspective on the haptic qualities of sculpture, the visitor is presented with a relay of sensations at the V&A Café, presumably encountering food cultures associated with North Africa and material culture with links to Italy. And yet, if we consider Appadurai's approach, the situation is hardly this simple. While Benzoni was a neoclassicist reviving the stylistic details and theories of Greek and Roman antiquity, the ingredients included in the harrisa butter squash dish, some of which are locally harvested, are nonetheless a product of a deeply globalized chain of commodity trade connected to no single point of origin. While harissa carries rhetorical associations with Tunisia, and squash is a food with direct ties to English cuisine, squash was in fact first native to North America and later popularized in Europe. Therefore, the national or regional associations of this dish are ultimately hybridized even if the squash in question was locally grown.

Although I have introduced the terms "local" and "cosmopolitan" as antipodes, at this point it is useful to problematize their relationship. If one can imagine the cosmopolitan individual as a citizen of the world, it is equally important to trouble this definition. Associations between food, cosmopolitanism, and nationalism are more complex than locating a point of origin, as demonstrated in a few brief examples from the wealth of literature dealing with this question. Jeffrey Pilcher describes the contests of cuisine that took place in the wake of the military conflict between Mexico and France, Cinco de Mayo (1862). After the battle, many elites and aspiring elites in Mexico "considered the mastery of French cuisine essential."[58] According to Pilcher, working-class taquerías served to "reclaim the honour of Mexico's national cuisine" in reaction to the growing fashion for French cuisine.[59] He describes the "cosmopolitan" tastes of elite Mexicans, which veered toward continental cuisine, as an expression of "the hegemony of French chefs over Mexican cuisine [which] did not go unchallenged."[60] Pilcher outlines the history of the taco as a newly emerged "national snack food" ushered in by Manuel Payno's 1891 volume *Los bandidos de Río Frío*, which mocks the standards of French cuisine in favor of Creole dishes.

In this setting, the associations between cosmopolitan and national foods are clearly at odds with one another and are also class specific. Pilcher's example points out the potentially negative and colonial associations of cosmopolitanism in food cultures. Josée Johnston and Shyon Baumann engage with the growing absorption of working class, so-called "ethnic" foods, and "comfort" foods into the realm of "high-end cuisine."[61] They align this trend with "cultural omnivorousness," defined by Richard Peterson et al. as a general shift in elite-class cultural consumption away from selective distinction that favors so-called high culture, and toward broad tastes and distinctions that are "increasingly diversified, inclusive, or omnivorous."[62] Rather than celebrating such "inclusive" dining as a democratizing move, Johnston and Baumann critique that "food is legitimized for omnivores when it can be framed as authentic or exotic," and that these values "work to validate a relatively narrow range of foods that require considerable cultural and/or economic capital on the part of individuals."[63] In an important footnote, the authors make connections between omnivorousness and cosmopolitanism, quoting Ulrich Beck's[64] useful and incisive definition of cosmopolitanism: "internal globalization, globalization from within the national societies."[65] To be a cultural omnivore may be to echo or unintentionally animate the destructive ideologies of globalization.

Conclusion

This discussion is intended to highlight the challenges inherent in designing museum restaurants that realize or promote institutional mandates. The V&A Café has an especially complex situation since it collides national and global associated foods and cultural objects with local and international visitors. By drawing on locally-grown produce and local inflections of national dishes, this site also aspires to engage with local context and cultures, including the different diasporas. The V&A Café deploys many of the tactics Kwon identifies— in particular the bodily, immersive qualities of the local site. In a way, however, the "site" activated in these museum restaurants is in fact the visitor's body, which, drawing on Duncan's ideas, can be said to perform a script through the symbolic and actual consumption of local and international cultures through observation and ingestion. These queries also serve to underscore the troubled nature of what it means to "be local"—that is, to be from or of a place, in a time of diasporas and migrations. Cultural institutions, such as museums, aim to demonstrate a commitment to local and national contexts, at a time of high cosmopolitanism through the symbolic and economic force of local foods hybridized with global dishes. Returning to the genealogy of the restaurant and incorporating the sensory turn in exhibition contexts can offer useful models for the future of food-based commensality in museums.

Although I have argued that the V&A Café uses food service in a complex, sophisticated, and rhetorical manner in order to give greater ballast to claims for local engagement with a global twist, I wish to stress that the foodways rehearsed and displayed in this setting are both a product of historical colonial enterprise that further commoditize the embodied consumption of culture in the museum setting. Museum professionals must be attentive to such associative values both in their programming and collections, and in the sites of hospitality that they offer to visitors. They should be aware of the "omnivorous" quality of cultural consumption and the potentially negative effects such attitudes can have. Framing "international" food practices in an aura of exoticism serves to undermine the genuinely *local* iterations of the foods associated with diasporic cultures. Rather than ornamenting diasporic food cultures with the freight of exoticism, museum restaurants should show how such cultures are uniquely inflected according to locality, and genuinely *a part of* the publics and constituencies that surround (and potentially support) the museum as an enterprise of public life.

Notes

1   The research on which this article is based was in part supported by the Hands-On Museum project, which is funded by the Social Sciences and Humanities Research Council of Canada (grant no. 410-2011-2645). The author thanks David Howes and Constance Classen for their interest in and support of this study.

2   V&A Mission and objectives, accessed Jan. 15, 2016,

3   Roland Barthes, "The Rhetoric of the Image," in *Image/Music/Text: Essays Selected and Translated by Stephen Heath* (London: Fontana Press, 1977), 32–51.

4   Ibid., 33.

5   Ibid., 47.

6   Tammy Jonas, "Eating the Vernacular, Being Cosmopolitan," *Cultural Studies Review* 19 no. 1 (2013): 117.

7   Ulf Hannerz, cited in Jonas, 2013, 117–118.

8 Homi K. Bhabha, Carl. A. Breckenridge, Dipesh Chakrabarty, and Sheldon Pollock, "Introduction," *Public Culture* 12 no. 3 (2000): 577–589.

9 Ibid., 577.

10 Ibid., 578.

11 Ibid., 582.

12 Miwon Kwon, *One Place After Another: Site-Specific Art and Locational Identity* (Cambridge; London: MIT Press, 2002).

13 Ibid., 12.

14 Hal Foster, *The Return of the Real: The Avant-Garde at the End of the Century*, (Cambridge and London: MIT Press, 1996).

15 Carol Duncan, "The Art Museum as Ritual," *Art Bulletin* 77 no. 1 (1995): 10–13.

16 For sources on the history of the restaurant, see: Rebecca Spang, *The Invention of the Restaurant: Paris and Modern Gastronomic Culture* (Cambridge: Cambridge University Press, 2000); Elliott Shore, "Dining Out: The Development of the Restaurant," in *Food: The History of Taste*, ed. by Paul Freedman (Berkeley: University of California Press, 2007); Amy B. Trubek, *Haute Cuisine: How the French Invented the Culinary Profession* (Philadelphia: University of Pennsylvania Press, 2000).

17 Stephen Mennell, *All Manners of Food: Eating and Taste in England and France from the Middle Ages to the Present* (Oxford: Basil Blackwell, 1985), 136.

18 Trubek, 31.

19 Spang,136.

20 Trubek, 36.

21 Mennell, 137.

22 Spang, 1.

23 Alain Drouard, "Chefs, Gourmets and Gourmands: French Cuisine in the 19th and 20th Centuries," in *Food: The History of Taste*, ed. by Paul Freedman (Berkeley: University of California Press, 2007), 269.

24 Shore, 304.

25 Tony Bennett, *The Birth of the Museum* (New York: Routledge, 1995).

26 Trubek, 40.

27 Spang, 72.

28 Constance Classen, "Museum Manners: The Sensory Life of the Early Museum," *Journal of Social History* 40, no. 4 (2007): 897.

29 Ibid.; see also: Fiona Candlin, *Art, Museums and Touch* (Manchester: Manchester University Press, 2010).

30 Classen, 18.

31 Classen, 279.

32 Candlin, 85.

33 Key pieces of legislation include the Canadian Charter of Rights and Freedoms (1982), which prohibits discrimination against the disabled, "the duty to accommodate" clause of the Canadian Human Rights Act (1985), and the Americans with Disabilities Act (1990). Kevin Hetherington outlines that the United Nations' International Year of Disabled Persons (1981), 1985's Carnegie Trust Fund report on accessibility to culture for disabled persons, and the Disability Discrimination Act (1995) have all influenced museum awareness and mandate related to accessibility in Britain.

34 Bennett, 1995.

35 Ibid., 4.

36 Ibid., 6.

37 Ibid., 100.

38 Duncan, 10–13.

39 Jim Drobnick, "The Museum as Smellscape," in *The Multisensory Museum: A Cross-disciplinary Perspective on Multiple Modalities of a Museum Experience*, ed. by Nina Levent and Alvaro Pascual-Leone (Lanham: Rowman and Littlefield, 2013), 177–196.

40 Ibid., 177.

41 Michael Conforti "The Idealist Enterprise and the Applied Arts," in *A Grand Design: The Art of the Victoria and Albert Museum*, ed. by Malcolm Baker and Brenda Richardson (New York: Harry N. Abrams, 1997), 24.

42 Michael Darby et al. *The Victoria and Albert Museum* (London: Scala; Philip Wilson, 1983), 5.

43 John Physick, *The Victoria and Albert Museum: The History of its Building* (Oxford: Phaidon, 1982), 30.

44 Ibid., 31.

45 It was designed by Francis Fowke and Henry Scott, and its façade was designed by Sir Aston Webb.

46 Darby et al., 3.

47 This is at least in part due to an ambitious series of renovations and extensions over many decades since it moved to its current location in 1857.

48 N.a. "100 Facts about the V&A," accessed May 18, 2015, http://www.vam.ac.uk/content/articles/0-9/100-facts-about-the-v-and-a/.

49 Physick, 100.

50 The Grill Room was so named because of an iron grill designed by Edward Poynter, which figured prominently in the space.

51 Physick, 136.

52 Immanuel Kant, *Critique of Judgment*, trans. James Creed Meredith (Oxford: Oxford University Press, (2007 [1790]), 42.

53 Physick, 138.

54 Arjun Appadurai, "Gastro-politics in Hindu South Asia," *American Ethnologist* 8 no. 3 (1981): 494–511.

55 Ibid., 494.

56 Harissa is a Tunisian spice mixture of Serrano peppers, roasted red peppers and spices.

57 Homi K. Bhabha, *The Location of Culture* (New York: Routledge, 2004), 7.

58 Jeffrey Pilcher, "Mexico City, 1891," *Victorian Review* 36, no. 1 (2010): 42.

59 Ibid.

60 Ibid., 43.

61 Josee Johnston and Shyon Baumann, "Democracy versus Distinction: A Study of Omnivorousness in Gourmet Food Writing," *American Journal of Sociology* 113, no. 1 (2007): 166.

62 Peterson cited in Johnston & Baumann, 168.

63 Ibid., 169.

64 Ulrich Beck, "The Cosmopolitan Society and Its Enemies," *Theory, Culture and Society* 19 (2002): 17–44.

65 Ibid., footnote 2.

17

Cooking as Art or the Art of Cooking[1]

Marta Arzak

A fortunate encounter and creative parallelisms

Publications about the interrelations between cooking and artistry are quite unusual, so prior to writing this essay I felt the need to conduct research on a topic with which I have long been familiar. I come from a family of chefs who have been running the Arzak restaurant in San Sebastian, Basque Country, Spain, since 1897. My father, Juan Maria Arzak, was one of the founders of the 1976 New Basque Cuisine movement. Today, he and my sister Elena Arzak work together creating a signature Basque cuisine, research-based, evolving and cutting edge.

I spent the vacations of my youth in the family restaurant, gaining insight into the close relation between food, cooking, and creativity. As an adult, I opted for a career in the visual arts, rather than the culinary arts; while studying art history and contemporary art, I became deeply interested in the connections between the two fields. My work at the Guggenheim Museum Bilbao has reinforced my skills in interpreting such links. Gradually, I began to collaborate as art adviser at Arzak, our family restaurant, and to curate projects and exhibitions that link art and gastronomy.[2] In this chapter I will summarize some of the projects with which I have been involved, where chefs and their creativity are the main protagonists.

Some people think that chefs have artistic personalities, and it is obvious that there are many parallelisms between cooking and artistic practices. Indeed, the analogies are undeniable at certain stages of the creative and working processes of both disciplines: the conceptualization of the idea, the production, and the materialization of it ending up in a dish or an artwork. Cooking food is a basic human need, an element of survival, but has always stimulated the senses, giving pleasure as well as sustenance. Nowadays, there is a new symbiotic relation between art and food caused by social and political changes that consequently evolve in society's need for new and continuous stimulus. The human brain is a "creative" muscle that interprets reality using the sensorium in multiple ways that vary between each of us, and that may provoke completely different gustatory and aesthetic experiences. Therefore, physiological and neurological issues influence an individual's interpretation of a dish and provide feedback to the chef; similar feedback occurs in certain artistic or aesthetic experiences, but the main difference between the two creative disciplines lies in taste and the role it plays in the creative process and in its result. In cuisine taste is the basis of everything, but in art it may be important in certain projects or artworks (e.g., a banquet orchestrated by an artist), but it is not always determinant.

documenta 12 and Ferran Adrià: A controversial initiative

In September 2006, chef Ferran Adrià phoned me saying that Roger M. Buergel, director of *documenta 12* (June 16 to September 23, 2007), had invited him to participate in that event not as *documenta*'s chef but as a thinker citing Adrià's "creative intelligence." Adrià is considered the chef who reinvented food; one of the world's greatest chefs. elBulli, his and Juli Soler's restaurant in Cala Montjoi, Roses, Spain will hold a prominent place in culinary history.

On that occasion, Buergel and his wife Ruth Noack, *documenta*'s commissioner, established three themes: modernity, bare life, and education. Buergel and Adrià agreed to work together in developing a proposal that is aligned with these themes as well as the chef's and elBulli's spirit. Adrià considered some options: an exhibition of the creative processes in the workshop and the restaurant, a film showcasing diners while eating at elBulli, an interactive display showing a menu designed by Adrià, or cooking just for one table as an art performance. All these options were eventually dismissed because of being just a representation of different experiences at elBulli rather than the real and direct experience of his cuisine. Finally, Adrià had the idea of converting elBulli in an external pavilion of *documenta* located in Cala Montjoi: the ideal exhibiting space for a chef is the restaurant itself, not only because the guest can experience the food best, but also because this context facilitates the real atmosphere and all technical conditions needed to create

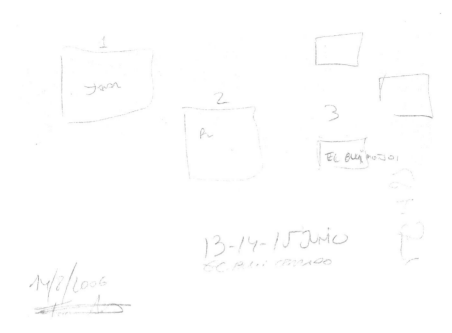

FIGURE 17.1 *Ferran Adrià's sketch showing different pavilions of* documenta 12 and elBulli as nr 3.

© *Ferran Adrià.*

the menu properly. Besides, Adrià had stopped cooking outside elBulli some time ago, and this option was the only possibility of showing the real essence of elBulli.

Concept development for *documenta*

Once Buergel and Noack approved this idea, Adrià asked me to join him on this extraordinary journey. My role was to accurately interpret the intersections between the art world and *haute cuisine* and to provide Adrià with the theoretical basis that would help him make his project feasible, to ensure that his proposal was coherent with both Buergel's intention and the nature of Adrià's creative process as a chef. We initiated an exploration and research process, similar to the lesson of anatomy that is extensively described in the book *Food for Thought, Thought for Food*.[3] The team explored the history of *documenta*, historical development of multiple artistic disciplines in Western culture, parallelisms and differences between the artistic and cooking disciplines, exhibiting practices in the art world, and concepts such as contextualization and de-contextualization. It was not our intention to equate cooking with art, but rather to identify the flexibility and permeability between different artistic disciplines in different moments of history.

There are many historical references about artistry and cooking practices. Greek historians documented the Babylonian and Egyptian banquets, but were the Greco-Roman ones the most lavish and magnificent due to their magnitude, recipes, displays of food, and the feasts organized around them.[4] For example, great masters like polymath Leonardo da Vinci or composer Gioacchino Rossini were also extraordinary gourmets and highly creative chefs.[5] Furthermore, visual artists have used and continue to use food and cooking in very diverse ways. In the past, food was depicted in still-life paintings and genre scenes mostly; then, in the twentieth century, numerous artists—starting with the futurists, the Dadaists, the surrealists and following with others like Janine Antoni, Joseph Beuys, Allan Krapov, Antoni Miralda, Juan Muñoz, Alicia Ríos, Martha Rossler or Rirkrit Tiravanija, among others— began using food, cooking, and the act of eating as media for conceptual, relational, political, or social representation and production purposes.

We found many analogies between creative and working processes in art and gastronomy: starting with the conceptualization of an idea, following with the manipulation of the materials or food, and ending up with the creation of a work of art or a dish and resulting in a product that is complete with sensory stimulation and sublimation of the senses.[6] The main difference lies in the senses, specifically in the supremacy of taste in gastronomy. Even though taste may be associated with some contemporary artworks, in cooking it is the basis of all production and consumption. After we analyzed the different typologies of art exhibits, we reached the conclusion that the logical and natural exhibition space for cooking was the restaurant itself. Removing creative cooking from its natural context would mean distorting its essence by trying to produce a substitute for it. Adrià always insisted that "cuisine is cuisine" and that he is a chef and not a painter, a sculptor, or a performer. In his opinion, cooking has its own disciplinary singularity, rules, and language in terms of creativity, representation, and display.

elBulli at *documenta*

The project presented by Ferran Adrià in *documenta 12* had at its center keystone "the table of *documenta*." Daily, Buergel and Noack selected and invited two *documenta* visitors to travel to Cala Montjoi and to have dinner at elBulli. Most of those selected were artists, art professionals, *documenta* visitors, and staff. elBulli restaurant was considered the "G pavilion," located in Cala Montjoi, 860 miles away from Kassel. At elBulli, *documenta* banners were installed and its logo was stamped on the menu of elBulli during the entire season of 2007. The catalog of the event was sold in elBulli and simultaneously the books of the restaurant were available at the art event in Kassel. The menu tasted in Cala Montjoi was exhibited outside the office of the director of *documenta* weekly.

This initiative was controversial and polemical because of the geographical distance and the restrictions of dining at elBulli. Many visitors to *documenta* felt frustrated (and so did we), but it was not possible to cancel the reservations made by clients of elBulli months ago. In fact, it is the frustration that is felt about long waiting lists of elBulli every year. The project was not only a dinner at elBulli but a global experience: trying to get a table, to get there, the expectations if succeeding in getting the table or the frustration resulting from not getting it, the first impressions while entering the restaurant, the scenography of the restaurant, the staff, and all feelings, emotions, sensations, thoughts, and conversations that come up during and after dinner. We were convinced that the project was the more ethical and coherent with Adrià's creative intelligence and the themes of *documenta*. Adrià said, "I'm showing that what I have been invited for and the basis of my work in 2007 is at elBulli." During a period of 100 days, two people had dinner daily at the "*documenta* table" of elBulli. The fact that these visitors were mostly artists and not gourmets, who make gastronomic trips regularly, that they did not know about elBulli's cuisine, allowed for a unique and pure experience and made them a valuable source of information. All their feedback in the form of letters, drawings, and written responses was collected in the book *Food for Thought, Thought for Food.*

After *documenta*

In 2011, elBulli closed as a restaurant and was transformed into the elBulli foundation: the creative laboratory, elBullilab, was opened in Barcelona in 2014. Another space, elBulli 1846, a space devoted to linking gastronomy with other creative disciplines will open in Cala Montjoi, elBulli's original location, in 2016. Adrià and his team participated actively in touring exhibitions. The exhibition *Ferran Adrià and elBulli. Risk, Freedom and Creativity* (Palau Robert, Barcelona) explored the creative universe of Adrià and the team of elBulli. Another exhibit, *elBulli: Ferran Adrià and the Art of Food* (Somerset House, London) showcased the art of cuisine by taking a behind-the-scenes look at the laboratory and kitchen of elBulli. Yet, another exhibition *Ferran Adrià: Notes on Creativity*, curated by Brett Littman at The Drawing Center of New York, featured Adrià's drawings, sketches, diagrams, and models and underscored the key role of drawing in his creative process. The exhibition *Ferrán Adrià.*

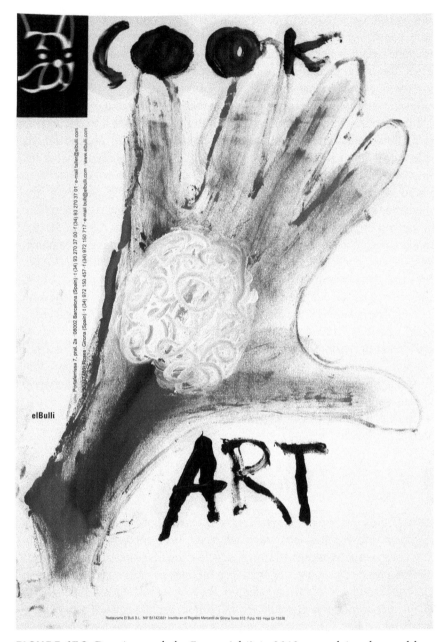

FIGURE 17.2 *Drawing made by Ferran Adrià in 2013 to explain when and how cooking began.*

© *Ferran Adrià.*

Auditando el proceso creativo, organized by Fundación Telefónica in 2014, is not on gastronomy but on the creative transformation of Adrià and the team of elBulli during twenty-five years.

Exhibiting *Frying Water*

The exhibition *Ura Frijitzen/Friendo agua* (Frying Water) aimed to metaphorically provide insight into how Elena Arzak, Xabier Gutiérrez and Igor Zalakain, chefs at the Arzak restaurant's laboratory, conduct their culinary research.[7] This symbolic representation of the laboratory was representative of these chefs' personalities and mental and creative processes. In principle, frying water is impossible. Actually it may seem impossible from a culinary perspective but also can give rise to something surprising and unexpected like serendipity. Elena Arzak, Xabier Gutiérrez and Igor Zalakain believe their work to be both team-based and individualistic, constantly immersed in a creative, intuitive, and reflective cycle. Consequently, and by showing the conceptualization of dishes rather than the complete culinary process, we tried to reveal what arises from the realms of imagination. The resulting exhibition was full of unanswered questions. Sometimes the research process is successful and other times it reaches a dead end; however, whatever happens the chef always benefits.

This unusual project was presented in the art gallery Espacio Marzana in Bilbao and at the Fundación Pilar i Joan Miró in Palma de Mallorca in response to the desire of these art spaces to share other creative languages besides art with their regular audiences. Also, it was a strategic opportunity to attract new audiences interested in cooking and gastronomy. At the Fundación Pilar i Joan Miró, the exhibition was located at Espai Zero, a room dedicated to young artists and other creative disciplines and whose working processes are in line with the experimental nature of Miró's artwork. It also coincided with the project *Pebre Bord!* (Paprika!), a campaign organized by FPJM (an art institution well-known for its educational vocation) in collaboration with the Slow Food Movement in the Balearic Islands.

The exhibition was divided into the following sections[8]:

1   "Fresh Recipes" "stored" in a refrigerator as a documentary resource of four dishes like *El círculo del chipirón* (The squid circle), *Rape con hilos y médula* (Monkfish with bone marrow), *Cordero con café cortado* (Lamb with macchiato coffee) and *Pompas de fresa* (Strawberry bubbles). Each recipe development had three phases: the concept; the composition or drawing; and the execution of the recipe. Visitors could pry into the contents of the refrigerator and take recipes home, never knowing whether they were real or fictitious.

2   "The Spice Room" housed a selection of various culinary products like spices, teas, flours, seeds, and salts, among others. These samples form part of the idea bank and often serve as an inspiration for the chefs. Aromas of spice and food scented the gallery space evoking the real spice room and the sense of smell that is intrinsic at a certain point in their creative process.

3   "Preparation in a Flash" was a speeded-up projection showing the multiple proofs and demonstrations of the different stages of preparation of a dish as well as the rhythm of work in the production process.

4   Getting the "Crack" was an audio recording reproducing some of the usual sounds in their working space, such as the breaking and cutting of different ingredients, sounds of electrical appliances, the crashing of diverse utensils, and cutlery, or the act of chewing and slurping.

5   "Culinary Terms" explained *tasting, smelling, curdling, removing, wrapping, emulsifying,* etc., and these are some of the terms that are used widely in the culinary lexicon. Chosen and written on a board randomly, they evoked the brainstorming and exchange of ideas that regularly happen in the laboratory.

6   "Deforming Form. Smashing Dishes" included stainless steel objects which were designed especially in the laboratory for presenting food in different ways. Models and prototypes made of steel were exhibited as an extension of an essential element to show and serve food: imagination. They also worked as playful objects that could be decorated and stuffed with unlikely suggestions and proposals.

7   "Dead End" included real images of tests, both successful and unsuccessful, and these were chosen randomly. Other images, taken by photographer Begoña Zubero, portrayed Elena Arzak, Xabier Gutiérrez and Igor Zalakain in a humorous attitude, at a reflective moment or at a dead end. In addition the three chefs were symbolically represented with their respective chef jackets welcoming or hosting the visitors.

This exhibition intended to demonstrate how during the creative process of culinary research, sometimes there are stages that need to be repeated, other times chefs succeed or fail, even unconsciously. All the sections were inevitably interrelated and formed part of the same integral process. It was clear that due to conservation and technical limitations of the exhibition spaces, food, represented through Arzak's dishes, could not be served in them. Metaphors, take-away recipes, representation of dishes and, above all, the sensorium through smell, sound, and sight was our best choice. One of

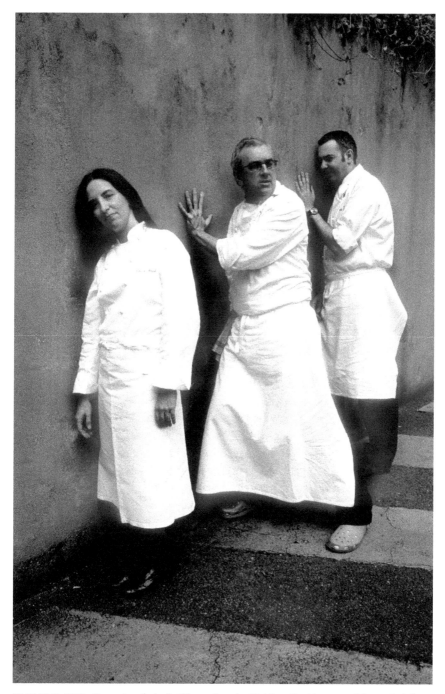

FIGURE 17.3 *Portrait of chefs Elena Arzak, Xabier Gutiérrez and Igor Zalakain for the exhibition* Frying Water.

© *Begoña Zubero.*

our main concerns was about the audience that would visit this kind of exhibition in an art space and how we could provide visitors with the best understanding and enjoyment of it. The audience included regular art museum and gallery visitors interested in contemporary art; artists, art professionals, and new visitors interested in food, cooking, and gastronomic issues, mostly chefs and culinary students.

A conversation with chefs about the art of cooking

For these chefs, Arzak, Gutiérrez, and Zalakain, the exhibition *Frying Water* was a reliable symbolic and conceptual representation of the creative processes at Arzak's laboratory. It was also challenging since it was the first time that they had exposed publicly their working method this way and it happened in an art gallery. Despite the initial fear, this laborious and intense exhibition development process helped them to order their ideas about their creative process and to translate them into concepts and a language accessible to a broader audience rather that the one attending professional gastronomic forums.

Recently, I had a chance to revisit the project with these chefs as well as discuss their craft. "How would you change the exhibit if you were to do it again?" I asked. In their opinion the project is valid in terms of the concept, but today they would try to introduce the visitor to a more multisensory, interactive, and surprising experience through technology, sustainability concepts, and joyful and participatory practices in cooking. Now diners are looking to and experimenting with other kinds of sensations and stimulus besides the gustatory ones. Gutiérrez went further: "I would change everything today. In terms of space, I feel uncomfortable to do it in an art space since when one speaks about creativity it makes no sense to speak neither about spaces nor about walls. I'm a dreamer and a creator. Regarding the contents, I would focus on 'observation' rather than in the complete processes. Observation and creativity are the most difficult parts of it (observation, creativity, experimentation and enjoyment) the essential and primordial stages."

"What do you think about the relation between art and cooking?" was my second question. "I didn't study Fine Arts," said Arzak. "I decided to be a chef because I loved cooking not because I wanted to become an artist. . . . Our main aim is to reach the public through creativity." Zalakain responded: "It's not the chef's responsibility or place to say if his work is art. For me visiting a market is like looking at a painting, you can see all that is life in there: culture, economy, people, products, gastronomy, social relations, etc. Chefs have had many professional claims. Until recently they had a low social status. Though, I think that is an exaggeration that chefs were considered in the same vein as philosophers or doctors, we just should try to reach our own status." "I'm not very interested in this matter, I've not even reflected on it. I don't consider myself an artist but a curious person," said Gutiérrez. Meanwhile, these and other chefs keep searching for the Holy Grail of creativity.

The act of eating together: Crisis or transformation?

The London-based Delfina Foundation launched a thematic residency focused on *The Politics of Food*[9] in 2014. I was invited to participate in the second season as food curator, specifically, in the section on Diet, to explore issues of nutrition, marketing, and identity.

The Basque Country, where I come from, is one of the top gastronomic destinations in Spain and worldwide, a pilgrimage place for gourmets and

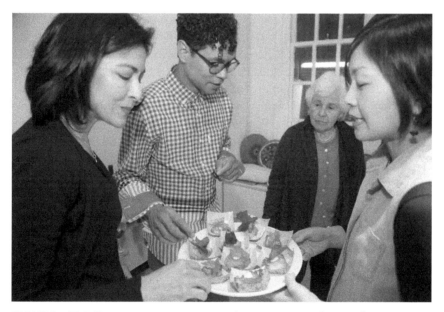

FIGURE 17.4 *Basque creative pintxos (tapas) tasting during the event* On Commensality: The Act of Eating Together. Crisis or Transformation? *at Delfina Foundation. In the image: Beatriz Mérida, Aaron Cezar, Delfina Entrecanales and chef Satoko Habara.*

© *Christa Holka.*

foodies. Here, everything revolves around food and cooking: births, funerals, popular festivals, businesses, gatherings of friends, and politics happen around the table. While we eat, we speak about food always. Thus, I focused the research project on the topic of *commensality*, as it is considered one of the main and primal acts on which human social relations are based. Together with Harry West, a food anthropologist from the University of London, we identified the focus of my investigation: Etymology and definition of the word "commensality," the history of the concept, crisis, or transformation of commensality.

The origin of the word "commensality" is in the late nineteenth century and its etymology refers to Medieval Latin *commensalis* (*com* "sharing" + *mensa* "a table") and some meanings suggest the following definition: the practice of eating together or as a social group. Human beings have eaten together throughout time and worldwide. When becoming omnivores (more or less over 2.5 million years ago) the act of eating together prevailed over the "erratic" feeding needed to survive. In the late Neolithic age Homo sapiens invented pots for storage and cooking. Starting with breastfeeding and continuing with daily meals, banquets or religious rituals, the forms and reasons why people eat together go from an embodied commensality to an enculturated one.

Eating and drinking at the same table is a fundamental social activity that generates and strengthens social relationships.[10] Also boundaries can include or exclude people according to, for example, social criteria. Some commercial and marketing issues may exclude commensals due to the high cost of some food products. Eating together has class connotations, links to social organization, and numerous forms of representation based on appearances, privileges, and ethical aspects. People's relationships to the way they eat can be compared to a spoken language, that is, we do not always remember the grammar but we speak automatically and fluently, and the same applies to manners around the table.

Physiological and neurological dimensions may explain the difference in our individual experiences of food. The brain creates tastes and smells, and even sight and sound are interpreted in the brain's cognitive process. How and what we eat generate a gustatory map in our minds that leads to certain forms of nutrition and diets. This gustatory map is reinforced by breastfeeding first and is completed by family food, when the enjoyment of recognizable food (family, school, neighborhood, and work) crystalizes in a culinary and gustatory identity. However, globalization, manufactured products, and transgenes are causing an increasing homogenization of taste.

Since food produces changes in our bodies, what we think about it and about its representation is linked to our act of eating, what we eat and what we do not eat. Our socioeconomic status conditions the way we eat as well.

Roughly speaking, people on low incomes may consume food that provides strength and that can be eaten "collectively"; those with an average income look for a balanced and varied diet and for a familiar commensality; and for high-income individuals beauty and luxury drive their choices of eating.

There has long been a dialog and a "flirt" between food and art. Lavish banquets were served at certain times, some artists were extraordinary gourmets, and chefs and others used food and eating as a topic of representation in still life and genre scenes. The emergence of the meals, dinners, and banquets orchestrated—and even sometimes cooked—by artists has its origins in the European avant-garde of the early twentieth century (Futurism, Dada and Surrealism). This tradition re-emerges in the conceptual and performance work of the 1960s and 1970s through artists such as Daniel Spoerri, Gordon Matta-Clark and Martha Rossler and continues with the socially engaged and the relational practices of the 1990s to the present— Michael Rakowitz, Lucy and Jorge Orta, Rirkrit Tiravanija, Meschac Gaba, Daniel Salomon, or Asunción Molinos Gordo.

Social formation of taste, its globalization and the increasing individualism in the alimentary politics and cultures constitute what we can denominate "crisis" or, I prefer to think, "transformation" of commensality. Eating is becoming an individual act rather than a collective one. Many people consider family meals, with all members around a table, an ideal while eating at work, in a restaurant, in an institutional dining room, at school, on the street, etc., is getting to be a common practice. Nevertheless, new emerging forms of eating in Western countries such as street food and on-line services of co-lunching facilitate and provide collective hospitality, communitarian culinary enjoyment. Therefore, hope is not lost.

At the end of my residency I organized and curated the event *On Commensality: The Act of Eating Together. Crisis or Transformation?* as part of the public programs of Delfina Foundation. The event was structured in two parts: a conversation between Harry West and myself discussing the concept of commensality and that aimed to work as the real starting point of my research on this topic rather than presenting its conclusions, followed by a practical example of commensality that consisted of a tasting of Basque cheese, creative pintxos (tapas), and red wine. The menu was as follows:

Idiazabal cheese
Iberico ham on bread pillow
Scorpion fish cake with kataifi pastry
King prawn and rice noodles
Dried onion sponge biscuit with marinated anchovies
Flax seed toast with cod
Fish and chips

Ox-cheek toast
Lemon tartlet
Charred sweets
Valbuena 5° 2006, Bodegas Vega Sicilia, wine

Chefs Elena Arzak, Mikel Sorazu and Satoko Habara collaborated on the menu, which intended to reflect some of the previously discussed ideas through food and wine. The menu was unfamiliar, as was the format of eating that was unusual in the United Kingdom.

On Commensality: The Act of Eating Together. Crisis or Transformation? was the starting point of an ongoing research. One of the questions in the follow-up questionnaire was "How does sharing of food and cooking of food connect you with other people or help to create social relationships?" Artist Roderick Coyne responded: "Eating, as well as being a necessary act for us all, is also a very intimate act. It is one of the few intimate acts that we are willing to perform in front of strangers, but it is the sharing of a meal with another or others that elevates the choice and pleasure of eating to the level of oblique dialogue. To those we know well we are able to give pleasure by providing them with dishes that we know they like. Food becomes a gift."

What is next?

I have shared a few cases of how chefs, whose working place is a restaurant, dealt with the conceptual and physical realities and limitations of museums and art spaces as a way of talking about the relationship between cooking and art. In this context the case of the Guggenheim Museum Bilbao is noteworthy. In October 1997 the opening gala dinner of the museum invited the participation of the main Basque chefs at that moment as a natural gesture of cultural identity and hospitality. Since then the support of gastronomy has evolved increasingly through the work of chef Josean Alija, who today runs the one-star Michelin restaurant Nerua as well as other food service spaces. During a 2015 interview with Juan Ignacio Vidarte, General Director of the museum, I asked him, "Are chefs artists?"

"It is a semantic debate; in my opinion the term 'artist' is overrated. It reminds me to the debate existing between sculptor Richard Serra and architect Frank Gehry. Serra accuses Gehry of meddling in the field of sculpture and Gehry replies that the difference is clear: the architect designs forms which have to be functional and has to take into account that his spaces have to include bathrooms, pipelines, etc., while a sculptor doesn't. They have different functions," Vidarte responded. In his opinion the main aim of a chef is to feed people and that is not an artistic practice. Of course there are chefs with specific creative personalities and creative processes. Vidarte considers cooking a creative discipline as do many others. Equally, there have been and are artists interested in cooking and food, but that does not make them real chefs. More importantly, the director of the Guggenheim museum questioned the importance of this debate. "Cooking does not need to be named art to be a worthy and a unique creative practice."

Regarding the coexistence of gastronomy and cooking within an art museum, Vidarte notes that the museum scene has allowed for more visibility for gastronomy and food services in recent years. However he has not yet seen fine cuisine in museums, with their own restaurants, food services and chefs, that share the museum identity, without competing, and finds common elements of inspiration and concerns linked to the museum's contemporary spirit. In the future Vidarte would like to see gastronomic spaces that are spaces for learning and sharing knowledge as this is one of many important goals of the Guggenheim Bilbao. It would be desirable that such spaces and experiences reinforced the educational function of gastronomic culture much in the same way the museum serves as an educational platform for the arts. It is undeniable that the dialog between both disciplines, art and gastronomy, is growing and that it will become richer still in years to come. Multisensoriality, hospitality, social and political aspects of food will play a crucial role in how food is presented and discussed in museums and art spaces.

Notes

1   I would like to thank the following: Elena and Juan Mari Arzak, Igor Zalakain, Xabier Gutiérrez, Satoko Haraba, Mikel Sorazu, Espacio Marzana, Iñaki Alvárez, Fundación Pilar i Joan Miro, Aina Pomar, Begoña Zubero, Christa Holka, Gabriela Ranelli, Ferran Adrià, Josep María Pinto, Delfina Entrecanales, Aaron Cezar, Delfina Foundation staff, Nina Levent, Bodegas Vega Sicilia, The Office of Cultural and Scientific Affairs of the Embassy of Spain in London, Harry West and Juan Ignacio Vidarte, among others.

2   In addition, my job as Associate Director of Education and Interpretation at the Guggenheim Museum Bilbao since its opening in 1997 has reinforced my skills in interpreting such links and my willingness in transmitting and sharing them with as many people as possible. Hence, gradually I began to collaborate as art adviser at Restaurant Arzak, to curate projects and exhibitions that link art and gastronomy—e.g., Chef Ferran Adrià's and elBulli's project for *documenta 12*, 2007, and the exhibition *Frying Water* in collaboration with Chefs Elena Arzak, Xabier Gutiérrez and Igor Zalakain at Espacio Marzana in Bilbao, 2008, and at Fundación Pilar i Joan Miró in Palma de Mallorca, 2010—and to organize some education and public programs at the Guggenheim Museum Bilbao focused on food and art. Recently I was fortunate to participate in the residency programme *The Politics of Food 2* at the Delfina Foundation.

3   Richard Hamilton and Vicente Todolí, eds., *Food for Thought, Thought for Food* (Actar, 2009).

4   Jean-Francois Revel, *Culture and Cuisine. A Journey through the History of Food* (New York: Da Capo Press, 1982).

5   See Dave Dewitt, *Da Vinci's Kitchen. A Secret History of Italian Cuisine* (Dallas: Benbella Books, 2006); Alessandro Falassi, *En la mesa con Rossini,* (Barcelona: Galaxia Gutenberg, 1993).

6   Jean-Anthelme Brillant Savarin, *Fisiología del gusto* (TRE, 2012).

7   This exhibition was presented in the art gallery Espacio Marzana, Bilbao (July 11 to September 19, 2008) and in the Fundación Pilar i Joan Miró, Palma de Mallorca (September 30, 2010 to January 10, 2011).

8   The text I wrote for this project and videos with Elena and Marta Arzak, Xabier Gutiérrez and Igor Zalakain are available at http://miro.palmademallorca.es/bloque.php?ldi=2&Cod_fam=10&Cod_sub=43&Cod_not=77

9   The Politics of Food program will devote one season every year over the course of four years to this topic. It brings together artists, anthropologists, curators, chefs, writers, scientists, and agronomists from around the world through residences, events, and exhibitions, broadening knowledge in these areas and offering a new and kaleidoscopic vision of the relation between food and art. The first season in winter 2014 introduced "a number of general environmental, economic and social concerns that have guided the overall programme" and the second season in spring 2015 "specifically explored the relationship between food and three sub-themes: *Sex, Diet & Disaster*". See http://delfinafoundation.com/programmes/public-and-thematic-programmes/theme-the-politics-of-food-season–1/

10 Kerner, S., Chu, C. and Warmind, M. (editors) (2015), *Commensality. From Everyday Food to Feast* (London and New York: Bloomsbury Academic).

18

The Art and Science of Plating

Charles Spence

Traditionally, decisions concerning the plating of the food in the restaurant were typically based on the intuitions of the chef, guided, if anything, by a series of rules of thumb perhaps vaguely remembered from cookery school (such as, for example, the rule that odd, rather than even, numbers of items should be served on the plate). Certainly, one finds a host of beautifully-illustrated books (what some call gastroporn, or food porn) on the bookstore shelves, all urging their readers to make their food look beautiful.[1] This is something that the painters of still life paintings with food have been doing for centuries.[2] In fact, some artists have recently been creating hyper-realistic renditions of food in painting, thus perhaps visually blurring the boundary between food and food art.

Food has not always been plated beautifully though. Back in the 1960s, for example: "The most common kind of French plating displayed all the ingredients, as they are side by side, placing the starches next to the vegetables, next to the meat or fish. The food would quite often also be stacked, by placing the main item on a bed of vegetables or potatoes" (Yang 2011). As Sebastian Lepinoy, Executive Chef at L'Atelier de Joel Robuchon put it in an interview, "20 years ago French presentation was virtually non-existent. If you ordered a coq au vin at a restaurant, it would be served just as if you had made it at home. The dishes were what they were. Presentation was very basic."[3]

The contemporary concern with the presentation of food (in the West) should, I think, really be traced back to the early 1970s, with the emergence of nouvelle cuisine (inspired, in part, by Japanese culinary practices), food photography, and the food media.[4] As Halligan (1990, 121) puts it: "Really, the concern with how the food looked can be traced back to the emergence of nouvelle cuisine. The pictures of these dishes have set themselves in the mind of the public. Nouvelle cuisine was essentially photogenic . . . Think of the glorious coloured photographs of these dishes, which have become eponymous with the purveying of recipes."[5]

The contemporary concern with making the plate beautiful started, then, with Paul Bocuse and his ilk. Though, as Yang (2011) notes about what has happened over the intervening years: "No doubt the pressures of earning awards and positive reviews have pushed French chefs to take a more artistic approach to plating." Some chefs undoubtedly love the attention that their beautifully-prepared dishes receive. Just take the following quote from Sebastian Lepinoy (again quoted in Yang, 2011): "I love serving our dishes to guests and watching their reactions. Usually, they will look at it first. Then discuss it with their friend, before pulling out a camera and taking a picture. It is great fun watching different responses."[6] Today, the trend toward beautiful plating is, if anything, even more pronounced, with a growing number of diners wanting to share pictures of the foods they eat with their social networks (see www.theartofplating.com).

The science of plating

While traditionally plating has been very much an art, guided by fashions and trends (just take, for example, the current trend for asymmetrical plating, or the use of unusual plateware), things are starting to change. In particular, over the last five years or so, psychologists and sensory scientists have started to take an interest in systematically assessing people's preferences when it comes to different plating arrangements. And while the intuitions of the chef often do turn out to be preferred by the general public (just as has been found to be the case in the visual arts), that has not always been the case. Asymmetric plating, for instance, generally gets a thumbs-down whenever we ask the participants in our laboratory, restaurant, or online studies what they think about it, and, more importantly, how much they would be willing to pay.[7] The scientists have also started to more systematically assess some of the rules of thumb as far as plating is concerned, again with mixed results. So, for example, while it is often claimed that odd numbers of elements are preferred on the plate this turns out, on closer inspection, not to be the case.

A growing number of chefs (such as Jozef Youssef of Kitchen Theory in London; see https://kitchen-theory.com/) are now starting to take the insights of such research on-board in the way in which they plate the food that is served to their guests. What is more, the rapid growth of online testing platforms offers the chef the opportunity to upload images of their latest culinary creations onto the internet one evening, and have the results of several hundred potential diners concerning how they would like the dish to be organized fed back to the kitchen the next morning, ready for that day's service.[8] Given the ease of data collection, and the growing public interest in the topic, my sense is that the science of plating, or rather the scientific approach to aesthetic plating, will continue to grow in the coming years. One presumes that it will only be a matter of time before these powerful new online approaches to data collection will be applied to the visual arts.

But can food be the object of aesthetic appreciation?

At one level, any one of us can obviously make a judgment call about whether the plating of a dish is beautiful or not. Most people also find it easy to judge which of an array of plates of foods looks the most attractive. However, just because we can rate how much we like a given plate of food, that does not necessarily, or immediately, make that an aesthetic judgment. Indeed, there is an ongoing debate concerning whether chefs, at least some of them, should be considered as artists. Or as Gopnik describes Spain's Adrià brothers: "If Albert is a Braque—a stolid man with a poetic imagination—Ferran is very much a Picasso, a grand maître who knows it."[9] Part of the problem here is the transitory nature of the chef's work. No sooner has a dish been created than it is consumed. A second more theoretically challenging issue relates to traditional notions of what can count as an object of aesthetic appreciation. A beautifully presented plate of food would not, for instance, seem to fit within Kant's influential framework outlined in his book *Critique of Judgment*. There the eminent philosopher stated that aesthetic judgments are characterized by three key features: 1) Their subjectivity; 2) Their disinterested nature; and 3) Their claim of universality.[10]

Palmer, Schloss, and Sammartino agree with Kant in arguing that aesthetic judgments are: "'disinterested' in the sense that they do not involve desire. Preferring a larger to a smaller piece of cake would not count as an aesthetic judgment in Kant's framework, because such a judgment is (presumably) about one's desire to consume the larger one."[11] Here, though, I would like to argue that a scientific approach to the aesthetics of plating *is* possible. While the participants in some studies have consumed the dishes that they have been asked to rate, in many others, the judgments are disinterested in the sense that people rate plates of food seen on a computer monitor that they know they have no realistic likelihood of consuming. What is more, and in contrast to the cake example, the amount of food in many of the scientific studies of plating tends to be kept more or less constant; all that varies, then, is the arrangement of the elements on the plate. Finally, here, it is perhaps also worth noting that there are occasions in which people will rate one plate as looking more visually appealing than another, even though it actually contains less food, again supporting the claim that their judgments are, in at least a certain sense, disinterested. All that being said, however, we will return later to the question of whether, in fact, any depiction of food can ever really be said to be "disinterested," given evidence concerning the notion of "embodied mental simulation."

Ultimately, though, it may be more fruitful to lay aside any philosophical arguments about whether food generally qualifies as an object of aesthetic appreciation, and to bypass the question of whether chefs should, or even can, be considered as artists, and instead to focus on applying the scientific methods of aesthetic appreciation to assessing people's responses to the attractiveness, or eye appeal, of different arrangements of food on the plate. The aim in the sections that follow is to determine whether there are any fundamental rules, or guidelines, concerning people's visual appreciation of food as it appears on the plate. The hope is that it might be possible, at least to a certain extent, to predict what is likely to look good on the plate, by studying what has previously been shown to look good on canvas.

Painting and plating: Do the same rules apply?

The scientific approach to aesthetics, and aesthetic judgments, has been popular for a number of years in the visual arts. As a starting point when it comes to studying plating, one might consider whether the principles of aesthetic preference gleaned from studies of the visual arts also apply when it comes to people's evaluations of plates of food. After all, both are judgments made on the basis of visual information; and, furthermore, factors such as balance, harmony, etc. that have been thoroughly studied when it comes to the visual arts are increasingly being experimented on with plating. However, before getting too excited, it ought to be stressed that there are a number of important differences between plating and painting that also need to be borne in mind.

One obvious difference is in terms of the frame surrounding the work, be it a painting, or a plate of food. The majority of paintings tend to be presented in a rectangular frame. By contrast, the majority of plates tend to be round and white. It will be important to bear in mind how the frame influences people's responses to what lies within that border.[12] Arnheim has described the frame of the painting as a "structural skeleton," and one might reasonably consider whether the rim of the plate serves much the same function—that is, of constraining how what falls within that "frame" will be evaluated. Certainly, people often judge those stimuli that have been placed in the middle of a frame as having a higher "goodness of fit." People also appear to prefer it when the elements in the paintings are arranged parallel to the surrounding frame.

A second important difference here concerns our preferences as far as color is concerned. Many of the studies that have assessed people's preferences for different colors (hues) reveal a general preference for cool colors such as blue, cyan, and green, over warm colors such as red, orange, and yellow. When evaluating abstract color patches, blue tends to be most preferred and yellow to yellow-green least preferred. However, when it comes to the colors of the food on the plate, there has, for a long time, been a general distaste expressed for those foods that are blue and cyan. Hence the preferred colors in paintings and on the plate likely differ. One possible explanation for such a difference comes from Palmer and Schloss's ecological valence theory.[13] The suggestion here being that people like/dislike a particular color to the degree that they like/dislike all of the environmental objects that are associated with that color. Perhaps people's liking for the colors of foods on the plate depends, then, on their liking for all of the foods that they have eaten that are associated with that color.

A third difference is that visual art, especially painting, is typically seen hanging vertically on the wall, whereas plates of food are typically seen while lying horizontally on the table in front of the diner. That said, many of the studies on the visual aesthetics of plating currently involve people inspecting plates of food seen on a monitor or digital screen, and hence closer to the vertical orientation. Whether this difference in orientation makes a difference to people's evaluations of whatever they are looking at has not, as yet, been assessed. However, beyond the key differences outlined above, there are many similarities between painting and plating. Below, a number of the principles that have emerged from studies of the visual arts are assessed in order to see whether they also play out in terms of modulating people's judgments concerning their liking for those dishes that have been presented visually.

Balanced plating

Many studies (of painting) have highlighted a preference for balance. So, for example, people generally prefer patterns of dots that are symmetrical over those that have been arranged asymmetrically. They also tend to prefer those shapes that are more symmetrical. As Zellner puts it: "Balance is a visual feature that has been found to be important in the aesthetic evaluation of a painting. A painting canvas, or in the case of food, a plate, is considered to be balanced when the elements are arranged around the center of the painting or plate in such a manner that they appear anchored or stable. The more balanced an artwork, the greater the aesthetic appeal."[14] During their training, many chefs will learn of the importance of balance on the plate.

In one study, researchers had people evaluate the visual attractiveness of a plate of food, and subsequently, its taste.[15] The plates of food (water chestnuts) were presented in either a balanced or unbalanced arrangement, and tahini (that was either colored or naturally-uncolored) was also placed on the plate. Unsurprisingly, the balanced presentation was rated as more visually attractive, though there was no effect on taste ratings. It is worth noting that the visual presentation was very simple, much simpler, in fact, than one would likely find in a restaurant setting. In order to try and address this concern, a somewhat more complex visual presentation was used in a subsequent study. There, the plating consisted of a balanced or unbalanced red pepper hummus placed on a romaine leaf with three baby carrots, three cherry tomatoes, and four pita chips. Somewhat surprisingly, in the latter study, the balanced presentation wasn't judged to be any more attractive, though the hummus was rated as tasting better when sampled from the balanced plate. Here, though, one might wonder whether the typical frame of the round plate reduces to some degree the potential salience of balance as a factor when compared, say, to a rectangular canvas.

Zellner and her colleagues went on to show that it might have been messiness, rather than balance, that affected the taste of food, as in their unbalanced presentation it rather looked like all of the food had slid to the bottom of the plate![16] So, in a second experiment, a chicken salad was served, with the balance held constant, but the neatness/messiness varied. People now had to judge how attractive the chicken salad looked, and their liking, with the salad being presented on a romaine leaf in either a neat mound in the center of the leaf/plate or spread out across the lettuce leaf in a messy but balanced manner. The neat presentation was not judged as any more attractive than the messy presentation, though the taste of the food in the neat presentation was rated higher. Zellner's recent suggestion, based on this series of studies, is that "although balance might be an important visual contributor to the attractiveness of visual art, it is less important than neatness when it comes to food presentation." (My colleagues and I take issue with this claim, though, since some of our latest results suggest that neat and balanced presentations are preferred over neat but unbalanced presentations.) In a final experiment, Zellner and her colleagues' participants looked at pictures from the first two experiments and rated how much care they thought had been taken by whoever had prepared the dish. This was judged higher in the neat than in the messy presentation. People also said that they would have been willing to pay more for the neat than for the messy presentation, and thought any restaurant preparing such food would be of higher quality. Thus neat food suggests higher quality, and a better taste. Interestingly, in our latest research, we have been able to show a clear preference for centered plating over asymmetric plating.

Attractive/creative plating

Debra Zellner and her colleagues assessed the impact of the attractiveness of the visual presentation on liking.[17] The diners in a restaurant were presented with a sautéed chicken breast with a *fines herbes* sauce, sautéed green beans with toasted almonds, and brown rice pilaf prepared and arranged in one of two ways by a chef at the Culinary Institute of America in New York City. There was a "standard" presentation of the dish, with the chicken breast and sauce placed at the bottom of the plate and the rice and beans situated in the two upper quadrants. The alternative, more creative presentation, had the rice situated in the center of the plate, with the chicken breast and sauce spiraling out, and with the beans situated around the edges of the plate. The latter presentation was judged significantly more attractive and liked more. What is more, the diners thought that the latter presentation had been prepared with more care. Disappointingly, though, they did not say that they would be willing to pay any more for the more attractive (creative) plating. The suggestion here being that regular customers to the restaurant were tested, and hence perhaps they had a clear notion of what the dishes in the restaurant ought to cost. Elsewhere, researchers have also found neat and attractive presentation to be preferred over neat but less attractive, or less aesthetically pleasing, plating.

The aesthetic oblique effect

People find it easier to perceive horizontal and vertical lines than their oblique counterparts. Interestingly, Latto et al. found that people preferred horizontal/vertical lines over oblique lines in a selection of Mondrian's paintings, an artist famous for his use of high contrast horizontal and vertical lines. Relevant to any consideration of the impact of the frame on preference, a number of the artist's paintings come in a lozenge, or diamond-shaped, format (that is, they have an oblique rather than a rectangular frame). Each of these paintings was presented to the participants rotated in each one of the eight possible orientations, separated by 45 degrees. The participants rated their liking for every one of the 64 images using a seven-point hedonic scale. A small but significant preference was documented for those pictures in which the lines were arranged horizontally and vertically (regardless of the orientation of the frame) over those where the lines in the painting were oriented obliquely instead. Subsequent analysis of the proportion of horizontal, vertical, and oblique lines in 88 paintings from twentieth-century paintings in the Israel Museum in Jerusalem revealed, once again, a preference amongst artists (or those who select their work) for the horizontal and vertical over the oblique.[18]

With reference to the more fundamental question of why it should be that people prefer lines that are vertical and horizontal, one suggestion is that people generally prefer those shapes and arrangements of shapes that they find easier to process. Note also that we have been exposed to more horizontal and vertical lines in the built environment, and so a familiarity account is also possible here.

Intriguingly, chef Jozef Youssef and his colleagues have recently assessed the oblique effect in plating.[19] A dish was served in either a round or linear formation on a round plate. The participants rotated the plate into their preferred orientation. The results revealed little evidence of there being much of a preference for a particular orientation in the case of the round presentation of the food. However, a clear preference was seen for an oblique line ascending to the right for the plate with a linear distribution of elements (see Figure 18.1). Across a number of dishes that people have rotated in our online research, the results often show a similar pattern. Should such results hold up in larger-scale studies, then this would seem to be an interesting way in which the aesthetics of paintings may differ from that of plating. Certainly, a casual inspection of plating arrangements shown in magazines and social media would seem to suggest that this preference for an oblique line ascending to the right may be intuitively used by chefs.

The golden ratio

It has often been suggested that, all other things being equal, stimuli that obey the golden ratio or golden section will be judged as more aesthetically appealing than those that do not. The golden ratio is obtained by dividing a line into two parts, such that the proportion of the entire line to the longer segment is equal to the proportion of the longer segment to the shorter segment, a ratio of roughly 1.6:1. However, it turns out that the evidence that has been published to date on this question (i.e., as to whether it is actually liked more) is not so clear, with many failures to demonstrate such a clear preference. Hence, the appropriateness of utilizing the golden ratio as a guideline when it comes to the plating of food should perhaps be treated with caution.[20] It was recently suggested that the optimum ratio of curry to rice would obey the golden ratio, though no empirical data in support of the claim was provided. While it may generally be true that shapes whose dimensions are around that of the golden ratio are preferred, it should be remembered that such preferences vary across both observers and situations.

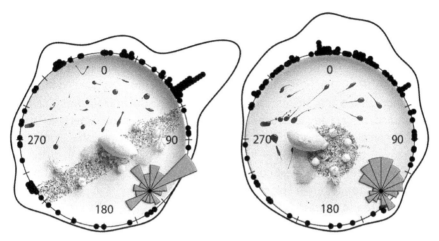

FIGURE 18.1 *Circular data plot and rose diagrams of the 100 plate orientations for each dish selected by participants in a recent study. The surrounding line shows an estimate of the underlying density of the data (the more datapoints at a given orientation, the greater the bulge in the line). The food has been added to the figure and oriented by the mean orientation in which the food was placed by the participants in the study. Notice the clear preference for the oblique line ascending to the right in the left-hand presentation.*

Figure reprinted with permission from Youssef et al. (2015) © Charles Spence.

Odd versus even

One of the rules of thumb that seemingly every professional chef has been taught is that odd numbers are preferred over even numbers of elements on the plate. Three scallops rather than four, say. We have recently put this suggestion to the test in a series of experiments at London's Science Museum. Across several studies, participants chose between odd and even numbers of scallops on the plate. However, the results failed to demonstrate a preference for odd over even numbers of elements. Instead, people's choices appeared to be driven primarily by the total amount of food on the plate.[21]

Contour curvature

Across a number of studies, and a variety of situations, people have been shown to prefer objects that present a curved contour over those with sharp, angular contours. The suggestion is that sharp contours are treated by the brain as potentially threatening, certainly more so than curved contours. When a sharp contour points toward the viewer then they generally like it less than when the image points away from them (presumably because it is viewed by the primitive brain as being a little less dangerous). We have recently demonstrated that this preference is true when it comes to triangular-shaped foods, as well as for triangular arrangements of sets of elements on the plate (see Figure 18.2). That is, food that points away from the observer is generally preferred to food that points toward the observer. Colombian chef Charles Michel and his colleagues recently conducted a series of experiments in which people viewed an image of a plate of food (actually the signature dish served by Albert Landgraf in his restaurant Epice in Sao Paulo, Brazil (http://www.theworlds50best.com/latinamerica/en/the-list/41–50/Epice.html). Participants rotated the plate into the presentation that they would have preferred to see the food. People preferred the plate to be presented in pretty much the same orientation as the chef had settled intuitively upon.[22] Such results can perhaps be seen as matching the findings of various other studies where people have been shown to prefer abstract works of art when presented in the orientation in which the artist intended the painting to be seen/hung.

Complexity

The suggestion that arises from studies of the visual arts is that a moderate level of visual complexity on the plate should be seen as more attractive than low or high complexity stimuli. This is, though, a measure that is a little difficult to assess objectively. Perhaps unsurprisingly, then, as yet, there has been relatively little discussion of the topic of complexity when it comes to the plating of food.

Food art

Some chefs have more or less obviously been inspired in their plating by the visual arts. The three Michelin-starred Italian chef, Massimo Bottura, for example, talks of his inspiration from contemporary art. He says, "The love I have for art is the one that pushes me further to delve deeper into the meanings of life. Art is the higher form of communication, in the widest possible way: you get inspired by jazz music, by contemporary art and then, hopefully, by my dishes!" (He laughs) "No, seriously, what I mean is that I try to interpret the artist's message and to make it mine, to translate it in life and in the dishes."[23]

But can making a plate of food resemble a piece of art actually add value to a dish? Chef Charles Michel and his colleagues conducted a series of

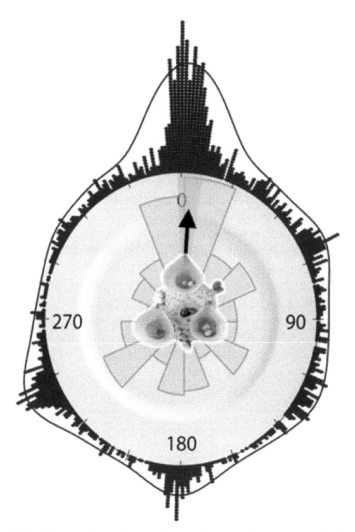

FIGURE 18.2 *Circular data plot and rose diagram showing the 1,667 plate orientations selected by participants. The surrounding line provides an estimate of the preferred orientation (indicated by the bulge of the line). The food has been added to the figure and oriented by 3.20° clockwise (the preferred orientation). An arrow indicates the mean angle that participants placed the food in (beneath which is a blue wedge indicating the lines 95 percent confidence intervals). In this case, then, the chef's decision to place the dish pointing at 12 o'clock was pretty much in line with the preferences demonstrated by the group.*

Figure reprinted with permission from Michel et al. (2015) © Charles Spence.

experiments that start to press this point using a salad that had been designed to imitate Kandinsky's painting "201" currently hanging in the Museum of Modern Art in New York (see Figure 18.3).[24] Studies conducted in the laboratory and restaurant setting have revealed that people are willing to pay more than twice as much for the artistic presentation than for the regular tossed salad. On occasion, the diners may even rate the elements as tasting better, and may even consume more. Linking back to one of the studies reported earlier, a neat but not especially attractive plate was not rated that highly. Hence, it would appear to be the aesthetic appeal rather than merely just the effort involved in plating that is valued by the diner. One can perhaps think of this transference effect in terms of the "art infusion" effect from the field of marketing.

An intriguing idea here, given how responsive the brain is to images of food,[25] is that one important factor influencing our aesthetic preferences is the amount of neural activity that the stimuli being judged give rise to in the brain of the observer. That said, a growing body of research suggests that the magnitude of the neural response often tracks the nutritional content of the food rather than its aesthetic appeal, and hence cannot be considered as "disinterested" in the Kantian sense. Thus, while the neuroaesthetics approach has made some headway when it comes to the visual arts, progress with regard to visual presentation in the culinary arts is still some way behind.

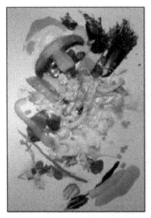 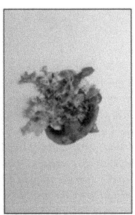 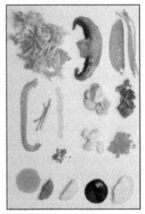

FIGURE 18.3 *The three different visual arrangements presented in the study inspired by one of Kandinsky's paintings. Note that the three arrangements consist of the same quantity of the same ingredients.*

Figure reprinted with permission from Michel et al. (2014) © Charles Spence.

Plating the table

The discussion in this chapter has restricted the frame to the rim of the plate; indeed, the majority of studies of plating have operated under the same constraints. One can, though, take a broader canvas—just think of the more traditional service *à la Francaise*, when all of the dishes were laid out at once, and the entire surface of the table became the frame on which the chef would aim to impress the eyes of the guests: "In the *ambigu*, the temporal succession of multiple courses is thus eliminated in favour of the visual effect of a unified tableau. Such meals are composed as a spectacle for the eyes and do not necessarily involve an oral consumption of food . . . They were modelled after painting, sculpture, and architecture and conform to those arts."[26]

One final point to bear in mind here relates to the impact of the size of the work of art on people's response. People respond differently to the same artwork as a function of whether they see it full size, versus a small rendition (on paper or screen). Whether the size of the image of a plate of food matters to the same extent is again unknown. However, the plating of food rarely reaches the grand scale of the large canvas. One of the best-known exceptions being the famous dessert of Grant Achatz served at his Alinea restaurant in Chicago. This dessert involves the chefs actually plating the table. Hence, the frame becomes the edge of the table. Chef Charles Michel has also been experimenting with large-scale plating of the table when he serves his Kandinsky-inspired salad in the UK. The response to this large-scale dish does, anecdotally, seem to be different to that when the dish is plated individually.

Embodied mental simulation and the aesthetic in visual representations of food

Ultimately, in questions concerning whether food can ever be considered as the subject of aesthetic appreciation, one key point turns out to be the fact that food is meant to be consumed, and hence the viewer/diner can perhaps *never* make a genuinely "disinterested" judgment about what they are looking at. However, here it is interesting to note that the marketing literature suggests that even when we see the picture of a food displayed on the side of product packaging or in an advertisement, our brains can't help but engage in a spot of "embodied mental simulation."[27] That is, we all simulate (consciously or otherwise) what it would be like to eat the food (i.e., the extent to which it affords eating). Consistent with this view, recent findings have even documented greater neural activity in the gustatory cortex following the presentation of a plate of food that is shown in a first- rather than third-person perspective. The headline of one recent article describing the hyper-realistic oil paintings of food created by one artist hints at "A feast for the eyes: Artist's incredible oil paintings of food look good enough to eat," might have contained more truth than any of us realize.

One might wonder, therefore, whether the food images we see in books, on Instagram platforms such as theartofplating.com, and even perhaps in the visual representations of food hanging in so many art galleries and museums— just think of all those still life paintings—might not also lead to "embodied mental simulation." Perhaps, though, the image has to pass some criterion of realism in order for such simulation processes to occur. But then again, perhaps not. The realism of food in painting has certainly varied quite considerably from one artist or epoch to another. It will, I think, therefore be interesting for future research to determine how realistic an image or representation of food has to be before it engages such neural processes. Until we have an answer to this question though one might have to allow the possibility that viewers of visual representations of food and drink can never truly be "disinterested," and hence that we can't make an aesthetic judgment about them.

Conclusions

In closing, I would like to stress my agreement with the line taken by Palmer et al. when they suggest that the "aesthetic response can be studied rigorously and meaningfully within the framework of scientific psychology." I too would like to extend their line that with the science of aesthetic plating, one is not trying to decide whether some plate of food is "objectively beautiful," "but rather to determine whether (or to what degree) some representative set of individuals judge or experience it as beautiful (or ugly)."[28] Ultimately, the approach outlined here can be thought of as part of interdisciplinary aesthetic science. In future research, it will be interesting to look more closely at any cross-cultural differences in people's preference for different visual arrangements of the elements on the plate. Analogous work on cross-cultural differences in people's appreciation for colors, art, and plateware are already well under way. One should perhaps also consider the impact of individual differences in terms of the viewer's level of expertise.

Of course, just because a growing body of scientific research now shows that symmetrical is generally preferred over asymmetrical, that ascending lines to the right are preferred over lines that point straight up or ascend to the left, that these observations do not start to become rules dictating the way in which food *should* be plated. For even if we are able to perfectly understand the rules and generalizations governing aesthetic plating, there will always be those who choose to be different, to go against the norm/conventions. In this, as in so many other ways, then, plating and painting share more in common than one might initially think.

As I hope the research outlined in this chapter has made clear, when thinking about plating beautifully, a number of lessons can be taken directly from the literature on people's aesthetic responses to paintings. That said, it is important not to underestimate the differences in our judgments and preferences that result from the rectangular frame viewed hanging vertically on the wall in the art gallery with the normally circular frame of the round white plate viewed resting horizontally on the table before us in the restaurant. One should not underestimate the impact of the environment (or context) in which we evaluate painting (normally the art gallery) or plate of food (the restaurant) on the judgments that we make either.[29]

One of the most interesting questions that this comparison of the viewer's response to painting and plating throws up, is whether the depiction of food in art can ever really be considered as truly disinterested, given the seeming ubiquity of "embodied mental simulation." The growing body of neuroscience and marketing data suggests that the visual presentation of images of food, be they on the side of the product packaging, be they on the plate, or presumably, be they in a painting or in a food image uploaded onto the internet elicit the embodied mental simulation of how much the viewer would like to eat, and how easy they would find it to consume, the food. One open empirical question here, then, for those working in the museum sector, is whether the museum-going visitors' "aesthetic" response to a still life with food would change as a function of whether or not they have just feasted at the museum restaurant, say?

Notes

1   It should, of course, be noted that there are also other books out there where this topic is studiously ignored. The fear here being that one does not want to encourage "the increasingly popular, and in some cases misguided, emphasis that some chefs have placed on the visual presentation of food." Dornenburg, A., & Page, K. (1996). *Culinary artistry*. New York, NY: John Wiley & Sons, 3.

2   Bendiner, K. (2004). *Food in painting: From the Renaissance to the present*. London, UK: Reaction Books.

3   The quotes here from Yang, J. (2011). The art of food presentation. *Crave (Hong Kong)*, downloaded from http://www.cravemag.com/features/the-art-of-food-presentation/ on 15/03/13.

4   Though see Deroy, O., Michel, C., Piqueras-Fiszman, B., & Spence, C.
     (2014). The plating manifesto (I): From decoration to creation. *Flavour*, 3:6,
     for evidence of a much earlier interest in visual presentation.

5   Is it any coincidence, one wonders, that this was also the time when proud
     chefs started to initial/monogram their plates? Halligan, M. (1990). *Eat my
     words*. London, UK: Angus & Robertson.

6   Yang, J. (2011). The art of food presentation. *Crave (Hong Kong)*, downloaded
     from http://www.cravemag.com/features/the-art-of-food-presentation/ on
     15/03/13.

7   Michel, C., Velasco, C., Fraemohs, P., & Spence, C. (2015). Studying the
     impact of plating and cutlery on ratings of the food served in naturalistic
     dining contexts. *Appetite*, 90, 45–50.

8   Spence, C., Piqueras-Fiszman, Michel, C., & Deroy, O. (2014). Plating
     manifesto (II): The art and science of plating. *Flavour*, 3:4.

9   Gopnik, A. (2011). Sweet revolution. *The New Yorker*, January 3. Downloaded
     from http://www.newyorker.com/reporting/2011/01/03/110103fa_fact_gopnik
     on 06/09/2015.

10   Kant, I. (1892/1951). *Critique of judgment*. New York, NY: Haffner.

11   Palmer, S. E., Schloss, K. B., & Sammartino, J. (2013). Visual aesthetics and
     human preference. *Annual Review of Psychology*, 64, 77–107.

12   As Arnheim (1988, 72) notes: "The most radical promoters of centric
     composition are the round enclosures—circular frames, disks, spherical
     volumes. Such fully symmetrical structures are entirely determined by their
     focus in the middle."; Arnheim, R. (1988). *The power of the center: A study
     of composition in the visual arts*. Berkeley, CA: University of California Press.

13   Palmer, S. E., & Schloss, K. B. (2010). An ecological valence theory of human
     color preference. *Proceedings of the National Academy of Sciences of the
     USA*, 107, 8877–8882.

14   Zellner, D. A. (2015). Effect of visual cues on sensory and hedonic evaluation
     of food. In A. Hirsch (Ed.), *Nutrition and chemosensation* (pp. 159–174). Boca
     Raton, FL: CRC Press.

15   Zellner, D. A., Lankford, M., Ambrose, L., & Locher, P. (2010). Art on the
     plate: Effect of balance and color on attractiveness of, willingness to try and
     liking for food. *Food Quality and Preference*, 21, 575–578.

16   Zellner, D. A., Siemers, E., Teran, V., Conroy, R., Lankford, M., Agrafiotis, A.,
     Ambrose, L., & Locher, P. (2011). Neatness counts. How plating affects liking
     for the taste of food. *Appetite*, 57, 642–648.

17   Zellner, D. A., Loss, C. R., Zearfoss J., & Remolina S. (2014). It tastes as
     good as it looks! The effect of food presentation on liking for the flavor of
     food. *Appetite*, 77C, 31–35.

18   Latto, R., Brain, D., & Kelly, B. (2000). An oblique effect in aesthetics:
     Homage to Mondrian (1872–1944). *Perception*, 29, 981–987; Latto, R., &
     Russell-Duff, K. (2002). An oblique effect in the selection of line orientation
     by twentieth century painters. *Empirical Studies of the Arts*, 20, 49–60.

19 Youssef, J., Juravle, G., Youssef, L., Woods, A., & Spence, C. (2015). On the art and science of naming and plating food. *Flavour*, 4:27.

20 Deroy, O., & Spence, C. (2014). Can you find the golden ratio in your plate? *Flavour*, 3:5.

21 Woods, A. T., Michel, C., & Spence, C. (2016). Odd versus even: A scientific study of the "rules" of plating. *PeerJ*, 4:e1526. https://doi.org/10.7717/peerj.1526

22 Michel, C., Woods, A. T., Neuhäeuser, M., Landgraf, A., & Spence, C. (2015). Orienting the plate: Online study assesses the importance of the orientation in the plating of food. *Food Quality & Preference*, 44, 194–202.

23 Quoted in Barba, E. D. (2013). My cuisine is tradition in evolution. Downloaded from https://www.finedininglovers.com/blog/news-trends/best-italian-restaurants-massimo-bottura/ on 10/05/2016.

24 Michel, C., Velasco, C., Gatti, E., & Spence, C. (2014). A taste of Kandinsky: Assessing the influence of the visual presentation of food on the diner's expectations and experiences. *Flavour*, 3:7. Note that the chef chose to invert Kandinsky's painting, to have what becomes a slice of mushroom in the salad presented in its natural upright orientation.

25 Spence, C., Okajima, K., Cheok, A. D., Petit, O., & Michel, C. (in press). Eating with our eyes: From visual hunger to digital satiation. *Brain & Cognition*.

26 El-Khoury, R. (2004). Delectable decoration: Taste and spectacle in Jean-François de Bastide's *La Petite Maison*. In J. Horwitz & P. Singley (Eds.), *Eating architecture* (pp. 301–311). Cambridge, MA: MIT Press.

27 Elder, R. S., & Krishna, A. (2012). The "visual depiction effect" in advertising: Facilitating embodied mental simulation through product orientation. *Journal of Consumer Research*, 38, 988–1003.

28 Palmer, S. E., Schloss, K. B., & Sammartino, J. (2013). Visual aesthetics and human preference. *Annual Review of Psychology*, 64, 77–107.

29 Spence, C., & Piqueras-Fiszman, B. (2014). *The perfect meal: The multisensory science of food and dining*. Oxford, UK: Wiley-Blackwell.

19

A Conversation with Four Pioneering Museum Chefs

Nina Levent with Josean Alija,
Petter Nilsson, Joris Bijdendijk
and Ali Loukzada

Museum restaurants and museum chefs found themselves in the midst of two very strong cultural currents: one relates to museums turning toward their audiences and making a dramatic shift from exhibiting objects to providing experiences; the other is society's growing interest in food, which has brought the culinary profession into the spotlight, making chefs into celebrities on par with artists, actors, and TV personalities. We certainly see these trends in redesigns and new museum buildings, such as New York City's Whitney Museum of American Art, which features the much talked about restaurant *Untitled*, and the re-opened San Francisco Museum of Modern Art, which now houses the restaurant *In Situ* with chef Corey Lee at its helm. Lee will be "curating" an a la carte menu of dishes recreated from "over 80 chefs from around the world," include Rene Redzepi, Alice Waters, Thomas Keller, and Andoni Luis Aduriz, among others.[1]

Almost 140 years since the opening of the first museum restaurant at London's Victoria and Albert Museum, the chefs at the helms of museum restaurants are breaking new ground for museum visitors and for foodies. This chapter brings together opinions of four chefs whose restaurants are in museums located in Spain, Holland, Sweden, and the United States. Two are connected with world-renowned museums, the Guggenheim Bilbao and the Rijksmuseum, Amsterdam. The other two work at smaller cultural venues with distinct collections and missions, the Rubin Museum of Art, dedicated to

Tibetan Art in New York City, and the Spritmuseum in Stockholm, dedicated to the regional history of alcohol. Also discussed is an unfolding trend that makes it possible for chefs and curators to be in a dynamic creative dialog, for guest chefs to be invited and celebrated much in the same way that museums celebrate artists and guest curators, for museum restaurants to contribute to the identity of a cultural giant but also to be a place that is about a chef's unique creativity and signature cuisine.

A conversation with chef Josean Alija, Nerua restaurant at the Guggenheim Bilbao

Chef Josean Alija runs Nerua, a celebrated restaurant located at the Guggenheim Bilbao. Nerua is one of the very few museum restaurants that boast a Michelin star. In 2015, Nerua has also been included in the World's 100 Best Restaurants list by the prestigious magazine *Restaurant*. Alija is praised for his purist style in which aromas, textures, and flavors are the main components, but also for his innovative avant-garde style.

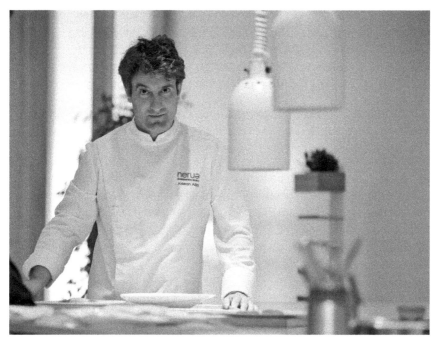

FIGURE 19.1 *Chef Josean Alija, Nerua, Guggenheim Museum, Bilbao.*
© *Andoni Epelde.*

Nina Levent (NL)   *How would you describe your approach to gastronomy?*

Josean Alija (JA)   Cooking brings people together to experience the transformation of products into a language that can be appreciated through the senses: touch, taste, smell, and sight. In my case, experience has led to the definition of a style, an identity of cooking. The word that comes to mind is *muina*, a Basque word that means nucleus, core, and essence. It is the term that best captures my way of understanding things, including gastronomy. This is the word that best defines me. Its soul, its heart, but also its brain and knowledge. This is a key to keeping restless attitude and creative process alive.

My cooking is a highly personal reflection of the world and the reality that surrounds me. It is based on loyalty to certain values that allow me to continue, always and constantly, along the same path. I understand cooking, the culinary experience overall, as the result of focusing attention on the purity of things.

Nerua, my restaurant, is a place that has been designed so that people can relate to each other as well as the culinary creations. A place that helps you to understand what is being served on a blank canvas, rounded off with brushstrokes of a landscape and seducing you with secrets and surprises. My cooking reflects seasonality and an obsession with revealing the essence of everything. Our gaze is fixed on nature, the plant world, and the sea. The process begins with observation, selecting the produce, studying and analyzing it in detail to reveal its essence. Playing with memory and recollections is important for the process. We designed a method where cooking takes place in a fun environment that has been created for enjoyment.

NL   *What does the proximity to the Guggenheim mean to you? How does Nerua and other food service fit within the Guggenheim museum in terms of its overall identity, its content, temporary exhibitions?*

JA   For us it is an honor to be in the museum and collaborate with our culinary offerings in the generation of an integrated experience for visitors. The direction of Guggenheim Bilbao Museum entrusted IXO Group to manage the catering services of the museum. Bixente Arrieta, cofounder of IXO Group, proposed three gastronomic concepts that bring added value to museum visitors.

Firstly, Bar Guggenheim Bilbao, a bar where you can enjoy an alternative way of eating, "the pintxos," the traditional Basque small plates that suppose a social ritual in this territory.

Then, Bistró Guggenheim Bilbao, which values a free-style cuisine, linked to its roots, to the memory of those dishes that are part of a culture and which have been adapted to an avant-garde context.

And finally Nerua, my place, where I can show my way of living and feeling gastronomy. At Nerua, we work freely with the restlessness of a chef, and our creations are related to the seasonality of produce. Knowledge is crucial in order to create, but creation cannot exist without freedom. We manage the creativity of our team independently, with the aim of showcasing our products and creating a discourse that helps people have a full sensory and cultural experience. We work respectfully and coherently, and this is what makes Nerua special.

As it happens in the artistic context, where you can find different movements and expressions, also in gastronomy you can find different languages. The gastronomy proposal in Guggenheim is an example of that reality.

NL   *Might you elaborate on specific examples of dishes and menus that make the restaurant complementary to the museum?*

JA   Our menus are developed with local products. The Bilbao setting allows me access to great produce. Only a few kilometers away, we have sea and farms that grow produce according to our needs. This allows me to work with seasonal ingredients and change the menu three times a year. Menus that are formed of nine to fourteen or twenty-one products, reflect the seasonality. The aim is to show and to enhance our culture by healthy and surprising cuisine that interacts with memories through the senses. I understand innovation as a way to progress without losing my style, authenticity, and the meaning of the experience. It is the perfect complement for the museum.

NL   *Have you worked with artists or curators at the museum? Have they directly or indirectly inspired you?*

JA   I enjoy seeing how each artist creates their language without losing their identity and to some extent I do the same. I do it by taking inspiration from nature and the feelings it evokes in me. I enjoy the whole process of cooking and, in particular, engaging with customers.

NL   *I have spoken with many visitors for whom a visit to a museum is a multi-sensory experience, that is never complete without a quiet time, food tasting, and conversation about art. Sometimes, we forget living in the world that preferences visual stimuli, that we are truly multi-sensory multi-dimensional creatures. What do you see observing and interacting with your customers?*

JA   We have learned a lot from our customers by listening to them, watching how they behave, getting closer to them so that our message and feelings resonate with them. Success has come through us becoming our own customers and analyzing each aspect of the experience step by step from the inside: space, atmosphere, how food is communicated. Empathy and customer relations are key to inspiring trust and enjoyment in customers. Success is fun—without fun, there is no enjoyment.

NL   *What is the difference between a chef in a restaurant and a chef in a restaurant that is located in a museum? What does a museum chef need to keep in mind when crafting the food experience?*

JA   The main difference is a commitment to the local surroundings, innovation and creativity, and an understanding of what the public is looking for. In my case, Nerua demonstrates my way of feeling and understanding cooking. It is a clear reflection of who I am. The team at Nerua is united by our passion for cooking and sharing food. A chef needs to have the complete trust of the museum in order to continue along their path.

NL   *The Nerua restaurant has become an important regional landmark for anyone who visits the region. Would you elaborate on the relationship between the restaurant and the local Basque cuisine?*

JA   I believe in a cuisine with local products; it is a way of showing a nation's identity and culture through a plate. My cuisine is one hundred percent Basque. It is the cuisine I believe in. The customers have turned Nerua into a reference for this region, because they feel identified with our work. We have created an experience of haute or avant-garde Basque cuisine. We are facing the risk of globalization: same products, same techniques, same presentations all over the world. Everything tends to be standardized. We are facing the risk of losing the essence and soul of the territory.

It is very interesting and incredibly enriching to have access to, and to share, knowledge globally. This is allowing cuisine and any other discipline to advance at a pace that would have been unthinkable. But what is really enriching, intelligent, and sustainable is to adapt that knowledge to the immediate surroundings. It is important to research products and species, which are underused or facing disappearance, to practice local innovative cuisine, to play with tastes, aromas, colors, and textures to achieve a new result with a known ingredient or produce.

NL   *What is the difference between being a chef in a museum restaurant and a chef in a restaurant outside the museum?*

JA   Every chef has to create a cuisine that is authentic to him. The authentic and pure things work. There is always space for good cuisine and gastronomy. This is how cultural heritage manifests itself in different fields, including gastronomy.

A conversation with chef Petter Nilsson, the Spritmuseum, Stockholm

Petter Nilsson is a Swedish chef who has made a name for himself in Paris, cooked in Belgium, Peru, and Lapland, and has recently returned to Stockholm to open a new restaurant within the city's Spritmuseum, a museum that pays homage to the history of spirits. The Spritmuseum team gave Nilsson free rein over the restaurant. Nilsson sees his new venture as a conclusion of all the restaurants that he has worked in and eaten at over the years.[2] The *New York Times* noted that "the waterfront museum located in refurbished navy sheds is not the first place you'd expect to find a groundbreaking chef."[3]

Nina Levent (NL)   *How would you describe your approach to gastronomy?*

Petter Nilsson (PN)   I would like to think that I have a natural approach. Natural in a sense of using produce from the farms around Stockholm as much as I can, and then adding the least "transformation" possible. Yet, I am creating something unique. I reserve the right to use intuition to make daily changes to the dishes.

NL   *How do you see your restaurant fitting within the Spritmuseum in terms of its overall identity? How do you work with curators at the museum?*

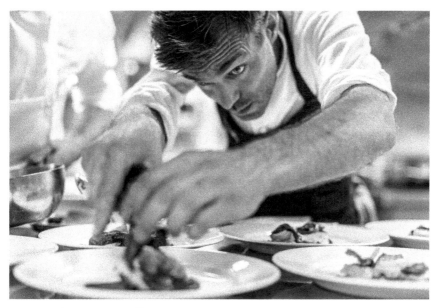

FIGURE 19.2 *Petter Nillson, Spritmuseum Restaurant.*
© *Spritmuseum.*

PN   Since the restaurant is situated in the museum of spirits, we have of course a natural link between the museum and the restaurant. We have a very close relationship and work together in the process of creating many temporary exhibits related to the history of alcohol. At least one person from the restaurant is always involved in the curatorial process and works on new exhibits. We also design dishes and snacks for the exhibition openings. One example is a crisp rice and barley porridge painted with food colors in the style of Frank Bowling during the artist's retrospective at the Spritmuseum. Another example is a black and white cauliflower dish that is an homage to the flooring pattern in Keith Haring's studio. This dish was developed for a group exhibit of artists whose work was inspired by Keith Haring.

NL   *For many, a visit to a museum is a multi-sensory experience that is never complete without a food tasting and conversation about art. How do you see the museum restaurant as a chef and a customer?*

PN   I have always seen museum restaurants as good places to spend time. No matter where in the world you are, museum restaurants purvey a certain cultural atmosphere. I think that having a place to digest the museum experience and discuss what you have just seen is of great value. In my opinion a museum visit is almost always a multi-sensory experience.

NL   *What is the difference between a chef in a restaurant and a chef in a restaurant that is located in a museum?*

PN   For a chef, a restaurant is always what you make of it, regardless of where it is located, be it in a museum or not.

A conversation with chef Joris Bijdendijk, RIJKS® Restaurant at the Rijksmuseum, Amsterdam

Joris Bijdendijk discovered his passion for cooking when he was 16 years old. As a young chef Bijdendijk learned to cook by working for great chefs. In 2012, at the age of 28, Bijdendijk began working as Executive Chef at Bridges, a legendary Amsterdam establishment where within a year he received his first Michelin star. Since 2014, Joris has been the Executive Chef at the RIJKS® restaurant in the Philips wing of the Rijksmuseum. At RIJKS® Bijdendijk works with traditional Dutch products. He is inspired by the flavors that have influenced the Dutch cuisine over the centuries and is guided by the philosophy of Slow Food.

Nina Levent (NL)   *How would you describe your approach to gastronomy?*

Joris Bijdendijk (JB)   For me gastronomy is about the products you use and the way you present them. The products should have the best possible quality. Don't use fifty ingredients in a langoustine (also known as scampi and Dublin Bay prawn) dish. Give it a nice garnish and a lovely sauce, but let the langoustine itself be worthy to taste.

NL   *What does heading a restaurant in the Rijksmuseum mean to you? How do you ensure the restaurant fits within the museum in terms of its exhibits and philosophy?*

JB   At RIJKS® we link our menu to the major exhibitions in the museum. In fact, we work parallel with the museum programming by having our own program of guest chefs cooking in our kitchen. A guest chef is invited to our kitchen for a couple of days to kick off the exhibition period or celebrate the opening of a new exhibit. We keep the dishes created by these chefs on our menu for the whole duration of the exhibition. This way museum visitors have a cultural experience in the Rijksmuseum followed by a complimentary gastronomy experience in the restaurant.

We work with guest chefs in a manner that is similar to how the museum works with curators or artists. Our program is closely connected to the museum calendar. RIJKS® has been open for a year now and we have welcomed several guest chefs. For our major exhibition "Late Rembrandt," paintings of Rembrandt's final years were brought together. To connect with the exhibit, we invited Margot Janse, an esteemed South African chef of Dutch origin. Margot was inspired by the exhibition and developed a special menu in response to Rembrandt's works where she introduced African ingredients such as baobab, bushu, and honeybush. Another example is the 2015 "Asia in Amsterdam": our guest chef was André Chiang, who was born in Taiwan, grew up in Japan, was trained in France, and now runs one of the best restaurants in Singapore. He was invited to develop dishes with Asian culinary inspiration.

NL   *Would you reflect on a challenge posed by cooking in the museum?*

JB   The challenge is that we actually have two different audiences. RIJKS® is a public restaurant for the locals. We also welcome a lot of museum visitors. These two groups have very different needs. Guests who spent the day wandering around the museum or planning to do so after the meal, often have less time for a lunch. Guests who live in the neighborhood or planned a special trip to Amsterdam for the restaurant often want to spend more time on a lunch of dinner.

NL   *What advice would you give other chefs working in museums?*

JB   Stick to the core values. Make sure the identities are the same for the museum, the restaurant, or café. Make sure that there is a logical link that connects this particular restaurant to this particular museum.

A conversation with chef Ali Loukzada, Café Serai at the Rubin Museum of Art, New York

Chef Ali Loukzada serves as Executive Chef at the Rubin Museum of Art. Born and raised in Mumbai, India, Loukzada spent his childhood working at family-owned restaurants. As a teenager Loukzada spent most of his time learning to cook with his mother and grandmother.

Prior to taking the helm of Café Serai, the Rubin Museum's Tibetian-inspired restaurant in 2011, Loukzada served as sous chef at Tabla Restaurant where he served as sous chef and combined his Indian roots with modern-day New York fare and, later, as sous chef at Stephen Starr's Modern Asian restaurant Buddakan. Describing his style Loukzada says: "My food will almost always have a balance of sweet, sour, salt, and spice. I try to layer these flavors in my dishes however I can. I also use the same preserving techniques that people have used in India for centuries to make pickles, preserves, and sweets"[4]

Nina Levent (NL)   *Would you describe your approach to cooking/gastronomy?*

Ali Loukzada (AL)   The term gastronomy originated from ancient Greek "the art or law of regulating the stomach." I would describe my cooking as Progressive Indian. Cooking in fine restaurants in New York City over this period of time has taught me that taking classic techniques and elevating and creating new steps that I apply with my own interpretation is the best approach to gastronomy. And that's what I work on improving every day!

NL   *What does cooking in Rubin Museum with its extensive collection of Himalayan Art mean to you?*

AL   Our menu at Café Serai is based around the changing seasons as well as the artwork that we have in the museum. Walking around the museum is always inspiring for me. I see artwork that may be painted on white china or on a canvas or maybe it is a statue, and I think about putting it on a plate with colors and forms that are very similar. Most of our dishes and some of the names of the dishes are inspired by artwork that has been or is being exhibited in the museum, such as the "lotus chicken liver" (I saw a painting of a lotus with its pink bud in the center and the flower and decided to make a chicken liver mousse that's pink with naan around it), or the "Buddhist beet salad" (a statue of the Buddha with its perfectly rounded belly was an inspiration for this dish). Others are inspired by the region, such as the "Himalayan bread sampler," and momos, which are typical dishes in Tibet, Nepal, and surrounding areas.

NL   *Have you worked with curators or artists at the Rubin Museum? Might you give examples of specific examples of dishes that make the restaurant complementary to the museum?*

AL   I always try to work with the curators and sometimes even the artists on the current exhibitions. One current example is the Steve McCurry photographs of his travels in India. I asked McCurry to share the most memorable dish that he had during his travels in India. It was a vegetable biryani that he had in Bombay, so we featured a traditional biryani dish encrusted with puff pastry, also known as dum biryani, at the museum with a cucumber and tomato raita!

NL   *Many feel that a museum experience is not complete without a quiet time, or a food tasting and conversation about art. What do you see observing and interacting with your customers at the Rubin Museum?*

AL   Both art and food are major components of any culture, so offering both experiences can really enhance the experience of our visitors. Because so much of the menu is inspired by the art at the Rubin Museum, dining really brings the entire experience together. For me, stepping into the museum was very natural. My background as an Indian allows me to relate to the artwork from India and neighboring countries such as China, Tibet, and Nepal. Growing up in India I was always surrounded by various religions, cultures, and festivals that are often featured in our exhibits. I was also trained as a French chef working in New York City's fine dining restaurants for several years, which made me a strong cook with French and modern techniques. Applying these techniques to Indian food worked out really well. So keeping my background and training in mind I try to give the visitors the best experience possible through our food, our pastries, and the service we offer our guests.

NL   *What is the difference between a chef in a restaurant and a chef in a restaurant that is located in a museum?*

AL   Being a chef in a restaurant is easy because you can create whatever you feel like and change the direction of the menu in whichever way you would like. Being a chef at a restaurant in a museum is more fun as it is also more challenging as one needs to relate to the museum's programming this season and new exhibitions. You have to be creative to connect the menu with every season that approaches and with upcoming exhibitions.

NL   *What advice would you give a young chef about to work in a museum restaurant?*

AL   Nothing is impossible. Stay organized, take a project with all possibilities and always be prepared to fail, but stay positive. What has always worked for me at this museum is to keep an open mind and approach food from all angles. For example, I don't look at an apple as an apple, because there are always a lot of ways you can transform an apple into a delicious dessert, pastry, jam, chutney, garnish, vinegar, or salad.

Final reflections

Museum restaurants play a role in communicating the museum content on par with museum galleries and museum education centers. Chefs and museum staff collaborate on menus that reflect current exhibits or are connected to the objects in the permanent collection.[5] Many chefs are in constant conversation with curators and museum staff about linking the dining experience with the gallery experience, and maintaining a consistent identity of all aspects of the cultural institution. Wim Pijbes, Rijksmuseum's General Director, noted that RIJKS® restaurant is the Rijksmuseum on your plate.[6]

Chefs speak about being inspired by art and objects at museums, as well as being able to relate deeply to the creativity of the artists on display. They can do so, because their own creative process is very similar: it is authentic to them and they incorporate many influences from nature, local traditions, and legendary chefs into their own signature cuisine. Museums that invite top chefs to run their restaurants are dealing with an independent creative force. Although the chef might be inspired by the museum, their restaurants first and foremost are the reflections of the chef's cooking style, his or her authenticity and innovative spirit. The chef as a sole creative force defines the dining experience.

The advice that is offered in these interviews to younger chefs is about being authentic and staying true to one's cooking style and core values. Each chef has defined and articulated a unique signature style. As content providers they are also at the forefront of conversations about sustainability, health, nutrition, local and seasonal ingredients, Slow Food, and hospitality. Like many artists and designers, the chefs speak about innovating every day, developing new menus, being inspired by nature, being restless, meeting a new creative challenge daily. Like museum educators and curators, the chefs strive to improve different aspects of their patrons' experience, including food, ambience, service, and communication. These chefs invite guest chefs to contribute to the menu or take over the kitchen for a day, an experience that is reminiscent of museums' artists' residencies.

As the conversations with this quartet of chefs indicate, a museum restaurant is not simply an extension of the museum experience, a post-visit culinary stop; a top museum restaurant like any restaurant can provide a complete sensory and dining experience. Their signature cuisine, driven by a visionary chef, draws patrons from beyond the museum crowd. These restaurants not only complement a museum, but also are regional and local gastronomic destinations of note. They attract new audiences to the museum as well as provide museum visitors with an unforgettable sensory experience.

Notes

1   Lucchesi, Paolo. *In Situ*: Corey Lee is opening a restaurant in SFMOMA. *SF GATE*, October 2, 2015.

2   McKeever, Amy. Petter Nilsson on Leaving La Gazzetta and His New Stockholm Restaurant, *Eater*, Feb 6, 2014, 10:20.

3   *New York Times*, April 8, 2015.

4   Kennedy, Marina. Chef Spotlight: Executive Chef ALI LOUKZADA of Cafe Serai in the Rubin Museum. January 12, 2015. *Broadway World*, Food and Wine.

5   Irina D. Mihalache. Eating in the Museum: New Practices in Visitor Engagement Through Food and Taste. *Arts & Food. Ritual since 1851.* Ed. Germano Celant. Milan 2015. 852–855.

6   Interview November 2015, http://blog.hotelschool.nl

20

From Georgian Dinners to Dinner with Dickens:

"*Don't* Preserve the Historic Kitchen! *Go* Into the Historic Kitchen!"

Irina D. Mihalache in conversation with Liz Driver, Director/Curator, Campbell House Museum

On Friday, March 31, 1972, something big was happening in Toronto: a late Georgian era house, built for Judge William Campbell and his wife Hannah Campbell in 1822, traveled one and a half kilometers, on dollies, to its new location at the corner of Queen and University. The Campbell House Museum, originally designed as a private residence and often used to entertain Toronto's early nineteenth-century socialites, was auctioned off and, for most of the twentieth century, functioned as office space and a factory, including a horseshoe nail company and an elevator company. Currently, the museum "is a vibrant public space where members of Toronto's diverse communities gather to discuss, to create, to perform, and to socialize, giving life to the words 'freedom of expression.'"[1] And what better way to socialize than with a glass of home-made shrub and a hefty portion of beef, roasted on the open fire in the museum's historic kitchen? If that is not enough engagement, one can enjoy a theater performance, which uses the whole house as the stage.

What museum visitors might not know is the work that goes into transforming a historic home, with only two full-time staff, into a multi-sensorial participatory environment.

The kitchens of the Campbell House Museum

Liz Driver (LD)   We have lots of food-related spaces in our house. The wonderful thing about Campbell House is that you enter through the front door and you are immediately aware that there is the historic dining room on the right, and the withdrawing room on the left, where people would have enjoyed tea or a drink of port. We have a historic kitchen and a ballroom! So we do lots of hospitality here. And we also have a modern dining room and we have a modern kitchen, which is completely outside the envelope of the original historic building.

Irina D. Mihalache (IDM)   *Maybe you can tell me a little bit more about these eating spaces.*

LD   *Don't* preserve the historic kitchen! No! *Go* into the historic kitchen. Start using it! What is the point of looking at things that don't have a use? I actually went through and I removed the items that were sort of broken and placed there just for display, and I added new utilitarian items. Sometimes, they are real artifacts, like a brass ladle. Other times I had reproduction ironware or tinware made. Because, of course, tinware especially, perishes. I really believe historic kitchens should work. You're going to be able, when you go on a tour with people, to say, "Wow, well we were baking in here yesterday and look! It looks like the fire's dead, but I'm just going to stir the ashes. See, there's still sparks. . . ." The working kitchen has such an impact on people's experience of our museum. They open the front door, they walk in and they say, "Ah! I love that smell! I can smell the wood fire." And this is especially true in a large city, of course, where you're not even allowed to build a wood-fired stove or fireplace any more.

IDM   *So what kind of activities do you have in your historic kitchen? And how do you integrate the historic kitchen with the new kitchen?*

LD   I love really true, careful interpretation. But I discovered that people actually liked to have cocktail parties in the historic kitchen. So they moved the table: they swung it to the back of the room [to create the bar]. I completely accept that, because, number one, my theory is that when people come to Campbell House, it doesn't matter whether they've come for a cocktail party, a business meeting, a wedding, a tour, an exhibition, or art opening, they're still drawn into the historic space and that makes them curious. And people love the historic kitchen the most. I think all kitchens are like that: they make people feel comfortable and intimate with each other and even more so if you are actually using it.

I'll tell you how I use those two spaces historically and in a contemporary way. At the beginning of a relationship with the Saint George's Society, they wanted to celebrate the two hundredth anniversary of Dickens' birth with an event and I suggested Dinner with Dickens for which we would roast beef on the open fire. I roasted the beef on the open fire and we did the vegetables in the modern kitchen. We couldn't seat sixty-five people in the historic kitchen so [first] we had everyone come into the kitchen and sample a hot punch from an original recipe that Dickens had in his papers. The guests watched the beef come off the fire, be carved on the historic kitchen table. They went and took their seats in the other room and we carried the beef in ritual fashion, one platter behind the other, and then distributed the platters on the tables for the guests to eat family style.

Theater and food

IDM   *Can you tell me a little bit more about the changes that you've made in terms of the food interpretation or food programming since you came to the museum?*

LD   Hannah and William Campbell built this house after their children had grown up. This was not a family home. This was a home for grown-ups, a home for entertaining. I've taken that as my leading idea. It fits very well with the fact that we're a part of the cultural activity in downtown Toronto. I think that food can be either the central purpose of an event or a program, or it could be any level of auxiliary. It can be nothing more than offering a cup of tea before a play or a lecture. Or we can have food tailored and customized to add meaning to the event, which is of course the most satisfying for everybody. What are some of the different things we've done in that respect? Well we've done quite a bit of dinner theater for Winterlicious.[2] The play that was proposed was *The Dining Room*, an American play about family life that is told around the dining table. It covered all these decades of history, 1930s through to the 60s or 70s. And so for the dinner that preceded it, we offered a menu from the 1930s, 40s and 50s: you could pick your appetizer, your main course, and your dessert. I researched and provided the recipes to the chef.

IDM   *Do you remember the dishes that you enjoyed the most researching for that event?*

LD   I think one recipe was for a meatloaf; there was also a tomato soup, and an orange chiffon cake. The play was centered on the concept of moving through time, and using food allows people to get right into it and notice different things about these historic times.

IDM   *And you also did an event with a Russian menu?*

LD   Oh yes! That was [a play by Brian Friel] called *Afterplay*, and was set in Moscow in the 1920s. And I asked a Russian culinary historian friend for advice. She had a reprint of a Russian cookbook from the era. She translated the recipes for tea-time treats for me and we made these two different kinds of Russian cakes. We served them [on plates set out] around a silver samovar that someone lent me! People came up the stairs and they saw the samovar, they got served this delicious tea out of it with the Russian cakes, and then they went in and they sat at little café tables. The play took place in a café. And so the audience became part of the café with the original Russian pastries.

Another play we did was *A Room of One's Own*, which is a monologue [by a character playing] Virginia Woolf. It takes place in the late 1920s at a British college. We transformed the ground floor of Campbell House to a 1920s common room and brought out our shabbiest old lamps and whatnot. It was as if the visitors came for tea before they were to hear Virginia Woolf's lecture. We offered them tea or sherry and cheese straws and rock cakes, or rock buns, which is a sort of raised scone. Most young people have never tasted sherry, but they were so game. They loved it! We were introducing them to the history of drinks and to the environment and the setting in which one would have tea and sherry at that time.

Some words of advice

IDM   *What would you like to share with museum professionals from other historic houses who are working with food?*

LD   Obviously, to serve food, you need to know your health permitting. In Toronto, you need a green pass from the City of Toronto Health to serve food to the public. I think it's wonderful to have a liquor license. People should just go out and get the license. My staff have the training so they can serve alcohol. I think it is also important to have a scholarly base: know what period you're representing, do your research. Try to be as true as possible both when you purchase your ingredients and with the methods you use to produce the food, in the equipment, in the environment that you create. You can't always be authentic: Sometimes I had to use paper plates. I try to avoid it, but we do make things in the modern kitchen. When you put on the event, whatever it is, try to find as many ways as you can to inform people about what they're eating and drinking. I often introduce the food and drinks: ". . . and you're having shrub. And shrub is made of . . ." Or leave the recipe out on the table where the visitors can access it. Also I have a kitchen tool box.

IDM   *What is a kitchen tool box?*

LD   It is a big plastic box for kitchen tools. In it you keep all your equipment so that you can remove it from your catering kitchen. Invariably, a kitchen in a museum is going to be used by a lot of different people, by caterers, by program officers. What it means is that you have a way of removing your valuable things, your museum supplies. It gives you a way of separating your museum equipment and functions from the catering functions.

IDM   *Lastly, how do you manage all your different identities?*

LD   I should say that a focus only on food is not a healthy thing. I like to bring food in on everything, if I can, so therefore I don't only want to be doing food at Campbell House.

Notes

1   "Mission," Campbell House Museum, http://www.campbellhousemuseum. ca/?page_id=10 [accessed January 22, 2016].
2   Winterlicious is an annual food event in Toronto, where restaurants and other cultural institutions participate with *prix fixe* menus at special prices.

21

White Onion, Cod, and Green Pepper Sauce:

A Recipe from Josean Alija

Josean Alija

Cod has a very interesting place in the history of Bilbao, with a very deep historical association with the city's culture. This fish is the basis of an important series of recipes that define the personality of the city. During Lent, fish was cooked in a fat flavored with garlic and chili to enhance its flavor. This way of cooking causes the cod to release a gelatin containing surfactants that binds water and oil, helped by movement: the forward and backward motion of the shaken earthenware cooking dish produces an exquisite emulsion—the pilpil sauce, one of the four most important sauces in Basque culinary culture. The skin of the fish plays a dual role, as waterproof protection and as a means of identification. The skin of the cod is also the part that holds the secret of pilpil, the "magic" serum.

The addition of green pepper to the sauce brings about a flavor similar to that of *piperrada* or *piperade*—a mixture of peppers and onion, a famous Basque accompaniment. The onion is a vegetable that has uplifted sauces throughout the history of cooking, which made me believe that I could turn it into a magnificent dish. Cut correctly with its layers overlapping, an onion bears a strong resemblance to a portion of cod. This idea led me to turn onion into cod: slightly crisp, fleshy slices covered in a cod skin on an emulsion of green pepper pilpil. This vegetable dish is associated with Bilbao, its cod culture and its many ways of preparing cod.

Cod and green pepper sauce

Cod skin stock

Ingredients　400 g cod skins, desalted and strained; 120 g water; 24 g spring onion; 3 g crushed garlic cloves; 1 pinch cayenne pepper.

Preparation　combine all ingredients in a vacuum bag, seal at 100% and cook at 62 °C in a Roner for 4 hours. Strain the stock, and then strain again through a Superbag[1] to remove any possible scales or particles. Let cool and refrigerate until needed.

Green pepper and basil leaves oil

Ingredients　100 g virgin olive oil; 150 g green pepper, deseeded and destalked; 25 g green coffee beans; 2 g basil leaves.

Preparation　grind the green coffee beans to a powder. Add the oil and green pepper and process at maximum speed for 15 seconds. Transfer to a vacuum bag, add basil leaves and vacuum seal at 100%. Cook in a steam oven at 100 °C for 1 hour. Then remove the contents from the bag and strain through a Superbag, pressing well so that all the liquid absorbed by the pepper is released. Decant liquid in a piston funnel to separate the water released by the pepper from the oil. Set aside the oil.

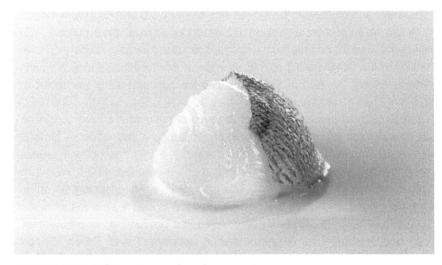

FIGURE 21.1 *White onion, cod, and green pepper sauce.*
© *López de Zubiría.*

Cod and green pepper sauce

Ingredients   200 g cod skin stock; 80 g green pepper oil; 2 g sliced garlic, germ removed; table salt.

Preparation   put the green pepper oil and the garlic in a pan and heat. When the oil begins to form an emulsion, remove from the heat, cool slightly, then strain the oil. Warm the cod skin stock. Process with a hand-held blender to aerate and lightly whip the stock. Drizzle the green pepper oil into the stock, blending until all oil is incorporated and an emulsion has formed. Season with salt. Set aside until needed.

Stewed brined onions

Oarweed stock

Ingredients   500 g water, 30 g salted oarweed (*Laminaria digitata*).

Preparation   soak the seaweed in a bowl with plenty of water for 5 minutes to desalt. Combine the seaweed and water in a vacuum bag. Seal at 100% and let stand at room temperature for 30 minutes. Cook in a Roner at 60 °C for 45 minutes. Strain the stock.

Brined onions

Ingredients   4 sweet onions, specially selected, 500 g 15% brine (150 g sea salt /1000 g water).

Preparation   Peel the onions and immerse them in the brine at room temperature. Place some weight on top of the onions to stop them from floating; leave them in the brine for 1 hour, then strain and set onions aside.

Stewed brined onions

Ingredients   4 brined onions, 200 g oarweed stock.

Preparation   place the brined onions in a vacuum bag and add the oarweed stock. The liquid should weigh 30% more than the combined weight of the onions. Vacuum seal at 100% and cook on a wire rack in a steam oven at 100 °C for 90 minutes. The time will vary depending on the onions. They should remain whole with a creamy texture, although a little firm to touch. Remove onions and drain on the rack for 10 minutes. Place them in a drying oven for 30–40 minutes at 80 °C to dry them slightly.

Cod skin confit

Spicy oil

Ingredients   200 g olive oil, 4 g crushed garlic, 2.5 g cayenne peppers.
Preparation   combine the ingredients in a pan and simmer for 30 minutes.
  Cool and strain.

Cod skin confit

Ingredients   2 cod skins, 20 g spicy oil.
Preparation   coat the skins with the spicy oil. Place between sheets of
  parchment paper, put into a vacuum bag and seal at 100%. Cook on a wire
  rack in a steam oven at 100 °C for 25 minutes. Open the bag, remove
  skins and cut to required size.

Finishing

Remove the outer layer of the onions. Cut the onions to resemble a piece of
cod fillet; cover with cling film and reheat on a tray in a steam oven at 100 °C
for 2 minutes. Remove them from the tray and aromatize on the grill over
holm oak-wood embers until they take on a chargrilled flavor. Place a piece
of cod confit skin on top of each onion so that they resemble pieces of cod
fillet with skin. Heat the cod and green pepper sauce and season with salt. Put
the spicy oil and green pepper oil ready in pipettes. Reheat onions under a
salamander grill.

Presentation

Place a few spoons of cod and green pepper sauce on the plate. Drizzle a
piece of the hot onion with a little spicy oil and place it over the cod and green
pepper sauce.

Note

1   A Superbag is a very fine and porous filter made from a flexible and heat-
    resistant material which is ideal for cooking stocks and fits well in different
    containers.

PART FIVE

Food and Art

22

Reflections on "Art and Appetite":

Painting America's Identity through Food

Judith A. Barter

The desire to combine my American cultural and art history knowledge with another of my passions, cooking, came to me in the shower. In 2001, I was about ready to go on sabbatical and wanted a break from looking only at art. Because of my interests in social and cultural history, and in cooking, I decided to spend a month at the Schlesinger Library at Harvard University reading food histories and old cookbooks. I concentrated on American food and alcohol histories, copying interesting recipes of all types. Eventually, I ordered dozens of cookbook reprints available through Dover reprints; used the online food history site at Michigan State University, as well as online sites at the American Antiquarian Society and the online menu collection at the New York Public Library. By far, the best source for the actual historic objects, menus, cookbooks, posters, trade cards and other ephemera was the Jan Langone collection at the William Clements Library at the University of Michigan.

Through these sources, I continued my research on food, thinking about how I could combine fascinating food history with American painting, to trace the history of American art alongside that of American foodways. I began to imagine what an exhibition combining food and art could look like. Ultimately, the exhibition *Art and Appetite: American Painting, Culture and Cuisine* that took place at The Art Institute of Chicago (November 2013 to January 2014) contained

118 objects, and the book is 248 pages. This case study shows how curatorial interest in interdisciplinary approaches to museum exhibitions and catalogs can allow curators to combine sensory experiences within an institutional setting. Using the traditional curatorial primary visual and art historical experience and combining it with new ideas can create new museum audiences. Like my reading and research, I wanted the exhibition to cover American food, eating, and art from colonial times through to Pop Art, when giant food forms became so important. I traveled to look at the most beautiful and compelling still life paintings of food in collections across the country. For a museum curator, quality and condition are paramount.

The great majority of these objects were nineteenth- and early twentieth-century still life paintings of fruit, or vegetables; sometimes incorporating wine, nuts, cheese, and other traditional nineteenth-century dessert items. But an exhibition of only still lifes of this type would be repetitive and dull indeed, and so I cast the net further afield to find paintings that showed meals, or kitchens, or food being used and consumed. So too, extending the nature of "food" paintings to include Pop Art sculptures, collage, and other genres enriched the exhibition visually and historically. These genre paintings relieved the "sameness" of still life paintings, and allowed a wider interpretation of cultural patterns. For example, two paintings in the collection of the Museum of Fine Arts Boston were essential early documents about behaviors around alcohol. The first, Henry Sargent's famous *The Dinner Party* (c. 1821), showed a male dinner party during dessert. As was the fashion, the tablecloth has been removed, wine and fruit have been served, a typical dessert of the early Republic. Another painting, Jerome Thompson's *A Pic Nick in the Woods of New England* (c. 1855), illustrates a New England picnic and provided corroboration for many mid-nineteenth-century American dishes. In the American fashion, before service in courses became popular, all the dishes are set out at once. The picture depicts soup, fowl, ham, oysters, and importantly, cider, whiskey, and wine. These beverages are somewhat hidden, perhaps because the painting corresponds with some of the earliest temperance laws passed in New England, although this large group is clearly enjoying the alcoholic beverages.

The popular dessert course consisting of fruit, cheese, and wine is the subject of John F. Francis's work. Francis made a career of painting bottles and glasses of wine and spirits, and was a temperance advocate! Instead of painting just fruit and vegetables, he chose this subject to show the temperate use of wine and spirits, mixed with water, and taken with cheese and fruit. A prominent Episcopalian, Francis took part in the debate over wine at Eucharist then raging in the Protestant churches. Indeed, this controversy led to the invention of alcohol-free grape juice, produced by the Reverend Welch and his son. Soon, Welch's unfermented grape juice replaced wine in many Protestant

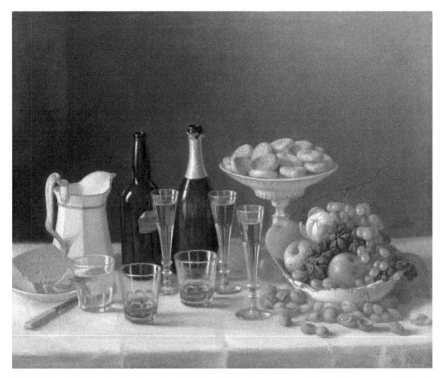

FIGURE 22.1 *John F. Francis (1808–1886), American,* Wine, Cheese, and Fruit, *1857, Oil on canvas, 63.5 × 76.2 cm (25 × 30 in).*

Restricted gift of Charles C. Haffner III and Mrs. Herbert Alexander Vance; Wesley M. Dixon, Jr. © The Art Institute of Chicago.

congregations. Here again, delving into the artists' interests and historical analysis of the elements of the composition enriches the visual experience, allowing a discussion of the importance of the temperance movement in the nineteenth century. Not only were there anti-saloon campaigns, but even the use of alcohol in the church and home was debated. Indeed, temperance as a social issue was second in importance only to the ongoing clash over the issue of slavery.

Genre paintings helped to interpret the use of food and food preparation. Mid-nineteenth-century works by Lily Martin Spencer depicted dining rooms and kitchens; Seymour Joseph Guy described high tea in a formal New York dining room of 1866; Edmund Tarbell and Willard Metcalf showed upper-class and working-class breakfasts; John Singer Sargent's painting of his dining room around 1885 showed the set table after luncheon. In particular, Doris Lee's *Thanksgiving* illustrates both class and gender in the kitchen.

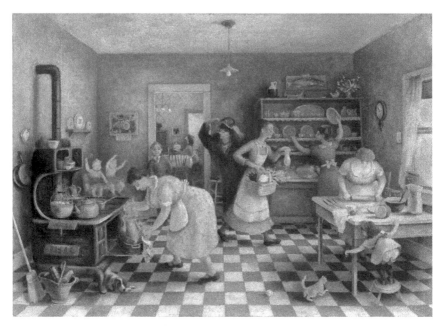

FIGURE 22.2 *Doris Lee (1905–1983), American,* Thanksgiving, *c. 1935, Oil on canvas, 71.3 × 101.8 cm (28 $\frac{1}{8}$ × 40 $\frac{1}{8}$ in).*

Mr. and Mrs. Frank G. Logan Purchase Prize Fund, 1935.313. © The Art Institute of Chicago.

The rural ladies are preparing this most important meal in a kitchen with an old wood stove and worn linoleum. The city-slickers who have just arrived are denoted by the differences between plain housedresses and the fashionable hat and fur worn by the woman stepping into the kitchen. All help us to understand the activities and settings of the traditional farm household, and the gendered spaces therein: kitchens and parlor were for ladies, while dining rooms with hanging game still lifes and carved sideboards spoke to masculinity and the symbolic hunt.

While genre pictures could anchor the time periods of menus as well as the type of meal, the still lifes themselves upon close inspection, did the same. Dissection of their subject matter allowed for wider cultural and historical interpretations than just formal analysis of shape and form. For example, Raphaelle Peale's *Still Life with Strawberries, Nuts &c.,* depicts Chinese export porcelain tea accouterments, an American-made covered glass vase possibly made at America's first glassworks and containing hot-house strawberries like those raised in the Peale family heated greenhouses at Belfield, their farm outside Philadelphia.

All these precious items speak to the pretentions of the American middle class, but also to the robust nature of American foreign trade, manufacturing,

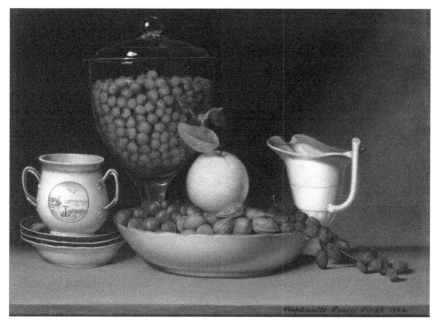

FIGURE 22.3 *Raphaelle Peale (1774–1825), American,* Still Life—Strawberries, Nuts &c., *1822, Oil on wood panel, 41.1 × 57.8 cm (16$\frac{3}{16}$ × 22$\frac{3}{4}$ in).*
Gift of Jamee J. and Marshall Field, 1991.100. © The Art Institute of Chicago.

and fertile farming after the War of 1812 when the United States mastered hegemony of the seas.

Raphaelle's uncle James Peale, also a painter, executed *Still Life: Balsam Apple and Vegetables* (1820s, Metropolitan Museum of Art) featuring a time-specific fall menu: eggplant, okra, tomatoes, cabbages, all members of the nightshade family. Included is what is called a balsam apple, actually a balsam pear, a beautiful but inedible, poisonous ornamental plant that Thomas Jefferson used at Monticello as a garden border around 1813. Properly explained to museum viewers, the picture can be interpreted as the introduction of danger into the edible American Garden of Eden. Indeed, at this time, President Madison and other agricultural experimenters decried the waste of American farmland and urged farmers to rotate crops, put nitrogen into the soil and allow fields to lay fallow. They also protested the American practice of depleting the soil, and moving further westward to new farmsteads, wasting national resources.

The symbolism of produce and fowl was addressed in other ways too. *Trompe l'oeil* paintings (fool the eye) echoed highly carved sideboards featuring dead rabbits, birds, foxes, etc. Paintings of hanging trophies of the hunt raised symbolic issues too. Two paintings from the collection of the Art Institute of Chicago, William Michael Harnett's *For Sunday's Dinner* (1881) and DeScott Evans's *The Irish Question*, feature foods that reflect on poverty and Irish migration to the United States.

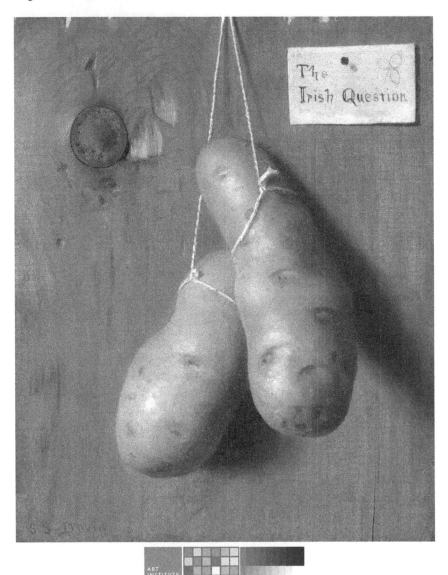

FIGURE 22.4 *De Scott Evans (1847–1898), American,* The Irish Question, *1880s, Oil on canvas, 30.5 × 25.4 cm (12 × 10 in).*

Restricted gift of Carol W. Wardlaw and Jill Burnside Zeno; Roger and J. Peter McCormick Endowments, 2004.3. © The Art Institute of Chicago.

In each case, the "food" element stood for timely political events. Evans's russet potatoes hanging by their "necks" offered a grim solution to Irish Home Rule and xenophobic attitudes about increasing Irish immigration to America during the period 1870–1885, and coincided with Charles Stewart Parnell's American tour. Irish independence was the subject of the day, but a note containing a shamrock leaf and the inscription "The Irish Question," next to the hanging potatoes makes clear one solution for the tremendous Irish immigration to the United States. Discrimination against the Irish during the 1870s and 1880s was rampant. These Irish were considered drunks, fueling the temperance crusade. *For Sunday's Dinner* makes use of the painted, skinny plucked chicken hanging by a leg against an old door with rusty hinges to address the poverty of immigrants like Irishman Harnett himself, and the goal of meat once a week for Sunday dinner. Most poor immigrants had no meat in their diet; to have a chicken in the Sunday pot was a symbol of success, even if the chicken was as scrawny as the cook.

Contemporary art allowed viewers to look back at the history of American food. Tom Wesselmann's paintings often critique the lost legacy of the Jeffersonian republican vision of a nation of farmers. One painting features a large bottle of Four Roses, a famous straight Kentucky bourbon label that was purchased by a large corporation in 1956. The corporation began bottling colored grain alcohol under the Four Roses label; instantly a famous and respected brand became known as "rot-gut." Other elements included in Wesselmann's *still–life No. 15*, are Gilbert Stuart's famous portrait of George Washington, a slick supermarket ad for plastic-looking steak, and flattened, colored blobs representing apples and lemons. All bespeak the mass produced food of the contemporary American diet. Huge *Green Beans* (1964, Museum of Contemporary Art, Chicago) or *Sculpture in the Form of a Fried Egg* (1966, Museum of Contemporary Art, Chicago) by Claes Oldenburg emphasized oversized, engineered American foodstuffs to allow us to equate commercially produced food with the plastic materials of which these works of art are made.

Ephemera provided important ways to connect the artworks to culture shifts. For example, Alice Waters' early menu for *Chez Panisse Presents an Evening of Garlic, Bastille Day, 14th of July* (1976, Janice Bluestein Longone Culinary Archive, Special Collections Library, University of Michigan) countered the Wesselmann and Oldenburg processed foods discussed above. Using menus and posters provided a doorway to emphasize the locally grown foods, fine ingredients and the "foodie" movement that began in the 1970s. Cookbooks also provided this emphasis and many late nineteenth- and early twentieth-century ethnic cookbooks, sometimes in their native language, were included. Early nineteenth-century menus from roadhouses and stagecoach stops provided viewers with knowledge of the incredible varieties of meats, fish, shellfish, and poultry served to protein-loving Americans. Americans also loved sweets and puddings and restaurant menus (few restaurants predate 1860) attest to this passion. For each object, a 150-word label was provided. Quotes from food writers, or artists writing about food were silkscreened on the walls. One of the favorites was Mark Twain's contention that on riverboat travel "scenery goes better with ham and eggs."

The exhibition also included decorative arts. Incorporating several table settings and furnished sideboards allowed objects depicted in the paintings to be exhibited next to their actual counterparts. Viewers understood that these objects existed, and were used every day. Table settings included flatware, pressed glass, cut glass, china services, oyster plates, and other accouterments.

The goal of using both the decorative arts and ephemera along with the paintings was two-fold. First, it lent richness and depth to the interpretation of the pictures, making them more "real" because of these historical associations. Secondly, it introduced a multi-media element into the exhibition so that it was not boringly all the same. Finally, these objects were things to which the viewing public generally had no access. Menus and cookbooks from library holdings, actual place settings from private and museum collections, product advertising trade cards—all these are objects usually contained in special libraries and archival collections and generally not seen or known by museum visitors.

The book for *Art and Appetite*, is of course, the lasting record of the exhibition. While the exhibition was arranged chronologically to take viewers through the history of American still life painting and food history, the book contained themes developed into chapters. The introductory section provided a history of American foods and diets from the colonial period to modern times. The first chapter explored the history and menus of Thanksgiving, the great American food-fest and a holiday devoted only to food. The paintings in this section ranged from works by Doris Lee and Norman Rockwell, to Alice Neel and Roy Lichtenstein. Chapter 2 provided a history of early horticulture and Enlightenment experimentation in Philadelphia and the resulting effects upon still life painting in the early Republic. Here the Peale family figured predominantly. Chapter 3 discussed art, food, and social refinement in Victorian America, including the gendered spaces of the home when entertaining, and new menus and patterns of service and utensils for eating. The chapter includes genre works by Lily Martin Spencer and Joseph Seymour Guy, as well as still lifes by Emmanuel Leutze and Robert Spear Dunning. Chapter 4 features one theme: the story of alcohol and temperance in still life painting. In the United States, from the 1830s on, temperance was a divisive topic imbued with moral meanings that finally culminated in Prohibition during the 1920s and 1930s. Chapter 5 reviews the popularity of *trompe l'oeil*

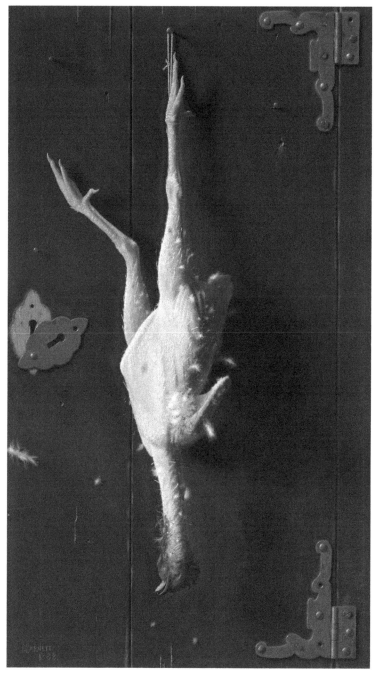

FIGURE 22.5 *William Michael Harnett (1848–1892), American (born Ireland),* For Sunday's Dinner, *1888, Oil on canvas, 94.3 × 53.6 cm (37$\frac{1}{8}$ × 21$\frac{1}{8}$ in).*

Wilson L. Mead Fund, 1958.296. © The Art Institute of Chicago.

paintings of food, their reception and popularity, their class affiliation and their political symbolism.

Chapter 6 focuses on the change in still life painting at the turn of the century. Gone are the excessively crowded still lifes of the Victorian period in favor of smaller, quieter studies of wrapped oranges, spilled boxes of candy or plums by Joseph Decker. Meals became smaller too; a breakfast tray with tea beside the bed by Edmund Tarbell, close up studies of simple biscuits and tea cups, or a market basket, all by John F. Peto, and glistening raw fish upon the countertop painted by William Merritt Chase. These simpler compositions formed a counterpart to the beginnings of the Arts and Crafts Movement and a reaction to the excesses of the Gilded Age.

Chapter 7 discusses eating in the modern era, traces the rise of American restaurant culture after 1880 and provides insight into how modernist painters such as Marsden Hartley or Thomas Hart Benton used food and dining symbolically in depictions of poverty, faith, and loss. The final chapter reviews Pop Art and popular culture in the 1960s, emphasizing mass production, canned and convenience foods. In the 1960s food becomes the subject of huge soft sculptures by Claes Oldenburg and others.

Partly because of the diversity of objects in the exhibition, all included in color in the book, and our decision to include several pages of relevant historic recipes at the end of each chapter, the book sold rapidly and well. The recipes selected covered the subjects included in the paintings and were chosen because they were unusual, or contained combinations of ingredients not common in cooking today. Many book purchasers commented that they could not wait to try them.

At the end of the exhibition, reproductions of trade cards with recipes included were free for taking. Once visitors entered the exhibition, they were sure to be entertained and learn a great deal. Each object in the exhibition had a label of at least 150 words to explain the picture and its relationship to food history. The book reinforced the exhibition labels with much more material, of course. At the exhibition exit was the usual museum shop, with cookbooks, aprons, chefs' hats, and reproductions of paintings. Visitors were also encouraged to go to the museum restaurant to try several new entrees based on recipes included in the book and exhibition.

But how could we make sure that people knew about and came to the exhibition? How to get the word out? Besides the usual street banners that the Art Institute hangs for every exhibition, the marketing department distributed the reproduced trade cards to restaurants all around the city, asking them to use them as table tents in their dining spaces. Through a partnership with restaurants in the city, the events related to the exhibition featured thirty of Chicago's finest chefs. Six chefs made two-minute videos discussing a work of art from the "food" viewpoint. These videos were sent out via email to members and mailing lists. I also made a video, a tongue-in-cheek cooking show-type video entitled, "Cooking with the Curator" that went viral on YouTube. I made recipes from the 1950s that were particularly awful, including "candle salad." These types of media events made the museum seem less elite and more welcoming to new audiences, showing them that art can be fun. We also put all the images in the exhibition, the recipes, and the menus into an exhibition with short commentaries on our website. Viewers could preview the exhibition, or review it after they had seen it.

For the opening events, we did away with the traditional sit-down dinner and instead had food stations where the Chicago chefs prepared favorite dishes. People could wander and explore the stations at their leisure. All these events made the museum environment seem less intimidating. Attendance for the exhibition was excellent, the book sold out (very rare in museum exhibitions) and at its second venue at the Amon Carter Museum in Fort Worth, Texas, *Art and Appetite* was the best-attended exhibition in that institution's history.

The conclusions that I drew from the experience were that museum audiences are open to multi-sensory experiences; that theme exhibitions may be more interesting to today's audience than monographic shows; that audiences want to understand the history behind objects (not just formal analysis); and that the combination of visual arts with other sensory explorations provides a richer experience for the museum audience.

23

Sweet Desserts and Representation of Desire

Nina Levent in conversation with artist Will Cotton

Will Cotton is a contemporary artist whose whole career revolves around his preoccupation with sweets and desserts. He connects a very traditional method of representation, realistic paintings on canvas, with contemporary discourses of desire, pleasure, the culture of fantasy, airbrushed beauty, and celebrity. Cotton's art comes out of a long tradition of realistic still lifes depicting edible objects, sumptuous, desirable, exotic, or rare. The tradition goes back to Dutch seventeenth-century still lifes, many in the Vanitas style that often boasted exquisite depictions of exotic fruit such as peeled lemon, ripe peaches, half-eaten berry pies, oysters, and rare birds—all objects of pleasure and symbols of indulgence. Cotton's work picks up on the two aspects of food objects: they are realistic and symbolic, they have recognizable physical qualities and larger meaning related to the psychology of human desire and pleasure. When it comes to pleasure, sweet dessert was invented and perfected for this very reason. Will Cotton has become a practitioner and an investigator of vivid and yet surreal scenarios created from sugar and flour.

The original inspiration for Cotton's hyper-realistic depiction of all things sweet, cakes, cotton candy, candy canes, ginger bread houses, ice cream was "Candy Land," a post-war classic children's board game. The game piqued the artist's imagination and led to a series of realistic depictions of Candy Land landscapes, complete with gingerbread houses covered with "snow" frosting, rivers of molasses, and ice cream floats. True to the tradition of realistic life painting Cotton builds complex life-size sets of cake and candy for his Candy

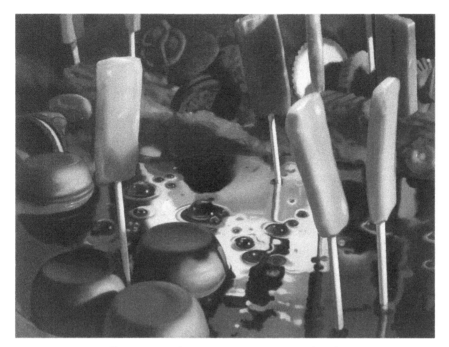

FIGURE 23.1 *Will Cotton*, Molasses Swamp II, *1999, Oil on linen, 36 × 48 in.*
Mary Boone Gallery © Will Cotton.

Land landscapes in his studio. The process of building them seems as all-consuming as the painting process; the result is a vivid hyper-real image that engages the viewer's senses, imagination, and fantasy. The physical presence and careful rendering of cupcake arrangements and frosted cake architectural structures makes them into something much more than an accurate rendering of a dessert menu item: they are the images of desire, the symbols of unattainable pleasure, objects of fiction, and catalysts for personal narratives.

At some point Cotton's landscapes became populated as the artist ventured into other classical genres, such as nude, mythological scenes, and portraiture. He has rendered female nudes reclining on the clouds made out of cotton candy, nudes partially covered with melting ice cream, portraits of women in elaborate headdresses of frosting and sugar, and most famously a series depicting the pop singer Katie Perry in various edible sugary outfits.

Nina Levent sat down with Will Cotton to discuss his inspiration, his process, and some of his recent projects.

Nina Levent (NL)   *When you began Candy Land paintings, did you sense that sweets, desserts, sugary foods had this great potential to be applied in a transformative way almost to every genre: dramatic landscape, pastoral* *painting, reclining nude, portraiture, mythological scenes, fashion design? What is the power of sweets?*

Will Cotton (WC)   Sweets' entire reason for being is exclusively to provide pleasure, not nutrition. In cuisine they're fairly unique in that respect, and as such, struck me as the right metaphor for all the aspects of desire, indulgence, and excess that I wanted to paint about. Like most American children I grew up playing Candy Land, so the idea that an entire landscape could be made of sweets was already in my mind. But I became interested in the possibility of a real Candy Land, and intrigued with the question of what it might be like to be in such a place. Would it be wonderful? Would it be terrible?

My first few paintings incorporating sweets were inspired by scenes lifted directly from the Candy Land board game: the molasses swamp, the ice cream floats. Those led me to thinking about what else you might find in a place like this, and the potential to pose questions about the nature of desire and imagined utopias. This in turn led me to the question of how I might populate these landscapes. And that's when the figures came in.

NL   *There is a lot of interest in embodied cognition and embodied aesthetics as researchers and artists explore how we experience art with all of our senses. Do you feel that aesthetic pleasure is something that goes beyond visual, engages our whole selves, and all of the senses?*

WC   I suppose the classic example of the power of the senses over the mind is the Proustian madeleine. In that literary incident it's the sense of taste that brings up a flood of memories and associations in the protagonist. That was the inspiration for my pop-up bakery project, which is the most deliberately multisensory piece I've worked on in an art context to date.

In the paintings my hope is that the viewer might have a similar experience, but in this case brought on by the visual image: a memory and set of associations reconfigured by the recognizable sweets and their unexpected function in the painting. It's important to me, in other words, that the subject of the painting always have a dual reading, to be understood as both cotton candy and clouds at the same time, for example.

NL   *You are well known for being a master realist painter, for working from life, for using, say, actual cotton candy instead of a lookalike. How important is it for your process to handle food? Are flavor and smell and texture important to your painting?*

WC   The visual symbolism contained within representations of sweets can run the gamut from the most simplistic child's drawing of a cake, to the very nuanced depictions based on careful observation in my own work. I've found

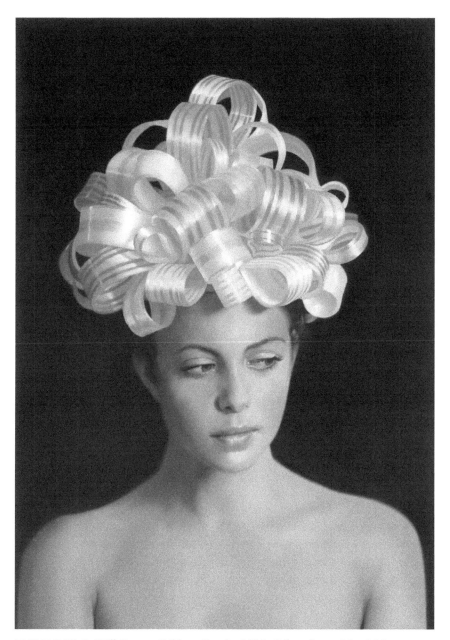

FIGURE 23.2 *Will Cotton*, Ribbon Candy, *2000, Oil on linen, 34 × 24 in.*
Mary Boone Gallery © Will Cotton.

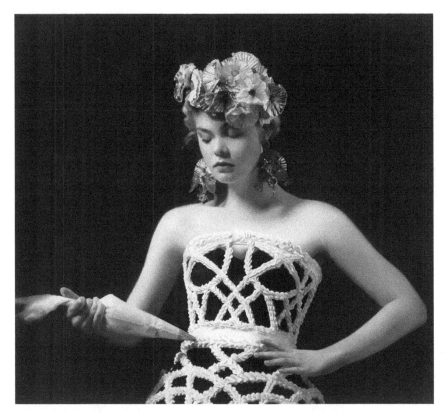

FIGURE 23.3 *Will Cotton,* Icing, *2014, Oil on linen, 72 × 80 in.*
Mary Boone Gallery © Will Cotton.

that the more specific I get (beginning with first baking the props myself, so
that they look just right), to carefully rendering surface details like shininess
etc., the more opportunity I have to bolster the narrative within the painting.
There's an experiential element too. It's important for me to be able to see, for
example, exactly what ice cream looks like as it melts off a hand. And how that
changes the model's facial expression. I believe that the painted image is
strongest when it's made from observation. So by building the props and using
the real materials as much as possible I can make the most convincing piece of
fiction.

NL *When you began your work with food in the mid–1990s, food was less
of a topic than it is now, and everything about food has become immediate
and culturally relevant. How has the unfolding conversation around food
influenced perception of your work and perhaps your own thinking?*

WC   I think the current conversation around real food and the symbolic use
of sweets in my paintings are really two separate things. I'm usually looking

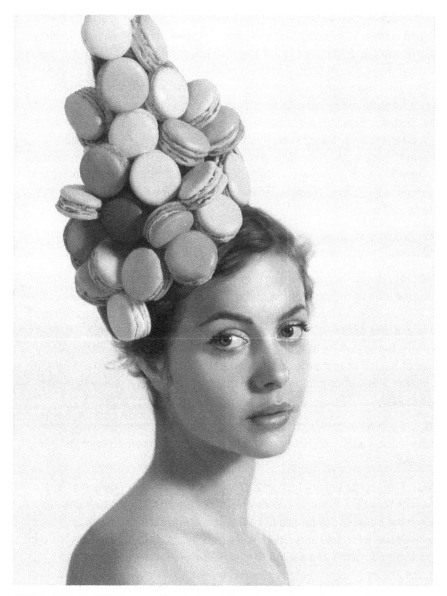

FIGURE 23.4 *Will Cotton*, The Deferred Promise of Complete Satisfaction, *2014, Oil on linen, 37 × 28 in.*

Mary Boone Gallery © Will Cotton.

for the archetypical example that will be most easily recognizable to the largest audience, as opposed to the latest marvel of molecular gastronomy.

In a number of the paintings lately, I've become more interested in issues of adornment. I've noticed that many of the pastries and cakes I've worked with put as much emphasis on the way they look as how they taste. The beautiful exterior is meant as an indication of the wonderful thing inside. I like to start a painting by asking myself a question. In this case, what would you wear in Candy Land? How might you adorn yourself? So I've been making headpieces, crowns, and dresses that strike me as the correct attire to wear in a land of sweets. There's perhaps less emphasis on location, but to me that's because those parameters have already been established in the previous work.

NL   *What is involved in your artistic process? Is it a collaborative effort? Why was it important for you to learn how to make pastry?*

WC   My preference is to make everything myself, to have the most control over the look of the prop or maquette. That's where the baking classes come in. But sometimes there's something I need that is beyond my capabilities. This was the case with the ribbon candy headpiece I painted in 2008. That's when a friend put me in touch with Dominique Ansel, who was the pastry chef at Boulud at that time. He agreed to try to make what I was looking for, and after a few attempts, made something spectacular. It was a fantastic collaboration.

NL   *If you were to design your own museum show, what kind of experience/s and environments would you want to create to engage your viewers?*

WC   The pop-up bakery I did in 2009 would work exceptionally well in a museum context. It truly incorporated all the senses. The kitchen was right out in the open so the smells of baked goods were always in the air. The pastries were for sale at typical bakery prices so that patrons might taste in addition to smelling and seeing the work. Several of my paintings and sculptures also helped set the scene. The reason for the museum setting is that unlike walking into a bakery, the visitor is expecting, and attuned, to having an art experience—to looking for meaning in the various sensory experiences being had.

24

Intoxicating Scenes:
Alcohol and Art in the Museum

Jim Drobnick

The art world is awash in alcohol. Beyond the traditional offerings of wine and spirits at openings, alcohol has acquired unprecedented prevalence in artistic practice and exhibition contexts during the last decade. The buildup to the current mix of art and alcohol, though, has been millennia in the making. Museum collections are populated by Greek kraters and Chinese cast bronzes that testify to the artistry and rituals associated with drinking in ancient times, as well as *vanitas* paintings featuring images of half-empty or toppled wine glasses that reflect upon the ephemerality of life. Scenes of riotous drinking and bohemian life appear in numerous genre paintings since the seventeenth century, and artists have famously contributed to advertising campaigns of alcoholic beverages such as Campari and Absolut. But what happens when alcohol leaps from the realm of two-dimensional representation into the hands and mouths of museumgoers, when drinking shifts from an activity gazed upon to one actually embodied within the museum's walls?

Alcohol in the museum reveals something of a contradiction. As Tony Bennett and other historians have pointed out, a number of museums in the nineteenth century were premised on creating a sober alternative to the pub and other drinking establishments.[1] Museums and alcohol did not mix because museums were positioned as a technology of civilization and moral betterment, as well as a means of social engineering. The goal was to steer the lower and working classes away from the activities of drinking, along with gambling, carnivals, and blood sports, in order to instill orderliness and cultivated values, and to channel potentially disruptive energies into productive, bourgeois-approved outlets. Restrictions against food and beverages in the galleries of the museum discouraged bodily enjoyment and focused visitors' attention upon the supposedly more intellectualized pursuit of autonomous visual pleasure. Training the senses by forbidding some and emphasizing others sought to achieve corollary effects in the psyche, behavior and morality of museumgoers whereby the adoption of the aesthetic gaze would remedy all manner of social ills. That the ills were caused by overcrowding in cities, alienating and dangerous work in factories, or rigid class-based stratifications did not seem to matter—regulating the disenfranchised with a sensory hierarchy that stigmatized the "lower" amusements of food and drink in favor of the "higher" delectations of sight was justification in itself.

Prohibitions against alcohol in museum exhibitions continue to this day but are relaxed when institutions court funders, art donors, and other supporters. For these upper echelon patrons, drinks are generously served in the galleries for special events such as society galas and fundraisers. These temporary intrusions are all the more special because the art rests tantalizingly nearby, and for a privileged elite the act of drinking breaches protocol applicable to everyone else. No one doubts, however, that the wealthy patrons, board members, and influential cliques of the museum community are trustworthy enough to handle themselves appropriately in the midst of the art. As opposed to the general public, their investment in the museum's well-being and alignment with its objectives is believed to be secure.

While the forbidding of drinking in the galleries dedicated to art remains standard in most museums, alcohol certainly is made available in their restaurants and cafés. These spaces, though, usually exist separately from those of exhibitions, either down the corridor, in a different wing, or on a distinct floor. They offer a respite from the galleries and the fatigue of looking, and typically are framed off through signage, passageways, decor, and other means. The architectural partitioning serves to contain the sounds of dining and the aromas of meals, and to keep them from circulating into other areas where they would disturb the rarified air of visual contemplation. Conservation dictates also require the separation of kitchen equipment and volatile food supplies so as to avoid endangering artworks on display or in storage. Yet it is sometimes the case that artworks are hung in museum restaurants, though such cafés would never be confused with an exhibition space proper. The precarity of such displays, unfortunately, confers upon the artworks a secondary rank, as if they did not deserve the protection or prime viewing conditions granted to more esteemed artists.

Contrary to the segregation prevalent to drinking alcohol in the museum restaurant, the artists' bars I will discuss appear within recognized exhibition areas. The overt separation of viewing from drinking does not apply. No hierarchy in status exists between the artists' bars and the other artworks on display, except, perhaps, in the dimension of participation and intimate engagement. Still, the artists' bars below uphold a similarity to bars in other contexts by providing a chance for visitors to relax and refresh. Yet, what is different? Intoxication becomes more than just a theme, subject, or symbol represented on canvas or manifested in an object; it becomes an experience and a life practice. Artists' bars are more than just a place and an occasion to drink, for the context of the museum and gallery heightens the scrutiny placed upon the phenomenon of the bar and compels visitors to also consider the aesthetics, social dynamics, and ideologies informing the activity of raising a glass or downing a pint. In contrast to the distance and disinterestedness of the modernist gaze, artists' bars oblige viewers to participate by sipping a cocktail or at least rub elbows with those who are.

The intimacy, physicality, and interactivity brought about by drinking would seem to be the perfect embodiment of conviviality that Nicolas Bourriaud (1998) defined when theorizing his version of relational aesthetics. The pleasant fellow-feeling brought about by artist-created microtopias, small-scale situations encouraging dialog and a rethinking of social relations, is an indicator of how the world could work outside of the competitiveness and ruthlessness of capitalism. While conviviality is certainly a part of the experience of artists' bars, there are undercurrents of tension that tend to disrupt a singularly congenial affective state, however positive on its surface. Alcohol's twofold nature—as a social lubricant and an unpredictable intoxicant—vexes initial assumptions about artists' bars solely functioning as a party or entertainment. In the case studies below, I will examine a series of artists' bars since 1970 that differently parse the meaning and use of alcohol. By enacting drinking in the museum or gallery context, artists' bars not only present an opportunity to imbibe, they extend a conceptual challenge to consider the act of drinking in personal, social, and political ways.

Tom Marioni: A watering hole for ideas

On a basic level, the museum is a social common ground, a meeting place. The question is, though, for whom? In the late 1960s and early 1970s, artists critical of the conservatism in mainstream museums sought to create their own alternative institutions, ones that would exhibit experimental artwork, cater specifically to the needs of artists, and develop an audience attuned to conceptual and post-media sensibilities. To establish these institutions, artists took on extra roles as administrators, fundraisers, publicists, publishers, and curators, but with a twist—they reimagined the roles while assuming them. Tom Marioni, an artist working in the San Francisco Bay area, influenced the turn towards self-run alternative spaces by founding the Museum of Conceptual Art (MOCA), which ran from 1970 to 1984. Not only did the museum show adventurous and emerging trends (it presented one of the first exhibitions of sound art), it also actualized Joseph Beuys' idea of "social sculpture" by becoming a work of art in all of its relationships and dealings.

As an early exemplar of the contemporary definition of the artist/curator, Marioni situated much of his practice at the intersection of art and life, often endorsed by the legitimacy of an institution, such as MOCA. His foremost and most longstanding project involved the staging of beer drinking "salons," which involved several museums and morphed through various iterations throughout his career. For *The Act of Drinking Beer with Friends is the Highest Form of Art* (1970), Marioni invited sixteen friends to the Oakland Museum for an after-hours private soiree. The result of their drinking—empty bottles and other detritus—remained on display for the general public to ponder. The success of the event led the artist to organize similar drinking occasions under the auspices of MOCA, which he cheekily admits was begun partly as an excuse to have parties.[2] On Wednesday afternoons, free beer was available for several years, a practice that was shifted in 1976 to Breen's, a bar located on the first floor of the museum's building. There Marioni met artists and held an "open house" where those in the neighborhood could gather, drink, and converse about art and current issues. The mood in all of these get-togethers was casual, for the intention was to deflate the pretensions of museum culture. Yet there were also rules: participants had to be invited and consume at least two drinks; only professional artists and writers could attend, though collectors could come if in disguise (to avoid the predictable hustling).[3]

The beer salons derived much of their power from the occupation of the museum's space and a commandeering of its sponsorship. For a couple of hours each week, the museum accommodated the presence of living, chatting, joking artists in its midst. Rather than featuring static, finished artworks, the drinking events enacted the relational processes that actually engendered works of art, as well as referenced the fluid network of artists that coalesced to form a community. That artists may drink with each other in the course of living and making art is unremarkable; when put in the context of the museum such drinking becomes significant. The pre-arranged time and place bestowed upon the drinking the appearance of ritual, though one that is secular and working class.[4] Not just a matter of "wasting time" or "getting wasted," the drinking salons hark back to the gatherings of Greek philosophers for whom wine served as the stimulus for dialog and debate.[5] It also reflects upon the aims of conceptual art and its privileging of ideas over objects. What better way than dialog, and freely flowing alcohol, to generate ideas? While conceptual art notably substituted text in lieu of representation or expression, Marioni carries forward the rationale to its logical conclusion: pure conversation.[6] The occasions were, as the artist opined, "drunken parties where ideas [were] born."[7] The beer salons thus foregrounded an essential but overlooked aspect of artists' practice—the simple life activities of camaraderie and talking that precede and inform the making of artworks. This is the immaterial or affective labor that artists (and curators) must perform to network and kindle opportunities.[8] In his role as both artist and curator, Marioni brings art world backstage socializing into the foreground, making the activities not only visible but available for participation.[9]

Yet, an air of exclusivity permeated Marioni's beer events. Like aristocratic salons, one needed to be a part of the scene, to know the right persons, in order to participate. Though the membership was fluid, and open to invitation, the impetus of the beer salons was to bring together working members of the creative community and was not intended for the general public. The exclusivity, however, carried a point. In the 1960s, many emerging artists considered the museum establishment to be an exclusive zone, hostile to vanguard art, disregarding of local and contemporary practitioners, and generally out of touch with the living aspects of art production. Unlike the confrontational tactics used by artists such as the Guerrilla Art Action Group to critique the museum's conservatism, Marioni chose a subtler method that nonetheless wielded a disrespectful edge and exposed the pervasive hierarchy. If funders and collectors could party in the museum, why not the artists who actually produced the artworks to be exhibited? Drinking beer in select artist groups thus performed an inversion of exclusivity—it was an intervention that privileged artists over other patrons, and left the residue for everyone else to envy.[10] The drinkers here were not "performing" bohemianism for an audience, they seized a space within the institution for their own friendship and pleasure. Insiders socialized while outsiders, strategically, missed out. In looking at the remnants of the party the following day, museumgoers could only imagine the revelry and contemplate the affiliations of artistic identity and help define "high" art.

Vera Frenkel: A drink while passing through

Walking toward the 2014 installation of Vera Frenkel's . . . *from the Transit Bar* (1992) in the Museum of Contemporary Canadian Art, one first encounters a mysterious jerry-rigged wall, buttressed by two-by-fours, and the muted strains of a melody.[11] The music increases after turning the corner and entering an unexpected and charming facsimile of a cocktail bar: a rectangular counter, set on a platform at a jaunty angle, surrounded by café tables, chairs, newspapers, video monitors, mood lighting, and the source of the music—a Disklavier piano. Akin to what may be found in an airport or an upscale train station, the bar features scattered luggage and overcoats, yet the illusion is decidedly imperfect. Real ferns and plywood cut-outs of palm trees cue an inherent artificiality, and jagged holes in the walls hint at unruly violence. In fact, the whole environment seems caught between construction and destruction as a section of terracotta-colored wall appears to be in the process of being repainted white, and gaps in the architecture expose supporting studs and equipment. Overall, comfort and estrangement interweave. One can certainly relax, down vodka or whisky shots, nibble on a few snacks, talk to the bartender and other museumgoers, and listen to the voices in the videos and the piano (sometimes played live)—yet there is an undercurrent of anxiety that disturbs the feeling of calmness. That combination of coziness and apprehension provides the perfect stimulus to compel the ordering of a drink, or perhaps a few.[12]

   . . . from the Transit Bar operates on several levels. It offers an unanticipated respite inside the museum where visitors can take a break and refresh their senses after the all-too common "museum fatigue." If museumgoing is often a hushed and solitary experience, this is a place for conversation and socializing. From a comfortable perch, one can leisurely watch the series of artist's videos on the backbeat of enjoying a time-out from the grind of aesthetic overload. The bar is also a convivial space. Alcohol entices people to linger and strike up conversations with old and new acquaintances. If there is hesitation about what one should talk about, Frenkel's mise-en-scène prompts visitors to consider the vagaries of travel, migration, and displacement. Six video monitors convey snippets of stories and remembrances by fourteen of the artist's friends who have experienced exile and discrimination. The memories, though, are complicated by being rendered into multiple languages. Originally taped in English, they have been given Polish and Yiddish voice-overs, as well as subtitles in English, French, and German, all of which increases the sense of "being other" and creating anticipation for the next intelligible phrase.[13] After spending a little time in the bar, and drinking one or more shots, a disquiet sets in: the clips rhythmically repeat and the mix of languages blurs intelligibility, all supplemented by the vodka or whisky buzz that may confuse the hearing of the stories with the memories of one's own examples of travel and trauma.[14]

   Within an exhibition, everyone is a traveler. Frenkel's bar underscores the fact that in the museum all visitors come from elsewhere, stay for a time, and then shuffle on. The Transit Bar self-reflexively confirms itself and its location as an inherently transitory space; its theatricality aims not to deceive but to trouble romanticized notions of global mobility. Being surrounded by testimonies of alienation is strategic, for it stresses the privilege of visitors' easy-going passage compared to those who are forced to move against their will because of war, hardship, or ethnic tensions. Even if one cannot immediately identify with the circumstances of migrants or refugees, Frenkel's lounge sports a self-published newspaper that, among other items, includes excerpts of the debate incurred by the then-current conservative Canadian government's plan to impede the workings of the Citizenship Act.[15] The issues thus envelop everyone, whether a potential immigrant or not, for the negotiations concerning immigrants implicate not just political leaders but those who elect and allow them to set policy. The current crises afflicting Syrian, Iraqi, Libyan, and Afghani refugees highlight the stakes involved and the relevance even for those far removed.

Why set up a bar, though, to engage issues of displacement? Drinking may be a singular lure, but its effects are more ambivalent. On the one hand, alcohol releases inhibitions to tell personal stories and loosens the reluctance to share with others, especially those newly met in transit. As the artist confides, "our alienation is such that only with strangers can we reveal ourselves."[16] The bartender, of course, is a prime contender for airing one's private feelings, and Frenkel often tends the bar herself to listen in on conversations and, perhaps, to induce them. Alcohol and an anonymous ear promote a type of "talking cure" in this context; one can freely express vexing experiences without fear of long-term consequences. Doubt may exist, however, about whether these revealings are true or fabricated. On the other hand, alcohol can drown distress and be used as a tactic for forgetting. Such drinking intends to disable language and remove from consciousness the persistent stain of trauma. For museumgoers, the extremes of derepression and anaesthetization are probably a stretch. These kinds of overindulgences may be invoked by . . . *from the Transit Bar*, but few participating in the installation's comforts would go that far. Nevertheless, one must account for the appeal of taking a drink amidst stories of persecution and xenophobia. Frenkel's comment about alienation provides a clue, not only about storytelling but also about the modern world generally. The worry about displacement permeates contemporary life, whether it is spectacularly writ in the media as millions flee civil war and failed states, or is intimately felt as a lack of belonging that troubles the mind and psyche. In the Transit Bar, alcohol may soothe the restlessness, but in the end, after the drink is finished, visitors know they will have to move on.

Meschac Gaba: Spiced critique

As temperatures soared into the mid-nineties, and humidity neared 100 percent, visitors to the opening of the 2003 Venice Biennale could be forgiven if looking at art seemed secondary to keeping hydrated and finding a cool, shady place to rest. The national pavilion for the Netherlands provided opportunities for both in the form of Meschac Gaba's *Ginger Bar* (2003). Shaped like the prow of a boat, the bar offered an artistically brewed cocktail of ginger, lemon, vodka, and water, served in a choice of either a brandy snifter or martini glass. Overall, the pavilion included Gaba among four other artists investigating the cracks in the sociopolitical program of multiculturalism, where even in a supposedly tolerant nation like the Netherlands attitudes of xenophobia, racism, and anti-immigrant prejudice staunchly remain.[17] Gaba, originally from Benin and residing in Rotterdam, addressed cultural difference, mobility, and acceptance not by directly invoking the issues but by surreptitiously infusing politics at the level of taste. While a lucky few could talk to the artist as he tended the bar during the Biennale's opening, most people were subtly introduced to the complex histories of colonization and globalization just by sipping the refreshing tonic.

Ginger served as a particularly apt ingredient to subvert the traditional summer staple of lemonade. The hot and pungent flavor referenced the artist's West African roots, where it is believed to have magical properties for increasing energy, stamina, and youthfulness. It also signaled the trade routes established since the fifteenth century to transport goods and people—reportedly, ginger was the first "oriental" spice transplanted to the New World for cultivation.[18] As the artist notes, "many Europeans consume ginger without knowing its origin and history of commercialization."[19] While its "spiciness" can upset the bland culinary preferences of some Westerners, for Gaba the herb both evoked the palate and sensibility of his homeland as well as represented an international adoption of difference: it was "truly creole."[20]

Displaying *Ginger Bar* in Venice, Gaba alluded to the city's main form of transportation and its past as a maritime power.[21] Beneath the evocation of spice trade routes and the globalization of taste, however, lay the calamities of colonization, slavery, diaspora, and postcolonial traumas. The trade in ginger connected disparate lands but it also, unfortunately, paralleled the trafficking of humans in that nefarious triangle of slaves, sugar, and rum circulating between Africa, the Caribbean, and Europe. At times, ginger played a notorious role: the Portuguese, for instance, added it to the diet of captured Africans in order to boost their fertility.[22] Gaba's bar dialogued with this history, though it refused Western triumphalist notions of mercantilism and discovery. The boat, for instance, was cut in half, with wooden shelves exposed like bare ribs so that it appeared to be, in the artist's description, just the "carcass" of a ship.[23] Such a skeleton was functional as well as metaphorical, for it held the numerous bottles of the artist's ginger tonic, lined up neatly in rows.[24] The array of bottles, however, bore an eerie resemblance to one of the most iconic images of the atrocity of slavery—the 1788 Brooks slave ship plan outlining how its human cargo could be most efficiently chained into place for the infamous (and deadly) Middle Passage.[25] In the heat of the summer, drinkers no doubt appreciated the ginger brew enabled by globalization, though the cost to generations of Africans was more covertly encoded into the very architecture of the bar.

As much as *Ginger Bar* offered a critique of colonialism and the slave trade, it also established itself as a social space within the art context. Admittedly, Gaba's bar was not situated in a museum, but it relates to my discussion because it continued the logic of his epic project *The Museum of Contemporary African Art* (MCAA) (1997–2002) completed one year prior. Here Gaba confronted the "Eurocentric African problem" in which museums in Europe tend to position Africa in a solely ahistorical or ethnographic mode, thus denying it political agency and contemporaneity.[26] MCAA was conceived as a museum built according to African sensibilities. Notably, Gaba did not include any dedicated exhibition space—all of the rooms blended museal operations, art, and life into interactive and participatory occasions. The museum featured a Music Room, Restaurant, Game Room, Salon, and Humanist Space, among others, and *Ginger Bar* continued MCAA's ethos as a public meeting place where socializing is a meaningful practice in itself. With this in mind, the label on Gaba's ginger vodka gained significance. Prominently displaying the phrases "No Name" and "Art is Fake," the artist equally distanced himself from the instrumentality of branding and the elevation of art to an autonomous domain. For Gaba, those unnamed experiences where aesthetics are imbricated into the everyday are the most transformative.[27]

Vodka, however, formed only a minor ingredient in *Ginger Bar*'s offering (it was included mostly as a flavoring and preservative).[28] On the one hand, it was no great loss as Absolut that year blitzed the Biennale for the opening and a concession stood nearby if one truly wanted to ramp up the drink's potency. On the other hand, the decision strategically reinforced Gaba's understated anti-colonialist critique. In an ingenious maneuver, to de-alcoholize is to de-colonize. Given that alcohol was a prime driver of the triangle economy in slavery, i.e., rum produced from the sugar grown by slave labor, to deprive the drink of its expected kick interrupted the exploitative operations between the first and third worlds. Would a "ginger vodka" without much vodka be considered false advertising? Only if the broader historical and geopolitical forces went unrecognized. *Ginger Bar* acknowledged the workings of the slave triangle, the legacy of colonialism, and the inequities of globalization precisely by refusing their intoxicating rewards.[29]

Erwin Wurm: Drinking alone

If the shortcomings of alcohol remain mostly subdued in the hospitality of artists' bars discussed so far, Erwin Wurm foregrounds the problems of addiction to the point of unavoidability. The Austrian artist dispenses with notions of cordiality in darkly humorous works that comment on the myth of alcohol, creativity, and the good life. *Drinking Sculptures* (2011) comprise a series of individual mini-bars fashioned out of 1970s-era dressers and credenzas turned on their sides, cut into, and manipulated, then mounted on metal stands. They open awkwardly to reveal bottles of liquor and glasses, and the instructions scrawled on the doors confirm the audience's role: "open the cabinet door/take a bottle of alcohol out/pour it in the glass/and get drunk." Lest anyone think the directions ironic or purely tongue in cheek, the artist adds "do it seriously."[30] That the units are named after artists notorious for their excessive drinking, such as Edvard Munch, Jackson Pollock, and Martin Kippenberger, nods to the ominous consequences of alcohol abuse.

The *Drinking Sculptures* continue Wurm's fascination with, and distortion of, domestic furnishings. Besides furniture, his oeuvre includes impossibly narrow houses, bloated cars, and wall-sized sweaters—all demonstrations of how the stuff of everyday life can shift from serving as dependable support to becoming cumbersome insubordinations. It is not just that the functional becomes dysfunctional, the homey becomes uncanny, it is that the armature designed to guarantee household and familial comfort becomes expressive of the very alienation it is meant to ameliorate. *Credenza*, for instance, in old Italian meant "belief" and originally signified the place where servants tested the food and drink for poisons before being presented to the master's table. The poisoning now, apparently, is self-administered, with the spirits contained in Wurm's cabinets—gin, tequila, Campari, whisky—conveying a dual nature as both solace and downfall.

The performance asked of the viewer inverts the norms of conviviality generally found in artists' bars by foregrounding an anti-social pathology. A bespoke bar may seem to be the ultimate in personalized convenience, yet the character traits invoked here of its users are those of self-destructive narcissists hiding booze (in artworks, no less) for their private indulgence. The mini-bars show the downside of the romance of drinking by exposing the isolation behind the bravado of masculine creativity. Drinking alone is a widely recognized sign of trouble, whether it be caused by depression, anomie, or physical pain. Finding refuge in alcohol may be more charitably termed self-medication, especially when confronted by the anxieties of the contemporary world that impinge on everyone no matter what their temperament. Rosalind Gill and Andy Pratt discuss how the injuries suffered under the precarious conditions of neo-liberal capitalism tend not to be of the physical kind, but those related to "exhaustion, burn-out, alcohol and drug-related problems, premature heart attacks and strokes, and a whole host of mental and emotional disorders related to anxiety and depression."[31] Drinking by artists and those working in the unstable fields of the cultural industry is thus not only more common, but perhaps even integrated into the management of the precarious workforce; that is, temporary, insecure laborers are *expected* to self-medicate.

Given the opportunity, would audiences get drunk as the artist planned? During the first exhibition of *Beauty Business* at the Middleheimmuseum in Antwerp, which included a number of the drinking sculptures, visitors not only accepted the challenge but became so unruly that some of the works were harmed and a section of the exhibition had to be shut down. Wurm attributed the damage by normally peaceful museumgoers to the "change of personalities" instigated by alcohol—where the anticipation of civilized habits can be overturned and chaos unleashed.[32] Yet, what constitutes appropriate conduct in this scenario? Since the artist encourages drinking and getting drunk, participation seems to inherently lead to rowdiness. And because the dressers and credenzas are already upended and lying on their sides unceremoniously, the museum bears the look of being "trashed" even before a bottle is found and a drink poured. The sculptures emphasize discomfort by forcing visitors to gracelessly sit, kneel, or step clumsily into leg-holes to access the promised liquor. It is one thing to valorize self-destructive artists by showing their artworks, but another to stage the spectacle of drunkenness on the museum's own premises.

In this vexed context, Wurm practices what he calls "critical cynicism" in which the taken-for-granted truths of existence are scrutinized and their ethical values interrogated.[33] For the built environment of the home, ethics are implied rather than explicitly stated, and one's behavior in its midst tends toward the routine rather than being consciously enacted. Nevertheless, the materiality of furniture encodes social ideals and influences one's personality, perhaps more effectively because of its subtlety. Where and how liquor is stashed and consumed signifies much about the moral principles that society wishes to advocate and the lifestyles that design magazines like *Wallpaper* and *Architectural Digest* promote. To what degree does the built environment enable, moderate, or conceal the consumption of alcohol? The excessive drinking habits of notable artists have tended to be public secrets, inexplicably adding to their aura. Does the reverse hold true—can drinking from an artwork in the museum make anyone something like an artistic legend too? Undoubtedly not, but in Wurm's devastatingly humorous sculptures, anti-social, self-destructive drinking appears to be an intrinsic part of the survival strategy in the precarious world of the beauty business, otherwise known as the art world. Operating at the intersection of fine art and household furniture, museum sobriety and private intoxication, *Drinking Sculptures* enmesh visitors in the hangover of modernist design.

Last call

Fifty years of artists' bars testify to alcohol's enduring and protean presence in contemporary artistic practice. These bars parallel the phenomena of food art and the related field of food studies by virtue of their focus on consumption, the body, sociality, and taste. Art installations offering food and alcohol pose an alternative to quiet, disembodied, monosensory visual contemplation by foregrounding performative, relational, and multisensory encounters. Visitors cannot remain distant, objective observers; to fully experience the art they must imbibe along with their fellow eaters and drinkers, interact with the preparers and servers, taste the flavors and feel the coenesthetic effects of what they consume. The conventional sense hierarchy becomes challenged, opened up, complexified, overturned. Sensory modes not traditionally granted aesthetic status gain primary significance as the bearers of artistic meaning. Focusing on taste not only generates appreciation of its particular empirical qualities, it also increases literacy about its capacity for symbolic, intellectual, and socio-cultural importance. Both food and alcohol-based art draw upon avant-garde and anti-modernist strains of artistic practice that merge art and life and that have recently moved from the periphery to the center in today's flourishing of post-media installation and performance.

Yet liquor possesses a consciousness-altering aspect that distinguishes artists' bars within the genre of food art and gives alcoholic artworks a character all their own. Much like the way in which drinking establishments form a distinct sector within the restaurant and food service industries, artists' bars occupy a singular position in food art because of the likelihood—or, perhaps, inevitability—of intoxication. Even in small amounts, alcohol can transform a banal situation, as philosopher John Dilworth describes, into one redolent with opportunity:

> [A]lcohol turns a sober or prosaic sensory experience into a less inhibited, mildly hallucinogenic experience in which the cognitive system of the drinker has been transformed into one having more dreamlike and suggestible characteristics. [It] provides a kind of permission, or entry ticket, into a parallel world where . . . a *free play of the imagination* can take place.[34]

Alcohol, then, does not just slake one's thirst, it enhances any occasion with mind- and mood-altering appeal and frames it as time when critical and analytical functions can be relaxed and new forms of "affective and cognitive exploration" advanced.[35] In artists' bars, the effect is further heightened by the free zone already implied by the context of art. If traditional museum experience involves a basic contrast between passive viewers gazing upon the end products of others' creative acts, artists' bars immerse visitors right in the middle of the creative experience itself, where the alcohol stimulates aliveness, spontaneity, and liberatory qualities.

As my examples have shown, however, artists' bars can engender positive and negative, contemplative and disruptive outcomes. This double-edged nature replicates what sociologists write about the counterparts of artists' bars—the taverns and drinking houses found in real life. On the one hand, pubs provide places where people can meet, engage in political discussion, form groups and social identities, and build organizations from the ground up, such as working-class unions. On the other, pubs are places regulated by the state because of their distribution of alcohol, which can then continue on a more interpersonal level via an intolerance for difference, such as local bars that are inhospitable to strangers, women, LGBTQ individuals, visible minorities, or those engaging in non-normative behaviors.[36] For artists' bars, the museum or gallery serves as both enabler and regulatory force. Those institutions, if they are going to host an artists' bar, have a vested interest in accommodating transgressions and provocations. Artists creating bars generally seek to set up a heterotopic space within the museum or gallery—one that fosters a rebellious spirit and does not prescribe limits upon the identities, discussions or activities of its patrons (with the exception of Marioni's exclusion of non-artists). A subtle antagonistic streak runs through the collaborative relationship of museum and artist that could be termed a soft institutional critique: museums temporarily relax their customary restrictions and artists take advantage of the opportunity to manipulate and push against the boundaries of that control.

What implications do artists' bars have for the museum? Are they simply an excuse to throw a party? Despite the cheeky pronouncements by some of the artists creating bars (in particular, Marioni), each artist creating an interactive drinking situation endows their work with ulterior motives and meanings. A museum could install a bar, and many have, but in the case of artworks authorship matters. The fact of artistic intention bestows a multi-dimensionality upon the bar that renders it both a place to procure alcohol and a deliberation about what the act of drinking signifies. Drinking, too, is a cultural practice, and it can be riven with sacred, political, moral, and numerous other implications. Those who rebuke artists for simply appropriating and transporting the social entity known as "the bar" into the museum and gallery context should recall the institutional theory of art and the tradition of the readymade—and be prepared to answer why, for instance, it is acceptable for popular objects and images to be repositioned as art but not cultural practices? The methodology of performance and installation inherently functions to take actions, gestures, and scenarios found in the world and then reconfigure them through the filter of art. In regard to artists' bars, the party as a topic is explored through the most pertinent of media—the practice of partying itself.

While there is little substantive art criticism specifically addressing artists' bars, some critics such as Hal Foster would no doubt dismissively lump these works into the general category of "party" or "festive" art that depoliticizes life through the act of aestheticization.[37] The argument generally involves the museum prescribing the manner of sociality and thus defusing any radical potential the jovial atmosphere might otherwise produce. True, museums usually close their doors before public bars do, and post guards among the collection who could act like bouncers if the need arose. But such a critique overlooks a few important features of artists' bars: the shock of finding them amidst the museum's galleries and mixed in with other, more traditional artworks; the randomness and volatility of conversations among strangers and friends; the differences in the style of participation between those who either launch headlong into drinking, remain on the periphery content with people-watching, or mingle with various intentions to connect with others and network. The sociality may be encouraged, but can never be fully determined. As for the politics of artists' bars, my examples above suggest that their potential resides more on the level of implication rather than didacticism. Who knows, for instance, what thoughts or actions may be generated out of the conversations inspired and influenced by vodka and whisky shots, cocktails and beer? Perhaps the museum is felt to be too genteel a place for dissensus to occur. Yet I would argue that artists' bars provoke a series of self-reflexive deliberations with political repercussions that people otherwise take for granted in the real-world equivalents: Shall I take another drink? How long shall I stay? Whom shall I talk to, and what will be the topic of conversation? Within the framework of the artists' bar, these questions about drinking, staying, and talking signify more deeply, for the questions take on an ethical self-consciousness about personal identity and comportment, the sense of time and engagement, and the purpose of sociality and communication.

While the legacy of museums practicing overt social engineering has softened since the nineteenth century, lubricated patrons no doubt would seem a prime receptacle for ideological messages. Can museums, however, instrumentalize the inviting, convivial scene of the artists' bars and co-opt the good-feeling for their own agendas? Museums certainly benefit from animating their spaces in adventurous manners, drawing in larger and more diverse communities, appealing to a younger, hipper demographic, and demonstrating their openness to innovative forms of participatory art. Yet artists' bars work against the museum, figuratively and literally. Their foregrounding of the "adult" pastime of drinking precludes children and thus full, family participation. The bars' presence causes disturbances in the spatial organization of the museum—creating a category crisis where the normal exhibition logic seemingly unravels and unexpected behaviors are invoked.[38] Even the artists fail to completely control what happens in their bars. While the artworks do convey the artists' aesthetic and social intentions and provide an overall atmosphere and platform for activity, visitors' own creative energies ultimately decide the actual outcomes. Alcohol can release an anarchic element in which participants explore uninhibited behaviors, act out different personalities, and otherwise improvise in the ambient setting of the bar. And to suggest that the museum overpowers the anarchic element fails to give credit to the artists for their work, as well as to the concrete experiences in the bar. Not everyone consumes to the point of blurred vision and slurred speech, but even a little alcohol can undermine the purity of the aesthetic gaze.[39]

Is the cordiality and fun offered by artists' bars suitable for the museum? Drinking involves an intoxicating pleasure, of course, which may be argued to be outside of the traditional remit of the museum. But the museum has always promoted pleasure; the question then becomes of what kind, and who gets to define it? Conventionally, the pleasure sanctioned by museums pertains primarily to the visual and the material, i.e., that which can be elaborated upon through categories such as virtuosity in execution, luxuriousness of media, intensity of expression, formal experimentation, and so on. At their root, these pleasures rely upon notions of autonomy, objectivity, and distance, whereby the viewer remains separate from the artwork and can evaluate it from a supposedly neutral and disinterested position. Artists' bars, by contrast, involve embodied pleasures. Visitors not only inhabit the work by sidling up to the bar and interacting with other patrons (and even the artists themselves who sometimes act as bartenders), they incorporate the work internally by consuming a drink. As much as the sense of distance collapses, so too does the facade of disinterestedness; upon the first sip, the alcohol kindles a series of soothing/stimulating bodily and psychological effects. Such embodiment is troubling to those constrained within the modernist, ocularcentric paradigm. To Hal Foster, the interdisciplinary and multisensorial aspects of these types of artworks render them "illegible," that is, unintelligible to formalist notions of aesthetics.[40] I would agree—these artworks are illegible to the modernist paradigm—but that is precisely their intention. Rather than following an arbitrarily limiting aesthetic, artists' bars pose a fundamental challenge and seek to establish a different paradigm of holistic, experiential, embodied practice. If the analytical tools associated with modernism are insufficient to addressing the complexities of experiential artworks, the fault lies not in the artworks but in the outdated critical purview.

A lingering judgment against the aesthetic legitimacy of experiential artworks relates to the assumption that visual pleasures are intellectual while embodied ones are not. Interestingly, purveyors of modernist aesthetics often utilize bodily metaphors to describe aesthetic experience. Kenneth Clark, for instance, recognized that "the rhythm of our breathing and the beat of our hearts are part of the [aesthetic] experience," and Theodor Adorno describes how great works cause a "tremor" in one's being that uncovers that the "truth embodied in the aesthetic image has real tangible possibilities."[41] Both authors confirm a physiological aspect to aesthetic experience, especially when encountering "great" works, yet these accounts are often taken metaphorically rather than literally. What if these embodied sensations were considered more than just a symptom, but the very initiator of intellection, analysis, and judgment? Given the importance of visceral response to the above and other art theorists, one would expect artworks, such as artists' bars, that provide palpable experiences to be accorded more validity. In many ways, experiential artworks do not just rethink the conventional nature of the aesthetic encounter, they actualize and form a logical endpoint to what many aestheticians already describe.

Artists' bars exemplify a notable genre of experiential artworks. Museums and galleries that stage these temporary installations foreground embodied aesthetic encounters to combine pleasure with the contemplation of how alcohol serves as a touchstone for complex social and political issues. The stimulation provided by alcohol adds a singular dimension to the experience—one that can be unpredictable, improvisational, even anarchic. It is through intoxication (whether mild or extreme) that a meeting place is constructed, conversations begun, self-reflection engaged, inhibitions lost, and the special cultural role of intoxication itself examined. If the variety of artists' bars demonstrates anything, it is the continued significance of alcohol in acts of philosophizing, aesthetics, and social commentary. To the museums, galleries, and artists who have realized these projects, then, I'd like to make a toast . . .

Notes

1   See Tony Bennett, *The Birth of the Museum*, London and New York: Routledge, 1995, and Peter Stallybrass and Allon White, *The Politics and Poetics of Transgression*, Ithaca: Cornell University Press, 1986.

2   Tom Marioni, *Beer, Art and Philosophy*, San Francisco: Crown Point Press, 2003, 93. At the San Francisco Museum of Modern Art, however, free beer was offered to the public for six weeks. Tom Marioni, "Interview by Robin White," *View* (1981): 18.

3   Since 1979, the beer salon experienced several changes in location and now resides in the artist's studio. It has also changed names to the Café Society and the current moniker Society of Independent Artists.

4   Marioni reflects that the Wednesday Benedictions he experienced as a child influenced the timing and regularity of the beer salons, along with the fact

that his Cincinnati birthplace was known as a German beer town. Marioni, *Beer, Art and Philosophy*, 39–40.

5   See Fritz Allhoff, ed., *Wine and Philosophy*, Malden, MA and Oxford: Blackwell, 2008.

6   On "dialogical aesthetics," see Grant H. Kester, *Conversation Pieces*, Berkeley: University of California Press, 2004.

7   Marioni, *View*, 3.

8   See Michael Hardt, "Affective Labor," *Boundary 2*, 26(2) (1999): 89–100 and Maurizio Lazzarato, "Immaterial Labour," trans. Paul Colilli and Ed Emery, 1996, http://www.generation-online.org/c/fcimmateriallabour3.htm [accessed June 15, 2015].

9   This is what Jennifer Fisher calls the "paracuratorial." See "Diane Borsato: Four Paracuratorial Performances," in Tanya Mars and Johanna Householder, eds., *More Caught in the Act*, Toronto: YYZ Books, forthcoming.

10   It should be noted that Marioni leveraged his own status as a museum director to organize these events, thus demonstrating a particular advantage of the hybridized artist/curator role.

11   . . . *from the Transit Bar* has been installed in a number of locations since it was created for documenta IX, each of which constructed a different entrance. The menu also included orange juice, Perrier, water, and chips.

12   In conjunction with Frenkel's exhibition, MOCCA also organized a workshop devoted to the "Art of Whisky" with drinks from both a local distillery and the Transit Bar.

13   The artist calls this technique of othering "embedded conflict." Vera Frenkel, interview with the author, January 20, 2016.

14   Interestingly enough, the literature on . . .*from the Transit Bar* is incongruously dry—no-one seems to have downed an actual drink.

15   It also contains a tracking of name changes over 150 years for the federal department handling Canadian citizenship, from "Immigration and Quarantine Services" (1867) to "Immigration and Colonization" (1917) to "Public Security" and "Human Resources" (1993). Such changes reveal much about how the government of each era considered persons entering the country. Vera Frenkel, *From the Transit Bar*, 6(1) (2014–15): 3.

16   Sigrid Schade, "Migration, Language and Memory in '. . . *from the Transit Bar*' at *DOCUMENTA IX*," in Sigrid Schade, ed., *Vera Frenkel*, Ostfildern: Hatje Cantz, 2013, 155.

17   "Biennale de Venetië 2003: We Are the World," http://www.galeries.nl/en.asp?exponr=12442&artistnr=3768 [accessed June 15, 2015].

18   David A. Bender, ed., "Ginger," *A Dictionary of Food and Nutrition*, Oxford and New York: Oxford University Press, 2009, 243.

19   Gaba, interview with Christine Y. Kim in "Meschac Gaba: Tresses," 2005, http://www.iniva.net/meschac/interview.pdf [accessed June 1, 2015].

20   Gaba, interview with Kim.

21 The Biennale's adjunct exhibition space, the Arsenale, in fact sheltered the production line for the massive fleet that garnered significant wealth over the course of several centuries.

22 Maguelonne Toussaint-Samat, *History of Food*, trans. Anthea Bell, Oxford and Cambridge: Blackwell, 1994, 497.

23 Gaba, interview with Kim.

24 The tonic predates the trend toward flavored vodkas and was concocted by the artist in collaboration with International Flavors and Fragrances and Distilleerderij van Toor.

25 1807 Commemorated: The History of the Slave Trade, "The *Brookes*—Visualising the Transatlantic Slave Trade," 2007, http://www.history.ac.uk/1807commemorated/exhibitions/museums/brookes.html [accessed June 1, 2015].

26 See Okwui Enwezor, "The Death of the African Archive and the Birth of the Museum: Considering Meschac Gaba's Museum of Contemporary African Art," in Kerryn Greenberg, ed., *Meschac Gaba: Museum of Contemporary African Art*, London: Tate, 2013, 29–49.

27 Gaba, interview with Kim.

28 Gaba, interview with Kim.

29 One could also argue that the act of drinking actually "consumed" the contents of the bar, thereby liberating its "cargo" from its containment on the "ship," and metaphorically depriving the slave traders of their commerce.

30 The works are fully titled *Performative Sculptures: Drinking Sculptures, the public is invited to open the drawers, take the glasses and bottles out and drink. The piece is realized when the performer is drunk.* See Middleheim Museum, *Erwin Wurm: Wear Me Out*, Ostfildern: Hatje Cantz, 2011.

31 Rosalind Gill and Andy Pratt, "Precarity and Cultural Work in the Social Factory? Immaterial Labour, Precariousness and Cultural Work," OnCurating, 16 (2013): 35, http://www.on-curating.org/files/oc/dateiverwaltung/old%20Issues/ONCURATING_Issue16.pdf [accessed September 1, 2015].

32 Julia Halperin, "Intoxicating Art: Erwin Wurm's 'Drinking Sculptures' Will Get Viewers Sloshed at Miami's Bass Museum," Blouin Art Info, September 24, 2011, http://ca.blouinartinfo.com/news/story/751202/intoxicating-art-erwin-wurms-drinking-sculptures-will-get [accessed August 15, 2015].

33 Stephanie Murg, "'I Call It Critical Cynicism': Sculptor Erwin Wurm on Not Trying to Be Funny," Blouin Art Info, February 10, 2013, http://www.blouinartinfo.com/news/story/865027/i-call-it-critical-cynicism-sculptor-erwin-wurm-on-not-trying [accessed August 15, 2015].

34 John Dilworth, "Mmmm . . . not Aha! Imaginative vs. Analytical Experiences of Wines," in Allhoff, *Wine and Philosophy*, 90–91, emphasis in original (Immanuel Kant is being quoted).

35 Dilworth, 91.

36 See Anthony Marcus, "Drinking Politics: Alcohol, Drugs and the Problem of US Civil Society," 255–276, and Sharryn Kasmir, "Drinking Rituals, Identity and Politics in a Basque Town," 201–223, in Thomas M. Wilson, ed., *Drinking Cultures*, Oxford and New York: Berg, 2005.

37 See Hal Foster, "Arty Party," *London Review of Books*, 25(23) (December 4, 2003): 21–22; Paul Ardenne, "When the Artist Parties, Is It Still a Celebration?" *Esse* 67 (Fall 2009): 10–21; Bennett Simpson, "Specific Spectacles: Art and Entertainment," *Artext* 71 (2000/2001): 70–77.

38 See Kali Tzortzi, *Museum Space*, Surrey: Ashgate, 2015.

39 Criticisms of the art bars' co-optation fail to explain how visual artworks avoid similar co-optation.

40 Foster, "Arty Party," 22.

41 Kenneth Clark, *The Nude*, Garden City: Doubleday, 1956, 54; Theodor Adorno, *Aesthetic Theory*, London and New York: Routledge and Kegan Paul, 1984, 346–347.

25

Tasting, Feasting, Connecting, and Providing as Art Experience

Sara Stern in conversation with Artist Jennifer Rubell

Jennifer Rubell makes large-scale installations, performances, sculptures, and happenings. Across all of these mediums, her projects simultaneously exaggerate and break down norms that circumscribe the traditional viewing, experiencing, and funding of contemporary art. Whether a lasting sculpture or an ephemeral food installation, most of Rubell's pieces involve the viewer in the realization of the work. Participants are invited to touch her sculptures, to ingest edible elements of her installations, to drink, to consume in myriad ways that erode the distance maintained in traditional viewing scenarios.

One significant facet of Rubell's practice focuses on what she refers to as large-scale food performances, frequently commissioned by museums and art organizations as site-specific works for gala events. Sometimes these projects take the form of deconstructed feasts that participants navigate, composing a meal along the way; other more recent pieces involve waiter-performers in multi-faceted performative situations.

Rubell treats the gala as if it were a readymade, a readymade that she takes apart and puts back together differently, leaving only the participants intact to navigate happenings that are part installation, part performance, and part meal.

Certain forms recur throughout Rubell's food performances, serving as both display devices and tools for facilitating different modes of viewer engagement. She piles food in tons, drips cheese, honey, and other viscous toppings from the ceiling, preciously arranges elements of the meal in grids or on pedestals before supplying participants with hammers to destroy previously pristine surfaces and objects. These signature Rubell gestures, which fluctuate between the sculptural and the performative, exaggerate and make visible the grandiosity of their context while also examining the museum or art gala and its relationship to the preservation of culture.

In our interview for this publication, Rubell discusses her process and various recurring themes, elements, and shifts in her work involving food and in her practice at large.

Sara Stern (SS) *How did you come to work with food in an art context?*

Jennifer Rubell (JR) I was really interested in food, not even necessarily as a medium, but as a thing. No other avenue led to a place where what I did would exist inside of a critical context. The great thing about the art world is that anything you put into it, regardless of medium, automatically exists within a critical context, and that was essential to me. So an art context was the only place where my work could land that made any sense to me.

SS *When you get a commission to do a project involving food, how do you begin?*

JR The process usually begins with somebody calling me up and inviting me to do a project. Almost all of the food projects I do are site-specific, in both small and big ways: physically site-specific, but also site-specific to the country, region, place, or city. I do an initial site visit, and develop an idea of how I want the project to exist inside the space, or what part of the space interests me. It becomes a very deep institutional engagement from the start. Sometimes I decide to do a project in certain gallery spaces that are programmed five years in advance, but have a window of one week when they are free, and I choose that as the place where I make a project. Or, in the case of my project at the Power Plant in Toronto in June 2015, I decided to use the theater space that is physically attached to the more traditional museum space.

So the biggest first decision is where exactly I will do the project, and then what I end up doing there is extremely site-specific because I work with people involved in food in that place. When it comes to food, I never bring something from somewhere else.

Next, I start to get in touch with whoever I think is really interesting in food. I don't think first, *I'd like twenty pig legs hanging inside of these niches. Let me see who can produce twenty pig legs for me.* Instead, I find the chef first. For example, Grant Van Gameren in my project in Toronto. He is really into pig, which got me thinking about pig. My first idea involved a whole pig spread-eagled on a canvas on the wall. And then there were certain constraints about cooking that whole pig, since there was no oven large enough. As decadent and extravagant as what I do may seem, I really push the boundaries of what is possible in food without resorting to absolutely ridiculously obscene things. I would never build an oven to roast a whole pig. I always find that something more interesting comes out of constraints.

Then the constraints of the space start to meet up with the constraints of food production. And through that process, something is arrived at that contains the original poetry of the thought, but that also exists inside of the space and inside of my aesthetic. So it is an extremely organic process.

SS   *There seems to be something very intuitive about the way that you work with food, as a medium for asking fundamental questions. For instance, "If I make a grid, how will people approach the table differently from if I made a pile?" Perhaps unlike minimalist sculpture, in which these questions revolve around the work unanswered, in enacting your projects with groups that ultimately must consume in order to have a meal, do you feel that there are answers to the questions you pose?*

JR   I don't think that there are answers. I think that the viewer becomes complicit in the questions in a more direct and explicit way. In my work, viewers can enter from any world or position. Someone might enter and say, "Wow, that's a lot of bananas."[1] And that to me is an absolutely valid point of entry. You can engage with my work on any level. I like when people who know nothing about art are wowed by a giant wall of donuts that they can eat.[2] That is exciting to me. And somebody who is thinking about the name

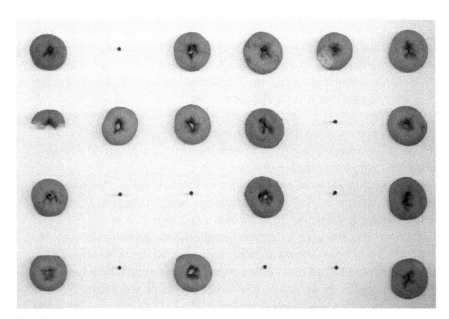

FIGURE 25.1 *Jennifer Rubell*, Old-fashioned, 2010.
© *Jennifer Rubell.*

of the donut which is also the title of the piece, "Old-Fashioned," as that relates to the binary quality of the grid, or "Old-Fashioned" as it relates to minimalism, or "Old-Fashioned" as it relates to hanging stuff on white walls, is also really interesting to me. The work I am most content with is work in which the "gee-whiz, that's a lot of donuts" person and the hard-core intellectual elite can dance together, and can feel comfortable together.

SS   *You often create situations for participants to interact with your installations, elements of a meal, waiters, and objects in particular ways. Have there been any moments in which people very drastically deviated from your intended prompt? Perhaps an instance that taught you something about food's effect on viewer-participants?*

JR   I do not create a prompt for a very specific behavior. I create a prompt for engagement. There has never been a moment that has really surprised me, but also, a prompt is not a script. People engage the way they engage. Actually, the more surprising thing is when participants stop short of the full engagement I might have imagined.

For instance, I made these "Drinking Paintings" at the Brooklyn Museum for "Icons" (2010), and people took drinks out of the "Drinking Paintings," but nobody threw drinks at the "Drinking Paintings." Then I showed the "Drinking Paintings" at Stephen Friedman gallery in London and people did throw their drinks at the paintings, which was really nice for me because it allowed the paintings to become what they are.

The idea of not engaging physically with art is so deeply ingrained within us that, if anything, I am surprised by how hesitant people are to destroy or to physically interact with the work when they come to a food performance of mine.

SS   *I am very interested in the moments in your work when there is a brief, beautiful residue of a form, just after something has been consumed and just before a surface gets destroyed. For example, in "Fecunditas" (2014), an enormous grid of deviled eggs lay underneath rubber chickens that participants had to beat to release smoked paprika, which coated the eggs and the table. Once people started to eat the eggs, a grid of ovals (absent eggs) formed against the layer of smoked paprika. Later in the event, the entire table was destroyed. Are those very brief, transient moments in which a pattern or form emerges out of absence or out of participation, part of your choreography?*

JR   That is completely inside of the conceptualization of the work. The more perfect the physical situation, the more exciting it is to destroy it. Destroying a big sloppy mess of stuff is not half as exciting as destroying this grid that was made through a meticulous and absurd process of first beating rubber chickens, and then eating the deviled eggs. But nonetheless, the grid

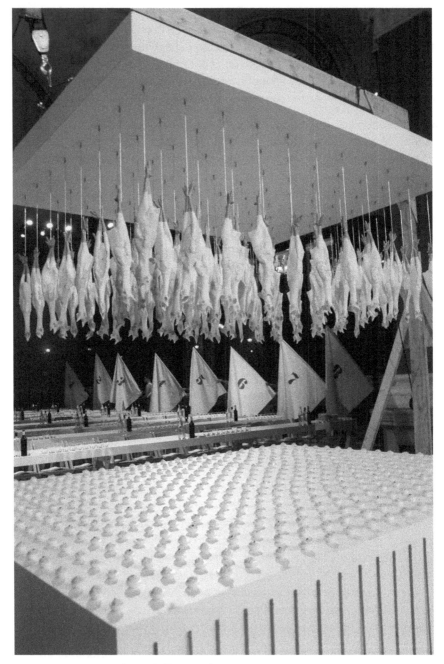

FIGURE 25.2 *Jennifer Rubell,* Fecunditas, *2014.*

Photograph by Wei Je © Jennifer Rubell.

remained there temporarily as this very poetic moment of absence—of the absence of the egg. So that is all very happily built in, but sometimes there are moments of unexpected poetry.

SS *In terms of your relationship with hospitality in your work, is the deconstructing of a meal, particularly in your earlier projects, a kind of exacting stripping away of elements of hospitality?*

JR Yes, I think that at a certain point, in any realm of human behavior, people just follow what came before. I am not talking about art—I am talking about life. You have a car because first there were horses with carriages, and then there were early cars, and then there were the next cars. And I think that this is also true of the way that we engage with food. The way that we might throw a banquet or gala probably grew out of nineteenth-century private, wealthy homes, which is absolutely not the way we live today, and not something I am particularly interested in. I am interested in the core functions of an event, and thinking about serving those core functions in a way that is actually more accurate [than a traditional gala].

Creating the possibility of engagement is a better representation of the true desires of the people who are there. So even though what I do looks very different from what a gala or event might traditionally look like, I think it is actually much closer to addressing people's needs and nothing more. By that, I mean that understanding participants' actual desires is a big source of material for my projects.

SS *Could you talk about what happens when a well-known work of art is made anew in food, materials that can be ingested?*

JR Each instance is different. "Icons" was the piece in which I was really engaging with previous artists. It was a really intuitive and obvious process. First, there is a lot of humor in my work. So in thinking about Bruce Nauman, a cheese head is just fantastic. But it had to be a head cast in something edible that would melt because I wanted a kind of gun-to-the-head effect. So I started by thinking about how many edible materials have a quality that would allow for melting. It was not time for something sweet yet, so of savory things, cheese seemed like something that would melt. I tried to do it in the most uncomplicated way possible, and then it got complicated because, as a matter of fact, there was only one cheese that would really hold its form as a head, and melt properly. It was so hard to find a cheese that would actually do what I wanted it to do that there was a moment when I thought it might not even be possible, but then Fontina came along and saved the day. I worked with some great cheese people, and learned so much. Things that are very simple can feel extremely poetic. To cast a solid head out of cheese, you cannot melt cheese and put it in the head because when you melt cheese, the milk solids actually separate from the fat, so it does not really become a solid again, which is very beautiful in terms of the process.

There is something about making art, even paintings: you have a blank canvas, then you do something on it, then that creates a problem that you solve, which creates another problem that you solve. That everyday quality of figuring something out by making it leads to a very beautiful place. It is a necessary way of getting to a beautiful place, because otherwise the work is purely conceptual, it's all in your head, and the materiality and aesthetics become secondary, which is a tremendous missed opportunity.

SS *And then with the chocolate facsimile of Koons' stainless steel Rabbit that you made for "*Creation*", you eat this thing that would normally be extremely expensive, untouchable, whole?*

JR Before eating it, you bash it in with a hammer, which is the even greater thing. Because you're eating all of it—all of this ends inside of your body, but before you get to that point, you're taking a hammer to it, and the hammer of course is related to the auction hammer. They all die by their own sword.

SS *Is there a feminist gesture for you in referencing male artists or male-dominated movements within these traditionally feminine realms of food and entertainment?*

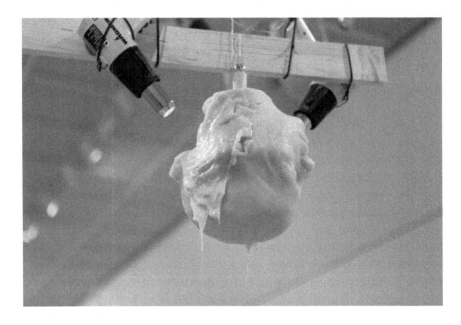

FIGURE 25.3 *Jennifer Rubell,* Icons, *2010.*
Photograph by Kevin Tachman © Jennifer Rubell.

JR Feminism is fundamentally a political position, and as with almost all political positions, it eliminates the nuance of ambivalence. It is really pretty black and white. In my work, I try to tell the truth, and not just the convenient parts of the truth. On the one hand, I am referencing the canon that I look up to, and the canon that I look up to is one hundred percent male. I don't know why, but it just is. Chances are good that they would all be men, because men have dominated the art world forever. So the gesture of destroying them I think has much more to do with the need to stop your heroes from being heroes in order to become your own hero. Which I think is a universal theme of children and parents, mentors and acolytes. And in terms of using a traditionally feminine medium, some days I feel like my use of food has to do with it being a traditionally female realm, but really the scale that I do it on does not read in any way as the woman behind the stove with the apron. And the woman behind the stove is feminine, but food on the level of gastronomy is dominated by men, so if I were to think of it as a feminist gesture, I would really be wrong.

SS *Do museums and arts organizations treat your projects as performances, installations, or some other hybrid? And how does your relationship with the institution inform your process?*

JR My relationship with the institution, and how they treat my project, does not influence my process. The museums see my work as a hybrid. I think something that is important to understand is that the gala is one of the most important things that happens for the museum all year. In some ways, it is more important than solo exhibitions of the greatest living artists. The people in the museum involved in it always go all the way up to the director and all the way down to the maintenance staff, so it involves nearly the entire museum. I care about their motivation in inviting me. Their motivation is very interesting, and their motivation is a part of my work, but it really just gives me an incredible opportunity to make work for museum spaces. And in an insane way, I have had as many solo exhibitions in major museums as the greatest living artists, which is very interesting. There is a huge opportunity for artists to engage with museums in the context of the gala. Usually there is a curator who works with me, and I also work with the events staff. The process of working with everybody is as interesting and exciting as any other part of the work, certainly as interesting as working with the materials or the social aspects.

Notes

1 As part of "American Morning" in 2008, her third breakfast at the Rubell Family Collection in Miami, Rubell installed a giant pile of bananas, alongside

a long table with boxes of cereal, milk bottles, bowls, spoons, cups, and a line of thirty coffee machines.

2 Rubell's 2010 project, "Old-Fashioned," involved an 8-foot by 60-foot wall with a precisely spaced grid of 1,521 basic old-fashioned donuts from Dunkin' Donuts. The project was first shown in 2009 at the RFC and then again in 2010 at LACMA.

26

Artists and Farmers:

Food Activism in Urban and Rural China

Michael Leung, Zhao Kunfang, and Jay Brown with introduction and conclusion by Nina Levent

Artists as farmers, artists on land, artists as food-and-land activists are all a part of a world-wide phenomenon connected to urbanization and food movements. On many continents artists and farmers find themselves on the economic and geographic margins of urban environments, being pushed out by developers and large-scale food production. Some artists leave urban centers to live on the land, alone or in communes, in search of renewal, relevance, self-reliance, and socially engaged art practice. Many seek an alternative to an art-market-driven practice, one that allows them to explore ideas and concepts that are outside the commercial sphere and to be immediately relevant to broader cultural discourses that include food, land, and environmental issues.

Rirkrit Tiravanija's involvement with rural land though the Land Foundation in Chiang Mai, Thailand is a long-term and ongoing project. Founded in 1998, the Land Foundation has a piece of land, cultivated with the intention to grow a creative community. Local and international artists have contributed creatively to the Land Foundation, including the Danish collective SUPERFLEX, whose artwork *Supergas* was designed to use animal dung to create biogas for cooking and lighting.

Biennials such as Kjerringøy Land Art Biennale in Norway, Mongolia 360° Land Art Biennial, and Echigo-Tsumari Art Triennial in Japan have offered platforms for many international artists whose practices deal with exploring land conservation and food production. The Echigo-Tsumari Art Triennial has perhaps the most direct relationship with farming, as it takes place in a rural region, a two-hour train ride north from Tokyo. Participants of the Triennial collaborate with the local population to create site-specific works in rice paddies and forests, on riversides and mountainsides, along streets, and in abandoned houses. Many of the resulting art works remain on view permanently and become a part of life in these farming communities and small towns.

Fernando Garcia Dory is a Spanish artist whose deep engagement with rural communities goes back to the 1990s. Garcia Dory is a self-identified "neo-pastoralist and agroecologist" who has been working with self-organized networks in rural communities, shepherds, and nomadic people. His projects included a functioning Shepherd School, a mobile cheese unit, a beehive, a seed network, a World Gathering of Nomadic Peoples, an establishment of the Spanish Federation of Shepherds with a meeting place at a museum, a proposal for a dairy museum and many others. These projects are micro-utopias with the contradiction and tensions that are inherent in artistic and museum interventions in agricultural systems, and Garcia Dory is very aware of these tensions.[1]

Unlike many social and political engagements of artists in rural areas, Futurefarmers, a multi-disciplinary design studio, does not align with policies or activist movements, but deconstructs existing food, farming, and transportation systems and networks, poses open questions, as well as provides playful entry points and tools to gain insight and re-imagine possibilities. Futurefarmers is a collective founded by artist Amy Franceschini in 1995 that now includes artists, researchers, designers, architects, soil scientists, and farmers. Flatbread Society is a permanent public art project of Futurefarmers collective initiated on waterfront development of Bjørvika, in Oslo, Norway in 2012. This dynamic site activation project comprises a Bakehouse, a cultivated grain field, an urban gardening community, and public programs. Among its public programs was the June 2015 procession of farmers who carried soil from more than fifty Norwegian farms through the city of Oslo to its new home, where the soil offerings were spread and a Declaration of Land Use was signed.

Unlike the work of Tiravanija, Garcia Dory, and Franceschini, the three case studies in this chapter discuss relatively recent and evolving hyper-local practices from China that grew organically with little or no reliance on art communities, public funding, or other systems. The issues and solutions these case studies explore are global and go beyond China: they are related to mega-cities and land grabbing, global heritage sites and economies around heritage sites, and the viability of rural economies. Included are the stories of an urban rooftop farm collective, a curator-led rural revival, and an artist residency on a small subsistence farm. The first case study, written by Michael Leung, an artist, activist, and founder of HK Farm, discusses his organization's development of an urban rooftop farming collective in Hong Kong. HK Farm works with farmers who have been displaced as a result of rapid development and land grabbing.

The artist collective supports these farmers by developing rooftop gardens that are both symbols of resistance and the last outpost of sustainable agriculture in a rapidly expanding metropolis, where every bit of arable land is fair game for developers. In the second case study, Zhao Kunfang traces the history and evolution of the Bishan Project, located in the rural Anhui province in Eastern China. A number of neighboring villages have become UNESCO heritage sites and must-see stops on the itineraries of millions of local and international tourists, turning their agricultural and traditional lifestyles into tourist and souvenir shop economies.[2] Bishan Project, which has since become a magnet for print and film coverage,[3] is the brainchild of Beijing-based curator Ou Ning; it is an attempt to create an experimental alternative model of agri-tourism and cultural development that supports the lifestyle of farmers without turning them and their village into tourist attractions. The third case study features Lijiang Studio; it is an artist-in-residence program on a small subsistence farm in Yunnan Province, Southwest China. Lijiang Studio was founded by Jay Brown, who has contributed this case study. The program offers income and opportunities for local farmers to expand their production both in material and symbolic ways, and for many international artists to observe, research, and respond to the environment of a small farm surrounded by traditional Naxi minority culture.

HK Farm, Hong Kong, China (*Michael Leung*)

HK Farm is composed of three principals, Glenn Eugen Ellingsen, Michael Leung, and Anthony Ko, who represent different disciplines and expertise including photography, design, educational workshops, and permaculture. Since HK Farm started in 2012, we have been farming on four very different types of buildings in Hong Kong—the sixth floor rooftop of an industrial building full of creative studios; the fifteenth floor rooftop of a residential high-rise with a temperamental lift; the rooftop of a six-floor tenement building sandwiched within a block that is acquired for development and future demolition; and a non-profit art space's triangular terrace on the third floor of an industrial building. In addition to being on different levels, these farms exist in different districts of Hong Kong, ranging from densely populated commercial districts to quiet, once-industrial neighborhoods. At each farm, nearby buildings always block the sunlight, encouraging the seasonal crops to shoot upwards, often at acute angles that point to the direction of the sunset, which is always met with a horizon of towering buildings. Welcome to urban farming in Hong Kong!

In Hong Kong, the flat rooftops are interesting spaces that expose flaws in the city's housing infrastructure and property pricing. Ad-hoc and self-built housing located on the roofs appeared in the 1950s and continue to be one of the solutions for affordable housing. (We shared our rooftop farm and cayenne chili peppers once with a Nepalese family who lived in a rooftop house and also tended a small garden.) A 2014 survey reported that Hong Kong's median home price was more than HK$ 4.02 million (US$ 519,000). Developer hegemony, oligarchy and the lack of any form of rent control have contributed to Hong Kong's global ranking as the number one city for most unaffordable housing. The city kept this number one rank for four consecutive years.[4]

The rooftop functions as the building's fire evacuation site and is managed by the tenants or owners of the top-floor apartment. Rooftops are often used for doing and hanging laundry, smoking and barbeques. It is common to find the elderly growing plants and produce for personal consumption. In the past few years, we have seen an increase in public and semi-public farms activating pockets of urban spaces to become sites of organic, collective, and creative agricultural activities. These agricultural hubs were recently mapped as part of The HK FARMers' *Almanac 2014–2015*, a conclusion to our one-year residency at Spring Workshop, a non-profit art space in Hong Kong.

In September 2014, we populated Spring Workshop's main terrace with self-made wooden planters filled with organic soil collected from remote farming areas now zoned for urban redevelopment in the North East New Territories (Hong Kong's countryside).[5] Developer and government collusion continues to evict farmers and villagers, resulting in the fencing of arable land and the reduction of Hong Kong's meager two percent food self-sufficiency rate.[6] Over the years, members of HK Farm constantly reflected what it meant to bring such "hostile" soil into an art space, especially during the occupation of four sites during the Umbrella Movement.[7] Working with guerrilla farmers, evicted farmers and a homeless farmer, each of our farm spaces seems to be connected by a network of "wormholes," creating passages and moments of mutual aid and support.

The concept of "wormholes" is central to HK Farm's activities. In physics, a wormhole or an Einstein-Rosen Bridge is a theoretical passage through space and time that creates a shortcut between two extremely remote distances across the universe. Physicists hypothesize that entering such a wormhole poses a risk of the wormhole collapsing, exposure to high levels of

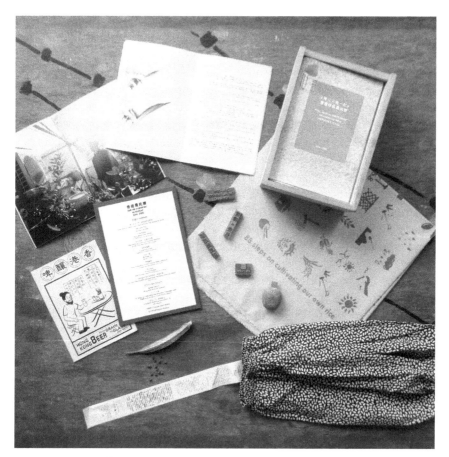

FIGURE 26.1 *The HK FARMers'* Almanac 2014–2015 *that includes ten contributors presented at Spring Workshop.*

radiation and dangerous contact with unknown matter. In the context of our urban farming practice, all the organic soil on our rooftops is from "hostile" spaces within this rampant neoliberal time of government and developer collusion. The "wormhole" in our practice refers to the tactful relocation of this nutritious soil from development sites to the rooftops; this practice physically and symbolically connects the ever changing urban with the endangered rural. Working with the soil, and the worms that joined the truck ride, permanently connects us to farms and farmers in the North East New Territories as well as other urban farms in Hong Kong. The wormholes channel knowledge and resources towards a more self-sustainable society.

Our farmer and artist residency program includes multidisciplinary and experimental approaches: community-based farming with security guards, an

Autumn Harvest Workshop that teaches planter-building and pesto-making, seed-bombing with primary school students, photo and film documentation, field trips to two farming spaces in China, a Talk-to-Your-Plant recording booth, and a Winter Discussion involving other self-organized farming groups. A culmination of this residency was a comprehensive almanac box set created during an intensive three-day book sprint. For the book sprint, the almanac team invited more than ten contributors into the Spring Workshop art space. The participants included translators, bread makers, writers, and activist farmers.[8]

In November 2014, Asia Art Archive, a non-profit art organization and library in Hong Kong and New York, invited me to join them on a tour as part of their "Learning and Participation" program. We visited a group of activist farmers known as Sangwoodgoon who "recognize the self-reliant act of farming and producing one's own food is an everyday act of protest."[9] In conversation with a large group of 15- to 18-year olds, farmers shared their experiences and how they involve various arts practices in their agricultural work. They distributed a self-published magazine to students that documented their five-month project and festival in collaboration with kaitak, Centre for Research and Development in Visual Arts, Hong Kong Baptist University. Sangwoodgoon farmers later participated in our almanac in the form of an artwork, a silkscreen printed *furoshiki* cloth showing the "88 Steps on Cultivating Our Own Rice."

The one-year residency program honed our sensibilities towards two places where art and farming intersect on multiple levels. One field trip brought all three members of HK Farm, artist and writer Elaine W. Ho, artist Nina Schuiki, and Athena Wu and Mimi Brown from Spring Workshop to Mirrored Gardens in Guangzhou, China, a place where "contemporary art practice, quotidian life and a kind of farming-oriented life practice, meet and overlap with each other."[10] During that visit and two of my subsequent trip to Mirrored Gardens, I became acquainted with and moved by the relationships formed by common sensibilities towards agriculture and the pace and constant deliberation in and around the permaculture farm space, situated next to an Olufar Elliason exhibition at the Mirrored Gardens. Large-scale exhibits housed in a village-like architecture interacted with the surrounding landscape and naturally intervened into communal spaces such as the Mirrored Gardens kitchen and a neighboring village.

Between 2012 and 2015, our rooftop and terrace farms existed in public and semi-public spaces, frequented by those familiar with urban agriculture, sustainability, and rooftop farming. After our one-year residency, we are now interested in bringing the rooftop down and directly engaging communities on the street level, from the bottom up. Soon, we will open a ground-floor street market stall in the old neighborhood of Yau Ma Tei, where I also live, to practice an alternative approach of community agriculture—one that includes the communing of a commercial premium space, advocating local production with a Gandhian philosophy[11] and collaborating with the local community with such an agricultural platform.[12]

The Bishan Project: Back to the land rural social reconstruction (*Zhao Kunfang*)

It was a rainy and humid late March morning in Bishan village. The rainy season seems to never subside early, persistently pouring until May. Riding a scooter and passing through township roads, there are endless seas of yellow rapeseed flowers around: strong, stimulating smells and the irritating buzz of busy bees. The mountains and even some buildings not far from the village are lost in the clouds and mist. Rain and wind blow upon my face and soak through my clothing; everything is damp. But all of this is nothing to stop the young, arty people and photography enthusiasts I pass by, on their hunt for the pleasant feeling of outdoor relaxation. They walk through farmlands in the rain, wear rapeseed flower wreaths, visit different villages by bicycle and never stop taking photos. It seems as if most of them have never been to the countryside before. I was on my way to help a friend who volunteers at Pig's Inn 3, a villa hotel in Bishan village. His other main activity is organizing a tiny independent, experimental art space, called WOW, and on that rainy and humid late March morning, I was going to help him prepare the solo exhibition of a local farmer-photographer.

Chinese urbanization has led an increasing number of rural people to migrate to cities in search of more opportunities for education and employment, leaving children and the elderly behind in villages. This reduction of the rural labor force certainly transforms traditional agriculture, and gave birth to agricultural tourism. Agricultural tourism is a fascinating product located somewhere between urban need and rural supply. In China, agricultural tourism, or the so-called "agritainment" is farm-based tourism, including guided tours through farms, participation in farm work and/or cooking, eating and living together with a farmer family. This growing phenomenon gives city slickers a taste of the beautified rural life while allowing farmers to diversify their revenue stream.

The development of rural tourism has been supported by governments, companies and institutions in multiple ways. Take Yi County in Anhui Province, where historical villages of Hongcun and Xidi, rich with the Ming and Qing dynasties' history, have been recognized as World Heritage Sites by UNESCO. Much of the tourism has been contracted by a Beijing-based real estate investment company that works with the local government. In order to attract more tourists to come and visit, the local government subsidizes farmers who grow rapeseed flowers in their fields.

From late March to early October is the peak season for the historical villages. Every day, each village has to accommodate thousands of visitors. Groups of students sit on the roads and paint the landscapes and photography enthusiasts walk round the village with their professional cameras. A large number of visitors occupy natural and public resources of the villages put into tourists use. Removing debris and drinking water resource pollution are the main problems caused by the over-development of tourism in these villages. Some villagers have sold their family houses to citizens for running tourism business (such as a hostel or restaurant) and they moved to a county town and live in small apartments. Although most villages in Yi County embrace tourism, a door was open for a different kind of cultural enterprise. In 2011, Beijing-based artist and curator Ou Ning together with Zuo Jing, founded the Bishan Project to experiment with alternative forms of cultural and economic development in Bishan Village.

Bishan Village is not unlike nearby Hongcun and Xidi villages, but it has not yet been developed for large-scale commercial tourism. In 2011, Ou Ning and Zuo Jing organized the First Bishan Harvestival to celebrate traditional rural culture in the village. The Harvestival attracted many Chinese artists, designers, architects, media, and international participants. Ou Ning wanted to share public and cultural resources with the Bishan villagers and engage them in the mutual enjoyment of rural life. He notes that the ideology of urbanization is very dominant and leads people to believe that successful lives can only happen in the city to the point that living in an old house becomes a sign of failure.[13] He said that transforming this kind of thinking is one of the goals of the Bishan Project.

Ou Ning has also attempted to establish Bishan Commune, a self-proclaimed utopian and anarchic society based upon the Bishan Project and Bishan Village. In his 2010 exhibition project in Shanghai. *Bishan Commune: How To Start Your Own Utopia,*[14] Ou Ning made bold statements about a proposed lifestyle for Bishan Commune. He advocated for living and farming together, sharing resources, building public areas for various cultural events. He named his house, a historical building now renovated to be a residential and work space, the Buffalo Institute. For Ou Ning, the Institute was the "brain" of Bishan Commune. He created Bishan Vouchers that represent the working hours, to be used in exchange for other living resources. He also expanded his vision by inviting designers to create the Bishan Commune Passport and Bishan clothing.

It became obvious that there was a huge gap between the villagers' expectations of Bishan's development and the utopian visions of Ou Ning and Zuo Jing. The villagers do not care about utopian ideas or about cultural development; they are mostly eager to change their financial situation and improve the lives of their families. Most of them wanted to engage in the business of tourism like their neighbors in Hongcun and Xidi. Having understood this fundamental disconnect, Ou Ning has adapted his goals to meet some of the villagers' expectations: in 2014 he invited Nanjing Librairie Avant-Garde, a

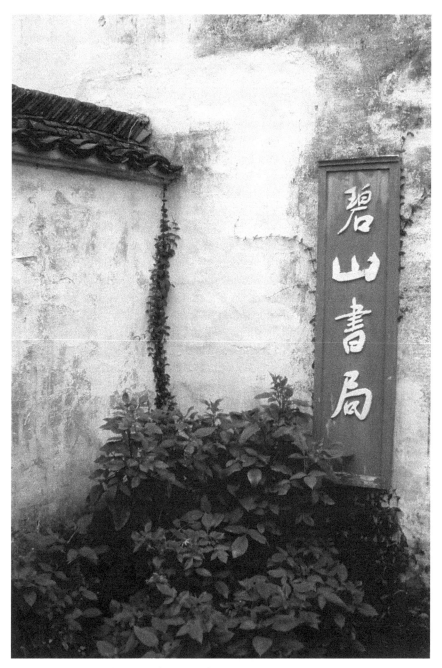

FIGURE 26.2 *Bishan Bookstore: The Nanjing Librairie Avant-Garde Bishan branch in a public ancestral hall of Bishan Village.*

© *Kunfang Zhao.*

famous Chinese book shop, to launch a Bishan branch of its bookstore. In May of 2015, Ou Ning restored a derelict public ancestral hall and transformed it into The School of Tillers. The newly restored structure contains an exhibition hall, library, learning center, café, and a store. As Bishan's "living room," The School of Tillers regularly hosts exhibitions and public lectures for both villagers and outsiders, supporting artists and scholars researching rural culture. The in-house shop sells local crafts and farm products and has more recently begun to organize a secondhand market. In order to avoid externally imposed gentrification in Bishan, Ou Ning encourages local farmers to open bed-and-breakfasts in their homes, enabling them to supplement their incomes. He hopes that the Bishan Project can go further still. Youth volunteers are recruited to participate in the project, and he catalyses pioneering work from young people in the rural area. One example is "Hun.Studio," founded by a 24-year-old architecture graduate and a local carpenter. They work together to design and produce furniture and sell their products on the Internet. The previously mentioned WOW art space has been created by a 21-year-old art student; it's located just next to rapeseed fields on the east side of the village.

Today's Bishan is gradually becoming a village for tourism, but perhaps an alternative version of agri-tourism. The primary reason why the visitors come to Bishan is not to see ancient architecture like those found in the neighboring villages, rather, they come to see modern uses of the old houses and the new possibilities opened in this traditional setting. The Bishan Bookstore is a popular spot for tourists. Guests love to read books in the restored ancestral hall, sip local tea at The School of Tillers, and stay at the Pig's Inn for a night. Just down the road from the Pig's Inn, observant visitors will discover WOW as a down-to-earth art space visualizing the endless possibilities of the village.

Because of the Bishan project, more and more young locals have started to pay attention to their hometown. They use their own savings to transform old shrines into cultural facilities and encourage university students to explore opportunities in rural villages. Ou Ning notes recently,[15] "Today's Chinese villages must not fall behind the times, so that the countryside can become an alternative to the city." While there are still many questions to be asked and avenues to be explored, the reconstruction of rural areas via art and culture opens up new ways for people to return to the land.

Lijiang Studio, an art residency program in Yunnan Province, China (*Jay Brown*)

Lijiang Studio is an artist-in-residence program—and perhaps an art practice itself—based since 2005 on a small subsistence farm in Yunnan Province, Southwest China, an area of confluence between the Tibetan Plateau, the

Han Chinese state, and upland Southeast Asia. Lijiang Studio, led by Jay Brown, rents a previously vacant courtyard house adjacent to a farming family, surnamed He, who have agreed to host the studio and support its activities in return for some employment at home and participation in the various possibilities the artists bring.

These neighbors of the studio, the He family, are farmers whose first language is Naxi, a Sino-Tibetan language spoken by about 300,000 people who live around the city of Lijiang. Just a few kilometers from the studio, Lijiang is a tourist destination, so there is a strong pull on their traditional culture from the state and globalizing capitalism, but there is also a strong sense of cultural identity. The He family was able to expand its food production to feed artists at the studio fairly easily by purchasing some chickens and another pig, and building a hoop house for year-round vegetables. For special events, the studio's neighbor He Xuemei, who the studio hires to cook, buys food at the market. Artists are not usually capable of helping in a material way to produce much food, although a group of artists trying to help plant or harvest can make things a lot more fun, and on a good day even speed things up. From a local point of view, one might say that the resident artists are focused on documenting, problematizing, and making the local food production more eventful.

It has been the dream of more than a few artists who've come to the studio to be self-sufficient, autonomous, connected to the land, and self-reliant. It has been the dream of many farmers to be free from the labor-intensive and cash-poor farmer's life that, in Chinese society, is considered very unfortunate. Lijiang Studio occupies some sloppy middle ground among these desires. There is often an impression that agriculture can lead to self-sufficiency or that mobility can lead to freedom, but that soon gets bogged down under issues of economic farm policies and a lack of social and cultural support for farmers. Luckily, it is usually at the dinner table where these questions get discussed, often in a very personal way.

The studio runs on a low budget. Artists pay their way and bring their own equipment. Funding to cover the overhead at the studio comes from supporters in the United States. The third component is the non-monetized resource embedded in the land, history, labor, culture, and people who live at and around the studio. The fantasies and realities of these actors collide in projects and relationships formed at Lijiang Studio as illustrated by these two artist residencies.

Katalog: World Heritage Beer Garden Picnic, 2008

The collective *Katalog*, consisting of Duskin Drum and Sarah Lewison, with the collaboration of Jay Brown, Li Lisha, Hu Jiamin, and Lijiang Studio's neighbors, the He family, took a mycelial approach to their work at the residency. Beginning with a commitment to social sculpture, they describe in the manifesto for the project:

SOCIAL MYCELIA: In our research, we ask questions about how it is possible to heighten awareness and demonstrate the kinds of social relations and co-dependencies shared by humans, plants, animals, microorganisms, water and soil. Our emphasis is on producing relationships rather than products, on reclaiming technological and scientific knowledge for ordinary people, and on the experimental creation of integrated appropriate human ecologies.[16]

During a residency spanning the better part of 2008, *Katalog* started with an investigation into the kind of co-dependencies at work around the studio, such as the energy cycle of photosynthesis by day and decomposition by night, asking where that fits into food and culture. *Katalog* was able to find meeting points between the highly domesticated labor-intensive agriculture of the farm and the wild mushroom foraging culture enjoyed in the mountains. They decided to install bio-remediating mushroom-growing sculptures interstitially at sites of erosion or pollution, and then plan picnics around the sculptures. *Katalog* started, from scratch, an extended process of growing mushrooms using available materials and putting the process on display through illustrations, foraging, research, readings, and interrogations of their own assumptions. *Katalog* produced a timeline of the history of NGO interventions in the Lashi basin, where Lijiang Studio is located, made a mobile natural history museum/lab, and printed small books and magazines illustrating their own work and drawing from sources such as E.F. Schumacher and the Chinese Environmental Protection Agency. During this period, they were able to investigate and document with video local experiences of development, meditate on what "basic needs" or perhaps "bare life" meant then and there, and help others around the village in its economy of mutual aid.

The World Heritage Beer Garden Picnic was conceived as a series of events of ecological remediation as aesthetic practice. Here again from its manifesto: "THE MUSHY GROUND: Customs, rituals, visual theory, theater and vernacular science are the fodder for reconfigurations of biological, social and economic life."[17] Our mongrel science questions standards, constructs and binaries. Later in their residency, as mushrooms were propagating and the mycelial masses of their practice took hold, preparations began for picnics, in which sculptures of growing mycelia were installed and celebrated as bio-remediating objects at sites of erosion or contamination. The final picnic turned into a social event for questioning The Picnic of the Future: A picnic is a time to drink and feast and rest and reflect. We want to know: What will we eat at the picnic of the future? Where will it come from?

It is possible to have a picnic that feeds and cares for the forests and water and soil, and also the humans?

Distortion of Distortion, artist's recipe book, 2013

Another food-based art project at Lijiang Studio took place in 2013 and was led by Emi Uemura. Emi's approach to working with food at Lijiang Studio was problematized by the fact that young farmers and food producers in first world societies are often starting farms without connection to traditional foodways, while Naxi families around Lijiang were often in the process of disconnecting from their traditions, either by choice or as a process of being forcibly disenfranchised from their land and culture.

The inquiry of the *Distortion of Distortion* project included travel, presentation, and discussion: farmers from Japan presented their own art works and projects at Lashihai. One farmer, Shimojima Wataru, had purchased a polluted mountain and remediated the site through planting so that it now produces food: this project took the better part of his daughter's lifetime. Two other farmers, Masayuki and Haruko Nagata, shared a film and their experience on an organic CSA farm growing out of the student protest movement in Tokyo in the1970s, and their current project mediating between local farmers and wild animals in Hokkaido. Another artist, Takuma Seiji, found a position as local historian in a town that provided him with free housing in exchange for his making maps and recording oral histories of the community. Experimenting with local recipes, researching their histories, as well as cooking for neighbors, led to the idea of a recipe book. The book is printed on handmade local paper printed with a laser printer. The illustrations were gathered from other visiting artists by carving into the small wooden stools popular locally and making woodblock prints from them.

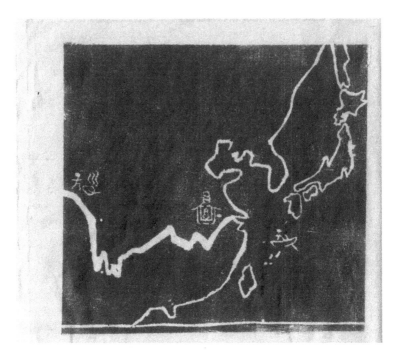

FIGURES 26.3 and 26.4 *Emi Uemura,* Distortion of Distortion Recipe Book, *2014. Woodblock print illustration for the recipe "Mock Miso."*

© *Jay Brown.*

Lessons from artists and farmers in China

What do these artistic practices mean for future museums? These creative practices and interventions have a lot to offer to various types of museums—art museums, historic farms that are stewards of farming traditions, history museums that have objects dealing with agricultural history, historic homes and plantations, botanical gardens, and small rural museums. Bishan Project is a trailblazer for many historic and heritage sites, including those named by UNESCO as heritage sites, that shows that there might be organic ways of blending a vibrant contemporary art and culture scene with the preservation of old structures and rural life. HK Farm is an example of linking artistic practice, radical social justice practice, and food activism that might be an inspiration for historic farm museums that seek to be relevant and make their collections and stories matter today. HK Farm also provides programming ideas for any museum that has a rooftop that can house a garden. Lijiang Studio and the artists who took their inspiration from local villagers and brought farmer wisdom from their own countries to share, remind us that the very local issues of land, food, and harvest are in fact global issues, and that hyper-local food and farm narratives resonate across oceans.

Notes

1 Claire Doherty (Ed.), *Out of Time and Out of Place. Public Art (Now)*. Art Books Publishing Now, 2015, 158–164, 192–203.

2 Oliver Wainwright, "Our cities are insufferable": Chinese artists go back to the land, *Guardian*, December 2, 2014.

3 *Down to the Countryside* (http://www.chinafile.com/multimedia/video/down-countryside), documentary film by Sun Yunfan and Leah Thompson, 2015.

4 http://www.scmp.com/property/hong-kong-china/article/1410730/hong-kong-ranks-worlds-no–1-most-unaffordable-housing?page=all

5 Hofan and Janice, "What's the fuss about the North East New Territories Development Plan?" http://goo.gl/R3bFsC [accessed October 19, 2015].

6 Elaine Yau, "Call for incentives to help farmers stay on the land and boost Hong Kong's self-sufficiency," http://goo.gl/i4yTEQ [accessed October 19, 2015].

7 The Umbrella Movement refers to the events that began with an oppressive electoral reform from the Mainland Chinese government on August 31, 2014, that led to a student strike and was followed by the occupation of four sites for 3 to 79 days.

8 "HK Farm," Spring Workshop, http://goo.gl/2521kD [accessed October 19, 2015].

9   Chung, Y. M. (2015). *The Role of Contemporary Art in 21st Century Education: Engaging Young People to Become Agents of Social Change* (Unpublished postgraduate project for independent study). The University of Hong Kong, Hong Kong. 22

10   "Mirrored Gardens," Vitamin Creative Space, http://goo.gl/7K7cjU [accessed October 19, 2015].

11   "Revival of Village Industries," Mahatma Gandhi, http://goo.gl/EE9NGe [accessed October 19, 2015].

12   The HK FARMers' Almanac is produced as a limited-edition volume-in-a-planter, to be shared among fellow agriculturists and other nurturing souls. Digital versions of all content as well as documentation from its publisher Spring Workshop will be downloadable from www.springworkshop.org/the-hk-farmers-almanac. HK Farm is an organization of Hong Kong farmers, artists, and designers founded in April 2012. Working in the city, we collaborate with communities and organizations to highlight the importance of urban agriculture and locally produced organic food. See www.hkfarm.org

13   *Down to the Countryside*, Sun Yunfan and Leah Thompson, 2015.

14   *Bishan Commune: How to Start Your Own Utopia,* A project for the exhibition Detour: The Moleskine Notebook Experience in Shanghai, 2010, on Moleskine sketchbook, 100 pages, 13x21cm, heavy acid-free paper.

15   *The Rural Developer* [BE/OL], http://v.qq.com/boke/page/h/0/k/h01615glx8k.html [accessed April 8, 2015].

16   *Katalog* Manifesto can be found online at http://www.carbonfarm.us/KATALOG/stmt.html

17   Again from the *Katalog* Manifesto.

27

Tasting Power, Tasting Territory

Nat Muller in conversation with the artistic duo Cooking Sections

"Food, glorious food" is the opening song from Lionel Bart's 1960s musical—later turned into a film—*Oliver!* based on Charles Dickens' classic *Oliver Twist*. As the rag-dressed orphans line-up for their daily bowl of unappetizing gruel they fantasize about luxurious and unattainable food items such as sausages with mustard, steak, puddings, jellies, and custards.

Food, like art, inspires an imaginary. It is here where the two realms most interestingly meet. There's a strong case to be made that it is precisely the rub between basic human necessity (nourishment) and the rituals accompanying the ingesting of food, be they social, dietary, cultural, religious, or other, make for an interesting feeding ground once they intersect with critical artistic practices. And while it is true that without food we will most definitely perish, without art we will lead gray and dreary existences. Art, like food, inspires meaning, ranging from pleasure and joy to dislikes and confusion. Increasingly artists are using food as a subject, a medium, or as Daniel Fernández Pascual and Alon Schwabe from Cooking Sections point out here, a tool, to explore a variety of current issues.

In the past few decades artists have, very interestingly, explored how topics such as cooking, feeding, and hospitality have altered audience experiences and participation in institutional and non-institutional settings—after all, one does not always expect to be breaking bread and sharing a meal in a museum.

Fernández Pascual and Schwabe take the relations between art, artist, audience, and institution a step further. Indeed, if we return to our orphans pining for delicacies that will elevate them out of their dreary tedium, it is clear that whomever controls the supply and demand of food, has power. Food, in other words, disciplines. Cooking Sections offers us what they call "edible cartographies," narratives of power and territory that take us on historical, political, economic, and—let's not forget—culinary journeys. From the British Empire and the Cold War Kitchen Debates between Richard Nixon and Nikita Khrushchev to the Spanish real estate crisis during the global economic downturn and the Israeli blockade of foodstuffs into Gaza. They map out—often playfully and deliciously—that what we eat and how we eat is in fact never innocent. Moreover, by articulating that food is power, but also fantasy, desire, and longing, we not only become aware of how certain ideologies and institutions shape the way food *is* in the world, but it also sharpens our own positioning within these food systems.

Nat Muller (NM) *As a collective you're interested in the overlap between visual art, architecture, and geopolitics. You both come from performance and architecture backgrounds; was it clear from the outset that you would be working with food and did you both have a personal affinity with it? How does working with food provide a particularly interesting angle to your concerns?*

Cooking Sections (CS) What formulated Cooking Sections and formed our collaboration is not food but rather our joint interests in landscape transformation, geography, and geopolitics, which we have individually explored through different media over the last ten years. "Food" became the current project as we found it a powerful lens and tool to shape research and discussions around topics we find relevant in contemporary society. In our practice we strive to apply the same method to research and presentation so they are reciprocal and bear equal weight. In that sense food becomes interesting to us when it serves both as the object of research and the means of representation. We are not food experts and really cannot tell you the difference between cocoa that was grown in Ecuador and the one from Saint Lucia. Yet, as food is something that encapsulates within it the past, present, and future of this planet, it seems to us a relevant angle when raising questions around space and power. The work we developed for Office*US*, the US Pavilion at the 2014 Venice Architecture Biennale, is a good example. Six practitioners were chosen, us included, and invited to reflect on an archive of one thousand buildings created by US-based architects in the last one hundred years. To do that, we chose to focus specifically on the spaces of production and consumption of food within them. This allowed us to hold specific discussions on architecture in the strict sense of the word, while exposing how architecture was used to influence and subvert much larger infrastructural systems around trade, economy, and culture at large.

NM *Many of your projects such as* When Agua de Murcia Lost its Virginity *(2014),* Boundary Gazpacho *(2013) and* Geopolitical Paella *(2012) are lecture/*

cooking performances. Can you talk us through the methodology and trajectory of these projects? How do you start your research, what is the relation between the performative elements of the lecture vis-à-vis the food component, and also, how do you develop your recipes?

CS   It always starts with a map; a coded representation and subjective perception of a place that is of interest to us. This can be a drawing, a satellite image, a video, or a carved piece of wood. Once we identify the place and subject of interest we start questioning the various renderings that have brought this place into our collective imagination and the power structures that stand behind them. Through that process you can start drawing direct links to legal, political, and spatial operations that have taken place. *When Agua de Murcia Lost its Virginity* investigates exactly such a moment, namely the "invention" of sangria as a "national" drink in Spain. It came out of a marketing apparatus to promote the newly invented Costa del Sol internationally within a Cold War scenario of military alliances with the US.[1] Yet, this quintessential alcoholic beverage, which was a way to use cheap wine and old fruit, is rarely drunk today by Spanish citizens. Nevertheless, Sangria Laws have been carefully formulated in the Spanish jurisdiction since 1970s, and in European Law even more recently in 2014 with a stricter version.[2] During the performance the moment of manufacturing sun and sand as a tourist attraction is brought back into existence through a series of music videos depicting the transformation of the coastal landscape, while the Sangria Law is demonstrated, literally, with several nonsensical non-sangria drinks. It is by carefully following the legal definition of sangria as a recipe that you can expose some of the interests behind its existence. In other instances like *Boundary Gazpacho* and *Geopolitical Paella* we tracked the formation of regions and their urban development, building up towards the 2008 Spanish housing crisis. The aim was to question the actual creation of profit margins, territorial boundaries, and corruption thresholds. Mixing up all these ingredients from very specific—as well as pointless—origins together introduces another reading of space and time while challenging the authoritarian role of the production of such spatio-temporal relations.

NM   *You use food to imaginatively illustrate power relations. The above projects offer alternative cartographies that we can actually taste, ingest, and digest. Can you elaborate on how this "mapping" of foodways, history, and power come together in a recipe and how this is a comment on the fluidity of the geopolitical world map? Then there is also the symbolism of translating materially what it means to be "power hungry" or "power starved."*

CS   It always starts with a map and ends with an edible map. We are used

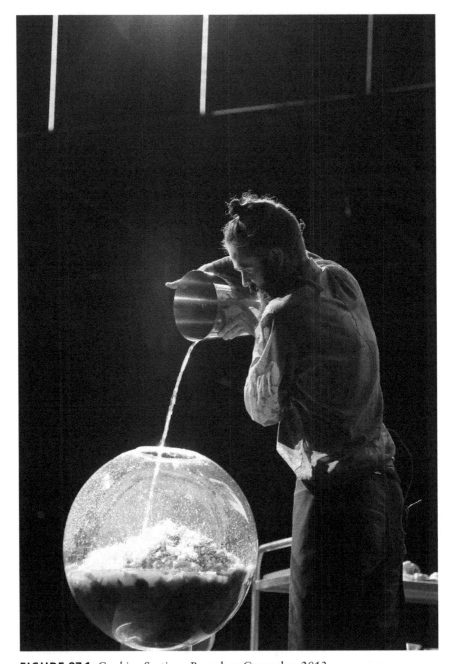

FIGURE 27.1 *Cooking Sections*, Boundary Gazpacho, 2013.

Photograph by TEDx Madrid © Cooking Sections (Daniel Fernández Pascual and Alon Schwabe).

to perceiving maps as knowledge-objects that inform us about unfamiliar territories. By making them into an edible object that can be made, ingested, and digested over and over we suggest that one can change the interaction with space. As part of many of our projects the recipe is given away so that people can go home and make the same thing themselves at home. Sourcing, cooking, or eating all the ingredients in a given recipe creates awareness of existing power structures and their direct connection to the environment. This is not to say that buying organic food or fair trade labels will save the planet, quite the contrary. It is about acknowledging the necessity to harness actions that introduce the production of food systems not through another market-oriented label, but through a new system that calls for a new set of practical priorities. Regarding symbolism, actually metaphors are something we usually try to avoid in our work. Instead, we aim to make material objects that speak by themselves.

NM   The Empire Remains *is an on-going multi-faceted project that examines the relations between colonialism, identity, market forces, and food with as point of departure the British Empire. What are the main questions you are interested in addressing here and how does a Christmas pudding fit into it all?*

CS   *The Empire Remains* is a long-term research project that began in 2013. It explores the infrastructure and cultural imaginaries set up by the British Empire to promote the food and agricultural industry between home and overseas territories. As a departure point, we have used the Empire Marketing Board, which was a British governmental agency established in 1920–30s to promote inter-imperial trade through powerful visual arts, film, and graphic propaganda. *The Empire Remains* traces the contemporary history of imperial bananas, sugar, tobacco, cacao, fruits, and spices and how these global food networks have evolved until today, and new economies and visions that have emerged out of these forms of trade. During the course of the project we are developing projects reflecting on the legacy of such trade networks and how they affect the world we live in.

The *Empire Remains Christmas Pudding* is a project we did in 2013 following the original recipe of the Empire Christmas Pudding that was invented by the Empire Marketing Board in 1928. The aim of the recipe was to increase the use of foodstuffs from the British Overseas Territories and Colonies, while placing the responsibility of the national economy in citizens' consumption habits. The recipe had 17 ingredients as well as 17 geographies, hence, the recipe becomes a map: the currants had to come from Australia, the sugar from British Guiana, the cloves from Zanzibar, etc. What we did was follow the same recipe today in London and figure out what happened to that marketing of origin and the networks involved in it. One of the interesting conclusions was that the contemporary version is actually not to promote origin, but to erase it. Most foodstuffs are simply "packed in the UK," "produced in the EU," or "Demerara-inspired." This allows changing the supplier constantly for obvious economic reasons without really lying to customers.

NM *What have you learned from your travels to former British colonies [in the Caribbean] and mandates [such as the British Mandate in Palestine]? What are the remains of Empire and how does that (still) affect local production?*

CS We could start by asking back: Are we living in a decolonized world at all? One of the most interesting things is to observe how cultural imaginaries are produced. When we traveled to some Caribbean islands, for instance Barbados, we did not encounter the "tropical" lush and wild vegetation you would expect. Instead, you realize that the entire island is covered in less than half a meter deep fertile soil. Hence, colonial enterprises realized that only sugar cane, a plant from the grasses family, could be successfully grown. What happened next, you already know. If you go there as a tourist, you might or might not realize the tremendous technological efforts of resorts trying to meet the desire for "tropical vegetation" through artificial irrigation. Now, what happens to the environmental landscape when Barbados cannot sell cane sugar under special tariffs to the UK in the way it used to until two decades ago? Then you have a spatial collapse yet to be re-imagined. Several crucial questions arise: What do you grow? Who is going to buy it? And more importantly, what do you do with tourists who expect you to grow something that their countries of origin no longer buy?

The case of Palestine is much more complicated, because you have a third player [Israel] appearing in the occupation of the land. However, you see similar colonial practices to control human bare life through local water and food resources, as we showed with our piece *Dietary Confinement*. We have been recently focusing on the global production of fertilizers extracted out of the Dead Sea. The environmental disaster that has been happening there since Mandate times has grown exponentially in the last decades. Hence, we are faced with the dilemma of destroying a unique ecosystem in order to feed the planet. Then what we question is whether we could come up with different approaches to landscape and food production beyond the economic powers controlling resources. That's what we are working on, the idea of becoming *Climavores*.

NM *Following the above question, food diversity and food sovereignty are at the forefront of global power politics. A wonderful, and quite ironic,*

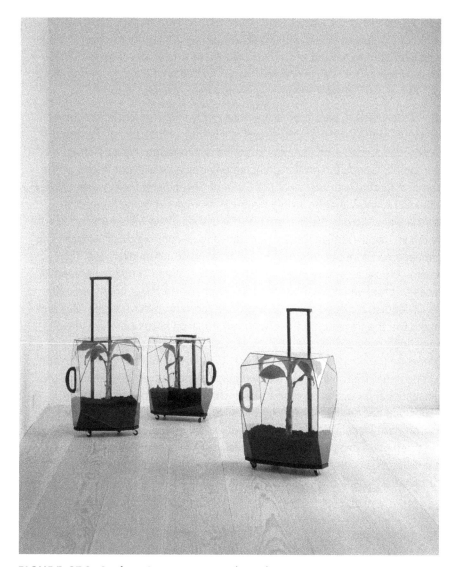

FIGURE 27.2 *Cooking Sections,* Cases of Confusion (50-40-20) (56-45-25) (55-40-20) , 2015. Stirring the Pot of Story: Food, History, Memory *at Delfina Foundation (London).*

Photograph by Sylvain Deleu © Cooking Sections (Daniel Fernández Pascual and Alon Schwabe).

example of this is the story of the Cavendish Banana and your installation Cases of Confusion (50-40-20) (56-45-25) (55-40-20) *commissioned for the exhibition* Stirring the Pot of Story: Food, History, Memory *(London, 2015), which I curated for the Delfina Foundation's Politics of Food Programme. Can you unpack the issues and thinking behind this particular work?*

CS　It started with gardener to the aristocracy and architect of The Great Exhibition of the Works of Industry of all Nations (1851) Joseph Paxton. He became fascinated with bananas in the early nineteenth century after he first saw the plant depicted on the Chinoiserie-Victorian wallpaper in one of the rooms of Chatsworth mansion, the Duke of Cavendish's Devonshire estate. Little did he know that he would become the man exporting Cavendish Banana plants across the planet from the Duke's glass-walled greenhouses. He did so using Wardian Cases, humidity and air-controlled portable devices that became an instrument for the colonization of nature overseas. This became crucial a century later, when Panama Disease [a fungus] erased all traces of other varieties of banana trees in major producer countries and the Cavendish replaced them, leaving little room for other species. But we asked: Did the traveling of the Cavendish Bananas save or undermine indigenous species? Inspired by this incredible Cavendish story, *Cases of Confusion (50-40-20) (56-45-25) (55-40-20)* as first shown at your exhibition in London, consisted of three hand-luggage Wardian-type suitcases for the transnational *bananization* of the world. The work questioned whether regulations against the smuggling of soil and seeds are really meant for environmental security or are actually driven by economic protectionism. The three glass carry-on suitcases were made following the dimensions that airlines EasyJet, British Airways, and Ryanair impose on air traffic and contained a banana plant inside.

Notes

1　Costa del Sol: the Sun Coast—a coastal strip in southeast Spain that includes the areas of Málaga, Marbella, Nerja, and Fuengirola.

2　Regulation (EU) No. 251/2014 of the European Parliament and of the Council of February 26, 2014 on the definition, description, presentation, labeling and the protection of geographical indications of aromatized wine products and repealing Council Regulation (EEC) No. 1601/91.

28

Last Course of the Volume

Nina Levent and Irina D. Mihalache

As a final treat for this volume, we would like to offer a triple course of experiences that denote important unfolding trends which are likely to impact museums' interaction with food in the coming years. These trends combine arts and sciences and include: the revisiting of historic food experiences; exploring performative elements of eating and hosting; experimental eating; mapping and researching food systems; and multisensorial reflections on food controversies.

Last Supper by Raul Ortega Ayala, Mexico City

Last Supper is a performance work by Raul Ortega Ayala who cooks and serves to twelve random people the recipes of the Last Supper that were suggested by food critic Daniel Rogov. The Last Supper performance begins with eating a sprig of parsley dipped into salt water, accompanied by a glass of wine; then, according to the custom of the time, the most revered person would break the matzo and dip it into the maror. To follow, the artist prepares and serves the guests a vegetable soup with goose fat and another glass of wine. For the main course, the artist serves roast lamb. The Last Supper ends by eating the ornaments on the table, which consists of fresh fruits, green almonds, and walnuts, as there was no tradition of dessert at the time.

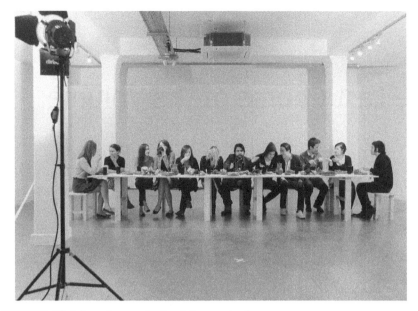

FIGURE 28.1 Last Supper *by Raul Ortega Ayala.*
© *Raul Ortega Ayala and Proyectos Monclova.*

Smog tasting by the Center for Genomic Gastronomy

The Center for Genomic Gastronomy is an independent research institute engaged in exploring biotechnologies and biodiversity that make up the human food systems of planet. They work at the intersection of food, culture, ecology, and technology. The Center is based at the Science Gallery at Trinity College in Dublin. *The Smog Tasting* project is part of a larger body of research into "aeroir," a play on the word *terroir* (taste of place) but in reference to atmospheric taste. A part of this project, smog meringues have been exhibited and served by the members of the Center in India, the US, Ireland, Belgium, and the UK.

Local, all natural smog tasting

This recipe was developed in Bangalore, India during a class at the Srishti School of Art, Design and Technology.

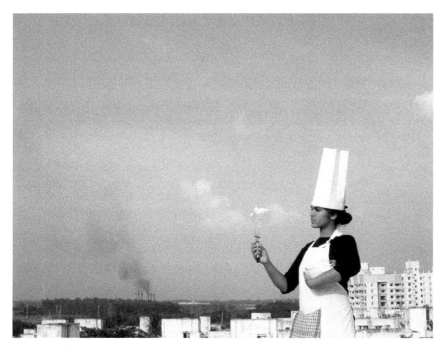

FIGURE 28.2 *Smog tasting.*
© *Center for Genomic Gastronomy.*

Instructions

1. Separate out 3 egg whites for each location you will be collecting smog from.
2. Go to the polluted location and stand in the smoggy area.
3. Whip the egg whites and begin adding 3/4 cup or 150 g white sugar for 3 egg whites.
4. At stiff peak stage, the meringue batter will consist of 90 percent air. In this case, polluted air.
5. Pipe onto baking trays and bake at 100 °C for 1.5 hours, and serve.
6. Or, box up the meringues and mail as Trojan horse treats to politicians or CEOs. The tragedy of the commons never tasted so good!

elBulli mimetic peanuts

Food critic Blake Gopnik describes this recipe as an elBulli classic, He writes:
"Seems to be a peanut, but is a crisp skin filled with a thin peanut cream."[1]

Serves 10	Preparation
For the fried peanut savory praline 500 g skinned raw peanuts 500 g sunflower oil	1. Combine the peanuts and oil in a small pan. 2. Place over a medium heat, stirring constantly. 3. When golden brown, spread over a tray lined with paper towel to soak up excess oil. 4. Blend in a liquidizer to a fine paste and strain. 5. Set aside.
For the fried peanut cream 200 g fried peanut savory praline (previously prepared) 165 g water 0.2 g Xantana 60 g virgin peanut oil	1. Combine the water and Xantana and process with a hand-held blender until lump-free. 2. Add the fried peanut savory praline while processing. 3. Gradually add the oil while processing. 4. Emulsify well. 5. Set aside.
For the fried peanut cream mimetic peanuts Fried peanut cream (previously prepared) Peanut-shaped silicone molds	1. Use a syringe to fill the peanut molds with the cream. Make sure that there are no air bubbles in the molds. 2. Freeze. 3. Once frozen, remove from the molds and store in an airtight container in the freezer. Make 20 mimetic peanuts.
For the powdered salt 30 g salt	1. Grind the salt to a fine powder in a liquidizer. 2. Store in an airtight container in a cool, dry place.
Extras 500 g mannitol	

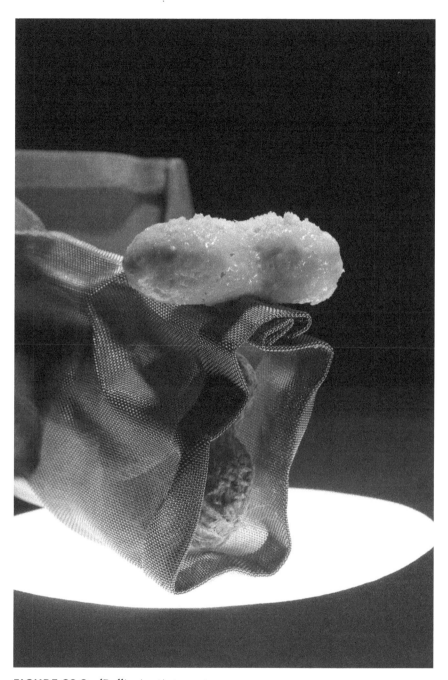

FIGURE 28.3 *elBulli mimetic peanuts.*
© *Francesc Guillamet Ferran.*

Finishing and presentation

1　Heat the mannitol in a small pan until it melts.

2　Use a needle to prick the frozen peanuts one at a time and dip them in the mannitol. One second is enough time for a fine layer to form.

3　Place the coated peanuts on a tray lined with parchment paper.

4　Leave to stand for 20 minutes so that the inside of the peanuts thaws.

5　Season with the powdered salt.

6　Serve 2 peanuts per person.

Temperature: Ambient
Season: All year round
Cutlery: None
How to eat: One at a time in two mouthfuls

Note

1　Blake Gopnik, "A Critic's Dinner," *Washington Post*, Wednesday, September 23, 2009.

List of Contributors

Josean Alija runs Nerua, a celebrated restaurant located at the Guggenheim Bilbao, as well as the Guggenheim Bilbao Bistro and *pintxo* bar. Nerua is one of the very few museum restaurants that have a Michelin star. In 2015, Nerua was also included on the "World's 100 Best Restaurants" list of the magazine *Restaurant*. Alija is praised for his purist style in which aromas, textures, and flavors are main components, but also for his innovative avant-garde style.

Marta Arzak is Associate Director for Education and Interpretation at the Guggenheim Museum Bilbao, where she has been working organizing the educational and cultural programming since its opening in 1997. Arzak is also interested in exploring the links between art, food, and cooking. She is art adviser at the Arzak restaurant in San Sebastián, Spain.

Judith A. Barter has been the Field-McCormick chair and curator of American Art at the Art Institute of Chicago since 1993. Her recent publications include *For Kith and Kin: The Folk Art Collection at the Art Institute of Chicago* (2012), *The Age of American Impressionism: Masterpieces from the Art Institute of Chicago* (2011), and *Art and Appetite: American Painting, Culture, and Cuisine* (2013). In 2005, Barter was selected Chicagoan of the year for arts accomplishments in 2005 by the *Chicago Tribune*.

Erin Betley is Biodiversity Specialist for the Center for Biodiversity and Conservation at the American Museum of Natural History and content research specialist for the traveling exhibition *Our Global Kitchen: Food, Nature, Culture*. She holds an MA in Conservation Biology from Columbia University and a BA in Biology from Boston University.

Jay Brown founded Lijiang Studio in 2004, an arts practice based in a rural farming village in southwest China's Yunnan Province. Since then, Lijiang Studio has facilitated and produced numerous residencies, exhibitions, and events in urban, rural, domestic, public, and private settings. Jay graduated from Princeton University in 2001 with a degree in Art History and certificate in East Asian Studies.

Mark Clintberg is an Assistant Professor at the Alberta College of Art + Design. In 2011, he conducted research at Oxford University, where he focused on gustatory taste as a device for interpreting seventeenth-century Dutch still-life paintings. Clintberg earned his PhD in the Department of Art History at Concordia University, in Montreal.

James I. Deutsch is a curator at the Smithsonian Center for Folklife and Cultural Heritage, where he has helped plan and develop programs and exhibitions for the Smithsonian Folklife Festival. He serves as an adjunct professor in the American Studies Department at George Washington University. Deutsch has also taught American Studies classes at universities in Armenia, Belarus, Bulgaria, Germany, Kyrgyzstan, Norway, Poland, and Turkey.

Jim Drobnick is a critic, curator, and Associate Professor of Contemporary Art and Theory at OCAD University, Toronto. He has published on the visual arts, performance, the senses and post-media practices. He co-founded the *Journal of Curatorial Studies* and DisplayCult, a curatorial collaborative.

Charlene D. Elliott is Professor in the Faculty of Arts at the University of Calgary and Canada Research Chair in Food Marketing, Policy and Children's Health. Her program of research focuses on food promotion, food policy, and food literacy, with a specific focus on children.

Scott Hill is curator at the Sydney Living Museums' Meroogal and Western suburbs portfolio. He has a long-standing interest in the interpretation of dining and other ephemeral elements within house museums. He holds degrees in architecture and has recently submitted his PhD on the significant early Australian colonial figure John Macarthur.

Paula J. Johnson is a Curator at the Smithsonian Institution's National Museum of American History and is currently researching and collecting objects relating to American food and wine history, as well as developing historical content for live culinary demonstrations.

Michael Leung is a designer, beekeeper and urban farmer. His work ranges from conceptual objects for the dead to urban agriculture projects. He is a visiting tutor at Baptist University, where he teaches Interdisciplinary Art in the Master of Visual Arts. Inspired by his current projects and previous experiences, Michael is now working on his first collection of fictional stories.

Nina Levent is the CEO of West & East Art Group and West & East Gallery and Incubator. Levent has served on the faculty of the New York Art Academy, and has been the Executive Director of Art Beyond Sight for fifteen years. She has also created and led more than 100 professional development workshops at such renowned museums as New York's Guggenheim, Whitney and Brooklyn museums; Washington, DC's National Gallery of Art; the San Francisco Museum of Modern Art; Walker Art Center and the Museum of Fine Art Houston.

Irina D. Mihalache is Assistant Professor in the Faculty of Information at the University of Toronto and her work focuses on eating practices in museum restaurants, food events in museums, and the history of museum communication. Her current work focuses on the culinary history of the Art Gallery of Ontario in Toronto.

Nat Muller is an independent curator and critic. She has written numerous essays and catalog entries on art and politics, artists from the Middle East and is obsessed with all things food. She has curated video and film screenings for projects and festivals internationally, including for Rotterdam's International Film Festival, Norwegian Short Film Festival and Video D.U.M.B.O. and has curated institutional and gallery shows across Europe and the Middle East. In 2015 she was Associate Curator for the Delfina Foundation's Politics of Food Program with a theme *Sex, Diet and Disaster.*

Jacqui Newling is interpretation curator at the Sydney Living Museums and is the institution's "resident gastronomer." She has a Master of Arts in Gastronomy and is conducting postgraduate research into early Australian colonial foodways at Sydney University. Jacqui blogs at *The Cook and the Curator* as "The Cook" and authored, *Eat your history: stories and recipes from Australian kitchens* (2015).

Christy Shields-Argelès is Assistant Professor at the American University of Paris and associated with the Interdisciplinary Institute of Contemporary Anthropology of the *Ecole des Hautes Etudes en Sciences Sociales* in Paris. She is currently working on an ethnographic investigation of taste as collaborative practice within the supply chain of *Comté*, a PDO cheese produced in the Jura Mountains of Eastern France.

Charles Spence is the head of the Crossmodal Research Laboratory at the Department of Experimental Psychology, Oxford University. He is interested in how our brains manage to process the information from each of our different senses to form rich multisensory experiences. His research focuses on how a better understanding of the human mind will lead to the better design of multisensory interfaces, products, environments, and foods in the future.

Eleanor Sterling is the Chief Conservation Scientist of the American Museum of Natural History's Center for Biodiversity and Conservation, with almost thirty years of teaching and research experience globally. She received her BA from Yale College and a joint PhD in Anthropology and Forestry and Environmental Studies from Yale University.

Sara Stern is an artist and writer from New York. She received her BA from Harvard University's Department of Visual and Environmental Studies in 2012, and is currently pursuing her MFA in the Visual Arts Program at Columbia University.

Jennifer Jacqueline Stratton is a documentary artist and researcher. She received her MFA from Duke University, where she is currently completing a postgraduate photography fellowship. Jennifer's work explores evolving connections and estrangements between communities, foodways, and environmental systems.

Van Troi Tran is lecturer and research assistant in Ethnology at Université Laval in Quebec City. He is the author of *Manger et boire aux Expositions universelles: Paris 1889, 1900* and has also published a number of articles on the history and anthropology of world's fairs. He is currently serving as president of the Folklore Studies Association of Canada.

L. Stephen Velasquez is Associate Curator in the Division of Home and Community Life at the National Museum of American History, Smithsonian Institution and is currently researching Mexican and Mexican American vineyard workers and wine makers.

Edward Whittall is a PhD Candidate at York University in Toronto. His dissertation research focuses on the intersection of food, performance, and place. He has written on the tensions between museum space and performance, as well as on food media and gender. He is an award-winning actor, and has trained and worked as a cook for over twenty-five years.

Elizabeth M. Williams is a founder and President of the SoFAB Institute in New Orleans. Much of her research and writing centers on the legal and policy issues related to food and foodways. She has written many articles for a variety of magazines and journals, has served as judge in many cooking competitions, and has consulted internationally on the food of New Orleans. She is a member of the Folklife Commission, State of Louisiana.

Ashley Rose Young is a PhD Candidate in History at Duke University. She earned her BA in History at Yale University and was a visiting scholar at the University of Oxford and Tulane University. Her dissertation focuses on the transatlantic history of food markets and street food culture in American port cities such as New Orleans and Baltimore.

Zhao Kunfang studied Cultural Studies and Culture, Material and Design course at Goldsmiths College and University College London. She joined Bishan Commune in the January of 2015. Her rich knowledge and experience with design, handicraft, contemporary art, and cultural studies contributed to rural reconstruction projects in Bishan, including the development of the School of Tillers and its first exhibitions.

Index

Lightning Source UK Ltd.
Milton Keynes UK
UKHW02f2336190618
324505UK00003B/169/P